Novels from Reagan's America

NOVELS FROM REAGAN'S AMERICA

A New Realism

Joseph Dewey

University Press of Florida
Gainesville · Tallahassee · Tampa · Boca Raton
Pensacola · Orlando · Miami · Jacksonville

04 03 02 01 00 99 6 5 4 3 2 1

Library of Congress Cataloging-in-Publication Data
Dewey, Joseph, 1957-
Novels from Reagan's America: a new realism / Joseph Dewey.
p. cm.
Includes bibliographical references (p.) and index.
ISBN 0-8130-1714-9 (cloth: alk. paper)
1. American fiction—20th century—History and criticism. 2. Realism in literature. 3. Politics and literature—United States—History—20th century. 4. Literature and society—United States—History—20th century. 5. National characteristics, American, in literature. 6. Reagan, Ronald—Influence. I. Title.
PS374.R37D49 1999
813'.540912—dc21 99-36889

The University Press of Florida is the scholarly publishing agency for the State University System of Florida, comprising Florida A & M University, Florida Atlantic University, Florida International University, Florida State University, University of Central Florida, University of Florida, University of North Florida, University of South Florida, and University of West Florida.

University Press of Florida
15 Northwest 15th Street
Gainesville, FL 32611-2079
http://www.upf.com

Beauty is momentary in the mind—
The fitful tracing of a portal;
But in the flesh it is immortal.
—Wallace Stevens, "Peter Quince at the Clavier"

Truman: Was nothing real?
Cristof: You were real. That's what made you so good to watch.
—*The Truman Show* (1998)

CONTENTS

spectacle: (n) 1. A specially prepared or elaborately prearranged display of a public nature designed to impress or entertain by its mass, proportions, or other dramatic quality
2. (n) a thing exhibited or set before the public gaze as remarkable
3. (pl) a means of seeing, a device for assisting defective vision

ACKNOWLEDGMENTS

Eloquence should always be set aside when it is time to say thanks. Many people helped produce this book. I would like to thank those who read early drafts and encouraged this project: the family of Robert Ferro, Brooke Horvath (Kent State University), Irving Malin (City College of New York), John Reese Moore (Hollins Critic), James Neilson (Trident College), Emmanuel S. Nelson (State University of New York at Cortland), John O'Brien (*Review of Contemporary Fiction*), Robert Phillips (*Mississippi Quarterly*), Richard Powers, the anonymous readers for the University Press of Florida who guided the manuscript to its final shape with generous and helpful advice, and the kind and gentle editors at the Press, particularly Susan Fernandez and Gillian Hillis, and freelance copyeditor Victoria Haire. Little could have been done, however, without massive technical assistance, and I would like to thank those who helped with computer searches and with manuscript preparation, including a generous thank you to Priscilla Stump and Rob Eckenrod, whose patience and technical savvy helped me complete this manuscript efficiently and correctly. Yet the manuscript would never have been finished without the wondrous inspiration of a family that taught me (and continues to teach me everyday) the lessons of spectacle realism: I would like to thank my wife, Julie, as well as my children, Carolyn and Mark, both kids of the 1980s.

Portions of chapter 3 appeared in the *Mississippi Quarterly*, and portions of chapter 8 appeared in the *Review of Contemporary Fiction*. Grateful thanks is given to both journals for permission to reprint the material here.

Introduction

Riding without Horses—A Reading of the 1980s

I discovered . . . that an audience has a feel to it and, in the parlance of theater, that the audience and I were together. . . . It was heady wine. Hell, with two more lines, I'd have had them riding through "every Middlesex village and farm"—without horses yet.

Ronald Reagan

What I'm trying to sell here is what everyone wants, happiness. . . . I don't want the public to see the world they live in while they're in the Park. I want them to feel they're in another world.

Walt Disney

We begin, perhaps unavoidably, with Dickens.

Surveying the wild contradictions of the 1980s, we pull together sufficient ironies to conclude (quite lamely) that it (like most decades) was the best of times and the worst of times. It was, for instance, a time for resurging chest-thumping, flag-pumping, beer commercial patriotism, for the chic bravado of a president fond of invoking Dirty Harry and Rambo as models of diplomatic tact, a time of jingoistic tribal rituals such as the Statue of Liberty Centennial Weekend spectacle and the Los Angeles Olympiad, a time when we publicly huffed and bluffed about a winnable nuclear war. Yet we closed the decade a debtor nation, humbled with a crippling dependence on foreign monies unmatched since we were a colony, and throughout the decade we found ourselves victimized again and again and again by the heavy shadow-strokes of international terrorism. It was a time when a president lauded the traditional ethic of hard work and entrepreneurial savvy—the same president who distanced himself from the routine of his own job (he was known for nodding off during staff meetings and for separating jellybeans by color during Cabinet briefings), who spent a full year of his eight-year term on vacation, and whose staff measured the enormity of a public crisis by whether the president needed to be awakened.

It was a time when we embraced a return to the conservative family values of Norman Rockwell's America, despite being a nation where fully half of all first marriages moved gracelessly toward divorce, where one-third of our children were being raised by single parents, where by decade's close we averaged more than a million legal abortions per year, where domestic entertainment technologies routinely took over the role of parenting as we charted the developmental problems of the first generation of "latch-key children." All the while we were inspired by a divorced president whose current family members were so estranged each from the other that their uneasy alliances were grist for enquiring minds. It was a time when the Christian agenda massaged its way into respectability and muscled its way into viability as a political engine—but only by first rejecting a born-again incumbent whose fundamentalist faith was an unquestioned source of integrity in an otherwise lackluster presidency and then embracing a president only casually affiliated with any organized denomination and who seldom attended church save as a photo-op.

It was a time that saw a startling reawakening of spiritualism, an upsurge in church memberships, an irruption of evangelical programming on cable television, as well as a widespread interest among Yuppies in nontraditional spirituality: channeling, meditation, crystallogy, pyramid power, angelology, psychic networks, herbal healing. Yet it was also a time of insatiable materialism, measured by the ostentation of these same Yuppies, by their fast-track wealth, and by their addiction to physical fitness that sanctioned lavishing preening attention to the body. It was a time when we rallied about an administration's bold experiment in supply-side economics that was at the same time being hooted as a dangerous shell game of mirage and voodoo arithmetic by economic advisers at the very center of that administration. It was a time for conspicuously public rituals of conscience-raising—the splashy spectacles of USA for Africa, Live Aid, Hands Across America, Farm-Aid, as well as massive antiapartheid rallies—and yet seldom have the needs of children, minorities, immigrants, the poor, the sick, the mentally ill, the homeless been so casually marginalized even as their numbers soared. In foreign affairs, it was a time when we trained our fiercest rhetoric at the Soviet Union, reviving the absolute zero of the Cold War, only to find by decade's end that our great agonist was a shadow-bear—and had been, all along. It was a time when we exorcised the heavy ghost of Vietnam—but via a delightful conquest of a Caribbean island resort barely the size of Detroit.

The contradictions go on and on, too many ultimately to help pin the decade. Of course, there is something a bit arrogant about the business of defining a decade so recently past. American culture has long been enamored with the decade as a significant unit of measure, each decimal unit of history with a particular logic and argument, a strategy perhaps coaxed by our uneasy awareness of our own adolescence. Just beyond the close of our second century, we are necessarily impatient with the slow slide of the century; the decade allows us a sort of microwaved history, part of our culture's Fotomat mentality that so often measures impatience in the minutes we must wait in a fast-food line. Thus, without irony, we christen the eight years of the Reagan presidency "the Reagan Era"—hanging on that handful of years a term usually reserved for far more impressive stretches of time and influence. After all, even sympathetic commentators acknowledge that the real glow of the Reagan presidency lasted barely twenty-one months, roughly from the second inauguration (January 1985) to the initial disclosures of the administration's realpolitik machinations that would become the substance of the Iran-Contra Hearings (November 1986).

It might seem, then, a most uncommon arrogance that drives us to define a decade just survived, to divine a narrative from people and events still familiar, still immediate. In such an imperfect remembrance of things so recently past, we necessarily gather up the trivial with the significant: the INF Treaty with Baby Jessica at the bottom of the well; the Beirut truckbombing with Vanna White; the New Coke with Bhopal; Teddy Ruxpin with John Hinckley; *Ishtar* with Christa McAuliffe; the advent of MTV with the lone figure standing against the blurred shadow of a government tank in Tiananmen Square. Decade assessment quickly degrades into a hyperserious game, an intriguing (if ultimately pointless) hybrid of Trivial Pursuit and Rubik's Cube—two of this decade's trendier pastimes. Amid this most imperfect rush to judgment, we attempt to choreograph such a cumbersome ensemble into some cooperative movement, some semblance of direction and plot. Such assessments, of course, are a most vulnerable type of history, history, indeed, that is still guessing. If centuries leave the wide, easy track of glaciers, decades move with the quirkiness of jackrabbits. To map out a decade just finished is to invite argument, not to end it. It is to sketch a rough draft of history, work that is treacherous and exhilarating, like drafting a wilderness map in roughest pencil. Part intuition, part guesswork, such decade-defining speaks a rough truth in its immediacy, in its very vulnerability to later correction. It is like a diary entry—flush from the experience, we fashion truths even as thought and reflection yield to the impulsive curve of emotion and intuition.

We begin with a natural curiosity, the need to sort through the inundation of images offered by a media machine that grew during the decade to Orwellian vastness. As domesticated technologies reached into our most private spheres, we surely overloaded on images: seabirds flailing about the oily surface of Prince William Sound; grainy black-and-white shots of the charred reactor tower at Chernobyl; the caved-in yellowed faces in AIDS hospices; Charles and Diana kissing coolly, stiffly on the palace balcony; the carefree dancing about the broken spine of the Berlin Wall; the heartbreaking detritus floating on the China Sea, sneakers and purses and shoes from the passengers of Korean Air Lines Flight 007. Add to that the winding parade of Andy Warholics visible only for their allotted fifteen minutes: Bernhard Goetz, Clara Peller, Jessica Hahn, Pia Zadora, Douglas Ginsburg, Janet Cooke, Pee-Wee Herman . . . on and on. In such an unrelenting fury, despite our best efforts to track the decade, it slips away, a spare shadow in a steady blizzard.

Given this onslaught, perhaps the work of structuring such a decade, the work of threading a convincing narrative, is not an arrogant act at all. Events, after all, do not move with the tight precision and reassuring predictability of circus acrobats on trapezes. Providing a narrative for the decade is a far more modest venture. After all, during the 1980s, we were stunned by scale. The slow boomerang of Halley's comet and the exodus of the Voyager space probes pushed our awareness beyond our familiar cosmos. In 1987 astronomers observed a supernova, the vast drama of the death of a star known as SN 1987A, in an explosion, a billion times brighter than the sun, that had actually happened (we were told) more than 50,000 years ago. Stephen Hawking introduced us, via a hip if improbable best-seller, to a "brief" history of time that so casually spanned eons. Information came to be processed in unimaginable volume, in massive gigabits. And, all about us, the apparent infinity of a parallel system premised by a webbing of worldwide computer networks began to open up. By decade's end, we were left threatened by inconsequence, diminished by the technologies so few understood or controlled. Meteorologists and earth scientists argued the consequences of global warming in terms of millions of years; we pondered the consequences of a "winnable" nuclear exchange—the unsettling dark of a 1,000-year nuclear winter; in 1989 we tracked an asteroid more than 100 yards wide pass "dangerously" close to us—a mere 450,000 miles away. During the decade, mechanical hearts began to beat in the shattered hulks of once-corpsed patients; experiments in recombinant DNA promised to our imperfect hands the trick of creation, so long the province of our deities; indeed, in 1987 the United States Patent Office issued the first patent for a genetically altered mammal. Amid such evidence of our vulnerabilities, our diminishing humanity, our imperiled condition, we need to tell the story of our passing moment, to know that our events had consequence, that we left an imprint, that, contrary to the bleak wisdom offered by one of the decade's cliché T-shirts ("Shit Happens"), we managed to find our way like kaleidoscope stones to the splendid arithmetic of design. In fashioning such a decade narrative, we act, then, not from our arrogance as much as from our vulnerabilities. And assembling such a narrative is akin to the electric thrill felt by those desperates left in midocean wreckage who gradually convince themselves those flashes of light on the horizon are, in fact, a coded message.

But the Reagan Era compels for special reasons. It was surely no ordinary decade. The Reagan Era testified to a tectonic shift in the national imaginative energy. It was supremely a *felt* decade. There are a few decades in our history—the Gilded Age and the 1920s come to mind—that find their way into the national imagination without a monumental war or devastating economic crisis to give them shape and heft and plot.[1] They are decades, to use James Combs's argument, that are emphatically re-creative, not creative, decades in which the country deliberately sought respite after harsh national traumas—the Civil War, Lincoln's shooting, and the fierce scarring of Reconstruction, in one case, and the devastating (and surrealistically pointless) attrition of World War I, on the other. Like the Gilded Age and the 1920s, the 1980s happened largely as an imagined event, its impact tracked not by historians or journalists so much as felt by those immediately within its pull. Surely not every presidency ministers to our imaginative life. Those chief executives who do not, of course, serve their time in office; we assess the Carter Years or the Bush Years, the Hayes Years or the Clinton Years, each by comparison a sort of joyless sentence (as the temporal term "years" suggests), endured by a citizenry often straining to engage that vision thing; they become terms of office attended to diligently by the elected president (and in some cases with substantive results) but without sparking the national imagination.

But the "era" is a far different construction, a far wider experience. It is a time when a president ignites an inexplicable exertion of emotional energy, taps into a need deeper than anything political or legislative. In the 1870s, Grant, whose political insouciance passed for radical disconnection, was sublimely suited after his work during the epochal struggle of the war to sit enskied in Washington. So supremely absented from the operations of his own appointees, he moved into the national imagination like some respected, if absentee, parent, thereby permitting, even excusing the giddiest exercises in material excess and moral license. Or Coolidge, ever silent, ever serious, ever restrained, seemed by the very excess of his restraint the perfect send-up, the perfect puckered straightman for a decade of jazzy kinesis. Reagan provided similar stimulus. With the dead-on instincts of a career actor for the emotional needs of an audience, Reagan rejuvenated the nation's energy, deliberately trafficking in our deepest emotions.[2] Thus, he measured his greatest success not by any legislative record (it was a rather standard record of considerable success and significant repudiation) but rather by the tonic revival of feeling. By any measure, it was a decade when we all *felt* better.

But it is not enough to decide that the Reagan Era was a sort of national daydream or a group sleepwalk or some fantasy construction masterminded by dream weavers in Reagan's camp who cynically cast about our national agenda the lightest skein of fantasy.[3] In such a reading, we sat about dumbly mesmerized by the polished performance of an actor, the simple projection of light and shadow, as he regaled us for the better part of a decade with apocryphal stories culled from old movies, amusing misstatements of fact and (un)expected gaffes, a stunning disregard for complexity, and an irrepressible (and inexplicable) optimism that proffered a worldview drawn in the bold colors of Crayolas. Such reductive analysis, however, misses the decade—misreads the text of the 1980s—to carp over the sorry wrongheadedness of the national fascination with what Reagan offered, for what Reagan meant to American culture, dismissing it all like some kind of irresistible hashish peddled by a consummate huckster/pusher.

Indeed, seldom has a decade in our nation's history been so embraced, so relished, and then so quickly regretted. The 1980s linger now largely in a wince of embarrassment. Such disdain, however, neglects the necessary component of our complicity, our awareness all the while that we were dealing with the mixed blessing of illusions. We participated in the decade. We elected to believe, for instance, in the elegant pseudoarithmetic of Reaganomics, historic cuts in taxes coupled with profligate spending, a sort of Master Carded "recovery" that violated the simplest rules of balancing a household checkbook. Or that sending the American military machine to rescue a dormful of American students improbably studying medicine in a Caribbean beach resort was, in fact, a military operation that could sponge clean the emotional debts of Vietnam. Or that we could protect ourselves from our considerable vulnerability from nuclear attack by stretching a great invisible shield in the sky. Or that we could make all the bad drugs go away by just saying *no*, Nancy Reagan like Peter Pan calling on all of us to clap to save Tinkerbell.

The point of the 1980s is that, inevitably, adults do clap—despite that hard core of our intelligence that finds suspect this whole notion of medical treatment dispensed by collective hand manipulations. Our complicity in the Reagan Era suggests that we were something other than enchanted, drugged, gullible, or simply victims of cynical fantasy wheelers intent on retaining political power. And so we need a new approach. The decade might more profitably be defined as a grateful giant step away from the rigid logistics of analytical thought to indulge the ludic possibilities of our rich imaginative inclinations. We wanted Reagan to happen. Undeniably—from the record of his two landslide elections, the record of the decade's polling in which we embraced him with steadily high approval numbers, the continuing awe he commands even at this writing, more than a decade after his peak years in office when there were serious clamors to add his face to the likenesses on Mount Rushmore and a public drive to repeal the Twenty-second Amendment that barred presidents from serving more than eight years—we licensed Reagan. Yet no one who moved through the media-saturated realscape of the decade could ignore the obvious: the worn public education system, the pillaged environment, the groaning national deficit, the crumbling urban infrastructure, the very public evidence of scandal amid administration insiders, the alarming escalation in AIDS infections, the unstoppable invasive stroke of terrorism overseas. We must, then, first find a logic for this striking contradiction: our cold understanding of the urgency of the problems within a most demanding immediate and, concomitantly, our willful step away.

To understand the dynamics that created Reagan's America, a construction jointly erected and collectively sustained, a fabulated zone that not only demanded the careful manipulation of possibilities but worked only if it received the cooperation of those who wanted/needed it, it is best to dispense with the patronizing metaphors of fantasy, theater, drugs, and dreams that currently dominate decade commentary and deal rather with the sort of landscape far closer to Reagan's America: that supreme postmodern landscape we call the theme park, a deliberate construction, an elaborate spectacle, a play zone without consequence that offers a necessary pause from the pressing responsibilities of the immediate and demands audience cooperation for its fullest effect, a landscape necessarily temporary but vitally restorative.[4] Although certainly the 1980s witnessed a national fascination with theme parks, vast theme malls, tony theme restaurants, urban revitalization theme neighborhoods, elaborate theme hotels—each a happy, insulated zone of artifice and play—we will draw our ties to that most formidable (and familiar) theme park, Disney World. (In a happy coincidence, the Disney empire, shaky at the decade's beginning, came back into its own during the entrepreneurial expansiveness and hard savvy of the Eisner years of mid-decade and became, once again, the premiere entertainment draw for our culture and Orlando the prime middle-class tourist destination.) There among the tourists who herd into the Magic Kingdom by the millions (and adults outnumber children four to one), we understand that our role is to participate, to accept what our more analytical nature denies as valid. As Baudrillard observes, the only real contents in Disney's magic kingdoms are the "masses themselves" (66), which he compares to petroleum products processed by a refinery. But it is, perhaps, more complicated. After all, we have a role to play in the Magic Kingdom: we listen reverently to a plastic contraption of wires and circuits and animal hair simulating Lincoln reading bits of his Second Inaugural Address, or we thrill to the audioanimatronics headhunters who prowl near the greenish waters of the jungle cruise, or we applaud (*think about that!*) a country music show staged entirely with puppet bears dressed in hillbilly getups, applaud, in fact, an engineered performance entirely untouched by the sort of human hands-on effort that might find applause rewarding. Our role, however, is not to quibble but rather to enjoy—to participate, to play.

It is at this decidedly odd juncture, where we find in striking confluence earnest play and sophisticated spectacle, that we turn to the literature of the era. What sort of literature is produced in a nation that commits itself to the seductive alogic of a play zone? In exploring the Reagan-Era-as-theme-park, we will trace how the decade witnessed a significant assertion of the realistic novel, so long eclipsed by the massive achievement of the postmodern novel. It is a critical commonplace that this flowering of realism in the 1980s was a corollary of Reagan's conservative nostalgia, an embarrassing throwback to a mossy literary artifact hopelessly out of sync with the trendy posteverything contemporary novel-qua-text.[5] Yet it will be argued here that this efflorescence of the realistic novel occurred not so much *because* of Reagan's America but rather against it.

We begin by drawing lines of comparison between Reagan's America, Disney's Magic Kingdom, and a postmodern text.[6] The vocabulary that defines, for instance, the audacious excess of the lexical play zone of the typical postmodern text shares much with the vocabulary that defines the vast sophisticated play zone of the contemporary theme park. And, oddly, Reagan (like Disney's imagineers or like any of the innovators of the postmodern novel) is profitably approached as a proprietor, a benevolent monomaniac who directed pleasure and coaxed happiness from a willing audience by creating a self-contained, structurally intricate totalized zone (Reagan's America), an alternate world wholly apart from the press and confusion of the "real world," not an illusion or a myth but rather a seductive world-apart that we "visited," whose immediacy (like that of a theme park) we felt comfortably surrounding us, a fantastic-real that succeeded only with our full awareness of its artificiality, our complicity to accept that patently fraudulent zone as authentic—or, more precisely, as authentic enough. The Reagan Era, then, (much like any vacation and much like the postmodern novel a generation ago) began with the conviction that we had reached a critical point of exhaustion—that we needed a break, we needed to play.

*   *   *

The threat is nearly invisible in ordinary ways. It is a crisis of confidence. It is a crisis that strikes at the very heart and soul and spirit of our national will. We can see this crisis in the growing doubt about the meaning of our lives and in the loss of a unity of purpose for our nation. The erosion of our confidence in the future is threatening to destroy the social and the political fabric of America.

Jimmy Carter, 15 July 1979

(Henry) felt stupendous . . . full of joy, and now a kind of heady romantic peace

> *seemed to be sweeping over him: ecstasy—yes . . . that was the only goddamn*
> *word for it.*
>
> Robert Coover, *The Universal Baseball Association*

Defining a narrative thread for the 1980s begins with the widely acknowledged political assessment that the conservative political earth-
slide of the general election of November 1980 had to do not so much
with any faith we had in the executorial promise of a former B-movie
actor and modestly competent two-term California governor as it did
with our wholehearted rejection of the taxing presence of Jimmy Carter.[7]
Indeed, politically, Carter's most intriguing achievement may have been
simply to make electable a longtime fringe curiosity such as Reagan, to
provide the rationale for according him such a thumping margin of victory.

Right or wrong, we closed the Carter Years convinced of our own exhaustion, our national spirits enervated, our expectations radically diminished too soon after the heady pageantry of the Bicentennial. We had
a dour sense of malaise that weighed us with a most intolerable reading
of the immediate as some unending, oppressively untidy problem. More
stern than inspirational, Carter had left us feeling tapped, impotent, the
world too big to know, too chaotic to order. Much of his term we had
spent managing what appeared to be rapidly depleting energy sources.
We seemed to be running out, running down, running scared. We closed
the decade with our thermostats down, our once-proud Skylab dropping
listlessly out of space, our hostages caged for more than a year, our
vaunted military machine in charred bits in the Iranian desert. For four
interminable years, we had been asked to sacrifice by a president who
had lost somewhere in the morass of Washington the coat hanger smile
that had so dazzled during his improbable marathon run for the presidency. We lumbered clumsily to decade's end, the decade of Vietnam's
messy nonclosure and Watergate's miasmic menace. We were shaken by
a nervous sense of uncontrollable inflation and unrelenting unemploy-
ment and of our own growing irrelevancy on the international stage. We
stared at unforgiving newspaper images of our president collapsing during a road race or fending off attacks from a killer rabbit. Checkmated by
his own oddly hostile party in Congress, shadowed by a strong wife,
bullied by international events in Afghanistan, Angola, and Iran, so obviously bamboozled in Panama, Carter had given us only a most agonizing
sense of our puniness.

Such bleak conditions are curiously similar to the logic of exhaustion dominant in the midcentury academic discourse that initially explicated the dissatisfactions with the conventions of realism.[8] Realism had flowered in our post–World War II taste for stark battle narratives (Shaw, Mailer, Jones, Bourjaily) and then later in the explorations of midlife gray-flannel traumas and of the need to locate a place for that troubled self within a troubling and complex social context (Cozzens, Cheever, O'Hara, Bellow). But by the early 1960s, such realistic fictions seemed no longer operable, diminished—we were told—by the very world of brutality and chance such books professed to record, a world now deemed impossible to define, much less understand and record. Actuality, as Philip Roth so eloquently spelled out, now stupefied, sickened, infuriated, and embarrassed. In ways that foreshadowed the heavy malaise and the sense of pinched possibilities at the close of the Carter Years, the simplest weight of realistic testimony so oppressed and enervated the spirit that such literary texts seemed suddenly intolerably heavy or, worse, redundant. After all, the tomes of O'Hara or Styron or Cheever or Bellow, for all their grand sense of dilemma and character, gave us back only that immediate, demanded a most tiring responsibility to engage the malaise and confusions and tawdriness of our own context, to accept our own puniness.

And so we turned away.

We turned, eventually ballasted by volumes of theoretical justification, to the massive baroque play of the postmodern novel, texts of daring inventive risks, texts that played out to their absurd conclusions the guerrilla logic of subversion present in the novel's evolution since Cervantes, novels that forsook deliberately the anchorage of believable characters, believable dilemmas, stage-managed suspense, and tidy closing epiphanies. As Tony Tanner summarized, "rather than simply attempting to transcribe the state of affairs, the majority of American writers tried to offset or challenge the realm of conditioned action with gestures of verbal autonomy" (344). Overtired of recording our collapsing expectations, oppressed by a tradition that bound us to a fidelity to a problematic immediate, given shelf after shelf of realistic fictions too impressed by such untidiness, by such confusion, by such complication, we were ready—like those long overdue for vacation—to be dazzled by artifice, by spectacle. Much like the country at the close of the Carter Years, we were ready to play, ready for the audacious, ready to step into the controlled arena of the managed funhouse.

Much critical exegesis has perceived the evolution of the subversive postmodern novel as a willful conflict with the established realistic novel: experience versus experiment, we trumpet, praxis versus form, the conservative entrenched versus the liberal avant-garde, vision versus technique—as if literary genres developed with the campy logic of a World Wrestling Federation undercard.[9] The oppositional logic of positioning postmodern novels against realistic novels, however, forces us to choose or leads us to believe that one genre triumphs at the expense of the other or that somehow we "lose" one tradition during the domination of the other. Such a hokey sense of battling books might appear a shade less antagonistic (and cheaply melodramatic) if we factor in the logic and spirit of the vacation, the human need to play. We do not need to choose. Nor do we need to dismiss, as John Gardner did so shrilly, the achievement of postmodern writers as morally bankrupt, "aesthetic gamesplayers . . . obscenely giggling and gesturing in the wings while the play of life goes on" (55). Work and play have always maintained a productive counterbalance, the responsibility to tend to the immediate held in balance by the need for leisure. Work and play stay in constant tension—much as the simplest workday balances time for recreation. Within any culture we accept the irregular patternings of vacation time; we do not all go on vacation at the same time, nor are we all ever devoted to the business of responsibilities. Indeed, one energy depends on the other for validity. It is a necessary, contemporaneous culture-wide cooperation.

Thus, despite the massive number of ludic texts during the 1960s and 1970s, for instance, we did not abandon, much less "lose," the realistic novel. That novel continued in the works of Updike, Styron, Auchincloss, Lurie, Bellow, Cheever, Malamud, and Welty, among others, reminding us (like phone calls from home during vacation) that the sphere of responsibilities and commitments and relationships awaited our eventual return. That pressing reality, however, could not diminish our relish of the interlude, that time apart and away, the restorative indulgence of the human need to recreate within the deliberately excessive lexical play zones of a generation of postmodern texts created and conceived as deliberate fabrications that each argues most empathically not the dilemma of its characters so much as the inexhaustible sport of the imagination unleashed—they are, supremely, mind-circuses, to borrow Lance Olsen's happy phrasing.

But we pay a most exacting price for either work or play in extreme.

The Carter Years could certainly be seen as the spiritless overexertion of the work ethic. Taking our cue from a yellow-pad president overcommitted to the sheer demands of running a government, we were left with the tiring sense of diminishment and the tedious attention to sacrifice that traditionally attend the miserly preoccupation with the burdens of the immediate. By term's end, we were ready to play. But by the close of the Reagan Era, we had wearied of play. Tired of the serious trivia of the controlled event, tired of the mantra "Don't Worry, Be Happy," tired of sustenance-by-sizzle, we grew restless within the play mentality—its highwater mark perhaps our uncertain reaction to the garish patriotic gore that attended the too-neat video-game war against a vastly overmatched Iraq (1991), a military spectacle grandly packaged as Operation Desert Storm, a near-effortless overexertion of military muscle played out conveniently on television in an uncomplicated 100-hour time span perfectly tailored for the diminished attention span of vacation time.

There were hints even during the 1988 general election that we were tiring of play, of the effortless hymning of morning in an America that was not so certainly luminous; we were growing leery of the reliability of soundbytes: Bush's labored flag factory photo-ops, the crude exploitation of the menacing visage of Willie Horton, the absurd contest for who could say the Pledge of Allegiance louder, who carried an ACLU card, who looked better riding an army tank, and who was and was not Senator Jack Kennedy. Too much play had left us feeling overmanaged, like visitors locked in the Magic Kingdom (or like readers sentenced—in both senses of the word—to shelves of postmodern experiments). By the early 1990s, we were ready to work, ready to accept like invigorating tonic the no-nonsense work ethic of Perot and then to elect the wunderwonk Clinton, eager as a graduate student to undertake the punishing routine of a hands-on presidency, ready for his sixteen-hour days, his endless roundtables of apparently invigorating policy talk. We were ready, in short, to return to the sphere of the immediate.

In embracing Reagan, then, we indulged the same need for play that had encouraged our fascination a generation earlier with the fantastic verbal privatescapes of the postmodern text. In neither case did we pretend the obligation of engaging the immediate was somehow void. Rather we determined to relish the happy logic of temporary disengagement. We were ready to play the role of what Maxine Feifer terms the "post-tourist." As Feifer points out, we no longer travel—with that antique, wholly quaint sense of being exposed to a distant people as a way to affirm ourselves as cultural beings capable of intellectual and spiritual education that results from experiencing firsthand another civilization's artifacts, natural wonders, and historic locales—a position that metaphorically suggests the role of a reader "visiting" realistic text-sites. Today, however, we tour; we satisfy a hunger for deliberate escape rather than any need for edification, a hard pursuit of diversion most fulfilled by our fascination with theme parks.

That popularity indicates our need for depthlessness, for noisy (and necessarily pointless) spectacle, our need to consume what are unabashedly signs, sophisticated substitutes for the authentic. We flock like the hypnotized to the otherwise swampy middle ranges of Florida, there to experience improbably a Mississippi riverboat, an Incan temple, a Parisian café, a frontier saloon, a jungle steamer, a Tahitian hut, and on and on. Such a place, we know, is bogus, is, in Baudrillard's apt phrasing, a "cadaver all in flux" (64). Yet we go to such a controlled and wholly manipulative zone knowing that we have a role to play in animating these moribund bits. We go knowing that we must agree to accept these fragments, these cleverly manufactured, radically decontextualized signs (rocketships, submarines, robot presidents, headhunters) as the real thing in order to tap the satisfying sense of escape that defines the post-tourist experience. The contemporary theme park is—like the postmodern text and Reagan's America—a triumph of form, of manufactured spectacle, a tonic collage of signs drawn from pop culture, cut and pasted with such skill and drawn before us with such velocity that sheer technique allows us to quash our certainty that this concoction is hardly "real" and to engage this wildly entrancing spectacle of excess. Repudiating the larger world of reference as too brutal to explore and too broken to repair, we step into a managed world, an enjoyable engaging alternative (w)hole. It is therapeutic: we go to disentangle ourselves from the sorry absurdities of our immediate; we go to be renewed, revived, delighted by effect, by edifices erected by the energy of the imagination, quite close to why we pick up a ludic text of Barth or Gass. Given the premise that the ordinary is sterile and impoverished—a premise that will be challenged by fictions examined here—we are thoroughly tamed by the pleasure of such a conspicuous text, or more specifically by our desire to be pleased, and ultimately by our willingness to be pleased.

And thus without trivializing any element, we find shared motivations in these three experiences: the Reagan presence, Disney's jungle steamer, and a postmodern text. Each is an act of willful disengagement, the welcome experience of the contrived. The pull away from each realistic landscape—the Carter Years or a household lodged deep in Middle America or a voluminous novel of, say, Styron—begins with a perceived crisis in the imagination, a perceived need for carnival excess, a need to celebrate the exuberance of contrivance. Within the gameworld of Reagan's America, we indulged the same fascination with surfaces, the same sense of deliberate depthlessness that so intrigues at Disney World and that so mesmerizes within a postmodern text. Stuck within a world that so persistently resists our most valiant attempts to define it and shape it, we withdraw to relish the festival spirit that is most clearly celebrated in our ability to erect vast, magic kingdoms.

Reagan's America, Disney World, a postmodern text: they are each about our right to spectacle, our right to succumb, our right to play in order to return ultimately to an immediate that endures (we know) just outside the confines of each insulated play zone. No one, after all, lives in Disney World, nor did we expect the considerable problems confronting the American agenda during the 1980s to go away even as we celebrated our national return to vigor, even as we reveled in the signature spectacles of the decade: Reagan's glitzy million-dollar coronations-qua-inaugurations; the quick-strike conquering of Grenada; the Soviet-less Los Angeles Olympiad; the Hands Across America weekend; the Statue of Liberty Centennial Weekend; the multinational commemoration of the D-Day Landing; the televised air war over Libya. By the same token, we do not expect a linguistically intriguing gametext will make any more tolerable or explicable the pressing weight of responsibilities and commitments that awaits us as soon as we close up even the most delightfully demanding hypercrafted autotelic text. Each example—Reagan's America, Disney World, the postmodern text—is a splendid space apart, a place where we can celebrate with the tonic irony of awareness the temporary privileging of the signifier, the temporary marginalizing of the signified, an environment of play where "reality" merits scare quotes for its sudden, splendid irrelevancy. Like any spirited postmodern text, like the gorgeous self-involved exhibitionism of Disney World, Reagan's America is/was a fashioned text, an open and blatant act of interpretation, a construction (like a theme park, like a postmodern text) of recontextualized bits of our high and low culture, borrowed for the most part from film and television (much like Disney World's rich complex of iconography and like most postmodern texts), all orchestrated in such a way that such a fabulation, so obviously estranged from the immediate, could be experienced not merely as a performance but as a "real" place comfortingly apart.

Even the decade's signal events that pressed us most disconcertingly into the immediate—the shooting of Reagan outside the Washington Hilton (March 1981); the deaths of more than 200 marines stationed as peacekeeping forces in Beirut (October 1983); the heartbreaking ninety-two-second ride of the *Challenger* shuttle (January 1986)—even those moments when we could not take easy refuge in the sunny audacity of the happyscape of Reagan's America we nevertheless reconfigured to allay their oppressive intervention. We converted work to play. Not surprisingly, given the decade's saturation by video coverage, two of the events were recorded live. Networks played ad nauseam the assassination attempt and the shuttle explosion until the horror of each became extratextual; like shampoo commercials, they became part of the white noise we can block out. Ultimately only the image, not the impact, lingered. We see them even now: the tangle of bone-white lines hanging smudged against the blue late-morning Florida sky; Reagan with that startled look, his arm crooked up uselessly to shield him. Conditioned by video replay, we no longer expect from such televised immediacy expanded awareness but accept rather the cold play of disengaged titillation. And the horror of so many marines dying in such a problematic mission in such a disconcerting position of helplessness was within forty-eight hours lost amid the garish spectacle of the safe thrill of the Grenada intervention, when more than 7,000 American troops stormed the beaches even as sunbathers and joggers with dogs watched in amazement. Whether such timing was deliberate is still debated, but in such a confluence of events the whole Beirut quagmire became like one of those nasty afternoon storms that pass over Disney's Magic Kingdom.

*   *   *

I wonder what it's all about, and why
We suffer so, when little things go wrong?
We make our life a struggle,
When life should be a song.

Poet Ronald Reagan, age sixteen, "Life"

I am moved by fancies that are curled
Around these images, and cling:

The notion of some infinitely gentle,
Infinitely suffering thing.

T. S. Eliot, "Preludes"

Reagan's America, of course, begins with the text of Ronald Reagan him/ itself. Like any postmodern text, like a stroll among the "worlds" of the Magic Kingdom, Reagan came to us a staggering bricolage, a depthless collage of decontextualized bits drawn from our cultural imagination, juxtaposed until that very instability of signs rendered for him a semblance of narrative consistency, a stable sense of character. This is not to reprise the tired quips about Reagan's mental stamina. It is rather to recognize the apparently effortless way he managed to assemble his public character from bits of our own media-driven memory, a sort of portrait of the artist as a plagiarist.[10] Like any postmodern text, like Disney World, Reagan is/was not so much about the bits but rather about how so many fragments worked together. For eight very public years, Reagan, whose actual biography was lost in the deliberate fog of an adulthood spent in Hollywood and by his actor's sense of the irrelevance of the private sphere, fashioned himself into a most intricate, wholly depthless postmodern text in which his public persona and his public agenda were crafted from cultural referents colliding freely under the benevolent free reign of an obvious unapologetic love of kitsch (a faith and a worldview no doubt drawn from the formidable span of thirty-three years Reagan spent in radio, film, and television).

He became for us a contrivance, a sort of Everytext—like any of the rides at Disney World, so apparently simple and yet so intricately fashioned, so stunningly affective and anything but a simple illusion. Stories he told of his own past, we would find out later, had actually come from narrative lines of old films. With the same innocuous straightforwardness, Reagan cut and pasted bits of our cultural imagination to direct and plot his foreign policy and his economic recovery program— decontextualizing such bits and then recontextualizing them against a new exotic backdrop. He drew from film (*Star Wars*, Clint Eastwood's Dirty Harry series, *Back to the Future*, the Rambo series, *Ghostbusters*, Errol Flynn adventure pics, Reagan's own modest canon of endeavors, and assorted western adventure classics and obscure World War II propaganda films), from television (including *The Untouchables*, *Gunsmoke*, *Wheel of Fortune*); from children's literature (specifically his own childhood love of Horatio Alger, Tom Swift, and Mark Twain); and from a hodgepodge of other potent cultural reservoirs (commercial advertising jingles, Louis L'Amour, Frank Sinatra, comic books, astrology, baseball, the Book of Revelation, and the cozy nostalgia of Norman Rockwell). We freely accepted this most bizarre pastiche, this serious play of effortlessly wrenching cultural signs out of context and giving them new, striking, unexpected (in)significance (invoking, for instance, Rambo in connection with the Beirut bombing or George Lucas's Evil Empire to characterize the Soviet Union or offering Norman Rockwell to help outline his economic recovery program or quoting *Back to the Future* as an inspirational point in a State of the Union message or comparing state dinner functions to movie sets or likening working with Gorbachev to costarring with Errol Flynn or invoking Bruce Springsteen's angry protest song "Born in the USA"—oddly enough—as an anthem for his conservative agenda or using again and again that Gipper line from *Knute Rockne—All American*).

Himself so artfully confected and managed (we recall his tight corps of stage managers who winced whenever Reagan would move off the prepared text or away from his omnipresent stack of notecards), Reagan in turn crafted from the stuff of other cultural referents—largely Frank Capra films and John Ford westerns and Norman Rockwell's *Saturday Evening Post* covers—the gleaming edifice of Reagan's America. This edifice was offered to us not as an inspiring vision of recovery or even as a bit of excessive (if excusable) political propaganda prompted by election year strategy but, rather, as an immediate reality, that is, as a sort of theme-park reality, a mesmerizing Theme-Park-on-the-Hill, an alternate world peopled by those with entrepreneurial savvy and an unquestioning love of country, by those moved by love of family and community, and by the abiding belief in a God who favors hard work and self-sacrifice. Like Disney World, Reagan's America was an environment of optimism and possibility so neat, so clean, so believable, so accessible that, much like those who travel to Orlando, we did not want to note its obvious disengagement from the immediate, its obvious hokey fraudulence. We wanted the feeling (if not the work) of prosperity; we wanted the feeling (if not the work) of reclaimed confidence and pride. We were told again and again that America was back, that America was strong, that America had rebounded under the caring auspices of the benevolent wealthy—and that that America was all about us, as "real" as any of the edifices of Disney's Main Street emporia. Standing there amid Reagan's

America (like pausing along Disney's Main Street or, for that matter, pausing amid the lexical exhibitionism of a postmodern text), we were compelled by the convincing scale of the exercise, the vastness of the spectacle itself.

Of course, whether speaking of Reagan's America or Disney World or a postmodern text, such *plaisir du texte* is not for everyone. To those unwilling to perform the necessary role of complicity (for instance, a Mondale/Cuomo Democrat or a middle-class family who goes to Florida for the beaches or a reader who savors the realistic novel), each of these postmodern texts is so excessive that it becomes deep parody, so conspicuous that it becomes camp, and the confidence that each text generates, the love of an artifice so garishly deliberate, is simply inexplicable. But surely the point of each postmodern exercise is not to disparage its obvious illusion, the preposterous composition of its play zone, but rather to succumb to it. Only those who deliberately resist the intention of Disney World would shuffle about the park niggling like a comptroller about the inflated cost of a soft drink or pointing out that clearly that is not a real bird in that "tree" that is so clearly not a real tree. Or, for that matter, only those most blind to the nervy intention of postmodern texts would page through any of those canonical exercises in narrative terrorism and grouse about their lack of resonant characters, linear narrative, or any coherent theme. And only those joylessly committed to the immediate would intrude into the playscape of Reagan's America as Walter Mondale did.

Fritz came to us in middecade like Tennessee Williams's Gentleman Caller, an emissary from reality most reluctantly invited. He pitched something he (unfortunately) chose to call the "New Realism" in a nasally Norwegian twang that could chip ice, and then insisted on doling out only tough gristle that refused to sizzle—talk of sacrifice and limits and inevitable taxes. Still in a vacation mode, we no more wanted to hear such dour realities than we would want to strain over the railings of the jungle steamer to glimpse the steel tracks on which our "boat" so effortlessly glides.

Under Reagan, whose stagey instincts and rich charisma frustrated any intellectual analysis of his appeal, we elected (literally and symbolically) not to disparage the illusion but rather to cooperate—that cooperation alone gave the decade the fragile legitimacy of a theme park. It is that very fragility, however, that is the subject of this book.

*   *   *

It is God who through his cataclysms unknots the equilibrium of terror in which humans are imprisoned.

Jean Baudrillard, *Simulacra and Simulation*

In the depth of accident, you be supple—never sleepy but at sleeping time.

Saul Bellow, *The Adventures of Augie March*

Surely to a child nothing would be more attractive than to live in Disney World, to settle amid the confected spectacles, amid the sweet insulation of its deep theater, the casual press of its unrelenting optimism, the sanguine celebration of form over content. It is, however, a far different matter to an adult. Even as so many of us so willfully succumbed to the seductive construct of Reagan's theme park and went about the serious business of cooperative play within such a managed zone of spectacle, others began the requisite counterbalancing. Not all of us went on vacation.

The novelists examined here authorize an exuberant binding to the very immediate made so splendidly irrelevant by the gaudy theater of play suggested by the Reagan Era. It is not that some of us simply tired of play. If that were the case, we would turn back to the immediate, to those novels examined here, much like those who complete a long day at Disney World and must turn, grimly, to face the parking lot, poorly prepared to reengage that larger field of reference not enclosed within the magic reach of the Master Proprietor, that larger immediate environment that we needed so desperately to deny in the first place. We turn to the immediate not simply because we weary of the deliberate artifice—whether Reagan's America, Disney World, or a postmodern text—but rather because amid the sheer excess of each magic zone we find ourselves gradually anesthetized to the very spectacles meant to enthrall us. The novelists herein discussed are hardly killjoys pointing out, with the smarmy attitude of a tsk-tsking playground monitor, that the dangerous trivia of each created play environment offers only spectacles that, although audacious and reviving, revel in the inauthentic and, thus, compel only mock emotions: feigned excitement, feigned awe, feigned thrills.

True, such deadening counterweight is often associated with the realistic novel. Turning from the lavish cerebral daring of postmodern texts to consider realistic fare might seem like abruptly leaving the circus to tidy up the elephant stables. We might feel abandoned to the burden of taking up what will most assuredly prove to be dreary pinched books, shabby testimonials undoubtedly coined in a dreary vernacular that make too much ado over dreary characters who toil at dreary jobs at the Winn-Dixie, who fret over their dreary disappointing children, or who wrestle over their dreary urges to sleep with a neighbor's ever-so-slightly-less-dreary spouse. These novels, however, reject such oppositional logic. As cultural documents of Reagan's America, they fully understand the power and the possibilities and the suasion of spectacle. They seek not to reject play but rather to reenchant work. These novels, so convinced of the significance of the immediate, caution that when the artifice becomes too slick—when we no longer care to distinguish bird calls from the stereo soundtrack piping from speakers hung between plastic branches, for instance, or when we find ourselves too fascinated by the backstage/onstage machinery that purrs so efficiently within a self-reflexive text, or when our national agenda turns out to be little more than the thin camp of nostalgia—we come to feel the oppression. We tire of contrived dilemmas—the utter lack of intensity as we engage pirates, octopi, ghosts, and bandits on slick mechanical rides, or the utter lack of intensity as we engage the baroque plotlines and simulated dilemmas faced by those curious noncharacters who turn so regularly into mesmerizing (if ultimately empty) experiments in language effect and sign theory, or (in the case of Reagan's America) the utter lack of intensity in processed optimism necessarily ungrounded in events and inspired by captivatingly lavish and surreally empty spectacles. In each play zone, we risk losing access to the possibility of depth, the empowering experience of pain, the instructive pulse of significant sorrow and meaningful joy. That is the work of the luminous argument of the novels explored here.

Luminous realism? Those two terms have seldom been linked. American realism, to borrow Harold Kolb's helpful phrasing, has been largely "descendental."[11] Acknowledging, of course, that any genre that can include Booth Tarkington and Saul Bellow, Edith Wharton and Jacqueline Susann, necessarily frustrates too-tidy observations, we will hazard nevertheless a directing generality: seldom has the traditional realistic vision tendered much reward for investigating the ordinary, a sphere that in its translation within the canonical texts of American realism (and of its darker offshoot, naturalism) emerges as a brutally oppressive environment of unsettling clout that works to crush whatever slender aspirations characters dare cling to. Since Huck Finn, realistic characters have struggled against their own evident inconsequentiality, the roiling unpredictability of random misfortune, have suffered against and within the immediate, a text-site that few readers would aspire to inhabit, peopled by misfits, criminals, the bored, and the ignoble who persist just below our concern.

Indeed, realism has given us largely casualties. This is not to demand from our literature the dopey idiocy of Pollyanna or to reanimate Howells's much maligned call for a realism sunny side up but rather to observe that the realistic tradition, in engaging the dark energy of experience, can leave even the most sanguine reader little to affirm. Characters are left shattered by experience, inhumed within saving illusions we see as lies or bitterly drained of any ideals, educated into limitations: Basil March, Silas Lapham, Carrie Meeber, Theron Ware, Jurgis Rudkus, Newland Archer, Antonia Shimerda, George Babbitt, Frederick Henry, Nick Carraway, Jack Burden, Morris Bober, Holden Caulfield, Ed Gentry. But these shattered ones are the fortunates. They at least survive their narratives. Consider realism's considerable obituary, those ultimately leveled by the immediate: McTeague, Studs Lonigan, Edna Pontellier, Maggie Johnson, Clyde Griffiths, Katherine Congreve, Peyton Loftis; Dick Hickock and Perry Smith (and, of course, the Clutters); Julian English; Randall Patrick McMurphy. Indeed, the saving heroic impulse within realistic texts since Huck Finn has been escape, the defiant (and desperate) gesture of flight that is so often deep (and unconvincing) retreat: Tom Joad, George Willard, Chief Bromden, Harry Angstrom, Yossarian, Augie March, Ezekiel Farragut, Cacciato. Adjustment, engagement, accommodation are acts of deep irony.

Surely, then, the signal theme of American realistic fictions from Henry Fleming to Moses Herzog has been the struggle of the fragile heart to maintain its tender integrity against an immediate that will not be coaxed to sympathy. Seldom in our realistic fiction does the immediate not frustrate, strangle, limit, terrorize, ultimately destroy. American realism has given us a century of characters full of disaster. They suffer without clear insight amid an immediate that has been at turns rendered metaphorically as a battlefield, a deserted railroad yard dirty with ashes, a desert, a squalid urban tenement, a cluttered row house, a jail cell, an asylum, a jungle, a feculent sewer, a dunghill. To be ordinary has been to be meager. Frankness as literary device inevitably ensures harshness. In what Donald Pizer terms the negative epiphanies of the realistic imperative, characters are left frustrated, denied, bewildered.

It will be the radical argument of our texts of the 1980s that as such realism has been truthful—but not entirely honest. As it turns out, life is more interesting than this. The realistic texts of the 1980s allowed the saving possibility of extending a generous benediction to such wounded lives, dared to intuit that when the sparest bit of (extra)ordinary sunlight touches the merest angle of the (un)spectacular immediate, it nevertheless sparkles. Such realistic texts propose, audaciously as it turns out, that endurance is not our sole option, that disappointment need not be the last word, that experience need not grind into drudgery, and that affirmation (not despair) and engagement (not retreat) are the more demanding responses. This is a period study. These books, by daring to stare into the crippling beauty of the immediate, by daring us to accept the risks of engagement, take issue with the decade's most significant emotional energy—optimism—and its dominant movement—withdrawal. Locked within the magic kingdom of the Reagan Era, we were given a fascinating confederacy of realistic novels in which characters risked engagement, made peace with the hobgoblins of chance and mortality that so bedeviled plotlines of inherited realistic narratives, and turned opened eyes toward an immediate that suddenly, unexpectedly shone with a dark but steadying radiance. Or we were given texts in which characters who refused such gestures were satirized, left distanced from reader sympathy. The Reagan Era made us all optimists; these texts argue that we deserved a better fate. Only against the gaudy, splashy spectacles of the Reagan Era, only in an era when optimism seemed so shallow, so heavily (and shabbily) spun, so patently theatrical—only in such a magic kingdom time could these works and their message—to step out from the magic kingdom—bear such heavy and significant weight.

This is not to suggest, of course, that the affirmation typical of these realistic works has never been sounded before in American literature. Surely American realists before the 1980s have suggested that experience wounds but reveals: such an argument is sustained within the deep reach of James's parlors and drawing rooms, by the harrowing beauty of Faulkner's Mississippi (and in the later work of southern writers such as Eudora Welty and Peter Taylor), within the urban epiphanies of Bellow's midcentury narratives, and in the broad range of John Updike's career-long explorations of the press and feel of the middle-class immediate.

Indeed, the earlier works of the some of the writers herein discussed—Anne Tyler and Reynolds Price, for example—tapped a splendid sense of the rewards of engaging a most daunting immediate. The point of this book is not to suggest that awareness and affirmation have never coexisted in American realistic narratives, but rather that these earlier isolated texts and these authors came to their cultural moments like mail delivered to the wrong address. It would take the showy excess of the Reagan Era to give cultural heft to this genre of realistic narratives. Reagan made significant—not possible—these luminous texts. As the appendix indicates, novelists in the 1980s collectively argued that realistic narratology need not only attack, expose, denounce, deflate, depress, distress, detonate, and deny; it might also find its way to affirm the shattering possibility that the immediate is an intriguing complex of dark compensations that compels not flight or fear but that rather educates and ultimately justifies wonder. To quote Bruce Springsteen, whose decade recordings brought such an argument to contemporary music, such texts addressed "those who have a notion / A notion deep inside / That it ain't no sin to be glad you're alive."

This genre needed the Reagan Era. These texts would emerge during a decade that offered so many distracting strategies for avoiding the immediate: in addition to Reagan's junk-bond optimism, there was the staggering proliferation of theme parks, the lure of the virtual realities of ever more sophisticated home and arcade game systems, the explosion of cable television technologies, the emerging webbing of the Internet, the dark cultural fascination with designer drugs, the splashy distracting excesses of Hollywood big-budget spectacles, the often bizarre expression of unconventional spirituality, and, far more disturbing, the emergence by decade's close of the unsettling ennui and chic angst of the alternative generation X that so wholeheartedly abandoned feigning even the slightest interest in the premise of affirmation and the notion of any value to the immediate. Amid such a decade, our writers fashioned a most defiant rejection of such strategies of retreat by reinvigorating the premise of the immediate; writers from far different backgrounds and literary interests (this book, for example, brings together Joyce Carol Oates *and* T. C. Boyle, Anne Tyler *and* Robert Ferro) confronted their cultural moment and forged a most radical body of realistic narratives that dared to remind us, pleasantly locked within the magic kingdom, that we cannot afford to take any of our sorry and splendid life for granted.

Yet, oddly, the luminous works of realism discussed here have been left largely without significant audience, privileged neither by book-stores nor by universities. Consider the consumer literature of the Reagan Era. Even a casual review reveals that the era's megabooks, its big-event best-sellers, only stroked our decade-long hunger to play. Best-seller lists were dominated by the industrial-strength puree processed endlessly by the Danielle Steel–Jackie Collins–Judith Krantz conglom-erate, the pleasant nullity of the middle-age romances of Robert James Waller, the prehistoric epics of Jean Auel, the hokey nightmare tomes of Stephen King, the techno-thrillers of Michael Crichton, the manipulative political endgames worked out by Robert Ludlow or Tom Clancy, and the potato epics of James Michener. Such works invoked the trappings of realism—recognizable characters, quickstepping linear plots, detailed settings with meticulous fidelity to specific time schemes, a reassuring sense of closure enhanced by clichéd lessons—yet they deliberately dis-pensed with the unsettling nuances of the immediate typical in the works we will examine. They are as "realistic" as the pirates in Disney's Carib-bean ride. Harlequin in intent, cinematic in execution, they most often morphed into low-level Hollywood offerings or, more fittingly, into high-profile television miniseries. These best-selling event-books partici-pated in the national urge to play: they were vacation books, subway/commuter books, beach books, terminal reading (airport, that is). Denied status as academic texts, denied serious examination even by book re-viewers, such "realistic" narratives reveled in their lucrative status as play.

Against such a decade at play, the realistic novels herein discussed engaged in the apparently unglittering counterforce of work, explored the immediate zone we had so cheerfully fled with the blessings of a president far more comfortable in his own tight zone of crafted play. Neither postmodern mind-circuses nor fluffed megabooks, these realis-tic novels have existed as of this writing in a most perplexing limbo state: they lacked the invasive muscle of the big best-sellers (although some bobbed uncertainly in the shallower end of best-seller charts), and they lacked the credentials to encourage, for the most part, any more critical attention than sympathetic reviews. Given the scholarly fascination with postmodern text explication (a generation of willing academics perform-ing the explicatory function of Disney's Birnbaum), given those canoni-cal postmodern mastertexts in which the placement of a comma can sus-tain pages of critical commentary, the novels considered here have stayed for the most part unexamined, much like the phenomenal world they so energetically engaged. They are not lost works ("lost," after all, suggests someone is looking for them), but rather they were just let go, allowed to move gracelessly out of print and to settle into the dust of library shelves.

So what sort of realism is offered here? It would be, perhaps, convenient to our narrative of the 1980s to draw pat lines of connection to the Gilded Age, the first great flowering of American realism. Comparisons can be made—and have been—between the Reagan Era and the time during and immediately after Grant. As we mentioned, the Gilded Age, like the Reagan Era, was a period of national restoration hard on the heels of divisive national traumas that seemed to justify playtime encouraged by a hands-off president more focused on the trappings of leadership than on its execution. Both eras found intoxicating the flashy thump of jingoism. Both were giddy eras of optimism that evolved under the benevolent auspices of fiercely pro-business governance, eras that encouraged the flaunting of the frivolous baubles of wealth and that celebrated like folk heroes entrepreneurial barons of industrial growth—even as the divisions widened between haves and have-nots.

But the realistic literature of that era is far different from the work produced in the Reagan era.[12] Certainly, both generations of realistic narratives demanded honest engagement against influences they both understood to be fraudulent: on the one hand, the exotic escapism and easy melodrama of post–Civil War romancers and, on the other, the verbal density and self-validating play of the postmodern avant-garde. But there are important differences. Encouraged by the revolution in photography and by the popular hunger for news, novels in the first great era of American realistic narratives offered the meticulous observation of the immediate plane (a bald exercise in work). Enthralled particularly by the sheer energy and special agonies occasioned within the new urban sites and as well as by the lore of the American outback beyond the Allegheny River unknown to the fashionable reading markets in New York and Boston, these writers brought literary expression into the immediate by rendering their settings carefully and accurately, by delving into character motivation, by excusing the author from intrusive commentary, by subjecting characters to the often joyless business of scientific observation, and by resisting the heavy gravitational pull of fairy-tale happy endings. Such books understood the reward of literary expression to be its impact, its ability to expound often difficult lessons about our shared capacity for indulging the material, for squandering the gift of love, for denying the supportive structuring of the family. Such lessons were administered to a reading audience like paregoric. The world, such narratives argued collectively, could not be prettied just for books; their saving gesture was the steadying faith in the ameliorative quality of honest perception, the long-shot possibility of eventual reform (moral and, in some cases, social and political) should we agree to see ourselves as we are.

How, then, are the realistic novels of the 1980s different? To be sure, the novels here are similarly constructed to reveal the immediate: recognizable characters struggle amid recognizable situations, stumbling with the imperfect grace that mar(k)s the awkward beauty of our own steps within the immediate, our own imperfect movement toward realizations that are hard-earned moments of heart-opening clarity. Like these ancestor texts, our realistic texts tangle with the traditional hobgoblins of chance and mortality. In addition, much like their nineteenth-century counterparts, these narratives are structurally and stylistically conservative, vibrant exercises in storytelling that develop a full company of characters who engage a reader's sympathy, that ignite the immediate by locating within its accidental arrangements of line, color, shadows, and objects the suggestion of the metaphoric, that manipulate the rich draw of suspense, and that move toward the necessary release of decisive closure. But the realistic novels of the 1980s brought together here undertake a far more intriguing work than merely pulling a perhaps reluctant audience toward the immediate, toward accepting what made such perfect sense during the Reagan Era to avoid. The novelists considered here seek nothing less than to transfer the understandable need for spectacle to the realm of the immediate, to bring together the apparently competing spheres of work and play.

It is not enough for these writers within the magic kingdom of Reagan's America to argue reengagement; that leads only to the disappointment associated with traditional realistic fare, the downbeat that inevitably concludes playtime. Nor do they invoke the angry rhetoric of condemnation and period satire; such hyperchurning so quickly becomes dated. Nor do they seek the dicey role of teacher/preacher outlining how we are to live, chiseling cold and careful moral fictions that deal too easily and too certainly with designating good and bad behavior. Nor do they seek to play the elaborate postmodern game of magic realism, that highly literary, highly artificial strategy of smuggling the inexplicable and the fantastic into the otherwise grim and ordinary. These works seek, rather, to reenchant the immediate. They are works of what we will call spectacle realism, a genre of realistic texts that offers an unapologetically ascendant sense of the immediate, a radical recognition born from full awareness of the flawed richness that, unsuspected and untapped, encloses each of us.

For our purposes, then, "spectacle" changes its grammatical occasion. It was surely the defining *noun* of the Reagan Era: those wondrous, gaudy, excessive (if empty) displays that, as we have argued, ultimately served to distract us from the immediate, to encourage the giddy celebration of disengagement. Our texts, however, alter "spectacle," subordinate it from noun to adjective. "Spectacle" here becomes a way to describe, to redefine, to reshape our understanding of the immediate. As a noun, "spectacle" may stun, but as an adjective it challenges. In shifting to the adjective position, "spectacle" functions now in a humbler but paradoxically grander way: it becomes a way of describing what is immediately about us, to remind us that the immediate, so long dismissed as shabby and disappointing, dazzles and amazes, devastates and elevates, challenges and confounds.

It may seem a bit fatuous to suggest the counterbalance to Reagan's postmodern America-as-theme-park would come from a resurgence of realistic narratives. After all, the decade suffocated us with realistic narratives. But we must be careful to separate spectacle realism from the oppressive invasion of disposable realistic narratives brought to our living rooms by cable technologies. During the 1980s we floundered in a webbing of realistic plots: the long-standing lineup of modest evening network melodramas and sitcoms supplemented by channels of cable programming, recycled offerings that returned Mary Richards and Matt Dillon to our cultural dialogue; developments in programming such as real-life docudramas, courtroom coverage, prime-time news shows, sensationalized "authentic reenactments" of crimes and rescues; hours and hours of talk shows that unspooled for public display the often aberrant private lives of countless guests drawn (amazingly) from the general population; the decade-long promotion of feel-good features, storytime interludes during news shows, both local and national; unedited, unending (and attractively inexpensive) broadcasts of legislative committee testimony and endless panel discussions on virtually all aspects of human behavior; infotainment shows that tracked with predatory ruthlessness the narrative lines of celebrities, athletes, and/or politicians; twenty-four-hour movie channels that showcased hour upon grinding hour even the dreariest Hollywood releases; the revolution in VCRs that domesticated those very same dreary releases, making them accessible and collectable; and, supremely, our fascination with video recorders that rendered us all characters in yet more realistic narratives, transforming our children's Tuesday evening soccer game into an epic narrative captured on tape for some unnamable posterity.

Surely, it could be reasoned that amid such an inundation of realistic narratives, realism might lose its suasive edge. It is clear, however, that compared to the luminous argument offered by our novelists, these realistic exercises are patently counterfeit. They indeed work against the respect for dilemma that distinguishes the argument of the novelists here examined. They are more part of the decade's counterforce of play. Guests on talk shows are given quick paramedic triage by today's guest counselor, or they are advised that they need professional straightening by well-intentioned (and thoroughly unschooled) audience members, or they are given a handy toll-free number for a local support group—there, dilemma solved. Characters within the packaged units of television programming have always recovered resolution within the required thirty- or sixty-minute time frame (twenty-two or forty-six minutes with commercials); news programs shape their features toward similarly convenient and tidy closure, save in far more compact time. The other realistic narratives cited are untrimmed testimonials, the negligible blather of the cable age. The complications of pain and wonder, the very experience of the immediate, receive only the blandest treatment from such programming: too intimidated by depth, too put out by complication, they tidy what is untidy and turn a viewing audience away from any respect for the freewheeling, splendidly contentious universe—harrowing and magnificent—that we must engage when comes the time to turn from our sets.[13]

It is exactly that question—what to do with the untidy, the unpackaged immediate—that finds its resonant response in the works of spectacle realism. These are novels that, when approached with the care that has long marked the explication of the gametexts of postmodernism, yield unsuspected depth, unsuspected urgency, and—far more intriguing—unsuspected vastness. These novelists recover the massive grace and wounding experience of the ordinary: love, family, work, and death. These novels provide a most important counterbalance to a culture on vacation by asserting with considerable audacity that spectacle is not found only in escape, that dazzle is not reserved for artifice—that the unrehearsed, the unprepared, the unpackaged immediate (of so little interest to Reagan's America and to Disney's World) can co-opt the logic of spectacle and can sustain, by its vast capacity to stun, the very need for wonder we seek to fulfill in our play. These are, to borrow from the lexicon of the decade, kinder, gentler fictions. They remind us that compared to the glitzy thrills of the playscape of Disney World, the ride home offers the possibility of a far more significant experience of vulnerability, unscripted encounters, imperfect anxieties, and, supremely, the possibility of legitimate emotion; so secure within the clean logic of the Magic Kingdom, we never suspect the open highway could be wider than we imagined and loaded with a magic of its own.

The argument here, of course, cannot possibly cover the breadth of the efflorescence of spectacle realism during the decade. Surely a book such as this might have included the spectacle realism found in the body of decade work of E. L. Doctorow, Louise Erdrich, Richard Ford, Mary Gordon, David Leavitt, Alison Lurie, Gloria Naylor, Jane Smiley, as well as in a formidable list of significant individual novels and in the continuing achievements of Bellow, Roth, and Updike. Two of the decade's literary phenomena, however, centered so obviously in the logic of realistic narrative, perhaps merit mention if only because they would so emphatically not fit the present work: namely, the grim urban realism of the celebrated Brat Pack (Bret Ellis Easton, Jay McInerny, Tama Janowitcz) and the realistic supertome of Tom Wolfe's 1987 blockbuster *The Bonfire of the Vanities*.

The much hyped works of the East Coast Brat Pack, the cluster of middecade realistic narratives that recorded with banal objectivity the drugged drift of the emerging Lost Generation X, could not reward the act of engagement apart from the grim smirk of revealing just how shoddy our materialistic lives had become. Within this fin-de-millennium ennui, these characters kick about a corpsed world and conclude with unearned anguish that we have been spiritually mall-ed. They respond to the excessive play of Reagan's America with too-hip cynicism, too-easy despair, and find attractive the alternatives of whining or escaping into drugs and sexual excess or making chic the mind-numbing indulgence of television. On the other hand, Wolfe's mammoth book, so self-consciously patterned after turn-of-the-century novels of muckraking social realism with its appropriately large-scale cast of characters and cinema-scope plot, exposed the underside of the Reagan Era fascination with wealth, of acquisition without conscience. Handsomely vast in scale, heavy with period particularity, eminently readable, the work offered only a handy lesson and an ensemble of marvelously striking characters—it indulged, in its own way, the play ethic but with a lesson attached, sort of like going to Colonial Williamsburg instead of to Disney World. So intent on its preaching imperative, it threatened to become an ungainly satire (as the later Brian DePalma movie revealed). It is surely not to deny the cultural weight of both of these expressions of realism to find their argument invalid here; but the present work surveys what is a much vaster and, ultimately, far more integral element of any narrative of the 1980s. The glittering charm of nihilism and the hard work of social realism, to borrow from the vocabulary of the 1980s, is simply out of the mainstream.

We will follow an emerging definition of spectacle realism by tracing a shared vision among eight writers whose works can represent a decade's argument. Chapter to chapter, we will follow the dark beauty of the struggle to engage, the slow and steady movement toward accepting what we each so inexplicably resist: the radical benediction of the immediate. The novels are treated here not in chronological order but are rather shaped into a thematic narrative that follows a movement outward, from withdrawal to engagement, a movement out from the magic kingdom, a narrative argument that begins with characters too drawn by the logic of disengagement—too locked within private magic kingdoms—to enter into the vibrant immediate. They are characters—Enid Stevick, John Wheelwright, Kate Vaiden—difficult to like, characters cut with deep irony, characters who resist learning; indeed education emerges as a controlling narrative structure for spectacle realism as a genre. We move to characters—Daniel Quinn, Mark Valerian, Maggie Moran, Depeyster Van Wart, Stuart Ressler, Jan O'Deigh—who each in turn come to feel the resonant reward of engaging what seems at first a most unspectacular immediate, an immediate that promises only the wounding gracelessness of unpredictable love and then the intrusive stroke of mortality. As we move from chapter to chapter, we will follow the gradual movement toward affirmation, the halting halfsteps, the false moves, the disastrous failures and luminous triumphs. We will move, chapter to chapter, from unflattering postures of withdrawal to heroic gestures of painful engagement.

It is a most demanding process—indeed, these books come to speak each to the other in unexpected ways. We cannot understand the shattering moment of vulnerability and engagement that marks Jan O'Deigh's closing affirmation that ends this volume without going through the painful retreat and withdrawal of Oates's Enid Stevick that begins it. Here, a gallery of characters must be educated, must be reminded that the value of experience, the pain and the joy of engagement, has always been its ability to alter our perceptions, to permit growth. These characters have similar dilemmas, test similar solutions, touch on shared opportunities, but move toward far different fates. Burned by experience, they each find the immediate supremely rejectable. We will follow as our writers school their characters in the difficult lesson of spectacle realism, in the luminous notion that confidence in the phenomenal world will reveal the (extra)ordinary in even the most perplexing immediate.

Not surprisingly, the problem cited again and again within these novels of spectacle realism is the self, that little engine of imaginative possibility that so energizes (indeed fashions) the postmodern funhouses. From Enid Stevick to Jan O'Deigh, these characters move (when and if they move at all) against the centrifugal force of collapsing into the self. To engage the immediate, these authors caution, is to engage each other—the anxious, imperfect exertions of the heart.

That is the work and the achievement of the novels of spectacle realism. Read collectively, these works are a most forceful argument for engagement and honesty. Certainly, it might be objected, in their mesmerizing narrative lines and with their humane characters muddling about the same dilemmas we must engage, these novels offer simply a different sort of play from the postmodern funhouses, a different sort of escapism from the mega-sellers, a different sort of cozy refuge from the taxing moments of our everyday. Surely, it can be argued, a Tyler novel or a Kennedy novel is just as much a controlled playscape as any fashioned by Barth or Pynchon or Gass. But compared to the deliberate systems of interior playscapes typical of the postmodern texts, the narratives here, if they are vacations, are more akin to trips to the wild seashore or to the open mountains or to the exhilarating treachery of whitewater—vacations that delight in negotiating demanding circumstances and risky engagements, vacations that require unblinking awareness, vacations that reward the willing engagement of the splendor and treachery of the unpackaged, the unrehearsed, the unscheduled.

Sounded against the shrill clanging anthems of Reagan's America, the noisy splash and dazzle of that manufactured counterfeit morning-in-America optimism, these writers intone a splendid counterascendant melody, one set in a most demanding minor key. Unlike the linguistic inventiveness and foregrounded stylistics of postmodern texts, these are works, these are characters, these are dilemmas that come to lodge in our hearts. They are works that offer not happy endings—that is the stuff and fluff of Disney and Reagan—but rather closings that satisfy our need to render from the improbable mess of the immediate the reassuring shape and feel of affirmation, endings that temper our keenest awareness with our deepest need for hope.

This, then, is the signature narrative of the realistic novels of the 1980s—and thus a significant element of any emerging definition of that era. These novels stand in striking counterforce to the junk-bond carnival of play erected and sustained through the decade and so wildly relished by a culture that perceived itself long overdue for such release. They are narratives that recognize that our problem was not that we craved the spectacles and the spirit of play but rather that we understood such giddy rejuvenation was our right only if we abdicated what we knew to be our immediate, disparaged its elusive, maddeningly imperfect benediction.

It is, perhaps, the unfortunate burden of our cultural imagination that the most familiar cultural epic that treats such a tension between work and play, between responsibilities and delight, is the 1939 MGM musical *The Wizard of Oz*, in which Dorothy Gale moves toward the bittersweet recognition that there is no place like home and makes her awkward (and sentimental) peace with the sloppy hogpens and carping relatives of her immediate world of Kansas; yet such saving wisdom comes even as we lose the vibrant color and absorbing spectacle of Oz and fade into the dreary spiritless black-and-whites of grunge-Kansas. Imagine, our narratives will argue, just the opposite. Imagine we are told that the color and the spectacle rest unsuspected in Kansas even as the glitzy (and tiresome) playscape of Oz stills into black-and-white dreariness. Imagine when Dorothy awakes on her dingy farm bed, her head swathed by a wet cloth, imagine that then the world suddenly, joyously leaps to color. In a decade when we so neatly veered away from any confrontation with the immediate because it was apparently known and so apparently thin, these narratives fetch us back into the immediate and dare us to participate in the imperfect, to feel its rushing urgency, to face full-front our own immediate world and there to touch, if even for a moment, the complex magic of spectacle.

1

Reading Ringside

Joyce Carol Oates, *You Must Remember This*

> *Moonlight and love songs never out of date.*
> *Hearts full of passion, jealousy, and hate.*
> *Woman needs man and man must have his mate*
> *That no one can deny.*
>
> Herman Hupfeld, "As Time Goes By"

We begin, appropriate to the logic of Reagan's America, in full retreat.

Readings of Joyce Carol Oates's decade masterwork *You Must Remember This* start to sound a little like the undercard down at the Armory: a lengthy lineup of contested pairs. The novel is apparently irresistibly contentious.[1] Perhaps encouraged by Oates's own controlling metaphor, the boxing ring, these critical stances pit attractive opposites to explicate Oates's massive narrative: power versus impotence, men versus women, innocence versus experience, emotion versus reason, self-interest versus idealism, lust versus love, nature versus art. Everything about the novel, it would seem, suggests rivalry and competition—we even share the live prime-time television event of Arthur Godfrey versus Julius LaRosa. But the opposition central to Oates's narrative—the main event, as it were— is surely the tension that unfolds between fact and fiction, or more precisely between the (f)actual and its suppression through elaborate strategies of what is best described as self-induced amnesia. It is a dilemma that will help establish the premise of spectacle realism.

Like the other narratives to be examined here, *You Must Remember This* is full of stunning events, each rendered quite graphic, quite immediate: statutory rape compounded by near-incest, fierce fights (some actually in the ring), automobile accidents, a backstreet abortion, messy suicides. Yet, within the narrative, these centering events stay secret, denied validity or confirmation. Among the characters—most of whom are in the same family (the Stevicks), and all of whom live within the same neighborhood of grim brown streets in Port Oriskany, New York—no two share an awareness of the same set of events. No one confides; no one even dares to encode into language (written or spoken) the dark evidences of human behavior so central to Oates's narrative. For instance, Enid Stevick, who in her early teens conducts a torrid two-year affair with her step-uncle, Felix, never tells anyone in her family about the relationship, even after the abortion that ends it. Her parents, Lyle and Hannah, assume she is so emotionally awkward that she can't get a date, and they take comfort in the interest her step-uncle shows in her. Enid does write about the shattering sexual encounters with her step-uncle in a notebook she keeps in her bedroom, but those entries are entirely in a private code—and even that notebook is consigned to a fire by Enid's mother, who, uncertain what it says, reduces it to ashes anyway in the uneasy aftermath of Enid's suicide attempt.

In addition to this clandestine affair, the narrative is replete with other secrets: Lyle's arrest on charges of being a Communist sympathizer and his subsequent suicide attempt; his aborted romance with a neighborhood woman; the affair Enid's brother Warren has with a married woman in Philadelphia (at least, we assume she is married, although her past may be yet another level of narrative secrecy); Felix's bloody bar fight that leaves him near death, a gruesome beating that the family calls his "accident." Rumors and lies shadow the narrative: we never know whether the gory boxing matches have really been fixed by Felix's "business" associates in the Port Oriskany syndicate; we are never sure where Felix gets his obvious money after his boxing career ends; we are never sure who torches the tony country inn Felix and his partners subsequently (and rather conveniently) buy for a song; Al Sansom, Felix's business partner, simply disappears after agreeing to turn state's evidence against the syndicate. Again and again, the plot shades into ambiguity; again and again, characters find their way to strategies of denial. With spooky neatness, event—the horrific, the immoral, the bloody—becomes nonevent, (f)acts become fictions.

Such a strategy of denial may account for the unsettling effect of the novel's ending. Seldom in Oates's massive canon has she offered so happy an ending. It is a most Reaganesque finish. In ways that even sympathetic readings acknowledge seem a bit contrived,[2] the Stevicks each move to luminous closure—a relentless rush to the very sort of fairy-tale areality denied in the strident opening lines: "Not once upon a time but a few years ago. Last year. Last week. Last Thursday" (9). Like some fairy godmother on a benevolence jag, Oates doles out to each Stevick that most splendid of narrative gifts: a future. Warren, a Korean war veteran and misfit law school activist, begins work with an underground movement opposing American nuclear weaponry; his sister, Lizzie, after a rocky start at local nightclubs, is set to embark on a singing career in New York, where she will marry her longtime manager; Felix, the calculating sexual predator who has pursued the intense sexual liaison with Enid, prepares to marry; Lyle and Hannah, after eighteen years of sexual abstinence as part of their Catholic marriage, make awkward love in a bomb shelter Lyle has constructed in the backyard; and, recovered from her affair and from the abortion, Enid buses out of Port Oriskany and matriculates at the Westcott School of Music in Rochester—she is prepared, as Linda Wagner-Martin argues, to reject the stranglehold of men and to assert her freedom. We close surrounded by shiny, smiley faces—an embarrassment of happiness.

What is it about such a sunny closing that bothers? It is as if Enid's mother had somehow managed to torch the previous 400 pages of Oates's narrative; it is as if all those events—horrific and disturbing, luminous and exhilarating—suddenly had never happened, all of them now as harmless as ash. As each character catapults so clumsily into good fortune, we begin to suspect a savaging irony. Warren is actually camped near a government weapons installation in Colorado, preparing to counter, along with a spare handful of others, the expanding American nuclear arsenal (specifically, a new Atlas intercontinental ballistic missile systems launch site) by swinging picket signs and by blocking the gates against construction vehicles hired to complete the site. And Felix, whose brief phone conversation with Enid to tell her of his approaching marriage never mentions their affair, apparently is convinced that his frank hunger to fuck (one of his favorite words) can be domesticated within a sanctioned union—despite textual evidence that, compelled by a voracious sexual rapacity, he was seeing another man's wife throughout his intense affair with Enid. And Lizzie, whose scratch talent has been heavily buttressed by a tacky Marilyn Monroe–makeover and by an overly rehearsed repertoire of mechanical dance steps, prepares to leave for New York with a shifty manager who only promises he will divorce his wife; in the meantime, the two of them will be sharing a hotel room.

And Lyle and Hannah finally achieve sexual exercise, but only within the cold entombment of a bomb shelter and even then only after Lyle, working feverishly against gravity to preserve his rapidly withering erection, hastily conjures a dreamvision of a much younger Hannah— her of the wet cotton panties and cooing willingness—an erotic confection that thankfully commands his sexual energies after he has tried unsuccessfully to whip himself up with briefer fantasies about total strangers, including a woman he had glimpsed at a funeral and even a nurse he recalls from his distant armed service days. Like Warren, like Felix, Lyle manages luminous closure (that magnificent emptying orgasm that closes the narrative) without maintaining any handle on the immediate. As Hannah stays dry as a sock, Lyle lustily fucks a mental image, in full retreat from the fat, heaving woman with her flopping, mottled skin who is underneath him, drawn into cramped carnal positionings, grunting beneath his suddenly lively thrusts.

But Enid, who commands the narrative center, is perhaps the most disturbing among Oates's self-induced amnesiacs. Off to music school, Enid decides she has suffered sufficiently and is now prepared to put her two years of emotionally excessive behavior into the cold void of non-event. The backstreet abortion has been harmlessly reconstructed into a nasty bout with "intestinal flu"; her steamy affair with Felix was never accorded status as event, never revealed within the iron imperative of language. She closes the novel happily entombed in one of the school's piano practice rooms—an insular zone apart, her magic kingdom—playing with rusty uncertainty bits of Mozart. She winces at her clinkers, her fingering slips. But she decides that if no one hears the mistakes, those mistakes never really happened.

That culminating moment defines the logic that permeates the narrative: our darkest behaviors, our darkest (f)acts need not be acknowledged; they are "mistakes" no one hears. With meticulous care, Oates buries each of her critical characters into protective shelters, magic kingdoms where each one denies the implications of the real. They are characters who simply would rather not know. At one point, Enid, feverish in her obsession with Felix, actually sees another woman's hair in hairpins in Felix's bathroom, uncontestable evidence that he is two-timing her, and yet says nothing. Whether it is Enid preparing to step away from white-hot experience into the chilly bell jar of the university to study, nunlike, within an aesthetics curriculum that promises only detachment from the practical world of experience; or Warren undertaking hopelessly naive political activism; or Felix moving without irony into the charade of married life; or Lyle digging an elaborate hole in the ground against nuclear apocalypse—Stevicks survive by playing (much as they do frequently in the narrative) a skewed game of hide-and-seek in which the point is *not* to find what is therefore left hidden. The immediate, so richly evoked by Oates's rendering of the western New York of her own childhood, is conjured here largely to be denied by characters who each close the narrative with the bent rictus of happy—and quite empty—smiles (like the punch drunks who, Felix muses, stumble into old age unable to remember anything, thus left in the soft protection of the moment).

The brutal immediacy of the boxing ring, which figures so prominently in graphic set pieces, would seem to promise a healthy counterforce to this shadow-thick world of evasion and denial.[3] The horrors inflicted so dramatically, so openly, within the public ring are of such magnitude that spectators with tender stomachs must retreat to handy rest rooms and spectators leave the cramped, smoky arena with bloodstains on their fancy coats and polished shoes. Boxing—with its combatants nearly naked, weaponless, bathed in harsh overhanging glare, engaged in the primitive ritual of a fight to the finish—would seem to bring into a narrative full of fictions the power of facticity, raw experience without translation, without euphemism. Indeed, Oates takes us through a grueling account of several ring events, including the bloody pummeling to death of a promising young boxer under the tutelage of Felix.

Yet, Oates uses the gameworld of the boxing ring to complement rather than refute her characters' withdrawal from experience. Boxing is simply another seductive escape from the real, another protective magic zone like Warren's political rallies, Lyle's backyard bomb shelter, or Enid's practice rooms. Far from the experience of the immediate, boxing is profoundly about performance, a comparatively mild simulation of the brutal forces that daily confound us. Boxing only parodies such openness; it is actually a closed exercise in control, a synthetic field of experience where, as Felix acknowledges, there can be no accidents, a tight little world where pain comes with explanation, where rules prevail, where preparation is rewarded, where skill matters, where event is provided structure, where pain is (reassuringly) the consequence of carelessness or error, where even death (as in the case of Felix's protégé Jo-Jo Pearl) is explicable, caused, earned—a world, in fact, far from the one we must engage daily.

Boxing is, in short, another marvelous dodge of *it*, that larger world of inexplicable forces that will eventually engulf Felix. He finds his promising career short-circuited one night in the ring when he actually gets angry, that is, when he drops the neater role of athlete and touches his darker humanity; that anger costs him a beating in the ring and convinces him to abandon his career. Boxing only "works," Felix tells Enid, if you stay cool. Certainly, Felix prowls coolly within the ring; but we watch him brought low outside its neat parameters first by his consuming hunger for an adolescent Enid and later by the experience of the abortion, of a death that will not abide rules. The boxing ring, then, recalls not so much the raw world of immediacy as it does a tightly contained (and so mesmerizing) magic kingdom, more like the rigged quiz show *The $64,000 Question* that the Stevicks (ironically) find enthralling and exciting; indeed, the fights Oates so vividly dramatizes are rank with rumors that Felix and his syndicate cronies have fixed them.

Appropriately, such a drama of evasion is staged against the backdrop of the 1950s. Oates reminds us that the decade's most public melodramas centered on figures—from Senator McCarthy to Charles Van Doren, from Richard Nixon to Edward Teller—who claimed legitimacy by brandishing "facts" that would later prove to be quite convincing fictions. Hard on the heels of a generation that had destroyed a menacing global presence by a strategy of resolute confrontation, whose only fear had been fear itself, here a culture went about the business of strategic withdrawal, deliberately refusing to think about the unthinkable amid a most unpleasant array of pressing "facts" about nuclear war cataloged by dozens of earnest government agencies and disseminated in lurid detail by newspapers and televisions, politicians and archbishops.

In Oates's reading of the 1950s (the decade that most shaped Reagan's worldview), distortions are given the validity and weight of evidence. Midnarrative, Lyle Stevick purchases a tiny Philco black-and-white television. Like so many other American families, the Stevicks, spellbound by that flickering matrix of colorless dots and gray shadows, begin to lose parameters, begin to move too casually from coverage of on-site nuclear testing to Lucy and Desi's flat, thus trivializing our most momentous (and terrifying) public events into harmless entertainments and reducing "reality" to flat, banal two-dimensional images, drained of color and pressed lifelessly under thick glass. Television, far from connecting the Stevicks to reality through the sudden muscle of a global reach, offers a most curious distancing, yet another shelter.

And the Cold War itself, which so (de)centers Lyle Stevick, proved another game of evasion, save on a global scale. The Stevick family watches on their tiny Philco the enthralling (and, we know now, deliberately contrived) melodrama of the McCarthy hearings, a virulent campaign that rested its case on a fire wall of unsubstantiated charges coaxed into sounding like the truth by the newly fanged media monster. The Cold War itself was executed only on paper in hot (and ultimately harmless) rhetoric, a paper war of newspaper screeds (like the ones Lyle reads so faithfully) and government pamphlets on the "facts" of the coming nuclear engagement (indeed, the necessity of putting the word within quotation marks indicates the era's blur of fact and fiction). Extrapolating with deliberate recklessness the barest scientific data, our government undertook the vast theater piece of a paper war, generating a most stubborn paranoia that drove us to undertake questionable military campaigns in obscure distant lands deemed suddenly critical, to execute domestic "spies" on the thinnest evidence, to drill a generation of bewildered students in civil defense skills, to test nuclear devices with grim recklessness, and all the while to promote backyard bomb shelters that could not, would not, afford even the meagerest hope of survival. In law school, Warren Stevick listens to a speaker who explains how any nuclear exchange would mock any attempts to prepare. Yet a generation ingested "facts" about Communist supremacy and Soviet strategy for world domination and the necessity of war preparation, facts that we recognize now as fictions.

The 1950s, then, offer a most appropriate backdrop for Oates's narrative and a most appropriate starting point for examining the 1980s. In that earlier decade (as in the 1980s), surrounded by facts, we dwelled nevertheless amid fictions. It was a suggestive, symbolic time where what was real went largely undetected, unacknowledged—much like the toxins that fly about the air of the industrial sections of Port Oriskany.

The few characters here who attempt to traffic in truth quickly pay a most disturbing price. In his used furniture shop, Lyle Stevick points out to an annoying elderly customer that the USSR and Red China occupy more area than the United States, a simple "matter of geography" (69) as handy as the world atlas that Lyle brandishes. For such efforts, Lyle finds himself within a Kafkaesque span of a handful of hours arrested as a

Communist sympathizer, subjected to five hours of ignoble grilling at the local police station, and ultimately released only because Lyle happens to reveal he had a son wounded in Korea and the police interrogator sympathizes and relents.

And there is Enid's music teacher, Mr. Lesnovich, who blasts Enid as she rhapsodizes on the refuge music offers her. Enid insists that could she master a difficult Chopin piece, suffering would never invade her life. He tells her baldly, baring discolored teeth, that such escapism is nonsense, that music cannot structure protection, that music is "only itself. . . . it carries you out of yourself but then you must return" (261). For his attempt at correcting Enid's delusion, he is left toiling joylessly through the monotony of endless rounds of thankless instruction amid the meager talents of Port Oriskany.

And there is Al Sansom, Felix's syndicate business partner in shady dealings that Oates deliberately obscures in the half-light of innuendo and gossip, who agrees to turn state's evidence when federal agents press too closely—to tell nothing but the truth. Before he comes to testify, however, he disappears mysteriously (but not unpredictably), his body never recovered, its demise explained only by the flimsiest webbing of denials and lies.

And there are the Rosenbergs, the real-life couple whose show trial and dramatic execution Enid follows. What sends the pair to the electric chair is not any deed they may have committed but rather their refusal to cooperate in the construction of the elaborate lie of nuclear paranoia that the justice system wanted so desperately to promote. Determined to tell the truth, like Lyle Stevick, like Mr. Lesnovich, like Al Sansom, they go off to their reward: brutal extinction.

Like the 1980s, the 1950s, then, marked an era of retreat when we met our most profound national fears with denial. Geraldine, Enid's sister who marries early and turns most powerfully fertile, tells Enid about childbirth—but then reassures her of the powerful dope available to allay such wracking pain. Indeed, the narrative explores how to circumvent the pain of emotional experience, how to dope up against experience itself; characters exploit all the traditional anesthetics: drugs, alcohol, religious extremism, suicide, and heavy doses of Ted Mack, Lucy, Groucho, and Uncle Miltie. As parents, Hannah and Lyle measure love by their ability to protect their children from disagreeable facticity: Hannah cautions her children not to look if the boxing matches get too bloody; Lyle quickly yanks (the ironically titled) *Life* magazine out of

Enid's hands when she lingers over the grainy black-and-white photo-graphs of Nazi extermination camps. Indeed, Lyle will dig the bomb shelter only because he sees the thing as an act of love.

But these censoring efforts pale next to the larger work of anesthetiz-ing the narrative line itself. The narrative is compelled by three explosive events: the passionate affair between Enid and Felix, Enid's unsuccessful suicide attempt, and Enid's bloody abortion.

The affair is a most intense exercise in erotic obsession that plays (we must assume deliberately) on two of the most forbidden sexual expres-sions: the violation of a minor and the violation between near-blood rela-tives. These sexual experiences are detailed graphically in set pieces that include depictions of oral sex and manual genital stimulation; the pain-ful, bloody initial penetration of Enid's hymen; the repeated grotesque insertions, inch by painful inch, of a generously endowed adult male into the tight fit of an early adolescent; the bloody towels from inter-course during Enid's period; the trembling onrush of orgasm that be-comes so fiercely addictive to both; Enid's fingernails clawing her step-uncle's muscled back; milky semen bunched at the tip of slippery rubbers; awkward attempts at saddle sex in the front seat of Felix's Cadillac in broad daylight; and later an aborted attempt at anal penetra-tion in a shower. We are spared nothing.

Enid's suicide attempt is given in a step-by-step account that actually leads off Oates's narrative as Enid methodically washes down forty-seven aspirin tablets. She is torn over her obsession with Felix, who had broken off the relationship and had even slapped her. We are given access to Enid's dark logic, the claustrophobic movement to closure, as she slowly chokes down the pills with gulps of tepid tap water. We are given the time and the date, we are given Enid's age and her weight, height, her outfit, even the whereabouts of her family (appropriately clustered about the television)—data that smack of the cold thorough-ness of a police report, chronicled in the sparest prose that compels us to step so immediately within the real thing. We are without explanation, without authorial direction. We share only the bits of dredged memory, until the empty aspirin bottle drops into the wastebasket beneath the sink.

The third centering event—the abortion of the baby—is delivered just as meticulously. We are privy to Enid's difficult decision, her careful preparation of an alibi to cover her recuperation, her packing, her meet-ing with the nurse and then the doctor as we are ushered through the back door of the backstreet clinic closed for the day. We stay with Enid as she slips on the papery hospital gown, endures the preprocedure examination of her vagina and anus, and responds mechanically to questions asked by a nurse and later by a nameless doctor. We stay with Enid until the anesthesia takes hold. Then we move through the three surreal days that mark Enid's uneven recovery: the draining pull of painkillers, the steady vaginal bleeding and the sanitary pads so full the bloody trickle eases down her thigh as she tries to sleep, the vicious cramps, the dry vomiting, the haunting deliriums.

Such raw experience, such undeniable event, such elemental (f)acts would seem to premise a most traditional (read, grim) exercise in realistic narrative. Yet, given the logic of Oates's 1950s and within the magic kingdom premise of the 1980s, here (f)acts slide (un)easily into fictions. The torrid affair is never discovered, never discussed, never acknowledged; the abortion, which costs Enid three weeks of schooling, is downgraded to a bout with "intestinal flu." To explain her suicide attempt, Enid fashions the flimsiest story of a bad headache, a dark bathroom, and an accidental overdose. Once Enid is discharged from the hospital, the unsettling conspiracy of her comforting family begins the steady work of forgetting the whole experience. The near-death, we are told, was "only a fiction" (210). Too easily, these characters traffic in evasion, euphemism, and outright deceit in a joint conspiracy of distancing. Denied access to language, event loses significance; the immediate cannot teach, cannot reveal.

Oates, however, counterpunches. We receive what each character dodges: the full brunt of experience, the necessary premise of spectacle realism. Through the pulling power of language, we watch the mess, the blood, the frustration, the heaving turmoil, the terror and acceleration, the dark power, the shuddering exhilaration; we read ringside, close enough to be moved viscerally by the blind fury of unalloyed facticity. It is, then, a contested narrative, a tensive interplay between honesty and dishonesty, much as, after his return from Korea, Warren is plagued by recurring eye trouble: one eye (importantly, his *right* eye) sees quite clearly; the other is muddled and uselessly out of focus.

Not surprisingly, none of the Stevicks, none of these artless dodgers, lays effective claim to reader sympathy. As such, Oates's narrative strategy recalls the book that Lyle Stevick invokes to justify his borderline misanthropy: Swift's *Gulliver's Travels*. Lemuel Gulliver is clearly offered as a monitory character, a character who after illuminating experience comes to conclusions that his author cannot afford to endorse. Much like Gulliver, the Stevicks voluntarily exile themselves to the margins. As they freely shade event into nonevent, Oates, as satirist, cautions that such resolutions, like Gulliver's immoderate rantings in the stables, represent a degree of despair, a strategy of disengagement that we cannot afford. After all, *Gulliver's Travels* is hardly comic if we assent to Gulliver's resolution. It is our job, then, to learn. As with Gulliver himself, the Stevicks diminish as the narrative draws to its close, damned by their limited perception, their self-inflicted myopia.

It is not too much, then, to suggest that the novel, for all the seductive noise of its plotting, is not even "about" the two major plotlines: Enid and Felix's steamy affair and Lyle's erotic infatuation with nuclear annihilation. That affair, like Lyle's nuclear armageddon, somehow manages both to happen and not to happen. The action is oddly lost, ultimately marginalized as irrelevant in a most risky game of hide-and-seek. And the stakes, Oates warns, are indeed high. We are told of an innocent hide-and-seek game that leaves a young Enid trapped and nearly asphyxiated in an abandoned icebox. Recall the earnest university art students who study Miriam Brancher's stunning naked body as she poses in frank and undeniable immediacy in their drafty studio. After class, Miriam winces as she moves about the canvasses to see how the students had refashioned, exaggerated, distorted her form even when they had the real thing before them. In the larger argument of Oates's controlling sense of spectacle realism addressed to a nation indulging a strikingly similar urgency, such strategic distancing ultimately diminishes our capacity to live, even to feel.

*　　*　　*

A man has to be realistic.

Lyle Stevick, as he digs his bomb shelter

What is this *it* that, like the midcentury bugaboo of nuclear annihilation, is so immediate, so unnerving, that these characters must keep *it* distant, invoking the Cold War logic of (un)thinking about *it*, of anxious confrontation through cool denial? Oates's reading of human nature, which will introduce the argument of spectacle realism, is premised upon accepting what we most resist: our animal nature. Unlike our spiritual and rational faculties that are so publicly developed in church and school (Lyle Stevick treasures, amid the third-rate poverty of his used furniture store, his long-ago schooling studying Schopenhauer and Spinoza; his brother Domenic is the family pride, a priest), our animal nature evolves amid shadows against the weight of our uneasiness, our inclination to shame. Like some monstrous Siamese twin, our noblest aspirations seem tethered to the gross weight of an animal nature that so tiresomely defecates, procreates, eats, bleeds, sleeps, hurts, erodes, and dies. This heaving animal pulls like some heavy undertow, a metaphor Oates develops in Enid's terrifying memories of swimming in Shoal Lake.

Within this animal nature lurks our vast, dark capacity for violence (so much a part of this century's history and so long a part of Oates's narrative interest), our hungry impulse to wound that which threatens us, to relish the sight, smell, and taste of blood, real or metaphoric. As animals, we stumble about the vocabulary of love as the flesh hungers for the comfort, the feel, the easy exertion of other flesh; what we term "love" is more a frank contest between consumed and consumer, a fierce experience of conquest that can just as quickly subside only to be triggered again by new prey. And, ultimately, as animals, we move inexorably toward generic death, helpless before its clumsy, necessary intervention.

Surely accounting for human behavior via this rubric of a contested struggle between flesh and spirit leaves as corollary a predictable mistrust of the information brought to us by our senses, as if their hungers were counterspies infiltrating our otherwise tight interior systems of rational and humane thought. What particularly draws Oates is the vision of Christian Catholicism. Schooled by its logic and wedged within the puritanical conservatism of the Eisenhower 1950s, the Stevicks evidence a vast discomfort with the body; they do not know what to do with its suspect pleasures, with the furious engine of its hunger and the bald helplessness they feel in its throes. Their God, it would seem, is a capricious (or perhaps careless) creator who leads them very much into temptation.

The Stevicks express these animal impulses in a number of ways: by their healthy appetites (despite their middling income, they eat to excess, consume alcohol, chain-smoke); by their voyeuristic fascination with the staged violence of the boxing ring; by their greed (particularly their ingrained certainty of the status conferred by money and their awkward shame over their own thin income); but most often by their driving sexuality. Daughter Geraldine, pregnant without benefit of clergy, is hurried off to a quick nuptial to begin the real work of serious reproduction; Felix is locked in the gravitational pull of Enid's tight adolescent body; the

young Enid masturbates until she drools; Lyle, a joyless career monoga-
mist, fantasizes about nuns naked under the habits, their bodies hairless
as porcelain dolls; Warren tries to help a depressed Miriam Brancher by
offering her his couch to sleep off a drinking binge, only to find himself
uncontrollably aroused the following morning while she showers. In
each case, the individual Stevick endures a distressing revulsion over the
sickness of the animal attraction.

Catholicism codifies the Stevicks' understanding of the animal: those
urgent signals, that uneasy helplessness, that inevitable pain. Indeed,
Father Domenic quizzes little Enid using the tight format of the Baltimore Catechism, where mysteries come with reassuringly direct answers, syllable crisp. Within such a steadying vision, the flesh's fallibility
becomes the precondition of redemption; its needs are sins; its indulgence, the premise of regret; its notion of love, dangerous and illusory; its
apparent potency, flimsy and ephemeral; its inevitable failure, punishment; its thorough vanquishing, our triumph. Flesh and spirit can be
separated. Thus, we are furiously embattled within.

Such a reading, of course, is wildly out of sync with experience: it is no
accident that Hannah Stevick, who closes the narrative going into business as a dressmaker, carefully snips Butterick patterns from large unwieldy bolts of cloth even as Enid strains to tell her of the unwanted
pregnancy with her step-uncle. Oates understands that, sheltered within
this Catholic hyperdrama of sin and redemption (itself a vast, insular
play zone), we protect ourselves from what we fear even more than the
anger of a bookkeeper-God: the helplessness we feel amid mere event not
explicated by the divine narrative of temptation and punishment. Pro-
moted by philosophers Lyle recalls from his university days, by ministers such as Father Domenic, and even by novelists (John Steinbeck's
tight allegorical reading of our Cain and Abel nature, *East of Eden*, is a gift
given to Enid as she departs for college), that pleasant fairy tale of our
internal civil war leads only to a particularly Stevick-styled game of hide-
and-seek. Helplessness *is* our lot. Domenic Stevick himself is felled too
young by the inexplicable intervention of the animal: his heart implodes
over a dinner of Virginia ham. Oates understands—as will each of our
spectacle realists—the terror over such helplessness. In a poignant moment, Lyle (drunk, naturally) confides to Felix that the greatest pain of
parenting was accepting his powerlessness to give his children even the
smallest measure of security.

To ease our sense of helplessness, we fashion a civil war between our flesh and our spirit. But, Oates argues, this "us-versus-us" interior psychodrama is not so much a civil war as it is a sort of Cold War: a long, drawn-out, mock nonwar between powers that turn out in the end to be allies. We demonize what we do not understand and cannot begin to control and thus sustain a melodramatic (and costly) campaign against its incursion. Much like the Communist hunters in 1950s America (and reprised by the Evil Empire rhetoric of Reagan's America), we demonize the part of ourselves that scares us most profoundly. Characters lock themselves within the isolating unnaturalness of self-battling. They hush their animal side, humiliated by its urges, unsettled by its expression. Neighbors whisper about the neighborhood sexual practices, both kinky and conservative; schoolkids spread rumors about teachers and students alike or snicker about girls who suddenly leave school; neighbors note babies born too early in a marriage or husbands away too long in the evenings. Unable to accept easily what they are compelled to do because they are flesh, the Stevicks give in to their "baser" instincts but then fiercely pretend such experiences never occurred, much as Lyle Stevick, who deals in the business of salvaging used furniture, works to enhance the illusion that such abused property is in fact "new."

This tension underscores our introduction to each of the Stevicks in the opening chapter. Hannah is introduced as a young adult visiting a friend's family in the country. While in their crude outhouse, she senses (quite accurately) a Peeping Tom, a pleasantly addled older relative who relishes such pathetic voyeurism. Her response is telling: she runs, refuses to return to her friend's house, hot with shame at being caught in such a vulnerable (and human) posture.

We meet Warren as a young boy with a harsh stammer who watches as neighborhood white kids chase an African American boy on a bike. The child, terrified, loses his balance and smacks into a slow-moving coal truck. Warren, stunned by the sudden intrusion of chance, tries to help the bloodied boy, who is obviously dead. The bystanders, however, accuse Warren of being among those who had taunted the boy. Terrified by such accusations, he runs. He tries to tell his family, but he stammers badly. The family's advice? Don't tell anyone. Forget it. Abdicate his status as witness. Still shaken, he is ministered to by his "loving" family—a special dinner with hot milk and honey and then the zany radio antics of Fibber McGee and Molly.

Then we meet Felix's father, Enid's grandfather, a man of considerable political weight in Port Oriskany, a man accustomed to power and control. Late in life, riddled with galloping kidney cancer, he arranges for his secretary to smuggle a revolver into the hospital, where, deeply ashamed of his illness and wasted away to under 100 pounds, he blows off his head one Christmas night. And the family's reaction? They smother event into nonevent within a collective conspiracy. Thirty years later, Enid even denies to curious classmates any familial tie to the man who was once Port Oriskany's mayor, despite the monumental twelve-story edifice of the Stevick Building downtown.

Finally, we meet Enid. She is contemplating the intricate patternings of her bedroom wallpaper, particularly its design of curling roses that permits the thinnest pathways along which she imagines herself walking. Locked amid the lower-class struggles of her family, oppressed by the evident poverty of her immediate world, her soul divides from its rude animal casing and slips away into the wallpaper, where it delights to the strains of haunting music no one else hears. Oates juxtaposes this intensely private (though thoroughly Stevick) exercise in retreat to a more public, collective exercise: the local plans for civil defense. Enid thinks about the bombs, terrifying in their immediacy—but, like a true Stevick, does so only briefly. She finds herself much preferring to drift off into her wallpaper, serenaded by private music. We close the chapter (appropriately) in a dream. Enid, running up a long flight of stairs, finds herself in an increasingly diminishing room. But, at the moment of utmost panic, she squeezes herself under the door, manages "to get out, get out, get out" (24)—the repetition enforcing what will become the master stratagem of the entire Stevick clan.

Oates, shaping what will emerge as the novel's sense of spectacle realism, finds such denial stifling. Released in middecade of an era entranced by retreat, the narrative recognizes that the most daunting obstacle facing any realistic fiction is that we are at base anxious creatures largely unwilling to engage life as it is actually lived, to accept the implications of what we experience. We are creatures that prefer dense shadows and cooler shadings. Oates reveals what we know in our hearts: that we are both flesh and spirit, that we are fashioned not by their competition but rather by the dark, imperfect rhythms of their cooperation. We are an imperfect moral system of inclination and interdiction, hunger and expression, appetite and denial. Our every gesture, from hope to love to faith, is triggered by the sensual but sustained by the spiritual. "They" are what we are. To suppress one destroys the fullest expression of the other. Oates valorizes clear vision the only way a satirist can: by showing the unexamined foolishness, the bland hypocrisy, the dangerous misperceptions of the benighted.

Consider, to take only one example, the aborted romance Lyle Stevick attempts with Mrs. French. With her summery perfume, her satiny jade-green kimono, her land-mine double entendres, her easy familiarity with Lyle (who comes to her house only to appraise her furniture), her intimate offer of sherry, Mrs. French (even her name!) is a most fetching possibility—and Lyle Stevick reacts with the spontaneous stirrings of his sensual nature. His is a frank hunger, a strange sensation for Lyle interred within a sexless marriage for close to twenty years, living most vividly within his relentlessly erotic imagination. Yet there he is on (appropriately enough) Eaton Boulevard, hungry and suddenly, splendidly vulnerable before a real (rather than imagined) woman, tuned by this woman's raw immediacy to stirrings that leave him hopelessly awkward, unable to gather thoughts into a recognizable sentence, tripping on his way out of the house, fearing the consequences of his riled thoughts. But later he is actually moved to tears. When he decides, after long nights of feverish indecision, to act on his impulse and to return to the house, only to find Mrs. French no longer receiving him as a guest, he dismisses the entire episode as folly ("it would not bear thinking about" [214]).

Ashamed of his foolishness, he denies the hot honesty of his emotional response any airing and returns to his chilled nonlife of rigid abstinence. Which, Oates inquires, is the honest gesture: Lyle's potent response to Mrs. French or his meek return to the comfortable rut of his tepid marriage, itself begun in a lie? Years earlier, Hannah, seeing Lyle falling in love with another woman (whose dark eyes still sear his dreams nearly twenty years after), tells him that she is pregnant with his child—despite his certainty that they had never had sex. Driven by social conventions and by his religious code of conduct, Lyle goes through with the marriage for what he derides bitterly years later as the Immaculate Conception. We see in Lyle's emotional résumé the (un)necessary conflict between animal and spirit—the restless shifting, the resistance, the ultimate oppression of one impulse or the other, the inability to accept both as ennobling. It is shortly after this aborted affair that Lyle begins his elected act of self-interment within his backyard shelter.

Or consider the chiaroscuro makeup of any of the secondary characters, who are each divided internally as deeply as Enid with her "twin" Angel-face (her schoolyard persona who enjoys shoplifting and cursing) or as Warren who returns from his Korean War experience with his body seamed, divided by a vivid white scar. Each character at first appears to be a tidy simple drama of flesh versus spirit, but each exists in a tension between such energies. For instance, Felix, within Lyle's reductive moral subtraction, is simply a man without a soul. He fucks and he fights. Surely Felix brings to the affair the hard physical element: an aggressive, mercenary lust; a distrust of emotions; a cavalier inability to commit to any relationship; a love of motion; a pure need to control; a brute faith in violence as the ultimate arbiter of otherwise complicated emotional moments. Yet he is also surprisingly tender and even considerate with his vulnerable step-niece, encourages and even pays for her study of music, empowers her by teaching her how to drive and how to aim and fire a gun, coaxes her back from her suicidal depression in visits to her hospital room, lavishes her and her family with gifts, offers her an exquisitely simple heart pendant as a birthday gift, and finds himself stunned into genuine grief first after a young boxer he instructs is killed in the ring and later after the experience of the abortion, revealing a heart at the moment of its deepest wounding. Indeed, in the emotional afterwash of the procedure, he finds himself impotent, the very source of his animal pride dead and useless. He deteriorates. His business acumen dulls, his apartment falls apart; he drifts, drinking to excess and picking fights in seedy bars. In his sorrow, he is compelled to confide in strangers on bar stools, although (in typical Stevick fashion) he cannot be honest but rather fabricates a sister who lost a baby. Despite that evasive maneuvering, his is grief at an operatic pitch. Even as characters sign off on experience, invoking the odd wisdom to forget, Oates as spectacle realist understands that it bears weight to remember, that in the sheer helplessness of animal desire rests our dignity, not our shame, and that animal connection and the unapologetic need for human touch is the fullest expression of our imperfect human soul.

Tension, then, not resolution, makes us most dramatically human. Warren quotes from the master realistic sculptor of another era, Auguste Rodin, "Every form thrusts outward at its maximum tension"— surely a reminder (lost to the Stevicks) that we are our noblest at the moment not of resolution (with the inevitability of unnatural suppression) but of tension. In this regard, it is particularly telling that at a family wedding reception, Enid and Felix first dance to "As Time Goes By," the song that furnishes the novel's title. Despite its cultural notoriety as a mawkish romantic ballad (in part by its immediate association with Bogart's hard-edged if soulful romantic futility), the song itself offers in fact a much darker picture—not of romance but of harsh animal passion as an undeniably pitched contest for domination. That it can be both—syrupy and brutal—makes it most appealing for Oates's argument (and for the argument of spectacle realism). It is only excusing either argument that diminishes the artifact. Like Oates's characters, the song must define itself within tension.

But Oates is not interested in merely haranguing us with the tired observation of so many traditional realistic narratives that we are animals. As each of our spectacle realists will argue, we are more than that. In a most unsettling moment here, Enid pauses to watch two mongrels fiercely copulating in the early spring, the male dog's penis "luridly pink and erect" (264) and the female crouched, submissive, whimpering. In a narrative studded by lurid, erect penises, Oates's point is that such animal copulations are hardly the dynamic emotional washing that shatters Enid and Felix both. Indeed, Oates acknowledges as much in the character of Claudette Sansom, Felix's spare-time mistress during his affair with Enid. Without any emotional involvement with Felix save boredom within her marriage, Claudette in bed is merely cinematic, going through all the posturings of love with Felix, faking the sounds, the appropriate writhings—but without intensity. The mongrels in heat and the renegade wife both cleave flesh from soul and sustain themselves on a thin plane of the purely animal. But Oates is not interested in merely moaning the conventional bromide of traditional realistic fictions that human love is inevitably darkened by animal lust. Indeed, she wants neither to dismiss nor to elevate the physical. She asks only that it be allowed its rightful place. To assume that flesh and spirit compete leaves us diminished, inevitably defeated creatures. Spectacle realism acknowledges what these characters refuse. We are both—much like the Philadelphia boardinghouse where Warren lives while he is in law school. It is a picturesque edifice until he must venture out on its roofing to rescue a drunken Miriam. From this vantage point, he finds the house a terrifying edifice of strange angles and sudden dropoffs. That house is not either but both. We are a similar construction. Although these characters resist it, that hard truth lurks about the action like the powerful revolver Felix shows Enid, a gun he never fires but rather keeps in a drawer, its power (un)leashed, (im)potent.

* * *

There's a space in your brain where you go when you're knocked out that is like
nothing else on earth and the secret is, it's sweet.

Felix Stevick, on boxing's appeal

Like *Gulliver's Travels* (and like each of our other texts), *You Must Remember This* seeks to instruct. We follow the education of Enid Stevick, who begins and ends as a dedicated student. Like Gulliver, she is a character of extremes in a book offering the larger wisdom of the mediated middle. As Enid reduces her complicated internal circuitry to little more than an on-off switch, we are reminded (by its absence) of Swift's sane sense of balance, that (regrettably or not) we are as much Yahoo as Houyhnhnm. Oates hints as much by titling (without irony) the lengthy middle section of the novel "Romance," although it includes a graphic recounting of the sweaty and often bloody sexual contests between Felix and Enid.

There is little doubt that Enid begins more spiritual than animal. Distanced from the immediate, inhumed within her magic kingdom, she is decidedly interior, enveloped by her extraordinary emotional sensitivity, by her mercurial temperament, by her exemplary dedication to learning, and by her strong Catholic faith. Early on, she exercises her considerable internal gifts: there are her odd excursions into the wallpaper; she is enthralled by the exotic sounds of the names of the lakes and mountains about her sister's rented cottage; she listens to her parents argue loudly in another room and, dismissing as unimportant the nature of the argument, imagines rather the sights and smells of the engagement itself; she takes an aesthete's offense at litter; she is immediately intoxicated by the atmosphere of her step-uncle's newly acquired inn and imagines dining long ago in its Victorian splendor (a dreadfully sentimental reaction that Oates quickly undercuts—the inn is a smoky ruin, damaged by arson); she responds powerfully to the spell of music, to the wonderful uselessness of exotic vocabulary words she writes out on sheets of paper. She is disengaged from the dingy world of Port Oriskany, a brown world she notices, if at all, with a cold awareness. Indeed, the day Felix comes to the lake and drunkenly seduces Enid, she was burned badly by the sun and is now coated in protective Noxzema. As a creature of the mind, Enid has little reference for death. Death is a game she plays in the YMCA pool, doing laps until she can no longer draw a deep breath and finds herself dizzy; later, she watches as bullies dangle a neighborhood boy helplessly, but harmlessly, over the city canal; it is a game she plays along the footbridge under the train tracks relishing the thought of the bridge's collapse when such an event is structurally impossible. Hers is a game-world, a mock world, protected, safe, insular, a magic kingdom. Not surprisingly, in the initial encounter with her step-uncle at the abandoned country inn, Enid is drawn to the empty upstairs suite through a game of hide-and-seek.

Before Felix so baldly intervenes, Enid simply neglects her physical side, unhappy with the lumpy weight of its presence—save in gym class where her sexual athletics with Felix are foreshadowed by her sweaty dedication to flamboyant gymnastics. She avoids mirrors. She bonds sparingly. Lyle and Hannah puzzle over their daughter's aloofness; Enid cannot coax a genuine tear when her older sister, Lizzie, moves out of the bedroom she and Enid had long shared. When Enid first dances with Felix, she is awkward and indeed ends up running out of the hall in middance and interring herself (Stevick-ly) in a handy bathroom, wracked by dry heaves. She calms herself (Stevick-ly) by locking herself into a storage room and playing Czerny finger exercises on a broken-down piano until her cuticles bleed. When she does feel the natural hot rush of the animal, she masturbates, slobbering, her eyes rolling. Before Felix, she is disgusted by the sexual act itself (she is put out that she has to listen to her sister and brother-in-law make noisy love at the summer cottage, and she is repelled by the notion of her parents engaged in such an act). She does not understand the sexual content of casual jokes made by other schoolkids; she is unfamiliar with even the introductory rituals of dating and knows the penis only through the cartoon distortions of schoolyard graffiti.

Much as the rock and roll that growls from Enid's portable radio stunned Eisenhower's America with its bald unleashing of the id, Felix tunes Enid to the devastating joy of the body—its stunning capacity for response, its violence, its hot need, its fiercesome beauty—the considerable suasion of the blood. Returning home from the Amory the night she first watches Felix fight, Enid involuntarily gags, feels a slimy coating in her throat that tastes, we are told, of blood. Indeed, she develops a taste for blood. Her eventual encounters with Felix include the bloody rite of deflowering and later awkward intercourse during her period. The affair is distinctly animal. But, for Enid, looking at Felix's body is like "looking into too bright a light" (187). Always a bright student, Enid is taught in a succession of dingy motel rooms the reality of her volcanic sexuality, her intuitive relish of the sensual; but Enid converts that experience into the bruising drama of the flesh against the soul. Enid learns, yes, but she accepts that such tonic wonder must be relished in secret, that its power renders her unfit, sinful. Felix is her fall (in a bit of authorial play, Oates lodges Felix in an apartment in the *Niagara* Towers). To her, the flesh is akin to the undertow, that heavy pull beneath the otherwise calm waters of Lake Shoal that drags to their death the unwary, the weak. She comes to see Felix as a viral condition that gradually abates. Before the abortion, she convinces herself that sex with Felix brought with it this sorry stroke of punishment—much as earlier when she had agreed to let a friend pierce her ears against her parents' wishes, she accepted the ensuing infection as earned punishment.

But Oates as spectacle realist is clearly uneasy within such logic, such simplification. Enid rejects what we so clearly see: whatever problems Felix represents within social and religious conventions (and they are considerable), his influence detonates her, taps energies she had never felt, reshuffles her assumptions, destroys her calming sense of control. After all, Felix, in the Latin so critical to the Catholicism that structures Enid reaction, means "fortunate." The helplessness that so shakes both of their lives is the fortuitous explosion of the deep emotion that alone justifies why we have hearts in the first place. That she cannot accept this, that she comes to loathe that part of her that responds to Felix and to accept that such a response can be isolated, controlled, and then excised, gives her closing "happiness" its savage irony. Felix introduces her to a shattering (im)potence that she attempts to combat, initially, by the dark alogic of suicide. When that attempt fails, Enid closes the narrative at the music school committing a far more devastating gesture of emotional suicide, one that leaves its victim alive.

But spectacle realism with its imperative to affirm will not allow the narrative to close on such a regrettable strategy of denial. We learn along with Enid. It is not easy. The affair pressures even the most liberal reader. The affair is love at its most sublime—and its most disturbing. We share the longing, the energy, the renewal Enid feels after each encounter. Filled with Felix (literally and metaphorically), she commits with new energy to her school studies, intuits new arguments in her music, renews ties to family and friends, and even lightens her intolerance for the ugly world of Port Oriskany. "If you would fill me with your life. Your warm coursing blood. O then I would never die: never! . . . I am safe inside your skin" (257). Yet despite Enid's elation, we are never far from the base expression of that same obsession. We share with stunning immediacy the problems of wedging an enlarged, quite adult, often bloody penis into a tight, decidedly adolescent "cunt." We follow as Enid, shaken at the age of fourteen by hot orgasms, sobs in gratitude. We are necessarily aware how this is statutory rape and near-blood incest. We are given the heated jealousies, the free cursing, and the stunning swiftness with which these two turn from sweaty fucking to snarling fighting, even bloodying each other.

It is not a pretty picture, nor a Crayola picture with bold and easy lines. In reading, we struggle between our sympathy and our disgust. We are torn until we realize that tension—not resolution—is Oates's argument. We must work to conclude what Enid resists: the contradictory nature of human love cannot afford to be rendered as melodrama. Oates cannot tolerate such division; at every moment she melds the spirit and the flesh, blurs the sacred and the secular. It is our lot, she reminds us, that the clanging bell that summons the boxers to the center of the ring in the smoky Armory sounds the same as the bell that summons Enid's fellow parishioners for Holy Communion in the incensed church.

*   *   *

Not that truth has the slightest effect upon our lives.

Lizzie Stevick, nightclub singer

If *You Must Remember This* can be seen as a novel directed to its cultural moment, surely the fate of the Stevicks cautions against the easy logic of withdrawal, against locking ourselves within the insular splendor of magic kingdoms. Enid—indeed the entire sorry cast of Stevicks—pays a most devastating price for her misguided decision to deny the animal, to confound the reality of attraction and its clumsy meshing of flesh and spirit by denying it articulation. The Stevicks damn themselves to isolation. They are a family riven by secrets; they are separated bits never cohering even into the simplest cooperation of a single honest conversation. The deep irony here, of course, is that Oates's narrative evidences that the rest of the Stevick clan is susceptible to the very same impulses. By playing dumb (as in speechless), by resisting the opportunity of confiding in her family, Enid stumbles about in the dark vacuum of her self-enclosed world, distanced, alone. We are reminded of the moment when Lyle decides that in the stranger Mrs. French he has finally found someone to whom he can reveal his considerable fears and frustrations, confidences he outlines only to himself, for when he goes to share it all with

Mrs. French he finds, through the impassive agency of her maid, that she is no longer even receiving him. Or the time Lyle phones Felix to have a drink with him—Felix is set to confront the messy reality of his ongoing affair with Enid, which he is sure Lyle has learned about, but Lyle only wants to talk about arranging a loan to start his bomb shelter.

Particularly poignant are Enid's similarly aborted attempts to share— to tell her parents near the close of the narrative that she is pregnant as her mother trims out dress patterns for her new business (Stevick-ly, she begins the business ashamed by such an assertion of individuality and thus keeps the business a secret from her own husband) and later while Lyle shows off the bomb shelter to her. She cannot share; her most critical revelations are cased uselessly in the italics that indicate mere mental noise. Conversation, when it does stir, either bogs down in happy talk about the everyday or aborts amid painfully ironic misunderstanding (when Enid suddenly begins to cry in the bomb shelter, her father assumes she is overwhelmed by the thought of atomic war). In a narrative that hinges on Enid's frequent physical couplings, that surrounds her with the pressing closeness of a family lodged in tight quarters, that gives her all the traditional gifts of otherness (a lover and later a child), Enid begins and ends quite alone.

But far more disturbing than such self-imposed isolation, Enid mistrusts the immediate, loses touch with the centering imperative of spectacle realism: the deep electricity of senses alert amid the unsuspected grandeur of the ordinary. In learning, as the narrative unfolds, to shut down the animal even as it asserts its joyous energy, Enid forfeits as well any involvement with that world accessed by those very senses. Oates understands the power of that complicated act of open engagement. When Lyle, typically entombed within his bomb shelter and admiring its tight construction, is momentarily mesmerized by the all-too-familiar sights of his own neighborhood seen through the clumsy apparatus of the shelter's periscope, he is comforted by the notion that soon bombs will level the whole area.

Enid is also decidedly numbed to the stunning wonder of the immediate. Indeed, following the amateur attempt to pierce her ears (numbed by crudely applying ice), Enid is left numb in her ear, her senses partly impaired. She has her moments: her heart suddenly warms as she rides the city bus along an otherwise nondescript neighborhood of Decker Boulevard, her eye suddenly stunned by its openness, smarting from the random arrangement of light and shadow and line—"her senses . . . alive, aroused" (60). Or we recall when Enid sits in a church she is oblivious to all but the powerful crashing chords of the great organ. Her bent fingers follow on the pew back the intricate lines of the enveloping music. Seduced by the marvelous dexterity of her fingers as they "play" the wooden pew, Enid slips easily away from the otherwise quotidian church service. She enters a mock world entirely self-generated and ruthlessly self-involved. Too abruptly the music ends, and Enid finds herself dropped back into what she sees as the thin banality about her, the simple drone of human voices.

That immediacy disappoints Enid drives a most telling wedge between character and author and ultimately between character and reader. At the high point of her entanglement with Felix, Enid joyfully feels that this love "set her in a relationship with the world that was unexpected, potent, mysterious. . . . Suddenly everything was vivid, piercing, tremulous with meaning: the faces of strangers in the street, the white-churning wake of a tugboat, even the yeasty gritty taste of the air on certain mornings" (225). Such sensual resuscitation makes her eventual denial, her self-entombing within the cloisters of Westcott, all the more disturbing. With Felix, she is introduced to the sheer beauty of the physical: she is stunned by Felix as he struts naked, unashamed, about their hotel rooms, his generous genitals swinging like fat fruit. Oates understands that beauty of the physical; she taps it in the breathtaking pictorial sweep of her descriptive eye, in her meticulous re-creation of the harsh choreography of the boxing events, in her graphic rendering of the surging power of physical love. The physical world attracts, dazzles, stuns, and—most important—alters; thus we touch the foundational premise of spectacle realism so much at odds with the larger logic of evasion and play of the Reagan Era.

Tucked away by narrative's close within the ivory-towered protection of the college campus, anticipating years of insulated instruction in the frictionless responsibilities of responding to music, Enid forsakes not only her step-uncle and her family but also the tumultuous life of experience. Enid finds her way to protective enclosure, to a sense of control that bars the violent and the bloody and the uneven shocks of chance, but that locks out as well the complex pleasure of engaging the everyday, that soft moment during Enid's rattling ride along Decker Boulevard. As such, she embodies the magic kingdom impulse of the Reagan Era, the serious play of retreat. She makes a most appropriate starting figure. She has much to learn, and she is walking away from it. The irony of Oates having Enid share her age and her biographical background is clear. Enid is Oates's dark twin, her Angel-face. Like some dark twin, Enid will give her life over to studying—not producing—music. It will be the cold life of secondhand study because Oates understands—and spectacle realism insists—that the heart and soul must be tied fully to the (c)rude experience of the immediate in order to produce original aesthetic artifacts. Oates appreciates the dignity in helplessness. When Lyle Stevick, the consummate shelter builder, emerges from an extended stay in his bomb shelter into the flood of natural light in his backyard, he feels a compelling vertigo, a moment's exposure standing there on the surface with only a thin membrane of skin and flesh to protect him. It is that exposure, that fragility, that characters seek to protect and that Oates seeks to expose because only by touching the contentious energy of that vulnerability can we find our way to the fully human.

*　　*　　*

> *Tokens dropped in the till, the bus rattling over the Decker Boulevard bridge, the look of the canal on winter mornings!—the surprise of the steep rock sides laced with ice glittering in the sun, mist rising thinly from the narrow channel of broken churned ice. . . . Enid leaned to the bus window transported, staring, her eyes narrowed in the pain of such brilliance, all her senses were alive, aroused.*
>
> You Must Remember This

Oates's novel, then, is a most skewed example of spectacle realism, one that extols the courage to accept the immediate for what it is—contradictory, uncontrollable, and stunningly powerful—through the argument of characters who elect to turn away. We learn the truth from practiced liars. The unflinching demand articulated by the title is directed quite personally to the reader—to you. You must remember what these characters so resolutely act to forget. We recall the dramatic sermon Warren hears at the front: a chaplain emotionally calls on the wounded never to forget, counsels, with a voice appropriately raw and hoarse, the "sacred obligation to remember." Of course, Warren, a Stevick, listens "dry-eyed" and even "antagonistic" (111).

In this regard, Oates's use of abortion as the climactic narrative event has a much larger sense. Within a narrative where characters work so diligently to bury the unpleasant, to deny the real, we close with an abortion, a medical procedure that is a most absolute exorcism, a calculated removal of that which upsets, that which speaks plainly, truthfully, of actions those involved wish to bury, to whisk away into the antiseptic nonspace of nonevent the product so often of the crossed pulls of flesh and spirit. We watch Enid's body, which had already begun its marvelous (and wholly natural) accommodation to maternity, struggle to adjust to being deprived suddenly of the fetus. We see that erasure is most unnatural. Abortion, after all, rests in the uneasy, shadowy between— where a life is somehow nonlife, where undeniable death is nondeath, where event itself becomes nonevent (Enid's official clinic paperwork lists the procedure as a routine D and C). Oates counterpoises the intrusive act of the abortionist to the revelatory act of the writer: the abortionist here works in the shadows in back alleys late at night behind doors barred against intrusion; he offers Enid neat erasure of the complications brought about by the unnerving helplessness because her flesh and spirit imploded. Oates, however, offers the honest glare of revelation, preserves all the evidence of event within her graphic narrative, and compels her reader to live where Enid will not: within the tension that the abortionist's snippings too easily remove.

But this larger authorial wisdom is offered not merely to deny sympathy to Oates's characters. We close the narrative surrounded by the dead—some buried, some not. Surely we see that each finds a way to happiness only through delusion and denial. But we understand the nature of the error; we are compelled to understand what has killed them (a narrative strand tracks Lyle's growing fears over a hacking cough, and he traces its beginnings to his job at a local factory). But, if we understand their anxieties over their vulnerability, their desperate need to control, we understand also what they have forfeited—and what is far more to the point, the characters themselves understand what they have aborted: nothing less than the immediate, with all its rich confusions, its sweet, violent unpredictability.

Embrace flesh and spirit—that, finally, is what we must remember as time goes by. Long before the tonic intervention of Felix, long before that emotional implosion sours, long before Enid fashions herself as a battleground, Enid herself tastes briefly the wild grace possible when flesh and spirit cooperate rather than compete, when the need to control gives way to the need to respond. In school, Enid tastes the deep thrill of the very helplessness she will struggle later to control. We are told of her remarkable athletic talent while executing elaborate maneuvers on her school's trampoline. It is an exercise that suggests the unexpected thrill of helplessness, the electricity of relinquishing control and handling moment-to-moment change within the decidedly unstable environment of the spontaneous and the unplanned. As her schoolmates watch in wonder, Enid abdicates her need to control and finds the experience of grace in the blind, exhilarating movement of her wildly creative flips, obedient (as she will be later with her step-uncle) only to the brute laws of the physical universe of matter in motion. When she most reluctantly dismounts from the trampoline, Enid is flushed by the excitement of the tension of the middle, where she is more than passive but decidedly less than in control, a wild cooperation of expectation and improvisation. It is vulnerability, the risk of accepting limited control and finding within its unpredictable rhythms the very stuff of a dark, striking beauty. Not surprisingly, given Oates's larger satire, the Port Oriskany school board later votes to remove the trampoline from the physical education curriculum—too dangerous, they argue, for a student has broken his back.

We close, then, with the first interpretative text-site of spectacle realism. Not the magic playscape of the boxing ring or the magic kingdom backyard bomb shelter or the hermetic zone of the piano practice room but rather the trampoline where flesh and spirit cooperate, recklessly, gloriously, where the dark press of contingency is undeniable, where flesh accommodates and indeed responds to the flamboyant rhythms of the unexpected, where "rules" are markedly ironic, where only those most willing to let themselves go are prone to the thrill and the pain of such vulnerability. That coming together of helplessness and dignity is, of course, the very definition of the human experience of love and death that so centers Oates's narrative, so terrorizes the Stevick clan, and so defines the texts of spectacle realism. Without despair, without humiliation, without embarrassment, without denial—and without warm milk and honey—Oates tells us that, as animals, we are helpless; chance and time happen to everyone. Why does Enid feel so compelled by the presence of her step-uncle? Why does business after business fail under Lyle's management? Why does Warren happen upon a drunk Miriam on the roof of the boardinghouse? Why does Felix suddenly lose control in the ring, get angry, and forfeit what promises to be a major boxing career? Frailty here is a measure of our strength. Oates refuses to dispense anesthetics. Oates demands our right to pain by offering characters numbed to their own plot. In shutting down, Enid convinces herself that the world gets tired of the noise of human pain; but Oates sees the error, the terrifying alternative: the chilling silence of each Stevick's self-dug burial plot. That noise of human pain is the very stuff of our existence and the very stuff of spectacle realism.

Shelters, thus, are for Stevicks—and for Reagan's America. We are born for the trampoline. Oates asks us to step (un)easily onto the trampoline, to relish the tonic rush of uncontrollable experience—to learn that, once engaged, the immediate can stun, revive, hurt, terrify, and transform. In one subplot, Al Sansom, Felix's doomed business partner, is fascinated by reports of UFOs tracking across the wide wastes of the American Southwest, that amid such arid nothingness might streak the evidence of the inexplicable, thus permitting the magic of surprise amid the starkly ordinary. By withholding her imprimatur from the Stevicks, Oates reminds us that the immediate does not need UFOs shooting across it to stir appropriate wonder. The Stevicks "die," each in his or her own fashion, so that we, the readers, might go about the clumsy process of living, so that we might engage what they refuse, embrace the helplessness that so terrifies them, the logic of the animal that so shames them. Like some eccentric undertaker, Oates ushers us past the embalmed, the soon-to-be buried—if only to help us recognize the (extra)ordinary miracle of living.

2

Strange Gods before Us

John Irving, *A Prayer for Owen Meany*

Watch out for people who call themselves religious; make sure you know what they mean—make sure they know what they mean!

John Wheelwright

It would appear to be something of a jolt to move from Enid Stevick, with her dark fascination with the volcanic beauty of the human animal, to John Wheelwright, the reclusive narrator of John Irving's *A Prayer for Owen Meany,* whose chief pastime is attending church services amid a life of elective celibacy. It may seem odd even to introduce an overtly Christian novel such as Irving's 1989 narrative into an exploration of spectacle realism. Fascinated as they are by the horizontal and suspicious of the vertical, realists—spectacle or otherwise—make lousy apostles. Indeed, the Christian vision as Irving uses it here ultimately finds suspect, even ironic, the deep interest in, the sheer celebration of, the plane of experience that so defines spectacle realism. Our agonies, our joys—each are essentially promissory; the premise of the afterlife compels us to postpone satisfaction, to qualify joy, to question happiness, to suspect love, to dismiss chance, to welcome death. But Irving reminds us, again through the narrative strategy of irony, that the contemporary Christian, stranded in the vast waiting for the Parousia, is actually quite similar to the spectacle realist—hungry for experience, engaged within the immediate, stunned by its freewheeling plot. They differ only in the Christian certainty that such plot posits an author, denies surprise, and presumes eventual closure. Thus, Irving's is a critical evolutionary point in our movement toward the affirmation of spectacle realism. Like Oates, Irving passionately engages a world of bruising violence, relentless absurdities, casual deceptions, and profound heartache. His characters, engaged in ways that Oates's shelter builders refuse, remind us that spectacle realism shares the hunger—if not the satisfactions—of the Christian sensibility so much a part of the American argument of the 1980s. It will be left to our later writers to bring together Oates's sense of the enthralling wonder of the immediate with Irving's willingness to engage that same bruising sphere of experience.

We begin with little Owen Meany, who so dominates the narrative. Early in Irving's novel, the title character, a diminutive teenager with an odd, fractured voice and an unnervingly calm conviction of himself as an instrument of God's will, volunteers to help a local repertory company stage Dickens's *A Christmas Carol*. The company needs someone to play the ominous Ghost of Christmas Yet to Come. It is a lightly regarded part because, as one disgruntled actor argues, no one sees your face, you haven't got any lines, and all you do is point. When Owen Meany volunteers, the director doubts that Owen can carry it off because of his height. Owen Meany asks only for a chance. "LAUGH, I'M OUT. SCARED, I'M IN" (180). Laughter or terror. As readers, we are given similar choices in responding to Owen Meany, to the boy who is told by his parents that he was conceived by virgin birth; to the adolescent who, after killing the young mother of a friend with an improbable line drive foul ball during a Little League game, conceives of himself as an instrument of God's will; to the young adult who finds himself visited by dreams prophesying his own heroic death, one that does occur much as the dreams foretell and on the very day they predict.

Surely, an eerie strangeness haunts the eccentric boy. Something in his presence commands attention. But if the narrative begins in barely restrained laughter—schoolfriends tease the tiny boy by lifting him up over their shoulders whenever the teacher leaves the room in Sunday school, they hang him by his collar on the school coatracks, and they suspend him helplessly from his jock during gym class—by the shattering closing scene, this business of elevating Owen Meany turns deadly serious as Owen sails out of his friend's arms toward a high window ledge in a makeshift public bathroom in a Phoenix airport to press himself against a live grenade lobbed by an emotionally damaged teenager just moments before it detonates, thus saving the lives of a group of terrified Asian refugee children.

Unnerved by the implications of Owen Meany's elevation, we are challenged to share in the narrator's certainty that the massive oddness, the undeniable heroism of Owen Meany legitimately express the sacred. If Owen is to be accepted as sacred, surely he must inspire a deep terror because he reminds a stubbornly secular reading audience of God's abiding muscle. But to step away from the narrator's certainty is to risk what Owen so fears in his audition: laughter—at his pretensions, his preposterous theatrics, his unapologetic arrogance. If accepting Owen thins Irving's ambitious work to a dreary novel dismissable, to borrow from the narrator's sour description of the 1960s, for its "mystical muddiness," its "aggressive" righteousness, and its "deadly absence of irony" (451), the alternative is bleaker. The liminal event in the life of the narrator John Wheelwright—the death of his young, beautiful mother by the foul ball hit by Owen Meany—bears the very signature of the contemporary world of accidents and random violence that recalls Oates's Port Oriskany. When Wheelwright brings a cousin of his to an emergency room, he surveys those injured in absurd mishaps, the sorry evidence of the irrational world we must engage, Irving's sense of the world's vicious Under Toad.[1] Any anxieties, however, would be surely resolved by the luminous argument of Owen Meany. The alternative to faith in his extraordinary posture is our too-familiar helplessness; Wheelwright's aunt, after the funeral of Wheelwright's mother, suddenly bolts up from a fetal curl on the living room couch, pounds the coffee table, and wails, "It doesn't make any *sense*" (129, italics Irving).

Like all Christian fiction (ultimately like all texts of spectacle realism), *A Prayer for Owen Meany* is a meditation on how to die, that most pressing expression of the (im)perfect immediate. Here, death comes in all styles—grisly and bloody, absurdly accidental, lingering and full of indignities. It is death, generic and explosively sudden, that compels Wheelwright to cling to Owen Meany. Dickens's lines, quoted by Wheelwright, sound Wheelwright's most fundamental fears, "Oh cold, cold, rigid, Dreadful Death, set up thine altar here, and dress it with such terrors as thou hast at thy command, for this is thy dominion" (181). Stunned one summer afternoon by the hollow crack of a bat swung in the late lingering innings of a meaningless baseball game, Wheelwright retreats into a desperate certainty about the talismanic figure of Owen Meany, who reassures him that death, no matter how absurdly pointless, nevertheless signifies.

Owen Meany tempts John Wheelwright—and, by extension, the reader—to traffic in explanation. Owen's certainty reassures Wheelwright from the moment a staggering concert of circumstances weaves a single deadly event that kills his young mother, Tabitha. Left suddenly quite alone, the young Wheelwright demands explanation. He reviews the team's responsibility—an easy grounder bobbled, an unexpected walk, a coach too eager to go home who sends in tiny Owen to pinch-hit, all meaningless events in a meaningless game in which Wheelwright and Owen's team was hopelessly behind. Not surprisingly, Wheelwright will find Owen's explanation more acceptable: Owen, spending the night with the Wheelwrights long before the game, hears a noise in the mother's room, stumbles into the room, and sees the Angel of Death preparing to take the woman's life. Because he interrupts that grisly business, he must complete the job through the apparent accident of the foul ball.

That baroque account with its seductive rhetoric of explanation convinces Wheelwright to accept Owen Meany as sacred phenomenon, an event on a par with the Incarnation. Yet events pressure the logic of explanation by revealing a larger universe of pure circumstance. For instance, the accidental death of a neighborhood dog grotesquely parodies the death of Wheelwright's mother. Owen Meany, never much of a football player (much as he was considered a marginal Little League player), without warning boots a football (much as he suddenly managed to connect with the baseball). It sails into the street, where the hapless dog follows, only to be hit by a diaper truck—a crushingly ironic intersection of new life and sudden, inexplicable death played out amid the offending tincture of human waste. The dead dog is immediately interred in a mock-reverent service—complete with an attending (although faintly appalled) clergy, the same one who later officiates at the mother's service. The death of that dog, despite such ornamental ritual, merely happens, much as when, earlier, during a sudden thunderstorm at her wedding reception, Tabitha is hit by a large hailstone. The death of the dog and the grazing by the hailstone are events that defy Owen Meany's reassuring testimony of the universe as a magnificent drama that, despite its dark, often ironic twists, argues an author and, hence, a plot.

In the hands of a less ironic novelist, these incidents might well have been placed before the baseball accident to exploit foreshadowing, to suggest a linkage in events. (Indeed, as part of a class he conducts on Thomas Hardy, Wheelwright comments on that author's "fondness for foreshadowing" [275]). But the foul ball starts the book, and the "foreshadowing" events come much later; thus, Irving, like all writers of spectacle realism, cautions that events in a secular universe cannot achieve design. We are, to borrow from Oates, bound for the terrifying grace of the trampoline world. That stochastic universe lurks just beyond the neat pattern Owen Meany offers, much as the virid violence of open wilderness frames a cleanly spun spiderweb.

The seduction of explanation, then, is at the heart of Owen's appeal to Wheelwright. Wheelwright insists from opening line to (melo)dramatic peroration that Owen Meany was central in his Christian reclamation. In 1968, in the men's room at that airport in (appropriately) Phoenix when Owen Meany, on special assignment with the army, heroically covers the grenade, in that deafening blast of light, God becomes for John Wheelwright an accessible commodity; random event suddenly staggers into neat configuration. It is a dramatic stroke that recalls inevitably Paul and the storied road to Damascus; indeed, Wheelwright notes that he commences his narrative just days after the Anglican observation of the Feast of the Conversion of St. Paul. Wheelwright's mother did not die from an errant foul ball but rather as part of a chain of events that culminates in Owen's saving of the Asian children. Inevitably, this central narrative line—reclaiming John Wheelwright into a churchgoing believer—risks the sentimental excesses of Dickens's Christmas classic, with Wheelwright, playing Scrooge at the casement window, delighting in his reclaimed soul in the aftermath of the radical event of Owen Meany. Critical responses certainly canonized Owen Meany. "You'd better believe that this wonderful little Owen guy was indeed the instrument of God, since our narrator does" (Pritchard, 38). Through the agency of Owen Meany, John Wheelwright discovers "the solace and power of Scripture" (Wall, 300). John Irving "loves" Owen Meany and John Wheelwright (Kazin, 30). Here is a delightful "juvenile" novel where the reader can revel in the uncomplicated exercise in lay preaching (Towers, 30). There is no complication here, "absolutely no irony" (Kazin, 30).

That is, until we begin to listen to Wheelwright.

Assumptions about an unambiguous, static narrative ignore the assessment of a good novel offered by Owen Meany himself: "any good book is always in motion" (290). Perhaps Irving offers more motion than we immediately perceive.[2] Perhaps we have been listening to the wrong story. After all, John Wheelwright decries his high school literature students for reading only for plot; perhaps we have read hypnotically, pulled by Owen's centripetal narrative that moves so inevitably to its heroic closure, but have ignored a far more unsettling parable about another man's struggle—and failure—to touch the sacred. Perhaps Owen Meany's story is really the story of John Wheelwright.

Despite Irving's repeated use in his fiction before *Owen Meany* of the narrator as part of an ironic strategy, critical responses to John Wheelwright have largely dismissed him as marginal, valuable primarily as a recorder of events.[3] But Owen Meany is an artifact, the product of Wheelwright's observation. We never share intimacy with Owen Meany; he is never ours to understand, to decode. When Wheelwright starts to work at Meany's granite quarry, he is assigned to the tombstone shop, not the quarry itself. It is easier, he is told, to start with the finished product. This is, of course, what Wheelwright does in his narrative. He commences with the uncontested elevation of Owen Meany, begins with the finished product. In ways that recall Oates's strategic use of satire, Irving carefully manipulates uncertainty over the presumptions of his own narrator. To us, Owen Meany is as much a dangerous counterfeit—a product of his own febrile imagination, his parents' monstrous superstitions, and his unabashed self-promotion—as he is an authentic, if unorthodox, lover of humanity, a genuine glimmer of the sacred, inexplicable and potent. There is no attempt to account for the deadly accuracy of his dreams concerning his own death, although psychiatrists, schoolteachers, and ministers each offer explanations. Clearly, resolving Owen Meany is not the narrative's interest; indeed, early on, when Wheelwright's cousins play hide-and-seek with young Owen, the tiny boy is never actually found. Rather, what is of more interest here is that we are in the hands of one who *has* settled Owen Meany. All of this makes Wheelwright a most critical psychology to explore.

John Wheelwright, by his own tedious testimony, is salvaged by the radical event of Owen Meany. We know he is a Christian only because he declares it—often.[4] Unlike the detonating recentering experience of traditional conversion narratives, Wheelwright converts pragmatically—before a job interview at a private school. He records the hours he logs in the local chapel tirelessly attending to the rituals of worship; he totes about with him a Book of Common Prayer. Yet the very narrative he relates questions whether Wheelwright is all that he assumes—much as when, unable to sleep, Wheelwright flips on the light in his grandmother's kitchen and sees himself splintered into multiple John Wheelwrights in a casement of Colonial-style windowpanes. With Owen Meany, John Wheelwright is exposed to a most disturbing mystery. Owen Meany is "so easy to lift up" (502), in the words of one of the schoolchildren who found lifting the tiny boy an ideal school prank. And surely Wheelwright lifts up Owen, offers us Owen Meany as an act of God, a saint. To concede Owen Meany such heightened spiritual status, to feel the terror rather than the laughter, would demand confirming Wheelwright as a reliable narrator, a practicing Christian, indeed our teacher in things spiritual. Is he, therefore, our spiritual wheelwright, setting right our broken systems of belief?

What sort of teacher is John Wheelwright? He attacks his students for their indifference (although he was himself a most mediocre student); he deflects their earnest questions with haughty disdain, mocks their dreary lack of insight, dismisses them as swine, plots to spring nasty surprise quizzes, smirks at their attempts to respond to his deliberately tricky questions, selects texts far beyond their intellectual development, and then lords over them his opinions, uncontested as they are. Indeed, he often aims a particularly impatient rhetorical question *at* the reader, treating us with the same disdain, the same rudeness as he does his students. Wheelwright as narrator is as caustic, as insensitive, and as uncontested as he is in the classroom, strutting about the private refuge of his own narrative with unexamined generalities all the while posturing with unchallenged arrogance.

If his teaching does not testify to his Christian sensibility, does John Wheelwright's regular chapel attendance, then, indicate his faith? Does his attending to the rituals of his religion, his careful attention to the calendar of church days, his deep involvement with the ceremony itself reveal his faith? Sadly, his religion comes to little more than an easy obedience to the simplest performance of rituals, which he defends not for their connection to the sacred but rather for their ability to "combat loneliness" (252). His is a disturbing sort of belief, one uncomplicated by the riskier uncertainties of faith. Whereas belief is sustained by unexamined certainty, faith must constantly struggle against the argument of doubt, which creates a tensive, supremely imperfect commitment, one tempered by constant challenge. In embracing Owen Meany as sacred, Wheelwright believes only because he has seen, which in Testamental writing is always the crudest pitch for faith. Faith demands the suspicion—not the certainty—that the world has plot.

It is a difference Irving finds critical; Wheelwright has no difficulty in asserting his belief, but as Owen Meany diagnoses, "THE TROUBLE WITH YOU IS, YOU DON'T HAVE ANY FAITH" (302). The difference between belief and faith is suggested metaphorically by the contrasting livelihoods of the Wheelwrights and the Meanys, one in timber and the other in granite. Lumber is acknowledged even by the Wheelwrights to be limited, exhaustible, unreliable for the long haul. It is flimsy and light-weight. It is all too easy to harvest; even the generally inept Wheelwright enjoys a summer of cutting down trees. Granite, on the other hand, goes deeper than the tenuous binding of mere roots. It goes earth deep; it is sterner stuff, massive and ponderous. It is far steadier, as a resource, vir-tually inexhaustible—but, of course, far more difficult to secure. The ex-traction process is not given over to amateurs such as Wheelwright, who is not even permitted to work the Meany quarry. Such demanding exca-vation suggests the difficult struggle to secure faith, the Christian virtue that structures, granitelike, the very foundation of Creation.

Belief without faith leaves Wheelwright a most ironic figure hunched over his empty pew. He is left suspended between an immediate that gives him no pause and an afterlife that gives him no joy, no security, no trust, no compassion. During chapel, he is easily distracted by disruptive children; he is annoyed by the canon conducting the service, by the te-dium of his sermon, by his bare singing talents, by the pea green color of his vestments; he is put off by the taste and size of the communion fare; he is harshly unforgiving about church elections that only recently turned him out of office. He is bothered by trivial word changes in hymns, by the unsightly pregnant condition of a minister, by the tedium of waiting in the communion line, by the unpleasant lighting in the church, by the warm press of humid summer air and the lack of air-conditioning. The church affords Wheelwright a pew to sit in, a sermon to endure, a bit of hard bread to gnaw, a prayer book to carry; but it cannot crack his soul and flood its sour darkness, converting the thin, clinging sort of belief that sustains Wheelwright into the assurance and joy promised to those Christians who have made a more authentic leap to faith.

Much as Oates provides a reworking of Swift, Irving works a rich sat-ire that depends on the participatory reader for the fullest effect.[5] When Owen Meany writes editorials for the academy newspaper, he finds ex-posing institutional hypocrisies is best achieved indirectly through irrev-erent undercutting. Even as Wheelwright approves Owen Meany as religious event, even as he ambles off to weekly church service, John Wheelwright reveals himself to be a sham Christian, lost in time (as the shattered chronology of his narrative line testifies), adrift in space (not wholly American, not wholly Canadian, defined more by what he abandons than what he can embrace, living in a sparely furnished room in an all-girl boardinghouse), friendless (indeed, Wheelwright denies those virtues where Irving heroes find redemption—family and friends),[6] yet confident over the certainty of God's presence in his soured, spoiled waste of a life.

In this, Wheelwright recalls not so much the easy sentimentality of the reclaimed Scrooge but rather the far darker figure of Jacob Marley, a spirit past redemption, a spirit damned to pay the penalty for his cloistered existence by lugging the awesome burden of such a wasted life for eternity. Irving quotes the most salient lines as part of the local theater production—"I wear the chain I forged in life," Marley intones, although Wheelwright could very well be speaking. "Mankind was my business—the common welfare my business; charity, mercy, forbearance, and benevolence were all my business" (215)—the tormented assessments of one man's misanthropy pointedly summarize Wheelwright's life. When he summers in the invigorating wilds of Canada's north country to escape the dripping humidity of Toronto, he ponders only the island's septic system. When Toronto is blanketed by lustrous snow, Wheelwright speaks rather of the "legion of dog turds" just underneath (87). If *Owen Meany* is John Wheelwright's story, the angry denunciation Wheelwright offers of Ronald Reagan boomerangs with unsuspected irony—such a phony Christian, he declaims, could "drive a *real* Christian crazy" (289, italics Irving).

* * *

If I were called upon to state in a few words the essence of everything I was trying to say as both novelist and preacher, it would be something like this: Listen to your life. See it for the fathomless mystery it is. In the boredom and pain of it no less than in the excitement and gladness: touch, taste, smell your way to the holy and hidden heart of it because in the last analysis all moments are key, and life itself is grace.

Frederick Buechner, *Now and Then*

If, as we have seen, Oates's characters smother event into nonevent by a conspiracy of secrecy and deception, Irving's characters deny event by shattering assumptions that surfaces reveal, that the text of appearances is even readable. In both novels, we play a rigged, skewed game of hide-and-seek with an immediate that stays sadly hidden.

To dramatize the seductive illusion of Owen Meany and the fraudulent role-playing of John Wheelwright-as-Christian, Irving draws heavily on the tension between authenticity and sham, the unreliability of surfaces, and the power of appearances to deceive. Here, the earnest (if hokey) world of church pageants and amateur theater makes for something of a subplot as Wheelwright's stepfather, Dan Needham, revives Gravesend's repertory company. For instance, when the company puts on *Angel Street*, a melodrama that was later turned into the eerie film *Gaslight*, Wheelwright's stepfather, just married and deeply in love, plays the maniacal husband bent on destroying the sanity of his wife, who is played by his real-life bride, Tabitha. The townspeople are so convinced by his villainous performance, they watch him with "evil looks" long after the performance (97). Or, during the church Christmas pageant, when Owen Meany steps unexpectedly out of his role as the Christ child to castigate his parents so sharply that he actually drives them from their seats, a man in the audience, convinced the moment was scripted, later congratulates Owen for such innovation in presenting the Nativity. Falling for an absorbing performance, coaxing authenticity from a convincing imitation, is central to Irving's argument about the impulse to believe in Owen Meany.

To underscore this, Irving not only gives Wheelwright a stepfather professionally committed to amateur theatrics but draws heavily ironic pictures of Wheelwright's mother and his real father, both leading double lives. Long before Wheelwright's birth, his mother moves about tiny Gravesend with easy respectability, a soaring soprano in the church choir, living quietly with her aristocratic parents whose porcelain lineage dates to the *Mayflower*. Her only indulgence is a weekly trip to Boston, to study voice. So demure is she that she brings from Boston colorful fashionable dresses—only to copy those dresses in black and white and then return the garish originals. Even her surprise pregnancy, announced without preamble at a family dinner, is quietly forgiven, an unfortunate indiscretion, she confesses, on the train on the way to Boston. Yet, as Wheelwright comes to know years after her death, Tabby (as her feline name suggests) had multiple lives. Wheelwright discovers that his mother had sung regularly in a swank Boston nightclub, where she was known only as the scintillating "Lady in Red," her smoldering voice and feline good looks recalled by male fans a dozen years after her death. In addition, he finds out that she conceived him not in some passing fling on the train but rather in an extended affair with the Congregational minister right in Gravesend. As Wheelwright gradually untangles the skein of deceptions, he is staggered to see how *"easily* and *gracefully"* she lied (313, italics Irving).

His biological father, the Reverend Lewis Merrill, despite his considerable local reputation in matters of divinity and theology, struggles as well against his public persona. The adulterous affair that produced Wheelwright is never acknowledged publicly. With a Hawthornesque touch, Merrill is stricken with a stammer that underscores his radical discomfort, his deep struggle with his faith. When asked to officiate at Tabitha's marriage to Dan Needham, he finds his text in the heavy sensuality of "The Song of Solomon" and closes with the instructions of John to "love one another as I have loved you." Reverend Merrill struggles with his unshakable attraction for Tabitha; indeed, he is horrified when, at that fateful Little League game, he waves across the field to Tabitha and in a moment of self-loathing prays to God to take Tabitha, to remove his temptation. That prayer, so apparently answered in Owen Meany's foul ball, haunts him even as he moves about his community playing a most convincing cleric.

And the larger world of *Owen Meany* is an unsettling environment of deceptions and too-convincing charades, where identities are never clear and seldom consistent, where frauds enthrall and fool the gullible even as Wheelwright protests the reassuring dependability of appearances. "We Wheelwrights do not scoff at the appearances of things. Things often are as they appear" (108). Consider the evidence Irving provides. Vacationing with a colleague's family at Georgian Bay, Wheelwright joins the family in trying to identify an animal slithering among the bushes around the family cabin—a duck? an otter? a muskrat?—but they can decide only that it is a female "something" (378); Owen Meany engages for a while in the rather lucrative business of manufacturing false identities by selling fake draft cards to minors; in the local repertory company, the Sunday school teacher plays a tart in a revealing French maid outfit, and lifelong residents intently fracture British accents; when Owen first meets Dan Needham, he mistakes a stuffed armadillo Dan gives him for some aquatic animal and then mistakes it for a living armadillo. Dan's company performs Somerset Maugham's *The Constant Wife,* a droll social comedy centered on a charade of a marriage in which a most conventional wife reveals herself to be anything but in dealing with an adulterous husband by agreeing to help cover his liaisons only if he agrees to her holiday with her lover. The Canadian Humane Society attempts to help stranded migrating hawks caught in the ice of a late winter storm, only to discover that the hawks are, in fact, vultures, which proceed to attack the society's assistants. The Tarzan adventure movies that play at Gravesend (oddly enough in a theater called The Idaho, although Wheelwright can find no connection to the state—yet another fractured identity, another nonsignifying name) Owen finds particularly fake, Tarzan wrestling the same tired lion in an obvious soundstage jungle.

Irving extends the argument of deception and gullibility well beyond Wheelwright's immediate world. Indeed, mid-twentieth-century American culture, sired by film and then raised by television, is rife with examples of stunningly bad performances that a gullible public happily embraces as authentic. Irving draws allusions to bad Hollywood biblical epics, forgettable adventure and mystery films, formulaic black-and-white sitcoms, lame 1950s variety entertainment shows, and even the chic bleak of heavy metal videos on MTV. The unlikely television phenomenon that most enthralls Owen is the glittery charade of Liberace. Owen watches this splendidly hokey exercise in hyperbole—although Wheelwright emotionlessly acknowledges the complicated double life of the entertainer revealed years later as Liberace neared his death from AIDS. More distressing, this manipulation of appearances defines the politics of Wheelwright's age (theater director Dan Needham actually comes to the academy to teach history). Apart from Wheelwright's frequent harangues against Reagan the actor, Owen comes to be quite disturbed over JFK's rhetoric of a bold new moral order when it is revealed much later that all the while he trafficked in the most banal philandering. There are larger, deeper deceptions: the Defense Department's elaborate justifications for Vietnam despite the rapidly dissolving moral clarity of the jungle war; the slapstick morality farce of Gary Hart; the baroque ruse of the Iran-Contra Affair; the command performance of Oliver North in military costuming before Congress—each of which comes under Wheelwright's scathing eye.

Yet, amid such slick deceptions and amateur performances (surely a handy metaphor for the larger frame of the slick play zone of the Reagan Era), Wheelwright comes to assert absolutely the sacred identity of Owen Meany; in such a world where sign and meaning routinely repulse rather than cooperate, Owen Meany alone is permitted to mean. It is a gesture of confidence dealt against Wheelwright's immediate world, a gesture made despite the evidence, a gesture that signals (in ways that recall Oates's Stevick clan) a heart in full retreat, a heart seeking the dubious shelter of a reassuring private construction. That Owen Meany, with his haunting dreams of his own death, convinces Wheelwright, who numbers Owen as his only friend, recalls a line from Maugham's *The Constant Wife*, quoted by Irving, "If John is going to deceive Constance, it's nice it should be somebody we all know" (103).

*   *   *

For what we need to know, of course, is not just that God exists, not just that beyond the steely brightness of the stars there is a cosmic intelligence of some kind that keeps the whole show going, but that there is a God right here in the thick of our day-to-day lives who . . . in one way or another is trying to get messages through our blindness as we move around down here knee-deep in the fragrant muck and misery and marvel of the world.

Frederick Buechner, *The Magnificent Defeat*

If we accept Owen Meany as religious event, the novel is lost to the argument of spectacle realism, which respects the dilemma of the immediate and the struggle to accommodate (not transcend) its pull. It is vital, then, for our purposes that Irving so dramatically defines Wheelwright as a problematic Christian.

In the Nativity pageant when Owen plays the Christ child, Wheelwright is assigned the role of Joseph—that biblical figure comes to assume unsuspected import. We watch as Wheelwright grows into that role, justifying his own sterile life by caricaturing Joseph as "that hapless follower, that stand-in, that guy along for the ride" (149) with "nothing to do, nothing to say, nothing to learn" (155). Such simplifying of the Joseph role reflects on Wheelwright's most imperfect understanding of his own faith. In the story of the silent Joseph, the contemporary Christian can find an exemplum of fidelity, compassion, and unquestioning, powerful faith. Joseph dedicates himself to a family he can never fully understand; he concedes control of his most deeply private sphere to sacred forces he could not, would not presume to decode, much less understand. In short, Joseph is the very antithesis of Wheelwright. Locked "in the midst of things we cannot understand" (124), to quote the scriptural reading from Tabitha's funeral, Wheelwright, unlike the long-suffering Joseph, demands explanation; God's design must be made clear . . . now. In this, he lacks patience—the fundamental virtue of the Christian who is necessarily suspended between the Incarnation and the promise of the Parousia. Unlike Joseph, who concedes limits and finds in such surrender the joyful dependency of trust, Wheelwright comes to discern the

pattern of God's actions, claims a clarity of vision that in its presump-
tiveness is more an occasion of sin. The novel closes with Wheelwright
praying God to return Owen Meany. "O God—please give him back!
I shall keep asking You" (543), which promises that he will continue
counterarguing God's design, unable to accept as unsearchable the ways
of the inscrutable Creator.

Indeed, the joyful dependency of the saint is suggested by the novel's
most developed symbolic pattern: armlessness. Armlessness is part of
the history of Gravesend; the Native American chief who handed over
the land to the Wheelwright ancestors signed the agreement by making
a crude form of an armless man. Tabitha's armless dressmaker's dummy
fascinates Owen, who even secures it after Tabitha's death; caught in
frequent silhouette, Owen often appears to be armless; Owen vandalizes
a parochial school playground statue of Mary Magdalene by removing
its arms; Owen returns the stuffed armadillo that Wheelwright offers
him as a gesture of friendship after the baseball accident—but without
one claw; the horrific explosion in the airport bathroom at the close blows
away Owen's arms. The condition of armlessness suggests the limits of
the created within events that cannot fully signify to our meager understanding. Interestingly, although Owen insists that he is helpless within
the unfolding plan of God's design ("GOD HAS TAKEN MY HANDS"
[301]), he is far from willing to accept such an invalid state. Indeed,
he goes about breaking off arms. As the Christmas pageant Christ,
"swaddled the length of his body, up to his armpits," Owen demands "to
have his arms free" (157). Later, clumsily, he will attach arms literally
when he affixes the arms from Mary Magdalene's statue to the dressmaker's dummy.

But the greatest failure of Wheelwright within the argument of Christianity is his resistance to the potent force of love—the stunning mystery
of (com)passion itself, the losing and finding of the self within the need
for another. In ways that recall Enid in the wild recoil from Felix, the
preoccupation with the self inures Wheelwright from the joy and the
grief of the heart, keeps him "safe" from the vulnerability inevitable in
any interaction with others. After his mother's death, Wheelwright divides his time between his adopted father's house and his grandmother's, never quite settling into one or the other. As an adult, Wheelwright shuns relationships with students and colleagues (in addition
to his disdain for his classes, he develops a caustic relationship with a
woman literature teacher); with his own shattered family (after years of

wondering about his biological father, he coldly rejects the earnest love offered by Reverend Merrill); even with his generation (by virtue of his draft deferment, Wheelwright is severed from the Vietnam War, the centering event of his generation). Wheelwright has no family; he attaches himself awkwardly to the summer retreat with the family of the school's headmistress, spends a cheerless month at their cabin, listening to their family stories—never a part, always apart. When a caring minister asks Wheelwright whether he loves anyone, Wheelwright names his stepfather and the headmistress, then quickly qualifies the intensity of that emotion and says that he more worries about them, specifically over their weight—he is too fat, she too thin.

In the narrative present, Wheelwright lives alone at a girls' boarding-house in a mock-sacerdotal pose of isolation and sterility that recalls Enid Stevick's acceptance of the renunciative life at the music school. There, in his magic kingdom, Wheelwright wonders as he passes among the noisy dining room tables whether someday the girls might actually talk to him. But Wheelwright has long forsworn intimacy. He confesses that he never quite managed to shed his virginity. Looking back, Wheelwright dismisses the pulsings of adolescent lust (as when he is drawn to his grandmother's maid) as "distasteful," even "evil" (233). He measures his potential for connection by the size of his erection (which, he concedes, is "not much" [62]). Now comfortably ensconced in middle age, he overhears his colleagues decide with derision that, so alone, he is what they term a "nonpracticing homosexual" (375). Unable to coax the trick of intimacy, preferring to pull himself into a tight, protective shell like the figure of the armadillo that so centers the early chapters of the book, Wheelwright hungers most for the sanctuary of his lonely church pew against the moment he must depart and confront all over again the world that so infuriates him. His chapel becomes another magic kingdom, another secure(d) place apart. He fumes over newspapers. He records with dreary accuracy the date, the weather, even the time of day, all of which merely suggests a man content with the parts but unable to find within such fragments the stirring of wonder. He needs the distracting miracle of Owen Meany, the show and sizzle, the lurid touches of spectacle (the noun), the vision and prophecy thing, to justify turning away from a world he judges—as Enid does—to be vacuous and entirely dismissable.

Yet even as we watch Wheelwright so foolishly deny engagement, Irving cannot entirely celebrate the tonic pull of love, cannot entirely endorse the argument of spectacle realism that finds (as we shall see) that connection compensates for the (im)perfect, (in)glorious, bruising absurdities of the immediate. This makes *A Prayer for Owen Meany* a critical step in our narrative of the 1980s. Wheelwright's cousin Hester is the one who most nearly approaches the argument of spectacle realism. Fashioning a clear picture of Hester is difficult because she is filtered through Wheelwright, a thorough misogynist who caricatures her as a dropout, an angry rebel, a loose woman-child dispensing her carnivorous sexuality on anyone (characterizations emphatically undermined by the very events Wheelwright narrates). But set against Wheelwright's isolation and sterility and against Owen Meany's maddening aloofness, Hester energizes the narrative with a frank embrace of the immediate that is at the very core of spectacle realism.

Unlike Wheelwright, who finds the world of pure contingency too hazardous and thus retreats to the private shrine of Owen Meany, Hester, with her strong shoulders, big bones, heavy jaw, and big hands, engages the world from earliest childhood. Battered about by her athletic brothers, rejected from the narrow sphere of her parents' love, her reputation wrecked by her own curiosity over the sexual hunger, Hester is most powerfully involved with this world (she alone of Irving's characters rejects the narcotic of television). Unlike those who rashly adore Owen or those who ridicule his oddness, Hester finds with Owen a most (un)complicated love. Still in early adolescence, Hester, hardened by a childhood pushed about by her brothers, is drawn simply to touch the tiny Owen. As Owen and Hester develop a powerful attraction for one another, Wheelwright naturally is stumped by the relationship. Yet even in the biased narrative glimpses we get from this fifth-Wheelwright, Owen and Hester's affection for one another is clear—raw, exasperating, supportive, unpredictable, deeply human. Unlike Enid, whose discovery of the sexual imperative is quickly lost as she encodes such energy into the cold logic of shame, Hester relishes its dark energy.

Well within the argument of spectacle realism, Hester—unlike Enid—is wary of assuming the spiritual; she finds spirit enough in the full-throttle engagement of the immediate. Whenever Owen talks mysteriously about his recurring dream, Hester dismisses him as an "asshole" and refuses to listen to "this shit" (417). Aggravated at his determination to die, she actually wrestles with him when he talks of God's directing him to an early death—hitting him hard enough to require four stitches, which later she tenderly kisses. She promises him in a most moving moment, "I'll marry you, I'll move to Arizona—I'll go anywhere with you, Owen. . . . I'll even get *pregnant*. . . . I'd do *anything* for you. . . . But I won't go to your fucking funeral" (469–70, italics Irving). Hester does not need Owen Meany as God's instrument; she finds sufficient purpose in the connection of their hearts and bodies (and in their passion, at one point she praises the generous size of Owen's penis). In any of our later texts, Hester would be the heroic center. Yet when Owen moves all too willingly to death and Wheelwright is left secure within the refuge of his mock shrine to Owen, Hester is left devastated, left quite alone.

Forsaking her attempts to be a coffeehouse folksinger (with its suggestion of engaging an imperfect immediate), Hester, glimpsed long after the death of Owen Meany, becomes a "fading queen of the grittiest and randiest sort of rock 'n' roll" band (452), whose ugly, often violent videos thread battle footage of Vietnam with images of Hester entering and leaving hotel rooms accompanied by young boys. After Owen, she attends to a barren life of meaningless intimacies with boys who are, she tells a predictably horrified Wheelwright, "easier to say goodbye to" (466). Touched deeply by intimacy, she has never found her way to the vocabulary for saying goodbye to Owen; one of her songs is titled "There's No Forgettin' Nineteen Sixty-Eight" (454).

If Owen Meany is both spiritual enough to compel Wheelwright to withdraw into a protective sanctuary yet immediate enough to shatter Hester's heart, how are we to respond to this curious figure? Although Donald Greiner finds Owen Meany a reprise of Hawthorne's Dimmesdale in his heroic assertion of the sacred in a secular world, Owen is perhaps more akin to the scarlet letter itself, a text that demands contradictory readings. Indeed, his initials—O.M.—suggest a most meditative icon, a resonating object that inspires reflection, not analysis. As Philip Page cogently argues, we can say with certainty only that Owen Meany is a far more ambiguous figure than Wheelwright allows. Yes, Owen casts a hard moral eye on his immediate world: he perceives early on the problem of Vietnam, military and moral; he speaks out fearlessly in his school newspaper column against the school administration's hypocrisies; he points out the massive contradictions in Christian doctrine; he dismisses his fellow students' fascination with drugstore pornography. Yes, Owen, a gifted student, nevertheless happily stays behind a grade to stay with the much less gifted Wheelwright; to help Wheelwright avoid the draft, Owen cuts off Wheelwright's trigger finger with an engraving saw even as he exclaims, "I LOVE YOU" (450); he shepherds Wheelwright through his education, ghostwriting essays and doing home-work, selecting his living accommodations, focusing his graduate work (on Thomas Hardy), indeed giving him a working argument for his thesis. Such unselfish concern surely touches on the miraculous in that it is asserted in our age of insulated self-interest.

Why is it, then, that at so many levels Owen Meany disturbs? There is his urgency to direct events along his own agenda, to break off the arms figuratively of those within his sphere of influence. His control of Wheelwright's life moves uncomfortably beyond magnanimous interest and verges on cold manipulation. There are other examples. Much to the chagrin of the rector, Owen takes over the traditional church Christmas pageant, redesigning staging and costuming, reassigning roles, this time with himself as the Christ child; later, he is offended when one candidate for the headmaster's job declines a "PRIVATE AUDIENCE" with Owen, finding inappropriate a separate interview with a student (283); one dark winter morning, he enlists the academy's basketball squad to move a faculty member's Volkswagen from its illegal parking spot to the stage of the school's theater.

What is far more disturbing is that this impulse to manipulate extends to the recurring dream foretelling his death. He does not simply allow the dream to manifest itself in his waking life, which, of course, would be a measure of faith. Rather, he makes sure the dream is staged exactly as he sees it. He drags Wheelwright to gyms for most of their schooling to practice a sort of joint dunk shot (he leaps into Wheelwright's arms and then slams the basketball through the net) until they can make the shot in under three seconds, necessary, he measures, to complete the dream of his handling the grenade. Moreover, Owen declines a generous scholarship offer from Harvard to attend what he concedes is the less spectacular University of New Hampshire, where to pay for his schooling he will have to join ROTC, thus moving himself into the armed forces as his dream demands; to make sure the ROTC program accepts him, he fudges his weight by consuming excess bananas and stretches his height by straining on his toes. As the day of his death approaches, Owen inexplicably calls Wheelwright in Massachusetts and convinces him to visit Arizona only because Wheelwright appears in his dream. In spite of his all-too-convincing spiritualism and his conversations with God, he directs, in effect, stages, the dream as he has seen it.

Owen is thus unseemly in his self-election. When he is crossed, he too-freely assumes the persecuted demeanor of the martyr. Swimming in a quarry lake with friends, the young Owen hides in the rocks underwater, and when no one rushes to rescue him he comes up sputtering, melodramatically declaiming, "YOU LET ME DROWN! . . . YOU DIDN'T DO ANYTHING! YOU JUST WATCHED ME DROWN! . . . REMEMBER THAT: YOU LET ME DIE" (30); later, as he is busted for running a fake ID service, he quotes (and not for the first time) Christ's dying words on the cross. His presumption of his role as God's instrument, his willingness to play neoredeemer to a world he so pointedly finds morally malignant, all define the movement toward his heroic gesture in Phoenix as a problematic act. Indeed, cradled in a nun's arms after the explosion, nearing the death that has so centered his life, Owen asks his commanding officer nearby, "PLEASE SEE TO IT THAT I GET SOME KIND OF MEDAL FOR THIS" (541), a special plea for recognition, a disconcerting reminder of Owen's egoism.

As instrument of God, Owen Meany cannot relish the miracle of the ordinary moment so vital to the Christian vision (and to spectacle realism) because to him there are no ordinary moments; he cannot find his way to any unexpected happy moment because to him there are no unexpected moments. Rather, Owen Meany propels himself grimly through time (Irving focuses on a succession of cheerless celebrations of New Year's Day) convinced of his own election, his own justification. For example, when Owen first meets Wheelwright's cousins, they play a happy tickling game; but when Owen is tickled, his response is to wet himself. According to Wheelwright, who himself seldom touches the simplest joy over the remarkable possibility of the present moment, "Owen's sense of his own destiny . . . robbed him of his capacity for *fun*" (373, italics Irving). Owen seldom laughs, save in the trenchant digs of his own withering wit. The gift of Christian laughter and its larger involvement in the affirmation of the gift of Creation, which parallels the premise of spectacle realism, is so lacking in Owen that, at one point, Wheelwright observes Owen had no use even for spring.

Of course, it is no great trick to object to the too-easy elevation of Owen Meany. After all, when Owen tries to make it into the army infantry, he is failed after he stumbles on the obstacle course—he cannot even pull himself above a five-foot wall. Wheelwright, without realizing the revealing irony, describes Owen Meany as a doll without "realistic joints" (14), suggesting a most malleable object, a narrator's plaything. Like the productions of amateur theater in Gravesend, the sacred Owen Meany, if examined closely, will reveal its sorry artificiality. In the Christmas pageant, the mystery of the Incarnation is re-created with stage tricks, poor contrivances of pulleys, and harshly amateurish special effects that include dangling above the stage a hapless student as the angel announcing the Nativity. During that Nativity pageant, Owen Meany decries the bulky costumes intended for the manger cows—they look too much like reindeer. It is an apparently minor objection, part of Owen Meany's irrepressible urge to control events. But the comment reveals Irving's larger tension: the confusion of the sacred (the cows present at the sacred event) and the secular (the reindeer, associated with the secular holiday).

Irving, finally, cannot confirm the gaudy seriousness with which Owen promotes himself as God's instrument. It is grand theater masquerading as religion. When the academy administration moves the morning chapel service to the better-lighted facilities offered by the school theater, the faculty suddenly finds itself unnaturally elevated, sitting not in pews but rather up on stage. Ironically, it is Owen who most vocally objects to the new platform that provides the headmaster with an "EXAGGERATED PLATFORM FROM WHICH TO SPEAK . . . THAT GIVES US ALL THE FEELING THAT WE'RE IN THE PRESENCE OF AN EXALTED PERSONAGE" (294). Such objections to the artificially heightened, to the sham spectacle of staged elevation, of course, recall the very business of elevation that Wheelwright invests in Owen. Owen is spectacle—the noun. Not surprisingly, Wheelwright approves of the new chapel service. "I confess, I rather liked the change" (294). But in leaving Wheelwright object-less, Irving finds most difficult the job of affirming within the precarious immediate the stuff of wonder. Rejecting Owen Meany leaves us little to accept—and that is the dilemma to which finally we turn.

* * *

When we take the little piece of time that we have in this world and pay attention to what it is telling us, not just to what it is telling us about the beauty of the sun as it sets, God knows, but to what it is telling us about the wildness and strangeness and pain of things, the tears of things, the lachrimae rerum, *as well as the joy of things.*

Frederick Buechner, *The Hungering Dark*

The trick of spectacle realism is to let go of Owen Meany but not the joy, to maintain the love of engagement and the respect for dilemma without the suasive cheat of demanding Owen as sacred presence. Profoundly moved by the Christian vision that accords plot to chance and offers a most stunning resolution to life after death, Irving, unlike writers we will treat later, cannot find a way to accommodate the initial terror over losing Owen Meany and being left within the apparent limits of the immediate. But for our purposes, writing within and against one of the most overtly religious decades in contemporary American cultural history, Irving sees that misappropriating the rhetoric of the sacred by mock Christians leaves us little to relish in the immediate. In this regard, *Owen Meany* very much addresses its own decade and will help advance our study. Although Irving uses John Kennedy and his generation's elevation of him as an example of such confusion (indeed, watching JFK's inauguration, Owen Meany quotes Isaiah's stirring passage—"for unto us a child is born"), the novel itself is far more a part of the often tacky religious dramas of the 1980s.

Even a most casual reading of the decade would indicate its religious nature. Evangelical rhetoric defined the politics of the resurgent (and triumphant) Right; fundamentalism abroad expressed itself most forcibly in devastating strokes of horrific terrorism; the hard realities of AIDS convinced earnest fundamentalists, armed with passages of scriptural support, to promote a pernicious interpretation of the retrovirus-as-vengeance; baby boomers, soul-tired of their generational materialism, turned with cloying naïveté toward arcane avenues of spiritual rejuvenation, to pyramid power, to water chambers, to crystal healing, to channeling; en masse, our most charismatic televangelists, whose vast commercial congregations were matters of demographics as much as faith, suddenly started acting like their own worst caricatures, a clutch of smarmy Elmer Gantrys. Add to this the censorship hysteria over the satanic element in the decade's heavy metal boom and later over the slippery definition of obscenity in the arts; the insurgent voice of American Catholic bishops introduced into the national argument over poverty, job opportunities, even nuclear war planning; the gale storm of John Paul II into international politics; the bloody holy war between Iran and Iraq; the militant rhetoric and often gruesome tactics of antiabortion activists' Operation Rescue; the evangelical fervor that attended massive relief efforts such as Live Aid and Hands Across America; the playful sacrilege of the early Madonna; the hokey high-mysticism of Shirley MacLaine's backlog of previous existences; Hollywood's fascination with paranormal phenomena and with ghosts in particular; the eerie 1987 pseudo-event of the Harmonic Convergence with white-robed minions gathered on hillsides; the uproar over Martin Scorsese's 1988 film *The Last Temptation of Christ;* and the cluster of former divinity students, practicing ministers, and even astrologers that animated the decade's presidential politics—and it becomes clear that the decade that commenced in the dark quiet jungles about the Jonestown compound and closed with Salman Rushdie improbably enough in hiding was strikingly religious in its vocabulary, its argument, its passions.

Amid such religious intensity, however, the decade also saw a most cynical manipulation of the images and the promises of religion, a twisting of its most fundamental language and symbols, an emptying of its spiritual intention by reducing it to a most blatant mercenary enterprise (in a stroke that would have seemed heavy-handed even in the clumsiest religious satire, a sprawling Christian theme park opened in middecade). Irving, who has so often tangled with just such big cultural issues (witness his timely treatments of radical feminism, Vietnam, abortion), challenges this apparent reawakening of the religious impulse, deflates its pretentious seriousness, and charges that the decade steadily confused the sacred with secular agendas and, more damning, that those most terribly certain of God's designs—from televangelists to terrorists—wrought the most damage. Hard certainty, as we shall see again and again, satisfies those most unavailable to the dark wonder of the immediate. Like Enid Stevick's Christian Catholicism, religious certainty renders uncomplicated what within the texts of spectacle realism stays a most enticing complicated immediate.

But Irving knows the spiritual hunger that can produce a pseudoevent such as Owen Meany—and this is where Irving cannot wholly accede to the argument of spectacle realism, why his fiction poses questions that only our later texts can resolve. Irving's fiction centers on the cold terror of living in a blasted secular wasteland, where the idea of a miracle has been pounded into hapless cliché by bland news anchors relaying accounts of house fires or highway traffic accidents or by the bloated rhetoric of medical technologists or NASA spokespersons; where the idea of "good faith" has slipped effortlessly into the droning white noise of television spots for real estate companies or law firms; where "You Gotta Believe" is heard not in church but in sports arenas to bolster long-shot teams heading for a championship showdown. Irving understands the hunger that compelled decade sightings of the shadowy face of Christ on the dented side of an abandoned meat freezer, and of the faces of long-dead children on the wide, empty screen of a drive-in movie theater, and the reports of church statues crying or bleeding.

But if he understands the hunger, or perhaps because he understands the hunger of John Wheelwright, Irving sees as well the danger of gullibility, the damning emptiness of counterfeit fulfillment. In such a decade of junk-bond spirituality where earnest religiosity turned into a most mesmerizing caricature of itself, where religion fell victim to the vanity and warm imaginations of ruthless self-promotions, where religion morphed into slick theater, Irving reveals in the harsh voice of his narrator the souring endgame of just such pretense and reveals within the drama of his narrative device the dangers of certainty in the inaccessible realm of the sacred. In an era when we all so needed to touch an Owen Meany, we turned rather to promote ourselves as our own best, last gods. In that way, we understand the title of Irving's novel: it is not a prayer offered *to* Owen Meany but a prayer offered *for* his presence in a life that, denied that plane, shrivels into terrifying thinness. For all the earnest assumptions of Owen Meany, the universe he passes through does not acknowledge his sense of design. His death in the airport men's room is surely a courageous act of selflessness, but it is no more than part of the weave of our daily record; events such as Owen's gutty sacrifice compel admiration but not adoration. We can accept Owen Meany as sacred, but Irving cautions that it is not Owen Meany that compels such belief but rather our own need. If we confuse the sacred and the secular, if we need Owen Meany or, as Owen himself says in his set piece on the feeling of betrayal after Kennedy's philandering was revealed, if we need to be suckered, it is because within this century's chilling intuition of God's essential unworkability, in a universe far wider and emptier than any other century ever suspected, we have been unable to argue ourselves out of the need to believe; we have yet to make our peace with an unsponsored immediate.

Elevating Owen Meany, like spinning the gorgeous illusion of Fitzgerald's Gatsby (which Wheelwright discusses with his class, focusing specifically on narrative unreliability), is the elaborate work of the secular confused by a manipulative narrator into an expression of the godlike, the sacred. Much as *The Great Gatsby* is in truth *A Prayer for Jimmy Gatz*, Wheelwright, like Nick, casts about an uncertain, if attractive, figure (Owen Meany/Jimmy Gatz) the certainty of election, thus providing a desiccated soul a rationale for accepting the spiritual dimension it so completely lacks. Nick and Wheelwright are unapologetic secular gospel writers, willingly myopic, who never see the ironic subtexts of the stories they relate. The easy undercutting of Wheelwright threatens to leave the novel as yet another savaging of those hyperserious born-agains who make such delightful (and easy) targets because of their blindness to their own thin performance. But Irving is clearly drawn by the power and the pain of those who struggle with the spiritual dimension against the rest of us who fashion lives untouched by the possibilities of such a dimension. Although the argument of Irving's novel is the danger of those, like Wheelwright and Owen (and the entire Stevick clan), who figure out the world and credit such design to a controlling deity, the novel does offer a character who struggles within the very doubt appropriate to the contemporary Christian, a character with important implications for the argument of spectacle realism. Reverend Lewis Merrill as both exemplary minister and profound sinner emerges as Irving's unheralded heroic center. Like Graham Greene's seedy priests (Owen writes a term paper on Greene), Merrill, confronted by the ambiguous argument of Owen Meany, refuses to define what such a figure signifies. "Owen was extraordinarily g-g-g-*gifted*—yes, gifted and powerfully sure of himself. No doubt he suffered some powerfully disturbing visions, too—and he was certainly emotional, he was very emotional" (463, italics Irving).

Rather than determining Owen, Reverend Merrill approaches Owen Meany with admiration, consternation, frank confusion, a mix of responses lacking in those who simply bow before Owen's daunting performance. During an academy exercise from which Owen has been excluded over some trumped-up charges, Merrill is asked (naturally by Owen himself) to offer a prayer for Owen Meany. Uncertain, Merrill leads a moment of silence that stretches to so radical a time that Merrill is considered out of order by the trustees who censured Owen. But that prayer for Owen Meany is a most appropriate response to Owen Meany. Against the tedious pages of testimony piled on by Wheelwright, against the deadly certainty of the passages from Owen's diary, this extended silence finds certainty impossible and articulates wordlessly the bald need we feel for a manifestation such as Owen Meany, how much we need Owen Meany to be authentic. Although Wheelwright (not surprisingly) dismisses Merrill for it, Merrill's force of faith is grounded in his own eloquent doubt. He finds God powerful but oddly distant, a Creator who loves despite. . . . Such doubt, for the superficial Christian such as Wheelwright, is hopelessly inappropriate. Merrill argues to Wheelwright that the enthusiastic embrace of the Church on the strength of Owen Meany's heroic act and his disturbing dream is a thin sort of conversion. A miracle cannot create faith; a miracle can only sustain faith. "You've witnessed what you c-c-c-call a miracle and now you believe— you believe everything. . . . But miracles don't c-c-c-*cause* belief—real miracles don't m-m-m-make faith out of thin air; you have to *already have faith* in order to believe in *real* miracles" (463, italics Irving).

Far more than the doubts that are part of his lifelong commitment to the spiritual definition of the human experience, Reverend Merrill suffers. He is, to borrow from Oates, a creature of the trampoline, compelled by the uneasy rhythms of flesh and spirit, the dark thrill of helplessness. Only Hester approaches his degree of the flattening pain of regret and loneliness—but Hester's agony is never pulled into the spiritual. Reverend Merrill lives for more than twenty years a traitor to his God as he wrestles with an irradicable sin and with the sense of his own imperfection, suggested by the errant lock of hair that disturbs his homily delivery every Sunday and his persistent stutter. Merrill breaks from his stale commitment to his dreary family for a brief affair with Tabby Wheelwright, a member of his church choir. Then he must endure as she abandons any thought of him; he must agree not to reveal his identity to his own son despite growing up in the same town. In quick succession, he is asked to perform the wedding ceremony in which Tabitha marries Dan Needham and then shortly after to officiate at her burial. In the initial reading, of course, Merrill appears a peripheral character. Only after his identity is disclosed late in the novel can his enormous suffering and unexpressed grief be fully understood by the reader, who has casually dismissed him as vitally unvital, much as Wheelwright has distanced the minister so completely from his experience that when he tries years after to reconstruct the fans in the bleachers the day of the baseball accident he does not even recall Merrill's presence.

The confrontation between father and son late in the novel reveals in harsh counterpoint the unsuspected stature of Merrill as the novel's struggling Christian and unmasks Wheelwright for the contemptuous parody of the Christian. As Merrill confesses the guilt he has carried since the day of the accident when he prayed thoughtlessly for God to kill the woman who so haunted his experience, Wheelwright dismisses such faith as thin and argues that Merrill's stale dedication to the church has denied him the willingness to believe in the possibility of a new miracle. What disturbs Wheelwright is not so much his father's dependent faith in God ("my bitter father could manage no better response than to whine to me about his lost faith" [482]) as his refusal to credit Owen at all. "What a *wimp* he was, Pastor Merrill; but how proud I felt of my mother—that she'd had the good sense to shrug him off" (482, italics Irving). The harsh misreading of Merrill is apparent. The experience of Merrill, the enormity of his simple human grief, his unceasing struggle with his faith, the powerful tragedy of his love darkened by his unshakable certainty of its sinfulness secure only a curt dismissal from Wheelwright, always short on the simplest expression of compassion.

To demonstrate Wheelwright's own dangerous sort of performance Christianity, Irving closes the narrative not with Owen's dramatic airport heroism but rather with one devastating act of performance, one ultimate parody that converts Merrill to a reckless certainty that surely marks the novel's deepest tragedy. In a perverse moment the night before Owen Meany is to be buried, Wheelwright, motivated by unarticulated anger over the poor stuff of his discovered father, decides to "help" the minister who struggles with faith by rigging a miracle of absurd dimensions. Wheelwright places his mother's dressmaker's dummy outside the minister's study and, after securing Merrill's attention by tossing a baseball through a chapel window, watches as Merrill, distraught over the conversation with his son, mistakes the dummy for the ghost of Tabitha and collapses in feverish certainty that the paranormal realm has at last touched his immediate. It is Wheelwright at his most cynical, his most misanthropic, his most Owen—foisting on another hungry soul the shadow-show of a rigged miracle, the shallowest appearance of the sacred. When the following day Merrill strides into the chapel to conduct the funeral service for Owen Meany, he delivers the service with unexpected animation, without stuttering; it is a most disturbing irony—a moment of triumph for Wheelwright (indeed, he feels secure in his conversion spoof) and a disturbing loss for the larger Christian struggle for the authentic experience, another victim of the contemporary hunger to touch, the impatient need for certainty.

* * *

Don't ask if you can believe until you've read The New York Times, *till after you've studied the daily record of the world's brokenness and corruption, which should always stand side by side with your Bible. Then ask yourself if you can believe in the Gospel of Jesus Christ again for that particular day. If your answer's always Yes, then you do not know what believing means.*

Frederick Buechner, *The Return of Ansel Gibbs*

We are left, then, with a sorry cast of imperfect Christians who, in their stark failure to affirm the authentic touch of the spiritual, turn away with varying degrees of frustration from the immediate world that so commands the center of spectacle realism or opt to traffic (like so many during the 1980s) in the most counterfeit manifestations, spectacles of the transcendent. In Irving's narrative, we are given a world where love interferes without benefit, where death stuns without illumination, where engagement of the immediate is harshly unfulfilling, where awareness of the immediate is grounds for retreat. It is a world curiously unable to reward engagement. We leave John Wheelwright as we left Enid Stevick—master of a private zone of spectacle, a play zone of controlled effect. We leave Hester blasted into indifference, stumbling without direction about a stark immediacy that cannot find its way to color. We leave Reverend Merrill, his face aglow, certain that he has at last redeemed the immediate, but only by brushing against a most ludicrous display of hokey spirituality. Suspended between Incarnation and Parousia, compelled (much as Wheelwright is) by a lifelong journey for a missing Father, we demand that our mean lives find direction, sustain plot. That it cannot be is the heartbreaking argument that waits just beyond the trick of Owen Meany. We are left in the same elegant helplessness that Oates records, a helplessness that is as ancient as the sorrowful lines from *The Medea* quoted during one of Dan Needham's rehearsals: "Many things the gods achieve beyond our judgment. . . . What we thought is not confirmed and what we thought not God contrives" (460). It seems that we cannot relinquish Owen Meany and hold on to joy.

Irving's response is far more problematic, far more guarded, far more wistful, far more contemporary; in this response he brings us to the brink of spectacle realism but cannot commit to its fullest argument. Despite Wheelwright's shallow assertion that, in the age of MTV, we have lost irony, irony most decidedly confounds the creation of Owen Meany. It is surely no coincidence that Owen Meany finds most appealing Frost's poem "Birches," which, like *A Prayer for Owen Meany*, tests the hunger to escape the random, pitilessly violent contemporary world, to get finally beyond the sense of life as a "pathless wood." But Frost resolves, much as Irving does in rejecting the riveting lie of the little Owen Meany, to be content in that horrific element, denied as part of the twentieth century the luxury of certainty.

Contentment, however, is far from the signature of spectacle realism. Here, the immediate is cause largely for regret. Irving's cautionary tale of the continuing struggle to touch the sacred is best summarized not in the hymns quoted at such tedious length by the insufferably religious narrator nor in the pages of self-involved entries of Owen's diary, but rather in the decidedly secular Broadway song lyrics Owen and Wheelwright overhear in a visit to a Boston music teacher as they search for clues to Wheelwright's father—"wouldn't it be lover-ly?" But spectacle realism cannot brook regrets. It will be the work of the novels to which we now turn to bring together Oates's sense of the stunning power of the accessible immediate with Irving's hunger for the generous benediction of the elusive sacred.

3

A Necessary Time to Bolt

Reynolds Price, *Kate Vaiden*

The best thing about my life up to here is, nobody believes it. I stopped trying to make people hear it long ago.

Kate Vaiden

Hers is a voice we have heard before. Like Enid Stevick, like John Wheelwright, Kate Vaiden dominates her narrative by smothering its events in the ruthless assertion of ego. Like those characters, Kate's young life is struck by horrific events that intervene because, as spectacle realism insists, we are passionate animals compelled by imperfect hearts with the roiling muscle of chance. And like those two, Kate rejects participation in that open realm of event, sequesters herself from others at a tender age (like Enid) to live out a life of chilled hibernation (like Wheelwright). Yet unlike Oates and Irving, Price cannot abide the quiet work of astringent irony to deflate the neat withdrawal of characters into magic kingdoms. Rather, he provides a narrative counterforce in the figure of Walter Porter, Kate's gay cousin who brings to her the benediction of love that she never earns, never solicits, and indeed ultimately spurns. Walter Porter will offer us our first sense of the exacting demand of spectacle realism. Like Reverend Merrill and Hester, Walter engages the immediate despite the cost, and in such a gesture touches the reader in ways that Enid Stevick and John Wheelwright surely frustrate. This makes *Kate Vaiden* a most logical next step in our look at spectacle realism.

We begin with Kate. Before she is eighteen, her young life has been shaped by the dark logic of suicide. Her world of rural North Carolina is shaken three times by the irrational stroke of self-destruction: when Kate is eleven, her father, distraught over her mother's infidelity, shoots himself after killing her; later, her first boyfriend, a marine recruit completing basic training on Parris Island before returning to elope with Kate, inexplicably stands up during a drill in which recruits must crawl under live machine gun fire, taking four shots in the back; and then, when Kate nears eighteen, the father of her child, desperate in part over her unwillingness to commit to any joint future, shoots away most of his heart in the bathtub of an apartment where Kate had taken refuge from him. In a novel that, like *You Must Remember This* and *A Prayer for Owen Meany*, is concerned with educating its central character, the act of suicide is critical for what it fails to teach Kate. Kate learns not the terrifying waste or the absolute price of withdrawing from experience; rather, she learns its persuasive argument—the necessity of sacrificing the self to preserve it. The shattering experiences of her adolescence teach her that to touch another, to allow another to touch her, is to be irreparably broken; they are the lessons of the trampoline, the lessons of the Little League ballfield.

Unwilling to surrender to such vulnerability, she denies touch, shrinks from it like an unwarranted invasion. In recounting her emotional experiences, Kate draws on the bloody language of warfare: violation, surrender, wounding, and attrition. Kate's adolescence is framed against the carnage of World War II; news from the front, carried on the family's enormous radio, counterpoints Kate's development. She begins to menstruate the year Germany invades Poland; she decides to live on her own on the day of Hiroshima. The murder-suicide of her parents, her sexual initiation with the doomed Gaston Stegall, the contradictory affair with Doug Lee that produces the child she will abandon—each experience teaches her that to be touched is to be diminished. Like the cloistered figures of Enid Stevick and John Wheelwright, Kate learns that the self is something to be protected. She cannot understand committing it to family or to love (people gazing at each other like "hypnotized frogs" [46]); she cannot coax pleasure from sexuality. Taught the simplest lesson (vulnerability destroys), Kate argues herself out of the worth of experiencing the emotions that can never be predicted, controlled, or explained—and that alone provide the (extra)ordinary experience of the immediate so vital to the premise of spectacle realism.

For example, first love teaches Kate not the stunning surprise of fusion but rather the dreary inevitability of fission. Her initial experience comes on a foxhunt with Gaston Stegall, two years her senior. Against a backdrop that suggests the animal instinct to hunt, Kate follows Gaston into the woods and spies him masturbating—"he held his penis like a wingshot quail and explored its considerable length with a finger from his other hand"; it seemed a "blind and feverish animal that might not survive." More curious than aroused (she asks, "Is it sick?"), Kate intervenes not to experiment with contact but rather to finish the job; she "milk[s]" him "dry" (40–42). This initiation (Kate is twelve) encodes the sexual act in a wonderless vocabulary of pain—Kate eases Gaston's "hurt"; erect, Gaston groans that he feels near death, that something is the matter "with this"—and isolation—as Kate completes the job, despite Gaston's enormous relief, both stay necessarily unviolated.

Over the next two years, Kate, although baffled by such need, is fascinated by the novelty of ministering to Gaston's struggling penis ("We stuck to the basic original idea, which was easing Gaston's body" [79]); Kate is less a lover, more an unlicensed paramedic performing crude triage. Their relationship is starkly phallocentric: Gaston's demanding organ is a "live handy pet with elaborate features" (41) that she must keep calm. Sexuality denied its tonic wonder is a paltry matter of unilateral relief, unburdening Gaston's pain, a submission to sparkless biology—as Kate defines it, "something your parents did to make you, and of course I'd seen dogs locked together and helpless" (37). Despite Gaston's cautious concern ("Ain't you hurting yet?"), Kate cannot concede the terrifying impulse to surrender ("I was not. I was happy" [74]). Such experience falls shy of the romantic, despite Kate's strained efforts to cull from her trysts with Gaston the stuff of the romances that she reads to pass the "hot empty day[s]" in her Macon summer (78). Indeed, at one point when she thinks of marriage (a "sickening trap"[84]), she reacts much like a threatened flank of a regiment—she attacks. She strikes Gaston hard in the mouth, drawing blood.

Kate dispenses with her virginity in a creek bed near where her parents died, the ascendant impulse to love plotted against the curving line of death. Further, she meets Gaston near a cemetery by a tall monument that marks the remains of a young boy killed by lightning on a clear day; nearby is "damp gray" quicksand where years earlier a pony, an animal Kate associates with sexuality, struggled to its death. And the act itself falls far short of Kate's expectations. Curious, she had listened to a smutty poem passed around the schoolyard, "Rhonda's Road to Womanhood," its rhymed couplets describing the lusty satisfactions of a secretary (ironically, Kate's eventual profession) once she finally yields her virginity. But the act itself does not engage Kate; during Gaston's heaving struggles on top of her, she pictures her own face in the beech leaves overhead. There is no epiphany, no bursting through the self, only Kate's banal invitation to repeat the act ("You just got to name your day" [77]), thereby relegating the act to dreary repetition. Later, Kate must remind herself to enjoy the act; it is a gift, she decides within the tight fascism of her ego, that she is giving not to Gaston but to herself. She admits only that Gaston's dependence satisfied her, his gratitude for her "slim supply of human traits" (83), his pleading, his spongy willingness to tolerate her quirks. "That was my main reward" (79). The sexual act never sparks into the sacramental as it does for Enid Stevick; Kate is far more like the celibate Wheelwright. When Kate studies Gaston's features "hoping to guess what people saw in love" (73), nothing strikes her; she will repeat that cool inventorying of a lover two years later on a train with Doug Lee and will reach similar conclusions ("I didn't see one cell I wanted" [181]) shortly before a stop where, without telling him, she bolts.[1]

What, then, are we to make of Kate's decision at the close of the novel to return to her North Carolina mountain town to find the son she abandoned some forty years earlier? It would seem a most miraculous change of heart, a gesture that would indicate admirable growth—in contrast to the experiences of Enid Stevick and John Wheelwright. Diagnosed at fifty-seven with cervical cancer and given only five years to live, Kate, touring the Vatican, pauses in the Catacombs to contemplate the brown bones of Peter, the "biggest quitter in human history" (288), whose storied repentance suggests to her the possibility of securing her own forgiveness. Flying home, Kate resolves to petition forgiveness from her son and then commence some elaborate happily-ever-after. Returning to North Carolina, she secures her son's phone number in Norfolk. She dials but receives only a recorded message and leaves a most curious message of her own: "I'm the burglar and will be right over" (306).

The book, however, does not close with this reunion. Kate tells us that she must prepare for that reunion by first writing out for her son the record of her life, thereby delaying reunion, she reckons, for a comfortable half year or so—precious time considering her terminal prognosis. Far from admitting another into her magic kingdom, Kate closes the narrative bolting her door and switching off the lamp, gestures that deny connection and illumination. The nearest she will permit her son is that anonymous message—itself an unambiguous warning that equates reunion with criminal trespass and the potential theft of valuables.

This quick (melo)dramatic turn to motherhood is, finally, suspect, much like the happy endings fashioned by the ironist Oates and the canonization of Owen Meany manipulated by Irving. After all, Kate is on a whirlwind tour of Rome; she is allowed but ten seconds to view the "few scraps" (280) of Peter's bones (as later she reads in a single sitting the Gospel of Luke, with its complex theme of forgiving the outcasts). Kate has never been strong on religion ("Church . . . is an optional thing I can take or leave" [203])—indeed, she is not even Catholic. Like Enid and John Wheelwright, Kate makes the greatest error in assuming the flesh and spirit are separate, unwilling, unable to touch the spiritual verve within an immediate that is unredeemed by a Creator. One Christmas night, she has a startling vision that, far from touching the spiritual, is a starkly physical image of Mary with her dress bunched up around her waist with the baby pushing its oily head out of its mother; during a Good Friday service, she wonders how iron nails might feel deep in her skin. Not surprisingly, there is little of the spiritual about Kate's epiphany in the Catacombs (appropriately, she is entombed). She is impressed not by the faith of Peter nor by the suffering he endured; rather, she is impressed by the aptness of her appropriating the Peter role. As a betrayer, she reasons, she will find her son and receive forgiveness, a sort of *Reader's Digest* (among her favorite reading) parable of the Prodigal Mother (Luke, whose gospel Kate admits reading, alone records the story of the Prodigal Son). Appropriately, she decides to reattempt motherhood as she flies over Greenland—despite its name, a forbidding, near-boundless sheath of ice. Kate, suddenly pressured by mortality, hungers for company; she is lonesome. But that is the same reductive affection she defined forty years earlier on the foxhunt with Gaston. Kate's "powerful lonesomeness" recalls the twisting pain of Gaston's unspent seed; Kate acts, yes, but only to take comfort. She postpones any reunion with her son from spring until fall, a movement away from the season of the ascendant promise of growth to a cooler time that bodes only the natural concession to dying.

And there she closes the novel—unable to establish community, unable, like Enid or Wheelwright, to allow her own life's events to teach her. Internal growth for Kate is best suggested by the malignant spread of the cervical cancer itself, destroying the very locus of maternal production. Unlike Defoe's *Moll Flanders* and Willa Cather's *Sapphira and the Slave Girl* (two novels Kate reads), which both move toward emotional reunions of mother and child, Kate staves off immediacy. Distance closes the novel, or rather the ironic closeness of the near-collision of voices on an answer-

ing machine, the possibility of touch neutralized by the easy manipulation of language.

The response to Kate, then, must be archaeological: we must turn over
the flinty bits of her heart and coax from them some degree of explanation. Like Enid and Wheelwright, Kate is hard to like. She is, by any
measure, a poor daughter who divides what little affection she can mus-
ter unevenly between her dead parents; she is an unreliable girlfriend; an
ungrateful ward; a maddeningly mercurial lover; an indifferent friend
who demands nevertheless enormous attention; a radical failure as a
mother. Relational identity fails her completely. She tries family after
family—some natural blood-kin (first with her Aunt Caroline, then with
her cousin Walter Porter in Norfolk, and finally with her own infant son);
others artificial, composed of caring strangers (with Daphne and Cliff
Baxter, whom she meets on a train to Norfolk; briefly with the family
maid; after Doug Lee's funeral, with her former schoolteacher Miss
Limer; later with the blind piano tuner Whitfield Eller, who had taken in
Doug Lee). But no arrangement will work.

Like Enid adrift within her wallpaper, like Wheelwright alone at
midweek chapel, Kate hungers most purely for solitude. Her earliest
memory is of being left alone at five months in the backyard under a pure
blue sky and feeling not panic but rather calm self-sufficiency. She recalls
Sunday breakfasts when, at three, she would realize that her parents had
a deep partnership that could never completely include her. Like Enid
Stevick, even before she moves into what will prove to be a most chaotic
puberty, she discovers masturbating—easy relief without the interfering
complications of a partner. She daydreams (long before Hiroshima, as
she confesses) about living alone in a ruined world. She confesses to
Gaston her sense of kinlessness—indeed, she calls her parents Dan and
Frances.

In this, Kate surely taxes gender definition. She tests the male urge to
be (the principle of autonomy) and troubles the female imperative to be
part (the principle of nurturing). Early on, she chafes against girlhood.
On a long train ride shortly before her parents' deaths, she recalls her
father's joke that kissing her elbow could change her into a boy (a contor-
tion she finds frustratingly impossible). As the train pulls along, she wills
herself into being a boy who, in her imagination, wants no friends and
whose feelings no one can hurt "though many had tried" (13)—the very
embodiment of isolation. Later, when she is the licensed driver for the
blind piano tuner, customers mistake her for "the prettiest man" they

have ever seen (252). The high point of her Christmas with her cousin Walter is his present of a pair of slacks. As she matures, she expresses only ironically the traditional feminine sensibilities: tenderness, domesticity, passivity, and the urgency toward communion. She bonds once—with a gray mare given to her as a gift from a distant cousin. She dreams of learning the horse's language (she reads *Doctor Doolittle*, a tale about another droll misanthrope soured sufficiently on human relations to turn to animals); but even that impulse fails her. She neglects the animal until it must be given away. She is, as she confesses, not a very good she—if a woman's identity is bound by her biological ability to bear children and by the demand to provide the appropriate nest. Such biological totalitarianism, however, too often drives a woman to reject as peripheral critical questions of who she is, thus allowing her rich, single voice to disappear within the casual welter of children and husband.[2]

But Kate most dramatically speaks. In reacting against any relationship as toxic, she argues a radical masculine sensibility: a peculiar hardness of heart, a fear of emotions, a compelling concern for strength or at least the appearance of it, a casual willingness to jerry-build a life from impulsive gestures, a determination to assert autonomy at the inestimable emotional cost to others, an unswerving perception of any relationship as a stifling trap, a narrow understanding of emotions as competition for supremacy, and a conviction that vulnerability leads only to diminishment. She is forever restless, bolting from emotional commitments, her "butt smoking" (284). She is always hungry (assigned to write on any of the deadly sins, Kate selects Gluttony and tells of a starving orphan who ate everything—including doors and hedges—but "never got fat" and "never got full" [147]; in any emotional crisis, Kate eats enormous meals yet stays "thin as a file" [53]).

This restlessness, this hunger, this rebellious discontent with the narrowest interpretation of female possibilities separates Kate, finally, from the other women who settle into the Macon dust, housewives casually defined and lightly valued, gender bound and fiercely unhappy—selfhood subsumed in the process of coupling and/or reproducing. When, at eighteen, Kate walks away from relationships and determines to fly solo (she admires Amelia Earhart), she would seem, to borrow from Price, to say "nonsense" to the "harem-wife-mother stereotype" (Humphries, 210). Indeed, after Gaston's suicide, Kate glimpses what a future as his wife might have offered. Gaston's father stops to see Kate, and Kate sees the mother, waiting docilely in the idling car, her teeth missing—voiceless and toothless, domestic and domesticated, in the passenger seat of a car going nowhere. Kate claims the male privilege of self-definition, the right to tell her story her way.

Why, then, is Kate so fiercely unhappy? That she is unhappy makes her crucial to our study. She reveals an Enid grown up, a feminine Wheelwright. With her own time dwindling, she is preoccupied with guilt; she repeatedly refers to Judgment Day as she prepares to reassert the maternal urge she could not coax forty years earlier. Happiness has eluded her in her forty years alone; she affirms only the donkey virtue of surviving great stretches of time ("You pray to die when you pass a calendar—all those separate days stacked before you, each one the same length and built from steel. But then you butt on through them somehow" [201]). In creating an I, Kate has committed a most elaborate act of strategic suicide: to protect the self, she has destroyed it. In a posture we have seen before, Kate is, finally, more dead than alive (she tends to fall into profound sleeps, "dead as a chloroformed dog" [129]); Kate elects at eighteen to pass on what she cannot control; she is numb (a word she uses when she cannot coax any response when she visits her father's grave); she inhumes her heart for forty years.

In so doing, she finds that time, which presses so heavily on her as a teenager, spins by furiously; this may account for why Price spends an enormous part of the book retelling Kate's adolescence and then runs rapidly through those forty years in the closing twenty pages. When, at eighteen, Kate bolts from the blind piano tuner's unexpected and wholly tender invitation to marry (extended to her, not surprisingly, as they pass a cemetery), she effectively shuts down her emotional life; without the burden of a beating heart, time is all too navigable. Kate at fifty-seven is a hollow monument that simply stands against time. Her description of her childhood bedroom, which she visits while looking for her son, eerily defines her own condition: "It might just as well have been a Williamsburg dummy, a rebuilt historic landmark, soul omitted" (280).

During that visit, Kate notices a houseplant, a Wandering Jew, that has been overtended, overwatered, and now hangs in limp and dying tangles—a victim not of neglect but of an overabundance of care. Similarly, Kate compassionately destroys her own wandering heart. Unlike Gaston, destroyed by the meanness he found in basic training; unlike her father, destroyed by the heart's (in)explicable fickleness; unlike Doug Lee, destroyed by a heart unable to trust its expression, Kate will not risk being broken by the abundant meanness she witnesses. Yet in that final act of bolting from the piano tuner, Kate commits suicide, like Gaston in boot camp, before she ever engages the war itself. Like Enid Stevick, like John Wheelwright, she survives by refusing her heart, like the Roanoke River whose unmatched beauty Kate fondly recalls but which is now dammed. Her odd pride in surviving her adolescence recalls an obscure Alfred Noyes's poem that Kate recites as a child: "A Victory Dance," in which the grotesque remains of dead soldiers watch with ironic pleasure the victory balls that signaled the end of the war. Kate's victory is a strategic martyrdom (she admires Joan of Arc), a variation on self-destruction (the blind piano tuner, when he hears Kate sing, predicts that someday she will sing *Madame Butterfly*). Kate commits suicide in self-defense. Determined to survive, she passes on the rawness of unplottable experience itself; she cites the power of the passage in Mark when Jesus at Gethsemane begs to avoid suffering. She retreats from experience, recalling the story Gaston tells of Robert E. Lee's young daughter who retreats deep into Virginia from the approaching Union army—retreating, only to die from cholera.

*   *   *

> Nobody my age could tell me what the seed was. The best guess seemed to be, the man peed in you; and that was the seed. But then there were all the times they didn't want babies but still sought it out. What troubled me to wonder was Why people do it when they *don't* want babies? *Why chase it down through pain and shame and public laughter?*
>
> Kate Vaiden

We have seen that novels of spectacle realism cannot tolerate such casual abdication of the difficult engagement of the splendid agonies of the immediate without the use of a most cutting irony. Yet here, despite Kate's excessive self-regard and deliberate self-destruction, despite asserting upon seeing her own newborn son that a baby was simply "something else I could hurt" (208), Kate is disarmingly seductive. Her drive to recount with deadpan honesty her every act of emotional treason against her family might salvage Kate from the more damning comparisons Price draws to her—to a dead river, a seahorse preserved in a block of glass, a dying houseplant, and an empty historical landmark eerily dead/alive simultaneously. The impulse to reconstruct her past in a voice so casual, so honest, so disarmingly immediate—that agenda of struggling with the past should reassure us that Kate means to use language for connection, to bolt ultimately to the reader.

Defining the problem of Kate, however, begins with just this gift for talk. Her schoolteacher, Miss Limer, sends home a note about her "tendency to talk" (33). Kate is a creature of language, a pure creation of words. Price offers no physical detailing of Kate—she is her voice, self-generating, self-sustaining, indefatigable. Kate does not act in the narrative present; rather, she talks. Again and again she is associated with the power of her voice. When she presses a distraught Doug Lee for why he continues to pursue her, he acknowledges the attractive power of her voice, "You could talk your way through granite rock" (216). In turn, Kate is fascinated by voices; they are her memories—her parents, her schoolteachers, her schoolfriends, each preserved for Kate not as a face but as a voice that she replays. She feels the enormous weight of her isolation only once: when she is living with her cousin Walter and Doug Lee and Walter is away on business and Doug Lee is asleep on the far side of the house, she feels the night press in on her as she realizes that she has never spent a night without a human within the sound of her voice. She panics and murmurs, "Help" (147).

Kate is unnervingly addicted to confession. Unlike the Stevicks who so gracelessly deconstruct events in a conspiracy of silence, Kate talks. Like some manic Ancient Mariner, she recounts her life in full on six separate occasions, reduces the act of autobiography to banal habit. Loops of narration, confessions within confessions, encircle her experience; given the seductive colloquial ease of Kate's voice, the plot is actually the telling of the events, not the events. Despite her apparent privileging of her abandoned son, he is simply the latest person she tells, save that now Kate talks against the prognosis of cancer, like Scheherazade from the *Arabian Nights* (a favorite reading of Kate as a child)—language itself now a vehicle for preserving the I against its "death," not the physical death from cancer but the spiritual death represented by committing it to an uncertain We. Elaborate confession, pages of introspection, are far easier than the simplest unscripted phone call that might admit another heart into her magic kingdom.

Language here is debased, counterfeit; it is never a vehicle for honest confession or humane engagement. The lives of Kate's immediate family are riven by buried secrets and piles of poor lies that try to exorcize infidelities. The first and last anecdotes Kate recounts about her parents center on secrets. Kate tells us early about her parents' first date. On the drive home, Kate's mother, Frances, needed to go to the bathroom. Uncertain over how best to handle the awkward situation, when Dan stops to buy cigarettes, she lifts the floorboard of the Model T and "lets loose" (4). She urinated, however, on the gearbox, and when Dan revved up the car and it heated up, the sickening smell of boiling urine overwhelmed the car. And, on the night Frances will die at the hands of a jealous Dan from the brutal exposure of her own secrets, she shows Kate how to make a "Buried Garden" (19) by pressing a small piece of broken glass against wildflowers buried in a bowl-shaped depression in the ground. After that evening's horrific events, Kate visits the spot and, indeed, the flowers stay remarkably fresh, suggesting that buried secrets never age, never disappear. Indeed, in Kate's experience, secrets corrode virtually every relationship, each a charade that, in turn, must be perpetuated by lying. Characters effortlessly opt for lies—to spouses, to children, to friends, to police officers.

In addition to secrets and lies, which both suggest the failure of language, there are Kate's frequent telegrams. Whenever Kate abandons without warning (usually without luggage) family, friends, and finally her child, she turns to the convenience of Western Union to relay her new location. Telegrams are fragments of language, harshly elliptical, nonengaging; they do not threaten even the possibility of disclosure, indeed, they are ways to subvert whatever potential language poses for fusion.

Secrets, lies, telegrams—language within Kate's experience is a convenience, a way to evade truths, to avoid the hard spontaneity of simple engagement. Language becomes ironically a way to say nothing. She dreams of using the potency of language to speak not to Gaston or Doug Lee or even her son but rather to her horse. She responds more powerfully to the smutty schoolyard poem than she does to the sexual act itself. As a voracious reader, she finds in her bookmobile romances delicious escapism. We recall a tender exchange between young Kate and her Aunt Caroline, who tries to explain to Kate why the family has so roundly expelled Walter from its circle of affection; but Caroline cannot speak directly to the question of Walter's homosexuality and must dither about in elaborate subterfuges, talking about Walter's tenderness, his love of dolls, his "friendship" with the young Doug Lee, how he "wasn't going to live the life people live—flocks of children and a woman" (62). Kate pretends to understand but of course does not ("I couldn't find so much as a seam to rip" [63]); the more language is heaped upon complicated experience, the more such experience eludes encoding. Years later (after working for a time in a library, with its suggestion of yet another magic kingdom) as she works in a law firm, Kate engages not people but rather clients—the perfect frictionless community created solely by language in a profession that goes about its happy charade of encoding the raw mess of human experience ("divorce, child custody, murders" [281]) into plausible explanation and clean affidavits.

Indeed, the central event of Kate's battlefield adolescence, her parents' murder-suicide, is never explained, certainly not in the obvious lies that the eyewitness Swift belabors in the kitchen the night of the shooting. His skin splotched like a leper, his eyes bolted to the floor, Swift is the very caricature of the unreliable narrator as he stumbles through a poor account of what happened in the cemetery when Dan caught Swift and Frances together. It is the familiar premise of spectacle realism: characters must engage, not simplify, the immediate. The reader, indeed Kate herself, will never wholly understand the murder-suicide—not from Swift's account and not even from a letter written by Dan himself the night before the murder-suicide. In the narrative present, Kate is given the letter by Swift, now decrepit in a nursing home. Withheld for so long, the letter promises resolution (indeed, Price encourages such expectation by having Kate refer to the mysterious letter early on but withholding its contents until nearly the close). The letter, finally revealed, is yet another aborted attempt to put into the sorry uselessness of language the dark confusions of a crippled heart. It reads like a telegram from a war zone, full of the uncertainty and the terror of living within a world that might detonate in a fragile moment. But, like any suicide note, it does not explain, does not help assess motive for the deaths. Reading it, Kate (as well as the reader) confesses, "I was still blind" (305).

Even love letters, those rich reserves of passionate rhetoric and unforced disclosure, cannot counter this premise of debased language. The letters of Kate's parents, from an eight-week separation shortly after Kate's birth, reveal little of the couple's potent, contradictory emotions. They are tepid letters that conceal more than they reveal. To read the exchange Kate offers as proof of her parents' happiness is to realize how much cannot be said: Frances's problems with Swift's lingering obsession over her, her dissatisfactions with the emotional poverty of her marriage; Dan's desperate uneasiness over his thinning trust in his wife's affections, his unholy dependence on her. The letters ironically insist only on reassurances. And Gaston's single letter from boot camp (much like the series of brief letters Doug Lee will later forward to the running Kate) is equally perfunctory, saying more in what must be withheld. Indeed, Gaston's letter indicates nothing that would anticipate (much less explain) his decision to stand up during the shooting drill. After Gaston's death, his father brings Kate a letter Gaston had written to her the night before his suicide. But Kate simply refuses it, denies it any privileged status.

When Kate uses language, when she indulges confession, it never secures another heart. People do not believe her; they abandon her in horror (as with her brief affair with the veteran Jay Mabry); they indulge cold pity; they even fall asleep. She fares no better with the reader. Kate stays distant. Consider the epigraph that begins this chapter, the very opening lines of Kate's narrative. She invites and then dismisses the reader in the same gesture. And as we move through her experiences, the more she explains, the more of her "facts" she sets out, the less we understand. We hear Kate's voice emerging from the warfare of her adolescence, much as the children in Macon during World War II listen to the "big, strong" (155) voices of Princess Elizabeth and Queen Wilhelmina on the radio as they address their populations during the German air war, voices that despite their clarity and apparent nearness are in fact dramatically separated from Macon. Kate's voice offers only the illusion of nearness. Indeed, Kate's signature speaking device, her effortless way with similes, represents another dodge, her separation into the world of "as if."[3] Kate's insistence on similes is never forced because it is simply part of her larger resistance to experience.

Such resistance extends to her need to understand events. Although she declares that in her profession as a legal secretary she can perceive the moment when clients start to lie, Kate labors under a destructive illusion of her own: she hungers (much like John Wheelwright) for the possibility of explanation. Pressured by the imminent closure of her own life-narrative, she is determined to bend her life to the logic of plot. Because of Kate's enormous faith in the suasive power of the tongue, she presumes explanation for experiences that we see so profoundly beggar explanation. She hungers to untangle the heart. She retells events with apparent candor, but the more she talks, the more the events themselves undermine the premise of accountability. Experience teaches her only irresolvable contradictions: hurt badly by abandonment, she will hurt others with the same gesture; loved, she will withhold her heart; touched, she will recoil; approached, she will bolt.

Tallying up her experience against her explanation cannot "solve" Kate. For all her folksy pretense to intimacy and full disclosure, her actions remain mysterious. The reader recalls Kate's difficulties with the Pythagorean theorem in high school math, the reassuring theorem that argues knowing two sides of a triangle will solve the mystery of the third. Such reliability is surely shaken by Kate; if the reader and her text form two sides, Kate is the defiant third side, unknowable as she deadpans her way through each impulsive urge to bolt. When Kate returns to Macon, pregnant with Doug Lee's child, her long-suffering Aunt Caroline bombards Kate for explanation: why did you leave us long ago? why did you leave Doug Lee? why have you come back here? did your parents have any influence in this? The questions, posed in controlled hysteria, only confirm the impossibility of explanation. Kate answers simply, "I left in August because Swift Porter hurt me badly after Gaston died. I know I never loved Douglas Lee. . . . I hope you'll love me like you did before. And I don't know where my parents *are*, except maybe Hell, much less what they mean" (198). It is language stripped to the point where the answer, despite responding exacting to what Kate is asked, reveals nothing.

Kate confesses ironically just such a predicament when, talking about the criminals she has met at the law office, she acknowledges, "the worse the crime, the less (they'll) know" (285). But she cannot accept that both self-destruction and the bothersome dilemma of attraction must necessarily beggar explanation. Like John Wheelwright, so profoundly disturbed by the random accident on the Little League field, Kate cannot abide mystery (she loves Nancy Drew). She assigns finally a reason for each act—those who come near her are simply doomed. To the reader, such "logic" is an unconvincing, disturbing assertion of egotism, the casual positioning of herself in the center of what is in truth a complicated emotional maelstrom, a gesture as oddly inappropriate as Owen Meany's assumption of the center of those events. Investing heavily in the possibility of explanation and finding problematic comfort in language, Kate thins into a voice, like Amelia Earhart disappearing into the cold Pacific void. Kate is determined to go it alone; it is ironic when she speaks so warmly of the community experience of World War II, which she calls a "long houseparty" because everyone helped out, saved tinfoil or bacon grease or knitted scarves or spotted airplanes. War, her experience should tell her, demands community; engagement, whether geopolitical or domestic, demands bonding.

*   *   *

*And I've got nobody but me, Kate Vaiden, to thank or blame. In many trips,
I know I've been led but not in love; I've flown that solo—pilot, navigator,
wrecking crew. I don't ask one other soul to applaud. I will say, though, it's let
me travel light.*

Kate Vaiden

Against Kate's interment within language, Price counterpoints the
struggle to touch—and thus introduces the critical imperative of spectacle realism to connect. To touch is to welcome invasion, to participate in
the shattering of the vast, empty circle of the self. Like Enid Stevick and
John Wheelwright, Kate plunges into the uncertain wonder of experience only to bail out. But the characters of Gaston, Dan, Frances, and
Doug Lee struggle with very emotions Kate rejects. Like Enid in her adolescence, like Irving's Hester and Reverend Merrill, they struggle with
the impulses of the heart that compel us to hazard the trick of unscripted
connection. They negotiate the graceful helplessness of the trampoline.
They serve in the war that Kate declines at eighteen (in her own boot
camp, as it were). These characters are not creatures of language (recall
Doug Lee's spare letters and Gaston's graduation pin for penmanship,
which suggests he is more involved with the medium than its message).
Unlike Kate, who ironically describes her own absorption into language
when she concedes, "Touch me; I answer" (3), these are touching creatures, some gentle as puppies, others wielding ice picks in the wild attempts to dislocate the self. Like Oates, Price encourages the reader to see
what the main character resists: the dark beauty possible only when we
get near enough to touch.

Kate cannot touch—when Gaston watches her clean the school's chalk
erasers, her arms coated in dust, he notes that she has "corpse-arms."
"You're dying from the fingers up" (68). Kate touches only one thing
(apart from Gaston's straining penis): the corpse of her cousin, "tender
and cool" (16), displayed in the family's dining room following a motorcycle accident. Indeed, the most destructive decision in Kate's experience
is a simple act of unreciprocated touch: she offers her newborn child her
finger and the baby turns away, justifying to Kate the logic of abandoning
it.

Kate learns only part of what her experience could teach (after all, she
is shuffled in and out of a number of schools, leaving her education hap-
hazard). What Kate never acknowledges—her fingers corpsed, her heart

estivating, her tongue unstoppable, her very womb tumorous—is the possibilities of helplessness, the very condition that so haunts Enid Stevick and John Wheelwright. There is, after all, no shortage of examples to teach her a more balanced vision. For all her professed independence, Kate depends to a remarkable degree on Good Samaritans (another of St. Luke's parables), who, despite Kate's characteristic ingratitude, provide a support system that ensures her charade of independence. They attend to Kate with inexplicable loyalty given Kate's response to such kindness with sudden disappearances clumsily papered over by telegrams.

Consider the examples. Walter, whose immense concern for Kate we will examine in a moment, understands her loneliness after the deaths of her parents and offers his home in distant Norfolk as refuge should she ever feel the need to bolt. When she does just that and arrives unannounced at his door, he notifies Caroline that Kate is safe, enrolls her in a private school, and goes about the business of making her feel part of his cobbled-together family. Fob, an even more distant cousin and a wealthy tobacco farmer, encourages Kate to "amount to something" (39), gives her outright the gift of the horse, and later supports her with considerable money from his farms. Noony, the black cook in Kate's adopted home, instructs Kate patiently in the ways of the heart and offers her refuge in her shack when Kate reappears in town pregnant and alone. Tim Slaughter, a Norfolk cabdriver, picks up Kate when she arrives there alone and without luggage and, without prompting and against Kate's suspicions, dedicates himself to her well-being, later taking her in when she abandons Doug Lee after he proposes marriage. Aunt Caroline takes in her sister, Kate's mother, and then Kate and then Kate's son when each in turn needs a home. Whitfield Eller, the blind piano tuner, gives Kate a place to stay, employment, and sincerely offers marriage when she finds her life ragged after Doug Lee's suicide. Daphne and Cliff Baxter, strangers Kate meets on the train to Norfolk facing drastic separation (Cliff is a day away from overseas duty), make room for her in their tiny hotel room during their last night together. And even the nameless tourist in Rome, the stranger in the raincoat, gives Kate his unused ticket to the Catacombs, which triggers Kate's impulse toward reunion. It is an amazing webbing of support and compassion that defies Kate's harsh dismissal of the heart.

Indeed, Kate cannot shake dark suspicions about these Good Samaritans: she is certain that Fob and then later Walter will expect some sexual favor (ironically, both are gay); when Tim Slaughter and later Whitfield Eller violate Kate's magic kingdom simply by touching her, she bolts within hours. In ways that recall the tensive irony of narrator and reader in Oates and Irving, we must learn the potential of touch by listening to one numb, by her own admission, to its possibilities, a narrative strategy that recalls the Emily Dickinson poem (which Price quotes) that particularly attracts Kate and could summarize our first three texts of spectacle realism: "Success is counted sweetest / By those who ne'er succeed."

Given such enormous exposure to those given so uncritically to the power of touch, Kate, like Enid the gifted student and John Wheelwright the professional academic, is ultimately a poor student. She never suspects the possibility of the bolting between hearts, largely because she exercises her heart only within the dark frame of the immediate family and later within the tight algebra of procreation. As texts of spectacle realism argue, the unexpected wonder of the relational world is seldom expressed in the unyielding frame of the family or in the sexual politicking that inevitably erodes coupling. Rather, it is felt in the compelling mystery of strangers opening themselves up to others—the fragile miracle of a moment's generosity, of unexpected, unambiguous simple kindness that we will see repeated again and again in the texts of spectacle realism.

Without surrendering to touch, Kate's much-vaunted strength—"you stand up at sunrise and meet what they send you and keep your hair combed" (88)—is a joyless, cowardly code of surviving within the tedium of time, of merely lasting. Thus, the testimony Kate offers, the text she fashions, is little more than a long suicide note. When Kate is in school, she is fascinated by a glass paperweight of Miss Limer's—a seahorse preserved on a bed of cotton, so apparently alive and yet quite dead, so apparently floating in the heavy glass square. Later, Miss Limer confesses to Kate that it is a memento mori of her own emotional catastrophe, a souvenir sent from her lover shortly before he married another woman, a wounding that left her within the dry logic of isolationism (her name suggests such souring). Miss Limer gives Kate the seahorse after the deaths of her parents. Kate suggests the seahorse: she hangs suspended in her text, immured in language—for all the apparent revelation, Kate stays untouched and untouchable, cool, distant, and unknown.

*   *   *

I was a better man with you as a woman than I ever was a man with a woman
as a man.

Michael Dorsey/Dorothy Michaels (*Tootsie*)

Kate, then, closes her narrative locked within the (ir)resolvable dilemma
that is characteristic of the challenge so often posed by spectacle realism:
the distrust of the unviolated self against the terror of commitment.[4]
Price, however, finds a way for the self to break free from its unendurable
loneliness into intimate communion and yet preserve its autonomy,
an achievement that reveals language's potential for fusion rather than
(like Kate's narrative) its poverty and the cool distance it places between
hearts. Dislocating the self, however, is not achieved by Kate; she is left
victim of her own experience. Rather, it is realized in the fusion of the
author and first-person narrator—a fusion to which Price himself tirelessly directed attention in interviews at the time of *Kate Vaiden*'s publication—that combines the imperatives of touch and tongue because touch
can come only through the magnificent accomplishment of language itself: the male author bonding to his female creation. In allowing Kate to
speak her own story, Price defies artificial boundaries imposed by gender
to create what he described as a "reversed gender novel." Price has de-
cried the "ghettoization" of the American novel that decreed men write
only about men, women about women. "Let men be men, women be
women," Price laments, thereby denying writers imaginative access to
"half the human race" and, as a result, to an "immensely useful species
of fiction"—creative androgyny that works through a most provocative
sense of empathy.[5] Nevertheless, for a male writer to enter the female
psyche might seem a dangerous act of trespass and forced colonization
or, worse, fraudulent masquerade. Price rejects such restrictions. He
treats directly the signal moments in female development: the sudden
onset of menstruation and the accompanying new odors and the subsequent strapping on of the "regulation outfit" that had more "straps than
a parachute" but was far "less fun to rig" (66); the initial tentative attempts at makeup before an unflattering mirror; the receptive sexual experience; the immediate certainty of conception; the annoying discom-
forts of pregnancy; the wet onrush of labor and the hot relief of delivery;
the struggle with the new demands of mothering; the harsh cooling of
menopause—an act of the imagination that requires completely abandoning male privilege. In stepping so compellingly within the interior

life of his female narrator, Price realizes the dislocation of the self so finally unavailable to his own character.

Although Kate manages to displace gender, in her own way "kisses her elbow" by embodying male stereotypes, she cannot make the leap beyond self-involvement; she never tests the vulnerability of abandoning the dead weight of her own created I. Thus, gender considerations are finally irrelevant as Kate is no longer fully human—recall the seahorse in paperweight whose sex Miss Limer cannot determine. Price, not Kate, achieves the unironic We, violates the self yet preserves intact its autonomy. Within *Kate Vaiden* itself, language performs what it cannot do for Kate despite her persistent urge to talk—the act of sympathetic bonding. Even as Kate tidies up her small and private room, locks up her magic kingdom against the impingement of mortality, Price bursts through as writer into what he has described as a "vast and common room" ("Men Creating Women," 20), to explore the fullest impulses of the human self by exploding gender altogether in a dramatic gesture that suggests the very ascendant imperative of spectacle realism.

Rejecting gender indoctrination is the novel's signal achievement and marks the way to our first encounter with the possibilities of spectacle realism. At last, we find its argument without the indirection of irony. To give Kate her voice, Price must correspond with his feminine nature without the bogus theatrics of high camp or the deliberate manipulation of image that so often occupies such exercises in the entertainment field. Here androgyny is intimacy—a triumphant private, not public, act of the imagination, a sort of (un)learning of social behaviors and an expanding beyond the tight magic kingdom of the self that has offered so secure a sinecure for Enid Stevick and John Wheelwright. In defying gender, Price illuminates the argument of spectacle realism: he refutes restrictions in order to explore in Kate not merely what makes her a woman but rather what destroys her as a human.

Yet such a reading frustrates. Must the potential for spectacle realism be relegated to a self-conscious aesthetic exercise, a highly artificial union of author and narrator that denies the tonic revelations of gender defiance any practical arena? Must spectacle realism stay, finally, a metaphor as the larger cast of characters retreats into familiar strategies of disengagement: suicide, alcohol, misanthropy, religious fanaticism, and a hard and thorough selfishness?

What makes *Kate Vaiden* a pivotal text for our study is that Price offers a character who does accept the imperative of engagement, who fronts with astonishing courage the vicissitudes of the immediate, and who manages, despite abundant justification for retreat, to embrace both experience and, in the process, a gathering of needful others. It is a defining moment for our study. Our interest lends unsuspected import to a secondary character, Kate's homosexual cousin Walter Porter, with whom Kate lives for four critical months following the death of Gaston. Against Kate's considerable centripetal collapse into the protected self, Price sets the ascendant example of Walter Porter, whose heart compels him outward not merely to construct the I (which he does with guts and dignity) but rather to complete it by insisting on a We within the same explosive universe of meanness that drives Kate (along with Enid Stevick and John Wheelwright) inward.

Unlike Kate, Walter can only define himself relationally (he sends birthday cards to "thousands of friends . . . he never saw [135]; he refuses to eat dessert without company) and, as such, brings to the narrative (and to our study) a tonic presence, a gift for sympathy, the very essence of the traditional feminine sensibility—and the foundational premise for the engagement strategy of spectacle realism. Unlike the narrow experiment in androgyny conducted by Price, Walter Porter offers the reader the far more compelling experience of it. And in the process Walter achieves what Enid Stevick and John Wheelwright refuse in their deliberate retreat; he survives the bruising experience of the heart in ways that Hester does not; and, unlike Reverend Merrill, he finds his way to the wonder of the immediate without the awkward intervention of any hokey spiritual dimension. His presence, slim as it is amid the noise of Kate's egoism, proffers our first gesture toward the ascendant vision of spectacle realism.

When Walter is first introduced some seventy-five pages into the plot, his family has already defined love of a most toxic sort: incest, betrayal, murder, suicide (indeed, the family poetry recitations feature Byron's lurid "Bride of Abydos"). We have heard of him—of the generous checks he sends to his family (despite their rejection of him), of the funeral pall he sends for the casket of one of Kate's cousins, a splendid spray of six dozen carnations ("red as your heart" [27]) that stays fresh long after the other flower arrangements have dried up in the Carolina heat. He steps into the narrative at Thanksgiving (that most relational of holidays) to reengage a family that years earlier drove him out with their ugly intolerance of his homosexuality. His return follows Kate's rather unspectacular introduction to sexuality during Gaston's foxhunt. Against that harsh reduction of love to predatory satisfaction, Walter brings an unabashed impulse to touch honestly without agenda. As Kate puts it, "Where other people would nod and smile, Walter would rise up from where he was reading and cross the room to touch you . . . warmth like a dog's, that constant but drier" (50). Although Kate denigrates Walter's impulse to touch (later, when Walter strokes her neck, she prepares for something "funny"), she is drawn immediately to him. Unlike the rest of the family, who attend with dry politeness to Kate in the aftermath of her parents' murder-suicide, Walter tries to comfort her by listening. In contrast to Kate's tendency to enforce distance through language, Walter enters empathetically into her private space (all he talks about is her schooling, her pain). And when he talks, he speaks the only kind words about the father, revealing an openness of heart that defies the colder judgments of the family, who demand that Dan be buried hundreds of miles away. Not surprisingly, when Kate bolts from Caroline's home, she goes to Walter, who on generous impulse gave her his address and phone number. Puzzled by why Walter became the pariah of the family, Kate asks her aunt what Walter did. The reply is revealing: "He treats every human soul as gentle as pups. That may have made some people mad" (60).

Comparisons against Kate are critical. As with Kate, experience has taught Walter the high cost of bearing a heart. He tells her, "You've been through some Hell . . . but Hell is a place I've served time in" (59). His homosexuality has cost him his family, his home, his roots. Unlike Enid, who obscures her past within the cloaking of secrecy, Walter will not pretend to be what he is not. He is, not surprisingly, the subject of cruel whispers so thick that Kate is stunned, once she actually meets Walter, to find the "great family sinner" (53) so nondescript.

More than merely bearing up under (and forgiving) the cold homophobia within his own family—his brother Swift will not be in the same room with him—Walter has involved himself since leaving Macon with the emotionally damaged orphan Doug Lee, seven years his junior. Despite the ugly comments that Kate overhears about Doug Lee and Walter as roommates in Norfolk, the relationship is decidedly nonsexual. Indeed, when Walter tells Kate about the relationship, what impresses the reader immediately is how little the bonding had to do with sexuality (in fact, they maintain separate bedrooms). Walter tells Kate that ten years earlier, as Doug Lee's Sunday school teacher, he could not bear to see the child placed in the state orphanage following his abandonment by his parents. Pained by the situation, pained by the "dim dormitory" and the "all-brown clothes" and the "third-hand shoes" (131), he negotiated an adoption arrangement that, after two years, was rescinded under the pressure of community whispers. Walter, however, would not allow Doug to be returned to the orphanage, and together (Walter was only eighteen) they bolted to Norfolk and there set up a loose sort of family. Unlike Kate, who at the same age will decide against commitment and will bolt rather in her own fashion, Walter bolts his heart to another in a gesture that has less to do with the sort of affection Kate understands—naked need, swollen ganglia, and the straining pain of unspent seed—and more to do with the sort of love she cannot understand—naked vulnerability, profound empathy, and the irrational gift of the heart.

Against Kate's willful deconstruction of family after family, Walter struggles to shape an extended family about Doug Lee and the runaway Kate. But Doug Lee—wounded by abandonment much like Kate—is hostile even to the idea of family. Price underscores their differences with the pictures on their bedroom walls in Norfolk: Walter displays trees, rooted and permanent, protective and organic, sheltering and living; Doug Lee displays ships, mobile and inanimate, harborless and solitary. In the four months Kate lives with them, Walter organizes poignant holiday dinners around Thanksgiving and then at Christmas, the latter in a friend's backwater fishing shack that offers an interlude of particular warmth against a brutal Virginia winter. Yet Doug Lee confides in Kate his callous dismissal of Walter's nurturing; debts to Walter, he says coldly to Kate, have been settled, we may suppose in acts of sexual gratification but more likely in Doug Lee's sense of "time served." Later, when Kate angrily rejects Walter's simple offer of help while she is pregnant by saying that he does not owe her anything, Walter is stunned to hear affection negotiated so casually. It's not that I owe you, he tells her with a genuine look, but that I love you. Even when Kate tells him so matter-of-factly that she is carrying Doug Lee's child, he accepts what must be devastating news of this frank betrayal of the trust he had placed in two of his closest relationships—indeed, he dismisses out of hand Kate's offer to abort the baby.

Yet Walter can seem to warn against the emotions, against the engaging of the immediate that is critical to spectacle realism; after all, he is so often used, betrayed, and then abandoned by those who form the center of his makeshift family. Doug Lee tries twice to kill him, once with a kitchen knife and once with an ice pick, and Kate fathers her child by

Walter's ward under his own roof. But against characters who are touched once by the fierce energy of the heart and recoil into protective magic kingdoms of self-enclosure or who are simply leveled by the heart's manic potency or those whose hearts are turned to ash—against, in short, the gallery of characters offered here—Walter argues the resilience of the human heart, the crossed rewards of engagement. In contrast to Kate, who keeps leaving families, families keep leaving Walter. Against the immense egoism of Kate's charade of autonomy, he acknowledges to Kate the fundamental blessing if "we reach out and take what's in front of our eyes" (171). Puzzled, Kate appropriately sees only the wall. Against Kate's strategic hiberation, Walter engages the heart's uncertainty, risks engagement for even the "chance to make something last" (171). Walter will not dodge living (even in his reading, against Kate's love of fluffy escapist fare, Walter reads *Strange Fruit*, Lillian Smith's disturbing 1944 novel of miscegenation that describes the destructive effects of racism in the South). Unlike Kate (indeed, unlike Enid Stevick and John Wheelwright), Walter counsels engagement; to a distraught Doug Lee, he points to the potential of suffering, "Only way to profit is to suffer" (223). And unlike Kate's thin heart, which is dead long before the cervical cancer will complete the job, Walter's great heart beats even after he is dead: he wills to Kate's son his considerable possessions and property. Wounded during the Easter season in the palm of the hand by an ice pick wielded by Doug Lee, Walter parallels, without irony, Jesus Christ (another disturbing androgynous presence). Like Christ, Walter defines the self in order to offer it to others.

There, of course, is the problem. It is easy to dismiss Walter, his naked displays of emotion (he actually swoons when he visits the grave of Kate's mother and then kisses the ground lavishly; his eyes brim with tears when Kate offers simple grace after Christmas dinner), his unabashed embrace of domesticity, his inexplicable loyalty to both Doug Lee and Kate. Unlike Owen Meany, who so grandly, so gaudily, assumes the role of saint, Walter Porter simply acts saintly. But contemporary readers are far more likely to credit the irrational meanness of Kate than equally inexplicable goodness; it reflects a problem as old as *Paradise Lost* (not lost on Price, himself a Miltonist): the wicked are far more attractive than the good. Kate acknowledges as much when she confesses her lifelong reading habit has convinced her that the "wicked alone bear reading about."[6]

Yet given Price's interest in the imaginative possibility of androgyny, the humane exploration of the vast common room shared by the sexes, Walter is far more than another dreary Tobacco Road Christ figure. His defiance of gender pulls him consistently toward rather than away from people. His strength is his great heart and its intuitive ability to live within the tension of masculine and feminine. Walter exhibits with unaffected directness the traditional gender definitions of the female: he is caring, emotional, fragile as a teacup (to borrow from his mother), instinctively nurturing, vulnerable, intuitively protective. But lest he appear to be a feminized male (or, to borrow from the decade's tired jargon—a wimp), he demonstrates as well the masculine hunger for unconditional autonomy, the courage to endure devastating public ridicule, and the strength to pursue unapologetically self-definition—his gutsy declaration of homosexuality in 1920s rural South (Kate's uncle, confronting his homosexuality, opted to hang himself). Touched again and again by catastrophe, Walter resists the temptation of surrender—alcohol; a convenient sham marriage; suicide, emotional or physical—and persists in his engagement of experience. Indeed, he possesses the only strength Kate does not: the strength to be weak, to relinquish the pretense of control by opening a heart completely, to trust in the heart against the considerable evidence of human meanness. That strength, Price argues (and spectacle realism affirms), is not what makes us male or female but what makes us finally human.

*   *   *

> Caroline smiled. . . . "Walter says you're lost."
> I said "Maybe so."
>
> *Kate Vaiden*

When Walter, who works for a railroad, inspects the Ringling Brothers' circus train before it transports its animals across the Shenandoahs, he is enthralled by a huge gorilla, "big-as-a-house" and "black as a hot night," who, behind bulletproof glass in a cage the size of a bungalow, is advertised as bloodthirsty in posters that show him dismembering a feathered native. But the circus manager contemptuously dismisses the gorilla as a "sissie" who refuses to act like a male gorilla. Yet, as Walter watches, the gorilla, with arms like the "hindquarters of a horse," lumbers to an inflated tractor tire that swings in his cage and effortlessly turns it inside out as easily as "you skin a fig—no six men could have done it" (50–51). When weeks later, Walter is cleaning up a train accident in the Shenandoahs, he jokes with Kate that the gorilla has been sprung free at last. That is the larger victory of the novel: setting free the androgynous voice, successfully balancing the strong/weak feminine and the weak/strong masculine, the I and the We. With the requisite courage, Price disturbs the easy assumptions of gender to explore the possibility of shared rather than tensive gender, to arrive (as Walter Porter does) at a necessary time to bolt, to dislocate the self, and to explore that facet of our human makeup not available to those too consciously bound to gender. The voice of Kate Vaiden may be intriguing because it is Kate's, but it is important, finally, because it is Price's.

But Price's achievement as authorial strategist and even Walter's position as narrative redemptor remain problematic. Our study cannot end here. We surely admire the imaginative energy necessary for Price to project his awareness into the feminine mystique; but it is a technical achievement, rather like being stunned by the blueprints for an airplane. And Walter's great heart poses even more of a dilemma. Its massive inclusiveness, its hunger for engagement are given to us unearned. We are simply told, for instance, by Doug Lee that Walter is the one person he has known "who couldn't say a mean word or do a mean thing" (138). That bald assertion, that verb selection ("could not") disturbs. And this is only one of several such testimonials offered on Walter, each given as affidavit, unchallenged and resting, we presume, on experiences to which we never gain narrative access.

Walter's willingness to engage experience, his willingness to forgive, his intuitive sensitivity to others, his sheer need to love despite the cost—these elements of the vision of spectacle realism are asserted here, because of Walter's position as secondary character. He is, to quote his cousin, like "good news daily" (62). It does not help, of course, that Price puts this narrative in the hands of one who would be predisposed to mock such a generous and open heart, a character who, at one point, given a gift of $500, is moved to count the money before accepting it. Kate's story, after all, is not Walter's; her decision to stave off reunion with her abandoned son testifies to how little impact Walter has had on her. But even if he touches us (and he surely does), we are not privy to his evolution; we learn his narrative only from the cryptic bits he confides to Kate, from family conversations that stay generously wide of the truth, from the malicious slant of town gossip, and from the heated rhetoric of Doug Lee's unresolved anger. Walter is simply not ours. Certainly, he illuminates the grim narrative line of Kate's confession, but he is rather like some light in an otherwise dark cave, a source of illumination appreciated but surely obscure.

We move now to William Kennedy's *Quinn's Book*, in which the evolution of young Daniel Quinn will flesh out Walter Porter—it is Daniel Quinn (rather than Kate) who will help us understand the achievement of Walter's great heart—and the deep error of Enid Stevick, John Wheelwright, and Kate Vaiden.

4

"The Twin-Peaked Glory of Bothness"

William Kennedy, *Quinn's Book*

Into the same rivers we step and we do not step.

Heraclitus, Fragment 110

Much in the spirit of Heraclitus, whose thinking so undergirds *Quinn's Book*, William Kennedy's 1988 novel is terribly familiar and yet radically different. It is a text of spectacle realism that draws on the narrative strategy of education, a novel that measures a central character's maturation against that character's willingness to engage rather than withdraw from a daunting immediate that, much as we have seen to this point, more than justifies by its brutal contingency strategic efforts to retreat from its alogic. Like Enid Stevick, John Wheelwright, and Kate Vaiden, Daniel Quinn is taught early about emotional betrayal, the heart's fallibility, the cutting intrusion of mortality—the elements of the (extra)ordinary immediate of spectacle realism. To this point, we have seen only the retreats into private zones—figural suicides who destroy what they act to protect. But unlike our other central characters, Quinn learns—or, more exactly, constructs his magic kingdom but ultimately steps out from its protective enclosure. Unlike Walter Porter, whose magnificent presence is muted against the noisy egoism of the title character, Quinn is a central character (it is, after all, *Quinn's* book) who moves from strategic retreat to reengage the immediate despite the horrific experiences he witnesses both privately as an orphan and as an ardent suitor of a most mercurial woman and later publicly as a newspaper correspondent during the Civil War. Ultimately, Quinn will learn to trust the pull of the imperfect heart against the far easier (and far emptier) trust in the self—all lessons of spectacle realism.[1] In doing so, Quinn will come to value, as we all must, contemplating rather than unraveling the mystery at the heart of experience.

Simplification, or, more specifically, the pretense to understanding, is again our focus. Quinn's Albany, much like our other settings, is a world where, despite meticulous detailing, surface only obscures, a world in which Quinn must make an uncertain peace with a lesson fundamental to spectacle realism: the concrete world is rather like an ocean wave. It appears to be a relatively coherent, closed system on a fixed, clean path but is in fact a churning, changing, open system that every moment redefines itself, that every moment justifies our attention and compels our wonder. It is a lesson we have seen other characters resist. But these texts have shown that only those most bankrupt of the imagination lay claim to the clarity of understanding, or, to quote Daniel Quinn, that "mystery reveals itself quickly only to those without the imagination to perpetuate it" (74). It is a terrifying, exhilarating, mysterious world that renders hard surface an illusion; understanding, reductive; the dictionary, ironic; and vision, even corrected and straining for a clear glimpse, marvelously fallible. It is, in short, a world that reminds us that clear sight is far from insight.

Recalling Irving's narrative, *Quinn's Book* takes place, in large measure, on stage: in theaters (on stage or backstage), on the public stage of sporting events, and in the more intimate theater of the parlors of the nouveau riche of Albany and Saratoga Spring. Quinn, an orphan brought to Albany with narrow expectations, comes of age in a world of frauds where acting is the norm, where reality is calculated pretense, where friends, even family, play at loyalty, where every relationship is an uneasy game of evasion defined by the shadowy dynamics of deceiver and deceived. Indeed, the Albany stage forms a subplot to Daniel Quinn's education. His first assignment as a reporter involves posing as a performer auditioning for the theater company. Quinn pretends to be an Irish singer to learn about a dark cabal known only as The Society, rumored to run Albany through terrorism. Earlier, Quinn meets his lifelong love, Maud Fallon, through her aunt, the flamboyant and notorious actress Magdalena Colón, a consummate performer with a hokey Spanish accent who is never really offstage. Maud herself is most at ease on stage, later finding notoriety (and substantial income) playing Prince Mazeppa. The high point of the melodrama, Mazeppa pulled naked across the stage by a live horse, is a sensational deception within a fraud: Maud is neither male nor naked, her sex and her nudity camouflaged by a flesh-colored body stocking.

The stage suggests an unreliable immediate where even the most transparent illusions demand to be taken as real. From the dramatic opening sequence on the swollen Hudson River, illusions confound Quinn; the more he sees (and he constantly demands to see the unfolding action), the less he comprehends. When, after her skiff capsizes and the drowned body of Magdalena is hauled from the icy Hudson, her death is only apparent; Quinn will watch as her "corpse" is brought back to life by the rough ministrations and generous endowments of his boss, canaller John McGee, in a hot act of necrophilia. Later, at a newspaper office that Quinn visits, a quirky investigative reporter named Dirck Staats is arrested in front of him and is quickly led off; moments later, the "police officers" are identified as local thugs for The Society who have kidnapped Dirck because he has so vigorously pursued its vast network of intrigue. Joshua the Rat, an escaped slave whose story threads Quinn's narrative, bravely works the lines of the Underground Railroad, responsible at Quinn's rough count for the rescue of more than 400 slaves. Later, John McGee, when he opens his gambling establishment in New York City, enlists the same Joshua to act as rat catcher for a bloody backroom sideshow that involves dropping rats into a ring with pit terriers. As Mick the Rat, Joshua reveals a savor of gratuitous violence and petty bloodletting that conflicts most oddly with his other role as life giver.

But Joshua is far from the only bifurcated character. As with our other texts, there are a cast of supporting characters and a textual geography that deny definition. Obadiah Griswold, whom Magdalena eventually marries, is a churchgoing member of Saratoga high society who nevertheless keeps a stunning array of pornography and enjoys licking behind the knees of his chambermaid. Phoebe Strong, mild-mannered social queen in Saratoga, publicly socializes with the notoriously irreverent Magdalena—yet pens an anonymous letter villifying Magdalena's character in a local newspaper. Hillegond Staats, Quinn's benefactor and pillar of Albany society as well as a reliable link in the Underground Railroad, is brutally strangled reportedly by an out-of-work actor posing as a priest but more likely by a local theater manager, a most feral sort who pursued the old woman with a bogus proposal of marriage to secure her fortune and yet who plays a most eloquent, elegant mourner during Hillegond's memorial service. In the Saratoga horse race that closes the novel, an unknown horse, a mysterious late entry, turns out to be a champion horse (named appropriately Zigzag Master) that was treated by a special dye to conceal its identifying markings. Indeed, earlier, Maud's horse had been drugged by an apparently harmless apple that had opium plugged in its core. In the closing sequence, at Magdalena's wake, itself an elaborate charade staged by Magdalena herself when she feels death approaching, magicians perform deft feats of optical daring and the dancing bear is, in fact, a Mexican dwarf in costume.

The world, then, is much like the Staats mansion that so intrigues the young Quinn—a baroque edifice of multiple wings and towers turned about a maze of corridors and tunnels where each step is an exhilarating act of faith. When a bizarre series of events compels the Staats family to disinter a relative who died heroically in his midteens some seventy years earlier during the American Revolution, the family (and young Quinn) is astounded by how the body has resisted putrefaction. Yet, without warning, the beautiful face begins to swell like a "loaf of leavening bread" (43), the entire body heaves, and the chest caves in, sending up a fine shower of silvery blue ash. With Quinn, experience never validates perception. Beginning with the catastrophe on the Albany bridge, Kennedy offers, like our other writers, a sobering vision of puny individuals up against the brutal energy of a raw world of inexplicable logic, where neat lines and clear sequence vanish in a chaotic swirl of sheer event.

Explanation, when it is offered, is lamely ironic. Conservative factions in Albany credit the unusually balmy December weather that loosens up the Hudson to the presence in their city of the erotic performer Magdalena. Accountability is mocked in the opening pages when the skiff carrying Magdalena suddenly spins out of control and in quick succession a great ice floe crashes into a bridge packed with Magdalena's fans; nature, we are told, has simply gone wild, the "cosmic, mythic rage against our vulnerable puniness" (9). The catastrophe leaves behind shaken survivors who claim such privileged status without clear reason. They survive only because they survive, much as Quinn does after a wave of cholera quietly, cleanly killed his entire family a scant year earlier. Kennedy's Albany is a harrowing, black comic world where an old woman, whose bonnet catches a random, harmless spark from the burning quay, tumbles headfirst into a shed full of hay and thus starts a massive conflagration that will ultimately devastate entire neighborhoods.

·As with the texts discussed earlier, characters in such an environment are brutalized by helplessness. Early on, we are told of an unfortunate

Swede who comes to be manacled to the runaway slave Joshua as he is being returned South. An immigrant coming off the boat, the Swede lost track of his young wife amid the dockside crowds in New York. Then he was swindled of his modest life savings. Despairing, he threw himself into a well, only to find himself pulled out by a "good samaritan" (38), whom he attacked, whereupon he was arrested for assault. He was being transported for trial when, improbably, shards of the exploding ice floe from the Hudson River catastrophe had struck the driver of the carriage, and freed him. Suddenly free, but still shackled to Joshua, he hides in the Staats mausoleum and there, ironically free of the law, nevertheless hangs himself, still in despair over his wife. Or we recall the spirit who communicates with Maud at the séance in Saratoga, telling of his botched suicide attempt after the wife he deeply loves leaves him: he throws himself in front of a thundering carriage, which tries to veer out of the way, throwing out and killing a woman passenger, who (it turns out) is the departing wife, the very woman he loves. A second carriage stops, the driver punches the grief-stricken husband, who, in turn, falls against a stone, quite dead.

In Kennedy's vision, however, such a brutal cosmos of happenstance is not nearly as terrifying as the human element it engenders, more specifically, our fathomless capacity to outdo the natural world for brutality and cruelty. When cholera sweeps Quinn's neighborhood, the family fears not so much the disease but looters who comb the streets looking for abandoned houses. At the height of the dramatic rescue of Magdalena from the Hudson, John McGee ferociously beats on the locked lid of her steamer trunk, certain it holds the actress's considerable cut from that evening's show. When Magdalena is pulled onto the Albany dock, apparently quite drowned, a woman, grieving over the death of her husband or perhaps her brother in the bridge collapse (we are, naturally, not given to know for sure), descends like a "jungle feline" (13) onto Magdalena's soggy corpse and bites a chunk of cold, wadded flesh clean out of the woman's cheek.

Such incidents, however, do not prepare Quinn for what the world will reveal to him. Quinn will be exposed to bigotry, xenophobia, racism, the boundless rapacity on petty and grand scale encouraged by ruthless capitalism, the enslavement of a significant percentage of the population of a supposedly free country and the brutalities of such institutionalized evil, fierce jingoism that expresses itself in casual atrocities against defenseless immigrants, labor riots in which the have-nots viciously turn against themselves, and the mushrooming holocaust unleashed by the primitive technological savagery of the Civil War. They are acts that follow the dark logic of that deranged woman on the dock—acts of communal cannibalism, where we relentlessly feed on each other.

Consider what Quinn witnesses. When the street riots that Quinn watches implode in Albany's poorest neighborhoods, disgruntled laborers see the great waves of destitute Irish immigrants only as threats to their meager employment at the local iron foundry. Surly xenophobia gives way to brutality when one dismissed worker splits with an ax the skull of an Irish foundry worker in front of his stunned family. The young Quinn, who begs to go out into the Albany streets despite the violence, sees firsthand the disturbing realities of the hardscrabble life of the famine Irish. But the Irish will reveal much more to Quinn. He witnesses the deliberately provocative staged event of the public funeral procession (the body lashed to three boards nailed together, the boards slanted "to allow . . . a full view of his final image" [121]). The more militant immigrants cart the bloodied corpse through the city's Irish neighborhoods, stirring the anger of a deeply oppressed neighborhood. The youngest son of the murdered immigrant vows hotly to a stunned Quinn to repay those responsible for his father's death; indeed, during the street riot that erupts over the funeral, the boy will be part of a mob that pummels the broken body of his father's attacker as other spectators cheer. With animal fury, the small boy will deliver a most brutal attack to the face of the near-comatose man—an act that recalls the dockside cannibalism on Magdalena.

Quinn is confounded not merely by such events but also by the disturbing characters he meets, characters who insist on being not only themselves but their opposite as well. The good will not stay good; the bad will not stay bad. It is as if each character were somehow a single twin, much as in the Staats mansion two portraits hang of Dirck Staats; in one he is fat, in the other thin. Indeed, twinning is a motif in the novel: Magdalena (who is herself a twin) travels with a maid who, for reasons we are not given, is made up to be her twin; twins wait to perform at the theater the day Quinn auditions as part of an undercover assignment. Joshua the Slave Runner is also Mick the Rat; Maud the spiritualist-medium is also Maud the erotic performer. Magdalena, after her rescue from the river, divides her stage performance between the frank discussion of her spiritual conversion at the river bottom and a hot rendition of the wildly erotic Spider Dance. Hillegond Staats, despite her ancient years, is described as "strapping" and "muscular," and, despite being a proper dowager of Albany society, she is driven by such erotic hunger that as she watches John McGee service the apparently dead Magdalena she goes "rigid . . . both hands gripping the inside of her thighs," stroking herself until her pelvis gyrates frenetically and she utters "soft gutteral noises" and demands that McGee service her as soon as he completes reviving Magdalena (29). McGee himself is utter chameleon, centerless and pure role—a canaller, a street brawler, an accomplished horse owner, a heavyweight boxing champion, a crooked politician, a gambler and saloon keeper, as well as a respected member of the emerging leisure class in New York society.

Ironically, we are given the unfolding record of such a twinned world through the eyes of Daniel Quinn, who persistently struggles against such puzzling logic. In ways that recall our other central characters, Quinn is not given to mystery; he investigates, hungers to reason events into plot. "The message emerging from my febrile imagination . . . was a single word 'linkage'; and from the moment I was able to read that word I became a man compelled to fuse disparate elements of this life, however improbable the joining, this done in a quest to impose meaning on things whose very existence I could not always verify" (130). What initially appeals to Quinn about journalism is its ability to empower event through the simple attentions of language. He admires the cold columned precision of the Albany daily where he works. Quinn is stunned by his ability to compose a sentence that confers both plot and significance on a simple bar fight. "He envisioned a thrilling future for himself, sitting alone in hotel rooms, ruminating on epic events, then imposing his conclusions on paper for the world to read in the morning newspaper" (170).

But events are not kind to Quinn's pretense to understanding. As with our other texts, events implode with jolting inexplicability. From the opening sequence on the docks of the collapsed bridge in Albany through his time as Civil War correspondent, Daniel Quinn is immersed in events that gracelessly deconstruct understanding; in this, he surely recalls that other literary naif whose initials he shares. To survive, Quinn must acquire the obscure clarity of the oxymoron, a flexible wisdom that understands that understanding itself is (im)possible. Such oxymoronic logic engages the immediate world premised by spectacle realism—it is the saving logic that characters to this point have not accessed. Such a vision is suggested by the startlingly flexible sight of the owls that roost in an upstairs bedroom in the Staats mansion. The bird, associated (oxymoronically) with both detached wisdom and predatory viciousness, is noted for its ability to "turn its head completely around and look backward" (234), to see naturally, easily, simultaneous realities. In Quinn's review of the Staats genealogy, he tells of cross-eyed Jacobus Staats, whose neighbors feared his offspring might be monsters able to "look both left and right at the same time they were looking straight ahead" (24). Yet Kennedy argues for exactly such a "monstrous" vision of the world, a vision that accepts a world of cooperative, not competitive, realities.

When Quinn returns to his childhood home for the first time since cholera swept his family, he wants to locate a birdcage his dying mother insisted he bury in the backyard against the threat of looters. When he unearths it, that rusted birdcage, so obviously useless and worthless, puzzles Quinn. Turning it over, he accidentally finds a false bottom and hidden in it a small disk. That strange disk bears an odd trompe d'oeil design that, as Quinn examines it, is at one moment a screaming mouth with "vicious eyes" and, when tilted, "a comic puppy with bulbous nose and tiny mouth" (73). Disappointed, Quinn has no use for the disk. Yet it will come to suggest the very open immediate plane of shifting signification into which Quinn (and the rest of us) must venture. Typically, Kennedy will place such talisman where it most belongs in an oxymoronic world—at the bottom of a birdcage. Not surprisingly, Quinn refuses the argument of the disk and keeps hold of it (he decides it must be a potato platter) but only for its tarnished beauty, which indicates his persistent love of the fetching surface. Only later, after he engages firsthand the senseless logic of a civil war (Kennedy's dominant oxymoron) and the senseless logic of love (Kennedy's other controlling oxymoron) will Quinn make peace with the disk and, thus, assume a pivotal role in our study of spectacle realism.

*　　*　　*

Cool things become warm, the warm grows cool; the moist dries, the parched becomes moist.

Heraclitus, Fragment 22

Certainly, the notion that the world is composed of complementary realities where the simplest sense perceptions are riven by disturbing questions of reliability; where the universe is best defined not as substance but as process—these are notions hardly original to spectacle realism or to Kennedy. Years before Heisenberg, we doubted the reliability of what we record. After all, Heraclitus pointed out long ago that the most reliable phenomena—wet and dry, day and night, hot and cold, young and old, sickness and health, left and right, fat and thin, sweet and bitter, hard and soft, up and down, even life and death—are only different angles of perception. Each set of phenomena apparently consists of opposites but the one turns into the other without clear discontinuity. Such conjectures could be applied to larger areas of human behavior—love and hate, wealth and indigence, intelligence and folly, war and peace, power and weakness, justice and injustice, good and evil, even right and wrong. Each of these "absolutes" is bound to its opposite, one depending on the other for verification and definition. Early on, Quinn records two disturbing dreams; in one, Maud dreams of a "voluptuous woman giving birth to an infant skeleton"; in the other, Quinn dreams of a woman who "owned bilateral pudenda" (31)—stark dream images that together suggest the inextricable braiding of living and dying. When Maud recalls a classics instructor who taught her the theory of "enantiodromia" (the process by which a thing becomes its opposite), Kennedy introduces the work of Heraclitus, the pre-Socratic thinker whose sole extant work, a collection of paradoxical epigrams, shapes a vision of just such a universe of constant flux where opposites are, in fact, shared, not competitive, realities.[2] Heraclitus suggested that every apparently reliable condition is simply a necessary part of a greater unity that is itself the perpetual and meaningful struggle among such oppositions, which forever encroach upon each other. The natural element of the cosmos, then, is conflict.

Daniel Quinn's America is a tensive, decidedly Heraclitian world of compelling opposites in constant conflict. From the streets of Albany's poorest neighborhoods to the sweeping battlefields of the American South, from the Albany foundry yards to the swanky hotels of Saratoga Spring, it is a divided world in deep conflict against itself, a conflict that nevertheless will yield to Quinn's eye by narrative's end a satisfying sense of design and cooperation, a world that rewards investigation by revealing not solution but mystery.

Each lesson Daniel Quinn must learn is inevitably cased as a Heraclitian oxymoron. A writer, he must learn that the word is usefully useless. A lover, he must learn that love makes for ultimate (non)sense. Women, he discovers, are erotic celibates, (in)vulnerable, as much sheer spirit as the clean curve of flesh. Love? It is selfish self-denial. Death? It is speechlessly generic and yet sacramental. Life, at its most exuberant, contains the stink of death; death, at its grimmest, reveals raucous insouciance. He must learn the wisdom of confusion, the certainty of uncertainty, the clarity of obfuscation. He must be taught the danger of absolutes—sacred and profane, spiritual and material, madness and sanity, good and evil. He must understand the danger of understanding; he must conclude that conclusion has a fatal lure. The oxymoron alone teaches him how to love properly the maddeningly elusive Maud, and it teaches him to forsake the artificial security and mock power of the world of journalism to pursue the world of the imagination. The oxymoron alone makes Daniel Quinn by the closing chapter what he most wants to be: a writer and ultimately a lover.

To negotiate such the oxymoronic world of (un)reliable absolutes, Daniel Quinn first experiments with the vehicle of language.[3] From the opening sentence, a most baroque construction that builds line upon line with steady compulsion, Kennedy draws attention to language, or, more specifically, to its efforts to keep apace of the events that implode about Quinn. Characters are most impressed by language, by the written or recorded word: they are actors, poetasters, songwriters, journalists, epistolarians. Will Canaday, the newspaper editor who takes Quinn under his tutelage, begins Quinn's education by giving him stacks of books and the newspaper to read. Quinn is most impressed by Dirck Staats, a "maestro of language, a champion of the heroic sentence" (102), who pens a multivolume history of The Society. When Maud was all of thirteen years old, she commanded a most articulate vocabulary, spoke three languages (as a child, she began to speak Latin without benefit of instruction), and, at the tender age of four, kept notebooks in an apparently invented language. And, unlike the experience of Kate Vaiden, language here connects: when Quinn is separated from Maud, they stay in touch through the tender vehicle of letters delivered by a most roundabout courier system of chance acquaintances. In fact, language here can even save lives: when Quinn discovers the mutilated body of Dirck in a deserted farmhouse, he fetches a wheelbarrow and pushes and pulls the battered reporter through miles of New York countryside, all the while talking to the barely conscious Dirck, a relentless, rambling monologue that keeps Dirck alert and alive, a delicate lifeline of words that ultimately saves Dirck's life.

But even as language thrives, bolts lovers, and even keeps alive a critically injured body, Kennedy, so much a Heraclitian, as well denies the power of language. Even as Quinn nurses through the ministrations of talk with Dirck, for example, he also engages in a disjointed, broken bit of nonconversation with a bearded old man he meets along the road. Trying to enlist help for the obviously wounded Dirck, Quinn cannot get the old man to understand his plight, and the dialogue collapses into a useless nonexchange. Language, it appears, is (un)helpful and (dis)connective. Ironically, of course, Kennedy understands the possibilities of language far better than his narrator. Consequently, we again learn indirectly through a tensive relationship between author and character. Quinn gradually comes to understand that language is powerful because it is powerless, critical because it can record accurately its inability to record accurately. That he learns at all, however, places him in a radical position within our study, and so we turn now to the business of that education.

* * *

> "Setting type isn't what I want to do," said Quinn, and he groped for the word that would define his goal. Editor? Not likely. Writer? Too ambitious. "I think just now I ought to learn how to be a paragraphist," he said.
>
> "You'd best learn to set those paragraphs in type if you want to earn a living, boy. Words are flimsy things. Type is solid and real."
>
> Quinn's Book

To frame this education, Kennedy moves Quinn (in Heraclitian fashion) between extremes: Dirck Staats and Will Canaday. Dirck, so passionately devoted to the word, testifies in his cryptic notebooks, written in his own code, to a tormented private paranoia, a Pynchonesque exercise in cabal-thought that is in truth a massive effort to defy Albany's neat exteriors by revealing a most sinister underworld. Yet such revelations relish the same sense of satisfaction of those who imagine Albany to be exactly what its comfortable exteriors profess. These readings are simply competing simplifications. The Society, as Dirck's ledgers reveal, is a brutal collective of some of Albany's most influential civic leaders. Their stranglehold on the night world of political Albany is tightened by brutalities against those who attempt to expose its syndicate webbing. Quinn will see the viciousness firsthand. When Dirck disappears, Quinn finds in an abandoned barn the body of a member of The Society who bungled Dirck's kidnapping, his stomach spliced open and set upon by feeding rats. A moment later, he discovers Dirck himself, mutilated, his tongue cut out. Yet, lest The Society yield a single interpretation, Quinn is told later that the cabal enthusiastically promotes Albany development and that Dirck's own father was a founder. Dirck's chronicle of The Society's villainy, despite its heft, is blinded, denying as it does the reliable record that "The Society was *not always* vile, and that *all* present members are not villainous men" (129, italics Kennedy). Dirck, we are told, sports "unusually small spectacles" (52), which he keeps propped uselessly on his forehead. Metaphorically blind, Dirck not surprisingly closes the narrative a mute, furiously scribbling the most banal conversation filler.

It is easy to dismiss Dirck Staats (he admits he is "odd as ripe birdseed" [53]), to see his paranoia as a tilting of the Celtic disk. But surely Will Canaday, who emerges as Quinn's teacher and surrogate father, who introduces Quinn to great books, and who paves the way for Quinn's success as war correspondent—surely Will Canaday enjoys the favor of the narrative. But given the Heraclitian reading, Will Canaday's newspaper is little better than Dirck's ledgers; indeed, at one point they are fused when Will devotes a twenty-page special edition to a translated version of Dirck's ledgers after Dirck disappears. Although the white-haired newspaper editor may appear benign (his name echoes "William Kennedy"), his versions of the truth published daily in his newspaper are as willfully nearsighted as anything Dirck concocts in his fanatical notebooks. The newspaper peddles a fashioned commodity that we collectively agree to call "event." The newspaper kills the wonder of experience—Canaday enters the narrative "cadaverous," covered by snow in the otherwise "lovely heat" of Hillegond Staats's mansion (20). The newspaper office is on a street prone to sudden flooding, but the newspaper offices themselves are up on the second floor—distanced from the raw element of furious chance—a protected, insulated magic kingdom.

When Quinn tours the offices, he is surprised by the tiny chaos of the worktables out of which the newspaper coaxed the geometry of its daily edition. Later, Kennedy excerpts columns from coverage of a boxing match between the immigrant John McGee and the reigning American champion. The boxing match, itself a meaningless competition quickly fought in a tavern and then quickly forgotten, is manipulated by a local sports reporter into an apocalyptic melodrama, a spectacle between America and the immigrant Irish; language, hyperbolic and purple, converts this banal sporting event into a showdown between peoples, between races; glorifies division; exaggerates cultural lines; simplifies realities; and lets us relish for an odd space of nontime the illusion of Clear Event. And when Will Canaday later witnesses the bloody labor riot in the Albany streets, he sees it as pure "madness," but his newspaper will bevel such chaos into a neat "feud between Papists and Americans" (127). Language reassures that what happens to us (even the horrific) can be carefully shaped by professional "paragraphists" into plot. It is a most pleasant narcotic. After all, hashish candy, which "produces the most perfect mental cheerfulness" (254), and patent medicine drops, guaranteed to alleviate a woman's menstrual periods or, failing that, to make unwanted pregnancies disappear, are advertised in the same Saratoga newspaper in which Quinn reads updates on the war in the South.

As spectacle realist, however, Kennedy cannot tolerate the radical arrogance of certainty, the cold eye of understanding. He will make clear the danger of language's pretense to certainty in the harrowing scene at the Albany Charity Bazaar. Quinn has returned North after two years with the Union troops, two years of filing reports from "death's center" (189), reports so vivid that they have made him a celebrity in Albany. The war itself we are not given firsthand. But we understand its effect: we lose for most of the novel's postwar sections the intimacy of first-person narration; Quinn distances himself within the insulating wrap of third person. Like Enid under the influence of her step-uncle, like Wheelwright in the afterburn of the Little League game, like Kate after her parents' murder-suicide, Quinn has been transformed by war, a transformation that, as Kennedy foreshadows, has gone terribly awry: at one point, Magdalena reads one of her cryptic original poems, "If a butterfly / Turned into a caterpillar / Where would be the loss? " (165–66). At the Albany Charity Bazaar, we assess the magnitude of just such a loss. At the bazaar, Canaday asks Quinn to speak to the Albany aristocracy gathered for a feel-good charity event to raise money for the war effort. Canaday tells him that, so far from the Southern front, they need the "war's reality." Quinn steps up to the platform and, surrounded by regimental flags pocked by bullet fire, offers a deliberately shocking picture of the violence, the carnality, the petty cruelties perpetrated by soldiers who find themselves in the absurdity of war. Pacing the platform, he tells them, "A pile of dead people, that's the reality I'm talking about. The bigger the pile, the bigger the reality" (222).

The speech, which runs for several pages, is in its thinness of wisdom and its narrowness of understanding like Dirck's ponderous notebooks, full of dark "truths" designed to shock from blindness those complacent enough to believe all is well. The war is far from civil—that is the "reality" Quinn offers—but that is little more than holding the Celtic disk to show only the screaming mouth. Quinn's "revelations," delivered in coarsest language, reduce the infinite technology of language to little more than a blasting tool. Women retreat from the gathering; men try to shout Quinn down. Quinn fancies himself educated by the war, but, within the Heraclitian vision, Quinn is now merely certain, (ab)using language to shatter others' comfortable securities. He stops reciting petty atrocities long enough to genuflect and cross himself, thus giving his remarks the imprimatur of holy truth. But as he delivers his screed, he recalls more the blackfaced minstrels that Quinn notices when he first tries to infiltrate the theater. It is a sorry performance in blackface. Coming off the podium, Quinn is immediately confronted by Will Canaday, who counsels him, "I think it is time you took up with your platter" (228).[4]

*   *   *

"Now, now, dearie," said Hillegond. . . . "Your auntie was dead, you know."
"I rather doubt it," said Maud. "I believe the symptoms of her life vanished, but not life itself."
"She's a savvy little brat, ain't she?" said John.

Quinn's Book

It is clear by now that texts of spectacle realism are, at heart, novels of education. But as we shall begin to see, the vocabulary of education hardly suffices. In text after text, characters, sunk within cynicism, detached from experience, blind to the immediate, must be not so much enlightened as disinterred, revived, resurrected.

Quinn provides a most helpful starting point. His education, indeed his resurrection, will be completed not by the disk but by a most significant, mysterious other. Since John McGee revived Magdalena by lusty violation, (res)erection (and the pun is deliberate in Kennedy) is kept vital within the narrative line. As Hillegond Staats observes, "All sorts of people come back from the dead to tell what it was like" (35). When Quinn returns from the war, his soul now a "lump of lead" (198), he is more dead than alive. When he first sees his long-lost Maud, she observes, "Daniel, I feared you were dead." Quinn responds cryptically, "I seem to have survived . . . but it may be an illusion" (198). To revive, Quinn must learn the lesson of community so available to Enid Stevick,

John Wheelwright, and Kate Vaiden—and so roundly rejected by each. Love, in the warm wisdom of Hillegond Staats, is "better than wheat" and "worth what it costs to find it" (135). Maud will instruct Quinn in the wisdom of the Celtic disk, to abide within what he cannot define, to live within the vulnerability of uncertainty. She admits, "I am never what I was. I am always new, always two. I am, and I am, and so I am" (164). In this, Maud embodies the disk, she is a flesh-and-blood oxymoron: helpless and fragile, yet resourceful and savvy; mysterious and enigmatic, yet bold and forthright; fiercely erotic and inviting, yet, as Quinn keeps discovering, distant and teasing; deeply dependent on Quinn, faithful over years that separate her from Quinn, yet hard-hearted and strikingly treacherous; eerily spiritual (she regularly converses with ghosts), yet vividly sensual as she shocks Albany with her Mazeppa.

Quinn keeps trying to hang the word "love" on this experience. We suspect simplification when, after Quinn assists in pulling Maud out of the Hudson, they kiss impulsively. After the kiss (which he presumes is similarly galvanizing to her), he imposes on Maud the role of damsel-in-distress dependent on his heroic rescue, a role apparently validated by events when John and Magdalena conspire to put Quinn off the canal boat as he sleeps when the four depart Albany. Awakening to find himself on the shore quite alone, tricked by those he trusted, Quinn weeps great "desolated" tears over the "theft of Maud" (60), the phrasing revealing the proprietary rights he has already assumed over a girl he barely knows. Stranded, he conjures dilemmas of Maud's impending ravishment. And he decides that now he has become a man, "solitary, furious, eccentric, growing bold" (61). It is an uncomfortable moment—the badly duped Quinn is so clearly misdirected. The "abduction" of Maud no more makes him a man than later the gift from Hillegond Staats of a writing desk and a dozen pen points will make him (as he trumpets) a writer.

Later, in Saratoga Spring, Quinn reunites with Maud. She is conducting a séance with the spirit of the man driven by love to kill quite by accident the very woman he loved—a story that could teach Quinn how devotion in our Heraclitian world leads oddly to destruction and solitude; how pure love is braided to death; how we keep killing what we love. These are lessons that would upset Quinn's neat simplifications. Yet despite witnessing Maud's dramatic conversation with the dead man, Quinn typically clings to set notions and tells her, "You cannot talk to spirits. Dead is dead" (157), most ironic in a novel where a variety of corpses (including Quinn himself when he returns from the war) are amazingly animated. But as Quinn watches Maud work the séance, so sensual and yet so spiritual, he perceives complications in her that can only be formulated in a page of Heraclitian epigrams that contradict each other but are nevertheless jointly true. "Her frown belongs to the devil. Her frown is paradise lost. . . . Her mouth is cruel with love. Her mouth is soft with invitation. . . . Her hair is devilishly angelic. . . . Her eyes are golden beauty. Her eyes are hard as Satan's heel. . . . Her hair is full of snakes. Her hair is a bed of warmth" (156–57). Yet, too much a reporter, he will dabble in such logic but will not commit himself to such twinned realities. He recommences the safer play of traditional romance: he makes plans to rent an open carriage with Maud, promenade through Saratoga Spring, stop for tea, and then stroll calmly until he finds an appropriately quiet spot where he will plant a conventional stolen kiss and declare his conventional eternal love for her and his tidy plans for their conventional future. Ever the oxymoron, she delivers to Quinn a most tectonic, most unconventional kiss in which Quinn tastes her tongue and that turns Quinn's teeth and gums to "sweet pain" (160), a most oxymoronic effect that nevertheless fails to budge Quinn's perception.

Ever obtuse, he plans their future, even as Maud dreams of a "living, pulsating, disembodied eye sitting on a large rock." The eye, she recognizes, is her own. When she reaches to return it to her socket, it melts into "corrupt slime" (171). It is, she sees, a hieroglyph that suggests vision and perception are not the same. Indeed, she traffics in the suggestive world of hieroglyphs that Quinn resists: she experiments with mesmerists trying to find the levels of her self; she communicates with the dead; she conducts séances; she explores her dreams. When Maud and Quinn stroll through the park, the two come upon the refuse of a spring picnic. Ever a literalist, Quinn observes succintly that it is a "mess"; Maud, more perceptive of the picnic that was abandoned with such haste, observes rather enigmatically (and in a fashion that recalls Heraclitus) such waste is "the remnants of beauty" (173). What exactly she means is, of course, unclear. That her remark *may* mean at all is critical as we are under the sway of Quinn, who moves about the world easily defining its realities, casually decoding meaning.

And even as Quinn plans a predictable romantic evening to propose marriage, Maud follows a bizarre gypsy ritual to divine the compatibility of their match by making a cake that uses water "in which she had lightly bathed her privities" (172). She exposes her breasts to the cake and draws her initials in the cake, slices out a piece and walks with it backward, puts it on her bedstand table and then eats it while she is naked. Then she waits, expecting the spectral double of the man she will marry to appear. But she falls asleep. Maud tries to explain the ritual to Quinn, but he quickly dismisses it and kisses her "lip and tongue" (175), an assertion of his growing sense of confident ownership. Maud resists Quinn's boldness and advises him to shave (he has never shaved). She assures him "it's time you learned" (175). Earlier, Magdalena discovered Maud's bedsheets stained by her first menstrual period, the bloodstain a "geography of long-awaited unknown" (169). It is time now for Quinn to enter, appropriately bleeding, into a similar geography. As Quinn takes each slow stroke and his blood scarlets the bone-white soap, he enjoys the illusion that he is cutting himself into adulthood. As the blood drips along his chin, Quinn (naturally) "trie[s] not to watch" (176). He emerges from the shave and, bandaged, pauses to look at the lawns of Obadiah Griswold's house, where he is staying, and admires its "symmetry" of grass and gardens, trellis and arches (177); it is his magic kingdom where clean lines cooperate into pleasant pattern. Overcome by his pleasant sense of a knowable world, he drops into an effortless sleep. When he awakes, all has changed. He finds Maud inexplicably gone and Obadiah Griswold suddenly, inexplicably hostile to him. Indeed, Obadiah, inexplicably snappish, tells him that Maud, with whom Quinn spent the morning, has been gone since the previous night.

He steps into a mysterious world beyond his neat illusion of control, a world where profound love is expressed in a hard act of abandonment, where explanation is crippled, where the fullest heart is best expressed by sheer heartlessness—the very trampoline world of spectacle realism. Of course, Quinn resists. He dismisses Maud in quick order. "Forget her. This part of my life is over" (181). He even dismisses the word "love," confident that he is done with its nonsense. This assertion, however, does not measure Quinn's education; rather, it is the same annoying assertion of certainty that underscores Quinn's later performance at the Albany Charity Bazaar. Like Dirck scribbling furiously in his notebooks, like Will Canaday calmly shoring up chaos into newspaper columns that divide the world into "rapscallions and heroes" (49), like the odd disk tilted only one way, his declaration represents only the simplest of available resolutions. Maud quickly moves from his heart's sustenance to its devastation.

The girl, he concludes, is "beyond [his] control" (181)—which is exactly the point Kennedy wants to teach Daniel Quinn.

When Quinn next meets Maud eight years later, she seems to validate his dismissal of her "love." He is a struggling newspaper reporter; she has become a sensation playing Mazeppa. Naturally, Quinn finds the display on stage disturbing. He comes backstage and offers his love to rescue her from such "raucous lasciviosity" (204). Yet he finds she is in hard control of her career and unwilling to give up its material comforts. She refuses his offer with a cutting remark about his income level, and he retreats. She is the same person who earlier kissed Quinn passionately and begged quietly to be his—here, she resists. Quinn is not prepared for such contraries. He walks out of the theater and, he assumes, out of her life.

But when Quinn returns to Albany from the war, Maud will intuit that carapaced heart, will see how he has drowned in the simple evil of the war, and how it has left him lifeless. Like the disinterred Amos Staats, Quinn comes to Maud a beautifully preserved body, quite dead. Like John McGee's ministrations to the drowned Magdalena, the vehicle Maud chooses to revive Quinn is the application of hard erotic heat. She summons him to her bedroom and exposes herself, wearing only a revealing chemisette. She cradles her own breasts lovingly, invites him to feel the pulse at her now-matured bosom, and with erotic ease exposes herself fully to his hard, dead eyes. To such a stunning display (the "triangulated center of his dreams" that he notes for its "emerging sunrise of irresistible invitation" [209]), Quinn offers only a crude architectural critique of her pudenda, a petty remark about her previous lovers, and a cynical crack about her once exposing herself in a similar fashion to a cake.

In the closing section in Saratoga Spring, Quinn, now carrying the disk, prepares to negotiate what he so long avoided: uncertainty itself. As Quinn approaches the city's racetrack, he observes two long lines of humanity intersecting, inextricably braiding: one, the wealthy white aristocracy of New York society headed with stately step to the elegant Opening Day festivities; the other, spirited African Americans singing and swaying to a rousing celebration of the national act of emancipation. It is a powerful emblem of the world of spectacle realism, a Heraclitian world of bound contraries—a single line that is both black and white, rich and poor, restrained and perfervid. Then a chance dialogue Quinn conducts with Maud's current love interest, a businessman who intends at midlife to switch careers and enter the tumultuous world of New York politics, introduces Quinn to the violation of continuity, into the broader Heraclitian sensibility of flux. Quinn asserts, "I date to this moment my change of mind on the word" (265). He sees his long devotion to newspaper work as a misplaced trust, the recording of experience as a "shallow sort of truth" (265). Such writing, he sees, is merely "true" (265). He decides that fiction, not fact, is the medium appropriate in the magnificent plane of a Heraclitian world. He embraces fascination, not revelation; mystery, not solution, and makes his first gesture at oxymoronic thought—"How could I ever come to know anything if I didn't know what I didn't know" (266).

After the horse race, itself riven by deception and ending with an appropriately oxymoronic twist (the winning horse is summarily destroyed), Quinn makes his peace with a reality that refuses definition, appropriately enough at Magdalena's staged wake, which so skews the very premise of reliability and perception. As Quinn settles down the afternoon of the party to write Magdalena's gag "obituary," he sees, in an epiphanic moment, that he has given his life over to observation, a fringe existence that has disengaged him from a rich, chaotic universe. Quinn now understands that recording the evident contradictions is not enough, that real wisdom finds the harmony lurking beneath such apparent chaos, and that intuiting such harmony is an act of the sole energy Quinn has yet to engage: the imagination. He stops writing the newspaper article and turns from the scrapbooks full of the factoids of Magdalena's life; he turns, rather, to writing Magdalena's "story" (280) as it had taken root in his imagination. "I might confront what was worth confronting, with no expectation of solving the mysteries, but content merely to stare at them until they became as beautiful and valuable as Magdalena had always been, and as Maud now was" (280). In oxymoronic fashion, he loses what he recovers: he abandons language even as he embraces it. He understands the writer is not to interfere, inflicting the clumsy tyranny of shape and order onto the unwinding of raw events, but rather to "kneel with awe and reverence" before the chaotic order of a world, compelled by the appropriately oxymoronic energy of "tragic laughter" (281).

Later, upstairs in the Griswold mansion, Quinn will slowly loosen the ribbon that holds the bodice of Maud's dress. Slowly, she will remove the ribbon from the dress and tie it around her neck and let the ribbon dangle freely along her torso. As he gently removes the rest of her clothing, only the ribbon remains. It falls the length of her body even as she rolls easily down to the bed. As he prepares to make love, Quinn lifts the ribbon aside; he treats her with the gentle anticipation of a reader opening a favorite book, gently turning aside the bookmark before consummation. Maud herself becomes Quinn's book. At last, Quinn fuses his two roles— writer and lover. And Quinn, long the master of the quick read, prepares at last to allow resolution to give way to wonder (as he approaches Maud at the close, he advises himself "Slow" [288]), to perpetuate the mystery that lurks at the core of the immediate. As Quinn makes love with Maud, a summer storm gathers, promising to break the long dry spell. Importantly, Kennedy, ever the Heraclitian, will not tolerate unalloyed love; in another room in the mansion, Obadiah Griswold hungrily licks the knees of a parlor maid.

Unlike with Enid Stevick, John Wheelwright, or Kate Vaiden, connection has been secured. Making love is a most appropriate close in a novel where the central character has had to forsake his deep trust in linkage. Making love, of course, suggests not the clunky connection of linkage but rather the sweeter bond of fusion, the Heraclitian oxymoron that separate elements become one and yet somehow stay two. To this point in the narrative, Quinn's involvement with Maud has been limited to kissing, or simple linkage. He is ready at last for the oxymoron, for a Heraclitian love that insists on and yet destroys boundaries. Quinn's fingers, dead at the tips since the accident during the crossing of the Hudson (recalling Kate's corpsed arms), show compelling evidence of revival that promises that Quinn is ready now to pursue the twin goals of his long education (both, not coincidentally, tied to the functioning of his reclaimed fingers): to love and to write. Alone of our characters to this point, Quinn has moved out from the magic kingdom.

*   *   *

> Now Double Alley's our Paradise Alley,
> For that's where we learned how to die.

Tavern song, quoted in *Quinn's Book*

But *Quinn's Book* can be approached as much about Quinn's age as it is about Quinn himself. Critical reactions cited, often with reservation, the novel's cutting and pasting of events marking Quinn's slow evolution with the public events of pre–Gilded Age America that he witnesses: labor riots, immigrant conditions, slavery and the Underground Railroad, the Civil War itself.[5] Clearly, Kennedy has an ambitious public agenda. He thus argues that the process of being coaxed away from the illusion of certainty is not only one that we each must undergo privately. It is a process that entire eras (such as pre–Gilded Age America and Kennedy's own, for that matter) must undergo. The lesson Quinn stumbles toward, to avoid gratuitous absolutes, can be pointed rather directly at these eras, both of unprecedented institutional simplifications when the wholesale indulgence of easy absolutes and the heroic resistance to complexity not only shaped a viable national political vision but (far more disturbing) helped define and conduct domestic as well as international policy. Kennedy comes at the Reagan Era through the remarkable parallel of history, finding in the mid-nineteenth-century embrace of melodramatic theater and the simultaneous rise of journalism important forebears of Reagan's play zone of disengagement, of our era's deep need for theater and its indulgence of the seductive diversion of the melodrama.

To understand Kennedy's critique of the Reagan Era, we need to consider the novel's subplot of the world of theater. Pre–Civil War America marked the emergence of popular stage, whose logic and metaphors would find significant resonance, oddly, more than 100 years later in the Reagan Era. Daniel Quinn comes of age in the time when American theater came of age, not the legitimate theater of repertory work but rather the lower-brow forms: medicine shows, dime museums, circuses, melodramas, and minstrel shows (indeed, the Albany theater is known as The Museum because it was for a short time a Barnumesque showplace for curiosities).[6] *Quinn's Book* exploits the form and expectations of the theater Daniel Quinn's world would be most familiar with—the melodrama—a form of theater-lite that has important implications for Kennedy's larger critique of the 1980s.

What did the melodrama offer? To attract and enthrall the lower-educated urban working class, melodramas emphasized manufactured plots rife with lurid events often compelled by staggering coincidences. Indeed, melodrama would come to tax the ingenuity of theater hands trying to realize the elaborate spectacles (the noun) with special effects that included great explosions, storms, volcanoes, trainwrecks, earthquakes, even great battles. The action came in swift, quick-cut sequencing. Such action theater forsook nuanced characters or behavioral shading or really anything approaching complexity for easy stereotypes and stock characters; such predictable confections operated without apology within an uncomplicated world of heroes and rapscallions. And whatever the stage devices, melodramas followed a formula: young lovers were separated by scurrilous villains who intrigued to keep them apart by abducting the girl/woman. Such nefarious schemes were eventually (and predictably) thwarted by the hero, a boy/man who, hopelessly smitten by love, survived by dint of his moral thought and resourcefulness any cataclysmic obstacles to rescue this damsel-in-distress and closed by claiming his love, her virtue intact. Audiences, breathlessly watching such a spectacle unfold, left the theater reassured that all along such chaotic events were guided by the providential hand of a greater God, who quietly determined that true love would eventually triumph and that villainy would fail.

The formula is, of course, a plot that clearly mimics the mainframe of Maud and Quinn's romance. And, through the narrative that chronicles this eventual reunion, we sit like theater audiences a century ago mesmerized by the sheer muscle of outrageous plot. In the first thirty pages alone, we experience spectacles: a treacherous river crossing, a deadly massive wall of careening river ice, a cataclysmic bridge collapse, a multiple drowning, a grisly act of cannibalism, a citywide fire, a bizarre act of necrophilia, a woman coming back from the dead, a suicide, an exhumed corpse that explodes in a shower of grayish ash, a passionate first kiss, a mysterious kidnapping. The novel indulges a wild excess of plot; any attempted summary is quickly defeated. Included here are cold-blooded murders (most never solved), a creepy syndicate-style crime machine that apparently runs Albany, a crusading newspaper editor, horrific kidnappings, labor strikes, bloody street riots, erotic seductions, heartbreaking betrayals; along the way, Kennedy enfolds narrative pieces on hyped prizefights, rigged horse races, spellbinding séances, desperate runaway slaves, lively amateur theater shows, and, almost incidentally, the American Civil War.

Yet the melodramatic model never quite works. To teach the dangerous lure of certainty, Kennedy exploits, skews the formula of the melodrama. Within Quinn's experience, unalloyed virtue is impossible to find. Villains are imperfectly defined. The good guys have the sour germ of evil within their character; the evil ones reveal with frustrating unpredictability odd glints of goodness. Quinn himself is hardly heroic. Like our other central characters, when he learns a bit, he thinks he has learned it all; consequently, like them, he is not particularly likable. As a lover, he is not consistent or persevering in his passion for Maud. And the damsel Maud is hardly in distress. She is resourceful and quite independent. And vice, so typically vanquished by the close of a melodrama, thrives unpunished, even unrecognized at the close. Events do not unfold with the melodrama's neat precision; they sort of shudder against each other in stark collision. And the resolution is at best problematic. We do move toward a reunion of sorts, but here that hard-won love is hardly pure and possesses a decided carnal dimension.

Kennedy does not, however, merely deconstruct the melodrama. As commentary on the Reagan Era, *Quinn's Book* cautions what happens when we attempt to impose the logic of theater onto the unfolding events of history. For Kennedy, the precursor of Reagan's efficient media machinery with its slick corps of spin doctors and opinion engineers is surely Canaday's newspaper, which puts a handy spin on the chaos in the streets and shapes unwieldy events into easy dramas. It is Kennedy's wider insight that the Reagan Era itself became a cultural exercise in melodramatic theater. We wanted to spot the Good Guys and the Bad Guys; we wanted the Good Guys to win; we wanted pure love to triumph. We wanted dilemmas, certainly, but those with clear sides and neat resolutions. We borrowed without apology from the mechanics of melodrama and from its rich sense of ritualized conflict, to give shape to events by processing them into a linked plot; by flattening national and international personages into convenient caricature; by redrawing into "sides" the whirl of forces that coaxes events; by insisting that events move with clear direction to neat resolution that framed a handy lesson.

Domestic and international policies were informed by a vocabulary borrowed oddly from the hokey space operas of George Lucas. With sudden ease, the world divided into darkness and light. We indulged (and financed) a great fantasy weapon system to do battle with the Evil Empire in the only place where such a melodramatic showdown most fittingly belonged—in the great open battleground of space.

We booed an international gang of heavies; like Quinn, we seldom ventured beyond surfaces: the beadle-browed Khomeini; the swarthy Khadafy in his hokey desert tents; the pock-faced Noriega in his comic-opera military uniform; the barrel-chested, stony-faced Soviet military (apparently sent up from Central Casting) to explain to the world press the destruction of the Korean jet airliner; the Cheshire-smile of China's cool despot Deng; and all those crazed international terrorists with olive complexions and heavy mustaches that we lumped with Hollywood (im)precision into the vague notion of "Islamic fanatics." We did not want to be bothered by the work of sorting through the contradictory realities of such political and religious entities. Like Quinn, we needed something to understand. Much as Montaigne warns in the essay Quinn reads (but disregards), we invented "false and fantastic subjects" to direct our fury, deceived ourselves for want of a legitimate object for our anxieties, as such objects, of course, do not exist. But after the toxic miasma of the Vietnam experience and the faltering guessing steps of Carter's foreign policy, we lost our taste for ambiguity; we relished the sheer certainty of the stance.

To complement such international bugaboos, we booed as well a cast of domestic villains flattened into cartoons: militant gays, welfare queens, inner-city gangs, drug abusers, career Washington bureaucrats who clogged the arteries of government, raging feminists, fanatic tree huggers more interested in spotted owls than in good jobs at good wages, doe-eyed nuclear protestors, the homeless who "elected" to live on the sidewalks and in the underpasses, and, of course, the hovering swarm of card-carrying members of the ACLU.

And in keeping with this indulgence of melodrama, the era teemed with easy heroes. Recall when, after the Albany fire, Will Canaday casually anoints Daniel Quinn as tomorrow's hero-of-the-day for wrestling a charred baby's corpse from a roaming street pig—a gesture Quinn concedes was driven not so much by altruistic heroism as by simple curiosity. In the 1980s, heroes were likewise effortlessly coined so that the very ease of coinage suggested unsettling inflation: Lech Walesa, Cory Aquino, Barney Clark, Donald Trump, Princess Di, "Gorby," Lee Iacocca, Christa McAuliffe. Plus: any one of the ordinary citizens who became the hero-du-jour in Reagan's State of the Union addresses; those stellar names who worked the big-budget relief efforts such as USA for Africa or Farm-Aid or Hands Across America; those anonymous revelers who danced like spidery shadows all about the Berlin Wall. From the dramatic (that finger-thin shadow of a sole Chinese figure standing defiant before a tank in Tiananmen Square) to the trivial (that bruised toddler pulled from a backyard well in Texas), we tossed up heroes with effortless ease and lingered within their reassuring argument—until, of course, tomorrow when a new figure emerged. Indeed, we manufactured most of the era's most durable heroes from the harmless stuff of entertainment and sports—Sylvester Stallone, Carl Lewis, Michael Jordan, Pete Rose, Madonna, Michael Jackson, Tom Cruise, Bill Cosby, Bruce Springsteen—not politicians, not social activists, not business leaders, really not anyone even "real."

Like Quinn, we wanted no complications. We did not want to see Lech Walesa or Cory Aquino or Mikhail Gorbachev struggle to make governments actually operate; we did not want to know that Trump and Millken and Boesky lorded over vast paper empires that fell with a tawdry flurry of bankruptcy papers; we did not want to acknowledge that Prince Charles had married out of monarchial obligation, not love, and that such an arranged union would fall of its own ugly irony; we did not want to know that the breakup of the Soviet Union was less the dramatic breakout of freedom as it was the banal erosion from bad economics and simmering ethnic unrest; we did not want to know Christa McAuliffe was a victim of engineering shortcuts and overburdened budgets; we did not want to know that Ethiopians still starved and that American farmers still struggled without relief. Like Quinn, we held the disk at one neat angle. We surely did not want to wrestle with the Heraclitian sensibility that argued such figures were authentic and fraudulent, heroic and absurd, powerful and useless, as much a gift as a hoax.

In the argument of *Quinn's Book*, within the magic kingdom of Reagan's America, we exploded into simplicity. Taxes could be cut, and spending could still be increased. Prosperity would trickle down from the superrich. Grenada settled the debt of Vietnam. A bigger defense budget would give us a better, more efficient military. Drug addiction could be curbed if we all just said No, the threat of AIDS could be eliminated if we all just abstained. We conflated military policy with the new rage of video games—yes, we could shoot down nasty incoming nuclear weapons far out in space with the appropriate shower of dramatic special effects. We believed that the possibilities of the individual, any individual, would be enhanced by eliminating government interference. Government would legislate its own withering. Greed was good. Junk bonds were secure. Pickle relish was a vegetable. There, amid such a carnival era, Kennedy offers a novel where those who manipulate such gratutious absolutes wreak the harshest damage: the cannibalism of class warfare that sends the poor in Albany to attack the poor(er) Irish immigrant camps; the fathomless cruelties of slavery that Quinn records, each act protected by legislative imperative that reduced the thorny moral problem to questions of property management; the draft riots in New York City triggered when disgruntled whites no longer see a war worth

fighting when its cause is freeing slaves; the holocaust of the Civil War—
each act matched in our decade by harsh xenophobia, jingoism, intolerance, tunnel vision, self-righteousness, fanaticism, racism, and inflexibil-
ity, each a sorry by-product of the simplifications of the Reagan Era's
contrived melodrama.

Although it may seem quaint to toss Heraclitus against the vast cultural text of the Reagan Era, Kennedy understands that in the happy
bromide "Don't Worry, Be Happy" rest anxieties that cannot be exorcised
until, like Quinn, we understand that the miracle of understanding is
to acknowledge how much we cannot understand—the very wisdom
of spectacle realism itself. Kennedy surely does not want to dismiss the
decade, simply level the theater. That would be cheap cynicism on a par
with Quinn's blackface performance at the charity bazaar. Rather,
Kennedy argues for balance. Kennedy spins a most fantastic tale of uncertainty and ambiguities, of contraries and contradictions, of (to borrow
from his earlier work *Legs*) the "twin-peaked glory of bothness," if only
to remind us that in such apparent discord the universe has always co-
erced its deepest harmony. As we sat mesmerized by the era, by the appealing spectacles of certainty, Kennedy reminds us that such intoxicating stagecraft is finally shabby pasteboard and wires, fancy lighting and
engrossing acting. Daniel Quinn invites us to do as a nation what he
comes to do by the close of his narrative: to step away from such hokey
manufactured wonders and into the far more intoxicating mystery of the
spectacle real.

And yet *Quinn's Book* cannot stand as a summary text of spectacle
realism. Quinn determines at narrative's end to "stare at the mysterious"
(282). But mystery is not the same as wonder. Kennedy's text is at best our
midway text. To introduce Quinn to the mesmerizing spectacle of the
immediate, Kennedy freely co-opts into his narrative line extraordinary
events at decided right angles with normative laws of cause and effect,
dazzling moments of spectacles (the noun) that hint at the inexplicable in
the universe. Despite Kennedy's commitment to a period piece that re-
creates meticulously the colors and edges of mid-nineteenth-century
Albany's gritty squalor, the narrative line is haunted by an effortless conversation with the inexplicable, the odd intervention of a system of logic
that defies our agreed-upon sense of the immediate.

Consider the evidence, the too-frequent intrusion of spectacles. There
are the mildly mysterious events: how Maud commands Latin without
instruction and how Amos Staats's corpse resists decay. But we are given

far eerier incidents. Quinn stares into the cold eye of Magdalena, whom he presumes is dead, and sees a vision of a procession that is remarkably similar to the procession later to the mausoleum of Amos Staats; Magdalena's vicious cheek wound is healed by a magic poultice of goat dung and chopped crickets; Hillegond Staats, under a trance, offers a startlingly accurate vision of where her kidnaped son, Dirck, is being kept; Maud communicates dramatically with a specter who speaks in thunderclaps sufficient to loosen the plaster in the Utica theater; later, Maud describes vividly the murder of Hillegond Staats, an event she did not witness, a description that strongly suggests the culpability of Joseph Moran, who in turn is inexplicably mauled by Hillegond's pet owls. Most disturbing (or perhaps intriguing), Quinn receives a dream vision in which the Celtic disk actually speaks a most cryptic message: "Under the arches of love, under the banner of blood" (129). These words apparently foretell the pivotal public address at the Albany Charity Bazaar (Quinn performs on a stage under banners pocked by Confederate gunfire) and the closing confluence with Maud (they meet under the trellis in Magdalena's gardens).

Given a narrative that so casually smuggles in the inexplicable strokes of the paranormal, we must take some caution in Quinn's education. The shabby stuff of magic can have no place ultimately in the argument of spectacle realism, which does not smuggle the extraordinary in the ordinary but rather finds the immediate (extra)ordinary enough. To find the (extra)ordinary, to tap the unsuspected spectacle in the immediate itself, to engage with full awareness the undeniable helplessness of the individual, to find the strategy to maintain that awareness and still dislocate the self within the sweet fusion of love, to reengage without simplification and without the showy intrusions of magic—it is to further this agenda that we turn now to our only work set entirely in the Reagan Era, a work that addresses the darkening advent of the AIDS pandemic.

5

Speaking the Language of Brightness

Robert Ferro, *Second Son*

"Romance in the 1980s: you—and you."

Robin Williams, comedian

We arrive, now, at our narrative midpoint. We have seen the spectacle immediate devalued, dismissed, denied. We have seen the vast cost of such withdrawal from experience. And we have felt the urgency of the writers, themselves locked within the massive magic kingdom of Reagan's America, who warn against such deliberate retreat, who see the consequences of characters who accept strategic withdrawal from the centering experiences of all realistic narratology (spectacle and otherwise): the inexplicable urge to love and the unjustifiable need to die. Too impressed by control, they have retreated to private zones akin to the happily empty clamor of Disney's Magic Kingdom, the impoverished optimism of Reagan's America, and the linguistic daring of any postmodern text-edifice. We have seen writers abandon characters to such private playscapes while challenging the participatory reader to learn what the characters resist: to engage the Heraclitian immediate that lifts as well as buries, an affirmation of the unsuspected dazzle of a most contradictory immediate that, despite its persistent resistance to our best efforts to bend it into plot and order, we cannot afford to take for granted. We have watched a quartet of characters who spend most of their narrative lives loving badly; we turn now to Mark Valerian, the first of a quintet of midlife characters, a character who spends most of his narrative dying badly.

In a poignant moment early in Robert Ferro's *Second Son*, Mark, a thirty-ish gay decorator who faces an unnamed terminal disease whose pathology (so graphically charted within the novel) unmistakably suggests AIDS, watches from the observation tower of his family's New Jersey summer house a stranger walking along the beach. This stranger sweeps the sand with a metal detector, looking for the slenderest evidence of something valuable amid the obvious wastes. As Mark watches, the young man suddenly stops, his machine apparently registering a find. But to retrieve the treasure, he finds the machine's metal scoops too cumbersome. He must drop to a crouch, forsake his tools altogether, and plunge into the sand with his open hand to secure the glinting object. In a line that resonates not only within Ferro's narrative but as well within the fiction of spectacle realism, we are told that "only the human hand will do" (4).

As Mark acknowledges, the moment is rich in "obvious metaphor" (5). Mark is "ill, dying perhaps" (4). To someone adjusting to the cutting intervention of mortality, the tableau of the stranger on the beach might indeed offer epiphanies about the uncompromising strategy to pursue so willingly the apparently futile search for treasure amid limitless dross and the need ultimately of the unsuspected power of the human hand to secure whatever treasure is available in such wastes. Yet, in keeping with the narrative pattern of spectacle realism thus far examined, it is a lesson missed by the centering consciousness. Like Enid Stevick on the Decker Boulevard bus, like John Wheelwright in the Phoenix airport bathroom, like Kate Vaiden in the cemetery, like Daniel Quinn puzzling over the Celtic disk, Mark Valerian is another poor student. He surely begins as a familiar figure: withdrawn, surrendered, self-pitying. Mark is drawn to the handsome stranger on the beach in a powerful mix of a desire he cannot express and a memory he cannot suppress of a more spontaneous time when such inclinations might have led to shuddering intimacy, the bathhouse days of indulgence and promiscuity lost now in a narrative that is set within the colder time of strategic withdrawal. In the face of illness, Mark has retreated to the protective isolation of his family's empty beach house, his magic kingdom. He watches the stranger from the security of distance, indulging only the oxymoronic "ranging intimacy" of binoculars (4). It is a mocking moment of ironic connection that insists (much like Kate's answering machine) on withdrawal and insulation even as our narrative center, heart suddenly "thumping" (5), remarks without irony on the unsuspected power of the human hand as an emblem of connection.

We have here elements familiar to the dilemma of spectacle realism. A character recoils before the experience of a harrowing immediate, the indignity of human helplessness, the disquieting vulnerability in the face of the graceless intrusion of too-early death. Again, a deeply sensitive central character succumbs to the impulse to withdraw despite the intuitive hunger for connection. Taught by a viral invasion the simplest lesson that connection leads to catastrophe, Mark joins our other narrative centers in the awkward posture of full retreat. Like them, Mark Valerian enters the narrative with especial claim to reader sympathy. Afflicted by a virus that promises only the grimmest indignities and then certain closure, denying him, as he reasons, half the time he should have been Mark Valerian; afflicted by virus that has made only logical his disturbing decision to withdraw; afflicted by a virus that makes problematic even the simplest exercise in social interaction by designating the sick as contagion, Mark Valerian should certainly lay claim to reader sympathy.

And yet, like our other characters, Mark Valerian reveals by midtext a decidedly unpromising mind-set that cannot be given license even under the difficult circumstances under which that consciousness has developed. As in our other texts, in *Second Son* a character is too stunned by the ample evidence of blind contingency, too willing to play its victim, too willing to demand a private place apart, too willing to indulge only the darkest surmises about a future that has so quickly become problematic. Like Enid Stevick, John Wheelwright, Kate Vaiden, Daniel Quinn, Mark Valerian begins his own narrative more dead than alive, another figural suicide willing to indulge the illusion of control despite his obvious helplessness before events.

Indeed, Mark's work as landscaper (much like Felix Stevick's boxing ring performances or Wheelwright's formula prayers or Kate's work as legal secretary or Daniel Quinn's reporting) allows him to meld into pleasing forms the otherwise messy natural world, here the unruly growth of his clients' gardens. And his work as interior decorator affords him the opportunity to fashion magic private spaces, to cast about otherwise careless interiors the pleasing harmony of his sense of order. Mark is a lover of beauty who conceives the point of existence as "the rearrangement of the furniture" (149), a fragile aesthetic sensibility that lingers lovingly only over the experience of the attractive. "Was not the absence of beauty the ugliest thing in life," he observes (22). Mark must come to make his peace with the (un)certain appeal of the apparent (dis)order of a natural world—the very world that has already begun to fail him—and to find the strength to do that by accepting any of a number of open hands, the very argument of spectacle realism.

* * *

> *"You are looking very well. Weren't you clever, dear, to survive."*
> *"I've a sorry tale to tell. I escaped more dead than alive."*
>
> Voltaire, *Candide* (epigraph to *Second Son*)

AIDS narratives, although surely fitting within any discussion of the decade, might appear at first to trouble the argument of the present study by resisting the affirmative premise of spectacle realism. The largest share of AIDS texts offers (understandably) the moving record of calamitous grief: bleak witness fictions of surviving lovers or family members or the candid journals of the patients themselves, testimonials that move inexorably toward closure, testimonials that are compelled largely by the need to wrest lives and loves from interment within the sprawling indexes of statistics generated weekly by the global reach of the virus.[1] But those so destroyed by the virus and those left behind must struggle to fashion even the slenderest affirmation; they must struggle against the considerable counterpressure of melancholy and anger directed at a virus that methodically, stupidly, destroys what gives it life. Indeed, the sheer magnitude of the illness—both the cold business of measuring the attrition and counting the dead and that steadily escalating statistical description of the virus's probable growth—threatens to turn even the premise of affirmation into shabby sentimentality. Even spectacle realism's saving impulse of (com)passion can be discounted as an agency of the very virus itself or denied its power by being perceived as impotent before the onslaught of the body's viral holocaust.

AIDS, it would seem, frustrates the very argument of spectacle realism. Why engage? What to affirm? Why confront the immediate? Why demand honesty? Why seek community when the disease has elicited calls for tattooing gays and quarantining the sick? Why bother with the intuitive need for confluence when confluence abets the virus? Why sift about such obvious waste like some ghastly Forrest Gump attempting to find the valuable something? Far better, far saner, far safer to withdraw. Perhaps the sole realistic AIDS texts are the shelves of publications generated by the medical community and by public health agencies. In a time of plague, engagement of the immediate produces not wonder but sobering caution.

Indeed, AIDS has fit far more conveniently postmodern treatment. With the virus's signature alphabet moniker, it has generated stunning language games that play with the "meaning" of the virus through the agency of puns, word games, euphemisms, inventive re/deconstructions that have found deep linguistic metaphors in the virus's method of transmission by allegorizing and extrapolating to inventive lengths virtually every critical area of the illness: anus, pen(is), bloodstream, sperm, bug, Trojans (as in horses and condoms), need(le)s, penetration, antibody, "spreading," and on and on.[2] Slippery medical uncertainties early on about the illness's pathology led to entrancing theories-qua-readings of the disease as a sort of deep text, an open and fluid information system, an interpretative construct/process that ruthlessly defies our need for epistemological certainty and offers a most absorbing intratexual gameworld where we find colliding bits of *Paradise Lost*, "The Wasteland," Revelation, traditional sonnets, classical elegies, and any of a number of war fictions. Of course, as asserted in the introduction, amid such games-playing, amid such magic kingdom erections (pardon the pun), intricate and fascinating though they may prove, we risk losing touch with the less inventive, less elaborate realities of the disease itself, the anxious humanity at the dark heart of the illness—patients that no more want to be language theories or word games than they want to be medical statistics or political buzzwords or religious metaphors.

It is difficult, then, to see how a work of AIDS fiction might fit into a discussion of spectacle realism. To place an AIDS text so squarely within a larger study of spectacle realism, however, is to argue that the pandemic has produced a response that finds necessary a strategy not of withdrawal but of engagement. Robert Ferro is particularly instructive in our look at Reagan Era literary texts that premise as therapeutic the turn to engaging difficult, indeed terrifying, realities against the inclination to withdraw into magic kingdoms. In his novels, we can trace the impact of his infection (he completed work on *Second Son* just months before his death from complications brought about by the virus), its impact on the work of a writer long enthralled by the pull of the imagination, whose work before his diagnosis frequently indulged a playful postmodern turn for free-splicing genres and invoking deliberate fantasy, and a playful indulgence of the paranormal. In novels before *Second Son*, Ferro had playfully indulged spectacles (the noun): voodoo practitioners, vivid erotic dream sequences, witches and curses and spells, eerie séances, ghost ships teeming with foggy apparitions that are able to defy the laws of materiality, involved drug hallucinations, even (in more spectacular indulgences) by vocal communications from distant planets and by secret golden temples built under New York's Central Park.[3] They are lush fictions that celebrated without bothersome explanation the interventions of magic, private zones of bold authorial play that flaunted the energy of imagination, that rejected outright the ordinary in flamboyant narrative gestures deemed the privilege of a liberated gay writer in post-Stonewall American culture: the right to fashion a work of splendid apartness, to reject the banality of the ordinary that so defined the dreary heterosexual world of marriage and family.

How does such a writer fit within a discussion of spectacle realism? Indeed, what is the position of a gay text within such a discussion of novels that do not otherwise privilege sexual identity as focus? What is, of course, at issue is not the place of AIDS within a discussion of the 1980s—its grim advent was surely one of the centering cultural events of the decade—but rather the position of a gay text within a discussion of heterosexual texts. Gay texts have long asserted—at times with anger, at times with pride, at times with frustration—their privileged positioning as a distinct genre critically different from mainstream representations of heterosexual relationships and heterosexual identity dramas. Should we, then, draw together, say, John Wheelwright or Daniel Quinn with Mark Valerian? Should not Mark Valerian's position as gay make him a different case whose frustrations, anxieties, and passions cannot, indeed should not, be lightly conflated with heterosexual dilemmas? Should *Second Son* be treated, as it has been for its short critical life, among other gay texts, the AIDS virus thus granting access to a mournful wasteland geography not accessible even to those heterosexuals most in sympathy?[4]

Clearly not. *Second Son* forsakes the centering dilemma of sexual identity and the consequences of asserting (or of not asserting) that sensibility. Mark Valerian's sexuality, in fact, is a matter of rather bland assertion—sexual acts within the novel are treated without sensationalism. In contrast to traditional outing narratives, Mark's family is never uneasy over the second son's sexuality. Nieces and nephews are casually introduced to Mark's companion, whose presence at the family beach house is accepted. Although the father maintains strong Catholic scruples against the lifestyle as inherently sinful, he has long since made peace with his son and hopes that his own iron faith might secure a cure for his sick son, that Mark's might prove a "light case" (29). Rather, what unsettles the Valerian family is the disquieting intervention of disease: a family that engages life with the furious energy of the upscale must confront the sudden graceless movement to the "unnaturalness" of "death out of order" (19) and the vaguely repellent testimony of Mark's infected body, with its splotchy lesions and raised moles and grayish tumors. These are not gay issues—and to quarantine from straight texts those gay texts that confront the human reality of helplessness is to deny the obvious. *Second Son*, like other texts of spectacle realism, is about (mis)handling the pressure of human vulnerability exposed so baldly by the evidence of mortality; it concerns the strength necessary to reignite wonder over an immediate world so easily canceled by death, a sense of wonder that comes largely from the stunning intervention of a significant other able to offer as counterforce the brittle magnificence of touch, of (com)passion.

Pressured by the sudden violent introduction to mortality, texts such as *Second Son* speak to the broad theme of vulnerability, the repugnant reality of a fragile human organism wasting away too soon, the gross failure of what turns out to be a most ephemeral construction—the human body—a theme available to anyone willing to walk through a hospital, hospice, rest home, or, in fact, any cemetery. As Ferro argues in the warm autumnal tenor of his text, which never mentions AIDS by name,[5] *Second Son* is supremely a work about lost time, about the necessary human(e) strategy of coaxing beauty from own our brevity. Like the other texts examined here, *Second Son* plays on the tension between the need to connect and the urge to withdraw; between the need to rage against the raw force of contingency and the urge to surrender to its difficult suasion. Like Walter Porter, like Daniel Quinn, Mark Valerian moves toward a resolution that stuns by empowering an immediate world that otherwise offers abundant reasons to deny it wonder. It is surely the great theme of spectacle realism (and of Ferro's text) to reveal the stunning poverty of apartness and to argue, much as Walter Porter discovers in fashioning family after imperfect family and much as Daniel Quinn realizes under the arches with Maud, the great human(e) struggle to secure a partness.

*   *   *

Can't beauty be enough?

Mark Valerian

It is a measure of Ferro's narrative skill that we so quickly second-guess the sympathy we initially extend to a character who, we are told within the first few paragraphs, is dying and who has recently witnessed the slow death of his mother after a series of cerebral hemorrhages. Reeling, Mark Valerian withdraws. With unacknowledged irony, he now lives year-round in a summer cottage, in his family's massive New Jersey beach house (not the family house, but rather the locus of its annual strategic withdrawal from the unbearable Philadelphia summers). A professional decorator, he tends to the upkeep of the beach house—work, given the ranging size of the house, that offers Mark, so suddenly aware of his temporality, a commitment to apparently perpetual care. Further, as he moves about the beach house deciding what will go where, when it will go there, how it will look, Mark, so suddenly aware of his helplessness, relishes how he can impose his will over a manageable domain. His is a magic kingdom where Mark regrets only how impure his aloneness has proven—violated so regularly by deliveries and interfering neighbors.

Mark savors the canopic atmosphere, the house haunted not only by its original proprietors (the Birds, the very name suggesting their unnatural confinement within the house) but by his mother, whose presence permeates each room like "perfume seeping through the house" (7). It is less a house, more a tomb in which the living have been interred (Mark is fascinated by the Egyptian burial rituals that included such interring of living and dead within the cold magnificence of the pyramids.) Mark even sleeps in his mother's bedroom. The beach house is a separate, controlled environment where change, when it comes, follows calm seasonal predictability and where change can be met and even countered from an apparent position of power (the cycle of screens and storm windows, of opening and closing shutters, of lawn mowers and snow shovels) and where the absolute closure he must confront given his medical diagnosis is easily denied as the seasons glide each into the next. Inhumed in his beach house tower, peering at the world through the protective security of his binoculars, Mark Valerian is Enid Stevick in the practice room; John Wheelwright at midweek chapel; Kate Vaiden in the

Catacombs; Daniel Quinn on stage at the Albany Charity Bazaar. He is, in short, a character more dead than alive, a character whose unfolding education is as much an act of generous resurrection.

Like these characters, Mark has abandoned even the pretense of affirmation; we follow the conversation in which Mark some time past told his father of his illness and we see how vehemently Mark denied the father's simplest argument of fighting this thing, how Mark rejected the barest optimism that might refuse despair, a "tendency to catastrophe" (22) that he ascribed to his mother's influence. Mark is in full retreat, resolving to live now for two years within a rigid monasticism (a re-claimed virginity that has made wonderless even the feeblest efforts at masturbation), watching the spectacle of the immediate with binoculars, de-animated into a brooding flesh-and-blood ghost who relishes his privileged position as sole proprietor of a house surrounded by "empty buildable lots" (9) and fronting the ocean, a house designed by Captain Bird to appear from any window to be a ship far at sea. It is a house that was built originally without the minimal connecting tissue, without electricity cables, plumbing, sewer lines, gas lines, telephone cables. Indeed, Mark is even kept distant even from the reader; despite sharing autobiographical similarities with Ferro, Mark is offered to us as if through binoculars, through the "ranging intimacy" of third person.[6]

That withdrawal into the beach house strains Mark's connections to his family—financial setbacks involving his father's business have raised the practical strategy of selling the beach house, which is in the children's names. Mark, alone of the Valerian siblings, vehemently and rather unreasonably bristles. When the father reveals an offer of a blank check for the house—a real opportunity for his company's financial recovery—Mark petulantly rejects it with a most distressing absoluteness, "No. I won't agree. Ever" (10). The heavy emotional stake he has claimed in this magic kingdom overrides any concern he has for the radical failure of his father's—indeed, his family's—business. Mark hotly insists that he is preserving the mother's memory, that he is maintaining the family; but clearly such an emotional reading of his lingering presence in the house is not shared by the other family members, who each have relationships, homes—his sister tells him that the Cape May cottage is "just a house" (14), and even the father makes few visits to the beach and has begun to make public his long-standing romantic interest in his secretary.

Ferro uses the father's failing business to suggest the catastrophic consequences of Mark's posturing, his gross failure early on to "merge." The near-bankrupt position into which Mr. Valerian's business has fallen plays on images that suggest a failed courtship, an unsuccessful merger, the withdrawal finally of the offer to couple. Mr. Valerian's mining equipment business, named Marval (a shortened version of the name of his wife, Margaret), assumes a distinctly feminine posture. It is pursued for "merger" by five brothers whose company, named Court Enterprises, is interested in Marval's accepting a new powerful mining drill (a suggestive phallic image, the drill is known for its remarkable hardness and for its various sizes). When this Court(ship) fails amid legal dealings, the impact on Mr. Valerian's business is catastrophic. At seventy-five, the father, at the very time he had expected to retire with splendid security, must liquidate his accumulated assets just to stay afloat. Ferro reminds us of the devastating consequences of the withdrawal of the offer to merge (indeed, the business deal collapses on the very day Mark is diagnosed). Clearly, Mark Valerian is in a posture of broken merger, protected within a beach house, invulnerable only because he has simply canceled out the possibility of experience. It is no surprise that Ferro has selected for Mark's family name a species of plant used as an aromatic for incense and perfume, used as a calmative for relieving stomach pain, and used as a sedative for inducing sleep—in each case suggesting the strategy of easing a difficult reality, the pleasant narcotic of disengagement.

The other Valerian offspring do not share Mark's sense of apartness. In addition to fashioning their own families (each of whose extensive genealogies we are given), the Valerian siblings have pursued professions that compel connections to the immediate. Mark's sister Vita is a psychologist tending to patients who, she understands, need her—"Each one wants a part of me every day" (150). To abandon her practice would make her less than "the shit they would smear on the walls" (150). Although divorced, Vita has her four daughters and maintains an amicable relationship with her ex-husband (who has since remarried and fashioned another family that is now included in Valerian get-togethers). A much older brother, whom Mark handily demonizes as reptilian largely because of his hands-on involvement with the ongoing catastrophe of his father's collapsing business (unlike the second son who so coldly retreats into the indifference of self-involvement), is a prominent lawyer with a taxing caseload and a dynastic sense of his own family, now extending into a second generation. A second sister, Tessa, has abandoned the fast track entirely to raise a family, which she does with generous heart.

It is Mark who makes of himself the exception, the precious sense of himself as the one left standing in musical chairs (24). Yet for nearly twenty years, he has relished a profession of constant travel, setting up temporary residency within others' spaces and remaking their untidy worlds into coordinated, artificial spheres of colors, line, and shadow. He never speaks of past commitments but rather of frictionless promiscuity. When Mark works, he works alone in the empty houses of strangers. By the close of part 1, we understand that Mark (like our other characters) has indeed acquired immunity: from family, from friendships (save the occasional passing fantasy, such as the moment "with" the beachcomber), and from any involvement within the immediate he too easily dismisses as toxic and ugly.

Yet such strategic withdrawal, much as we have seen in other texts to this point, does not enjoy the imprimatur of the novelist. Ferro—himself dying—will not brook withdrawal, and Mark's strategy works against even his own inclination to connect. Early in the novel, Mark is on his way to a Philadelphia hospital for a battery of tests. He sees (again from protective insulation, this time from a moving taxi) a striking figure—a black man with "big brown eyes, round and calm in a smooth face . . . softened in the start of a smile" (56). Mark's gaze lingers. They exchange smiles even as the man moves into the sidewalk crowd. Later, at the hospital, Mark is asked to produce a semen sample. He is given a cup and is escorted to a white-tiled hospital lavatory, but he is unable to get hard— there is no "substance, fullness, heat" (57). Mark weeps, and in his tears he thinks momentarily of the black man. Anger gives way as desire sweeps him sufficient to produce the sample—"the connection," we are told, "was made" (58).

The profound irony of such a connection is clear. Masturbation, used by characters in each of our texts, suggests only the hard abandonment of the human community and the denial of the complication of bonding in favor of clean paramedic satisfaction. Mark sits on the hospital toilet, plastic cup in one hand, his own cock in the other—mocking the opening prescription that only the human hand will do. Such heatless (dis)connection is underscored here by the oppressively antiseptic whiteness of the hospital room and by Mark's subsequent hostile encounter with a perfunctory doctor too overwhelmed by the caseload of AIDS patients to deal in politeness. Determined to stay apart, Mark settles the natural inclination to confluence by the triage of sanitary masturbation and, in a most self-absorbed snit, departs the hospital, which later will be the setting for his difficult movement toward education.

*   *   *

> The open mouths of rivers where they join the sea.
> The places where water comes together
> With other water. Those places stand out
> In my mind like holy places.
>
> Raymond Carver, "Where Water Comes Together
> with Other Water"

Mark begins the business of reengagement, ironically, during a job assignment that takes him away to the splendid isolation of a Rome villa that he is to renovate. Typically, Mark spends his free time on the villa's terrace observing the city through binoculars—nuns hanging sheets, old men tending terrace gardens (each ironically suggesting sublimated fertility). It is surely not the Rome of romantic escapades that Mark recalls; the virus has shut down the night world that Mark remembers once provided torrid opportunities for cruising. The city is further menaced from the imminent crossing of the radiation cloud from Chernobyl. Typically Valerian, against such a toxic outside, Mark fashions within the borrowed apartment a snug place apart, a carefully appointed magic kingdom of his own design. Unfazed by the immediate, he admires the dazzling vermilion sunsets caused by the hanging radiation steam. The terrace apartment becomes another tidy, color-coordinated, haunted enclave (he decorates the rooms with his mother in mind), its sense of magic disengagement made complete by a local clairvoyant, whose Tarot pack assures Mark that the radiation from Chernobyl—"loaded with plutonium and totally dangerous" (76)—will nevertheless eliminate the virus and that indeed Mark might already have urinated the virus out of his system entirely. Under the irresistible lure of this magic kingdom, Mark resolves he simply will not be sick.

This willed insulation, this magic play zone, is violated only by letters from a school friend, a writer living in Florida named Matthew Black with whom Mark maintains an entirely epistolary relationship that suggests (like binoculars) both intimacy and cool distancing. One of these letters informs Mark that a friend of Matthew's will visit Mark in Rome.

William Mackey will dramatically alter the dynamics of Mark Valerian's withdrawal. Bill, a set designer and theatrical lighting specialist, has also tested positive; but, unlike Mark, who tracks his infection to a casual encounter during a New Year's orgy, Bill has been infected from a long-time companion who has only recently died. Unlike Mark, Bill has dared to risk the vulnerabilities of engagement. Mark's interest in Bill (naturally) ignites from Mark's shallow aesthetic reaction—Bill's beauty is the "basis of their friendship" (77). But it evolves quickly. They make love that first night. Ferro manipulates expectations of romance. It is, after all, springtime in Rome. After only days earlier fleeing a gay movie theater when he was groped in the dark, Mark now experiences physical love for the first time in two years. They make love "with the collected, considerate reserve of elderly lovers who worry for each other's hearts or brittle bones" (90). Their mutual infection may curb the athleticism of their coupling but not its intensity.

We must, however, resist finding this serendipitous match a narrative solution. Too much about this coupling suggests escape and fantasy. Ferro places the ignition of this passion at midtext. Something disturbs. Mark and Bill make love initially within a protective space created on the terrace by a dense trellis Mark designed. Mark compares Bill to a lovely being lowered from the sky on piano wire. "Share the fantasy," Mark advises Matthew in a letter that he signs Mrs. John Huston (93). But the fantasy, the romance, the sheer ease with which Rome is invested with Hollywood wonder, cannot be offered untroubled by irony. In the colder light of the morning after, the two compare lesions from a virus that will not be coaxed by the indulgence of fantasy. They share coffee while listening to heavy chimes from the nearby clock tower of St. Peter's. The stern tower chimes with a "clarity lacking in everything else" (86), an undeniable temporal presence that Ferro underscores by actually enumerating each of the tower's fourteen solemn rings. As Mark and Bill soak in the Rome morning, the city is being poisoned by deadly radiation (Mark notes the vegetable crops that are devastated, the milk that will have to be dumped, the children that have been kept home from school). The messy business of Mark's own dying is now little more than a bad dream he has of a slow train headed for a cavernous train station. Far from Cape May, far from his family, far from his doctors, Mark relishes his apparent dodge. After a night with Bill, Mark considers the massive radiation cloud curative, the clock chimes musical, and the retrovirus itself negligible. In words that carry ironic weight within the larger play zone of the Reagan Era and its own wonderland campaign against the national crisis in drug abuse, Mark decides on the villa terrace, as he calmly soaks in the radiation he assumes is therapeutic, that the most pointed response to intrusive mortality is to "just say no" (87).

Mark and Bill will expand their magic kingdom to include an impulsive trip to Venice that, under the threat of Chernobyl, is hardly romantic and far more (like the beach house, like Rome) haunted, emptied of the complicating press of people. Nevertheless, amid the emptied city, they tour like lovers; they lunch at exotic places; they hold each other. When overtired, Mark simply holds fast to Bill's limp genitalia—they care for each other in moments of fatigue or late-night aches in ways that surely signal Mark's emotional growth since clutching his own cock in the hospital lavatory. But even as they linger within such romantic magic, we understand the natural force of Mark's heart has simply convinced him to renovate his own interior space by allowing a door and admitting another—it is as if Kate's glass paperweight had two seahorses.

But we also understand an important step has been realized. The transformative nature of Mark's gesture of bonding is suggested during the couple's night ride along the deserted back canals. As they sit under a blanket in the security of each other's arms, their gondolier begins to sing in a "sweet supple tenor." Suddenly, what seems to be an echo of their gondolier takes dimension as a separate voice, a distant and muffled other whose voice, coming from another gondola somewhere in front of them, subtly braids with their own gondolier's—an effortless merger that rises toward powerful climax as the boats themselves converge, the voices moving in a "lovely aria" there along the silvery canal waters, against the narrow channel walls, in the unexpected and wholly thrilling miracle of accidental confluence in the most unpromising terrain (Mark and Bill note the mucky pollution awash in the canal's night water). "To be ill in his company," Mark writes in a letter," is to be well in relation to each other" (99).

But as seductive as that magic is, Ferro understands the limits of such insulated play zones. Mark and Bill manage to be both a part and yet apart. Mark must come home—the romance must be legitimized within the context that first created the logic of Mark's withdrawal. We quickly see why the Venice interlude is midtext. When Mark returns stateside and introduces his family to Bill, we see a Mark remarkably similar to the hypersensitive Mark of the opening pages. He has still mastered only the logic of disconnection, his embrace of Bill is protective and exclusionary.

Given the chance to hold his grandniece, he declines; he vents to his brother with hypersensitive dramatics over the issue of whether Bill is sick; and when he considers his illness, he still rages against the feeling of being cheated. At midtext, he has much to learn.

But, as with our other texts, we have a character more interested in dodging instruction. We move immediately into another magic kingdom Mark and Bill will construct—in the cabin of Bill's dead lover, Fred, in the remote reaches of the Berkshires. Mark naturally embraces the sheltered isolation; although the cabin is accessible via a road system, the two opt to leave their car and take a canoe, relishing the artificial sense of retreat. The cabin is set back beneath a heavy canopy of ancient trees. And much as Ferro poisoned the magic kingdoms of Rome and Venice with the iso-tope-rich radiation clouds, here the pastoral landscape cannot fit neatly into Mark's decorator's sense of design. The area is preternaturally quiet, moribund—they hear no birds, indeed no sounds at all. The cold lake water is flat and dead as glass. The heavy tree growth about the cabin is black and dead, fallen trees deep into rotting. The wild growth itself has exploded into a surreal thickness. The ancient plumbing in the cabin makes risky the water supply. There is no electricity, no heating. And once again it is a borrowed magic space, and one that is once again haunted: it is Fred's cabin. His family, all now dead, built the imposing structure. The dried wood of the foundation creaks; the house makes "small sudden cries" (135). Like the Cape May beach house, the cabin is another canopic world—indeed, Mark and Bill are there to scatter Fred's ashes on the lake; the bone-white urn is part of the furniture scheme. (Later, the solemn lake ritual turns grotesque as the ashes refuse to sink and end up hanging on the water, Mark notes, like vomit). In the pitch-dark nights, they listen to the unnerving screech of owls. When Mark and Bill bed together, in a tight embrace because of the damp cold, they sleep clutching each other as if "falling over a waterfall" (135).

But we are reminded of the potential power of Mark's connection to Bill. In a moment that recalls the gondoliers, Mark, canoeing alone in the middle of the lake, talks quietly to himself and is stunned when Bill, watching him from the dock, answers. The acoustics of the empty woods carry Mark's voice unsuspected to an audience—"it thrilled Mark the few times it happened, that on remarking to himself how quiet or beau-tiful it all was, Bill answered him" (136). And, later, in a stupendous (and heavily contrived) gesture of his love, Bill will surprise Mark by rigging, with the help of a generator and "miles of extension cord," "a necklace of lights" that runs along the graceful curve of the bank of the lake (146). Using his background in theater design, Bill later adds a pump to rig a water jet that shoots sixty feet up and that, when caught by the late afternoon sun, spokes into a "wedge of rainbow" (146)—it is pure spectacle, the noun. The Massachusetts lake becomes a most magic kingdom: in a most mysterious moment on the dock as Bill and Mark listen to Fred's favorite Chopin études as a memorial to him, a stray black cat suddenly jumps into Mark's lap, purrs warmly, and stirs Mark into an erection, which the cat grips before curling its thick back and stretching, its sphincter wide open. Under the tonic influence of this magic play zone, this is no simple stray cat but is accepted without questions as the restless spirit of the departed Fred.

When Mark's sister Vita comes up to Massachusetts for a visit, however, we are provided an important check on this decadent indulgence of contrived spectacle. Mark dismisses a "stupendous" waterfall that Vita finds so mesmerizing—"This is a pathetic natural occurrence" (147). He wants to show her the dazzling artifice of Bill's lakeside light show lambent against a wilderness stupidly bleeding into dusk. Vita is surely impressed by the show ("This place is magic"), but disturbed by its hokiness, its unnaturalness, its inappropriateness ("It would not occur to anyone to string electric lights around a pond in the middle of nowhere"). Even as Mark speaks of the lights as living things that speak "the language of brightness," that in Bill he has at last found a man who, like himself, understands "the point of existence is the rearrangement of the furniture" (149), Vita demurs. Such aesthetics, we understand, have justified Mark's lifelong retreat, his persistent preference for controlled enclosures, the artificial splendor suggested by the hokey spectacle of the strings of lights powered by a soundless (and appropriately) insulated generator. Vita points out in a sentence that surely speaks to the heart of spectacle realism, "Some people prefer disorder" (149), a sentence of considerable import, we gather, because of how roundly Mark and Bill ignore its suggestive insight.

We close this section uncertain; coaxed like Vita (whose name surely suggests the living sphere from which Mark retreats) by the magic spell of this exercise in retreat, willing to suspend the necessary inclinations we may have to engage the immediate (Vita, after all, describes her caseload as something out of *Snakepit*), we accord love at this narrative juncture the only power we know in our clearer moments it lacks: the ability to mend the immediate, to make it perfect. How desperately we want to end the narrative at the close of part 3 with Vita observing that in the Berkshires, far from hospitals, the illness seems to be waning. "Whatever you're doing . . . it seems to be working" (151). But it is Ferro's point that the magic of retreat cannot be sustained; the string of lights, after all, is a temporary effect compared to the thundering rainbows tossed up effortlessly and continuously by the waterfall that Vita watches. To close, we turn, as we must in AIDS narratives, to a far more immediate landscape in part 4: the very hospital that Mark found so violently sterile and inhospitable early on. It is time to move out from the magic kingdom.

*   *   *

Mark, I don't want to upset you, but it's time we faced facts.

George Valerian, Sr.

As with so many AIDS narratives, Ferro's closing chapter begins ominously: the early autumn weather in the Berkshires turns inhospitably cold; the magic black cat disappears; Mark acknowledges that his body is turning into a "map of the disease" with new lesions, raised tumors, bumpy moles. He acknowledges "it had gone through him and would not stop" (156), a decided turn toward engagement of the immediate from the same character who had a scant fifty pages earlier believed the virus could be simply pissed clean out of his system.

The education of Mark Valerian begins in earnest when Ferro gets his character—literally and metaphorically—to the hospital. Pneumonia hospitalizes Bill. That very real crisis compels Mark to reenter the sterile ugliness of a city hospital, an environment, for Ferro's purpose, of diagnosis and recovery peopled by those who struggle within the urgent moment to maintain (rather than relinquish) engagement with a most difficult immediate. Within the hospital, Mark is far from his magic kingdoms. Reminders of the infection are all about the hospital ward. The AIDS patients' doors are marked in harsh red warning signs; the entire hospital staff is gloved, masked, gowned. The atmosphere offends Mark's sensibilities: he objects to the hospital outfits as ugly and excessive; he suffers amid the smokers in the waiting room; he finds himself no longer in control as he tries to resist doctors' efforts to get him to leave Bill's room. When Bill's lung collapses during a routine bronchoscopy, Mark struggles against anxieties unfamiliar to one so determined to this

narrative point to withdraw. He waits now helplessly, feeling alone, terrified—like our other characters—by the sudden intervention of a ruthless mortality he had worked so diligently to deny.

Without medical explanation, Bill recovers as quickly as he lapsed; his
lungs reinflate on their own. The medical reversal, itself part of the
unscripted (dis)order of the natural world Mark so wholly disparages,
Bill credits weakly to "air faeries" in a moment of enchantment that
might have seemed appropriate along the Venice canals or by the lake in
the Berkshires but that is now strikingly out of place within the tiled
polish of the isolation ward. In this hospital sequence, Mark is exposed
(to use the language of infection so central to Ferro's metaphor) to critical
elements of spectacle realism: he witnesses the crippling beauty of the
harsh ad-lib of the natural world; he feels the sheer human helplessness
that he has so deftly avoided; he touches the small gratitude of the human heart that does not need to go it alone. In these closing pages, we
move not toward magic cats or Tarot cards or strings of flickering lights
or even air faeries—but rather toward the human assertion of (com)pas-
sion: Mark's wearying round-the-clock hospital vigil and, in the wake of
Bill's unexpected recovery, a quick interlude of sexual contact (Mark fel-
lates Bill when Bill exposes his erection in triumph) in the very hospital
bed in the very isolation ward where Fred died some time ago. That quieter spectacle moment reminds us what Mark must come to accept: the
fugal impulses of living and dying that make up the rhythm of the immediate.

As Bill recovers, we are tempted to co-opt the sense of enchantment.
But Ferro cannot permit such hokey magic. We close this hospital sequence on a far less enchanted note. As a gesture of encouragement (and
a promising gesture of an evolving heart), Mark visits another AIDS patient, a young man (half Mark's age) dying quite alone. Mark enters the
darkened room and stares into the boy's discolored face. It is far from the
beauty his eye has always demanded. In trying to conduct the simplest
conversation, Mark finds the boy angry, deeply resentful. The boy has
surrendered so completely to the imminent stroke of a death he finds
savagely unfair that his sole consolation as he wastes away is that everyone will face the same fate—"All of them deader than doornails" (167).
The boy savages Mark's sense of enchantment so soon after the magic
recovery of Bill: "Your lover will die, then you will; then all of them, one
after another" (167). Mark resists, but the boy will have none of Mark's

magic. "Fuck you. . . . It's better to die anyway. . . . This slimy, evil world; this cesspool, this stink and slime" (168).

Here we have the counterforce to Bill's magic air faeries: the wholesale abandonment of possibilities, the absolute dismissal of the immediate. The boy's remarks cut to the heart of Mark's self-enthronement. "Do you know some magic way? Are you any different from anyone else?" (167). Only when Mark prepares to depart does the boy set aside his prickly anger to hold Mark's open hand—only the human hand will do. That gesture, compelled not by passion but rather by compassion, holds far more promise than the earlier fellatio episode. Moved by this encounter, Mark returns to Bill's room and falls, in tears, into Bill's arms. Suddenly the narrative dispenses with the easy skein of enchantment: there are no air faeries, no protective insularity—only vulnerability, the exposure to an ugly immediate that coaxes, nevertheless, a most poignant and unexpected moment of confluence.

The showdown with the Valerian family that follows Bill's release from the hospital tracks a remarkably similar course. Mark visits his father for lunch, only to find all the family gathered. Mark feels immediately exposed; this family conclave takes place not within his fiefdom at Cape May but rather within the family home in Philadelphia. Out of his element, feeling ambushed, Mark tenses as he quickly determines the subject of this family gathering. The time has come to sell the beach house—and Mark reacts with bristling heat. He still has not learned. It is an uncomfortable moment of emotional pleading that puts the reader in a most difficult position; after all, we hear apparently what Mark will not (momentarily distracted by the room's elegant furnishing, he actually misses some of what his father says): each member of the family trying to calm Mark, reassuring him of their love, telling him that only the perilous financial collapse of the family business has compelled so drastic an action ("the whole goddamn mess is about to go under" [197]). We hear the father relent despite financial desperation ("I am at the end of my rope" [198]) and agree only to mortgage the beach house, a far more burdensome course for him but one that pacifies Mark, preserves intact his magic kingdom—a magic reprieve on par with the notion of air faeries reinflating Bill's collapsed lungs.

Paralleling the brutal scene in the hospital with the dying boy, Mark pursues his father, insisting (although the family has bowed to his intractable position) that all along the father has loathed him because of his homosexuality and has resisted any effort to bring Mark into his business because, as Mark cattily observes, he "was just a woman" (199). The father denies such a "cock-eyed" way of looking at things, but Mark persists until the father unloads a devastating critique of Mark's profession as a landscape decorator (which, from the position of a lifelong commitment to the harder business of engineering, appears to him—as he says—to be little more than glorified ditchdigging) and his vast disappointment, with a sweeping gesture about his own opulent home, that his son would never achieve this. It is as brutal an assessment of Mark's life as the dying boy offers from the pool of shadows in the hospital bed—brutal, but honest.

Mark's reaction—a sobbing fit—moves toward a (predictable) (melo)-dramatic explosion against the hapless father. Mark wails that the family is just waiting for him to die, a most immoderate response to a father's honesty. The father quickly assures Mark that such is not the case (indeed, the logic track from the father's observation about the modest prospects of a professional decorator to the notion he therefore wants Mark to die is difficult to trace); all the family quickly acts to console the piqued second son. But Mark is far too impressed by his own dilemma and angrily tells the distraught father that he and Bill are "going away" (204)—an abrupt announcement (predictably to flee) that he knows will cause only further agony for a father already fingering the ends of the rope. What finally stops this slide and completes the education of Mark Valerian is an improbable exchange of letters with his friend, Matthew Black, about a ludicrous venture to launch a rocketful of gays toward a planet that Matthew claims is known as Splendora near the star Sirius.

*   *   *

Doesn't it seem as if autumn were the real creator, more creative than spring, which all at once is; more creative, when it comes with its will to change and destroy the much too-finished, much-too-satisfied picture of summer.

Rainer Maria Rilke

By every measure, Mark Valerian should be enthralled by even the possibility of Splendora. Everything we know about his character suggests that should a rocket of unhappy gays be launched to a distant planet peopled only by gorgeous, terribly polite, thoroughly gay humanoids ("long, lean, delicate, in the sense of a swimmer's body as opposed to a fullback's" [189]), a magic kingdom planet faraway where the misfit

Earthlings could live in harmony and health in the protective pocket of deep space, Mark Valerian would be among the first to volunteer. As Matthew Black fills his letters with details of the so-called Lambda Project, Splendora becomes a significant element of the closing chapters; but it is far from a campy comic relief sci-fi fantasy amid the novel's darker argument, a narrative version of the enchanting distraction of the strings of lights that bespeckle the dusky rim of Fred's lake.[7] Matthew Black, a fortyish recluse-writer tending to a mother dying slowly in a rest home, offers a disturbing study in Mark Valerian's impulse to seclusion taken to its logical and menacing conclusion—and provides our study with the clearest glimpse yet of the darker logic of the Reagan Era's magic kingdom.

What is Matthew Black offering? To understand Splendora, we must make sense of the character of Matthew Black. We know from the caustic commentary of his letters that he is wholly uninterested in connection; he dislikes the bay on which he lives because it is so often violated by noisy families ("When the wind is wrong you can hear children having a good time, which after a crying baby is the most irritating sound known to man" [142]). He fights with his elderly neighbor over a screen of trees he has planted to ensure his privacy—"his" leaves drop on the neighbor's lawn (in response, he "accidentally" nips the woman's dog with his lawn mower and coldly wishes on her the living death his hospitalized mother is enduring). When he vacations, he heads to Mexico, to scuba dive, to relish the underwater privacy afforded by miles of coral reefs. Apart from weekly visits from his infirm mother, he is quite alone. When his sister comes to spell him in the tending of the mother, he goes off on solitary jaunts. Gay, he disparages the possibility of romance ("What is needed is a condom bodysuit" [143]); he settles for the easy friction of anonymous sexual engagement. At a bar in Gainesville he is nearly swooning when he believes he is to have a parking lot encounter with a patron, who at the last moment retreats to the security of the bar.

Perhaps because of the grinding business of witnessing his mother's slide toward death in a rest home that is haunted by the moans of the forgotten dying, perhaps because of the monasticism forced on him given the dangerous reality of promiscuity, perhaps because he is himself infected with the virus, when Matthew concocts Splendora it is far more than a feathery fantasy. To read the letters of Matthew Black (his very name indicates the dark tenor of his position) is to read a brooding apocalyptic jeremiad that not only describes a projected trip away from Earth but envisions an Earth that is itself left a ruined, contaminated shell damned by nuclear annihilation or by environmental collapse. This unavoidable catastrophe draws from him only the darkest satisfactions, much as he smugly observes that the *Challenger* astronauts who vaulted for the sky ended up being "hauled out of the sea like tuna" (66). In offering Splendora, Matthew not merely indulges the longing as a gay for a climate of toleration but turns on the Earth that has made toleration inaccessible and pronounces a sentence of absolute doom.

Like the resentful boy in the hospital who sees all the people about him someday dead as flies, Matthew offers a death wish—save that his is tendered for an entire species ("total planetary blight. Rather like Mars" [207]). A writer, he exerts his imagination professionally to fashion private zones, text-sites, under his control—a man remarkably like Mark Valerian (and, of course, our other central characters). In his vision of the quicksilver demise of the Earth, Matthew abandons the immediate as hopelessly poisonous, the logical extension of Mark's own secret delight in withdrawal, his odd distaste for the (im)perfect (dis)order of the natural realm, his fondness for those tight spheres that fall entirely under his control, his bristling rejection of his family's simplest gesture of support and kindness. But even as Bill succumbs to the fantasy, toys with the idea of committing money to the project, Mark intuits the danger of Matthew's offer and ultimately declines to participate; such magic, he says, is madness. Splendora is simply not for him. "I would like to believe in this. . . . But I think not. . . . I don't believe this has anything to do with me, with us. It is not real. Or if it is, it is not real enough, or real to anyone but you and your Lambdans" (209–10).

The narrative now moves quietly toward engaging the immediate. Counterbalancing Matthew's menacing fantasy of Splendora, we are introduced to the benign figure of Dr. Theo Thompson. Amid the flurry of Splendora letters, Mark goes in for a checkup. He notices that Dr. Thompson has stopped dying his mustache and has let it grow its natural bone-white, has in effect stopped prettying up the natural, resisting the natural rhythms of time. We are then treated to a page-long summary of Dr. Thompson's meticulous examination of Mark, an inventory that includes weighing Mark and taking his blood pressure (numbers we are given), palpating his liver and spleen, checking his throat glands and his newest lesions, and sharing his pride over the regularity and consistency of his most recent bowel movements. We are given in short a most immediate, a most physical Mark.

Set against the alternative of Splendora is the possibility extended to Mark through Dr. Thompson of a new blood treatment using Interferon that promises little but the tenuous promise of "perhaps." It is a largely untested treatment that may involve retaining fluids, organ shutdowns, fever, breathing impairment, constant nausea. And, more important, the blood treatment demands that Mark's family participates in a search for compatible blood types. No longer can Mark rely on the tight private sphere he has enclosed about Bill. The long-shot blood treatment represents to Mark what the planned refinancing of the beach house offers to the father: a chance to fight, not the magic of rejuvenation (as Mark decides when he sees his invigorated father preparing at the age of seventy-five to scrap back from financial ruin) but rather the struggle for rejuvenation. Undertaking the treatment program pulls Mark toward what he has resisted: the hard realities of his own illness, the embrace of his own imperfect family, the pettiness of his dogged strategy to defy their attempts at care and concern as intrusive. He finds them each willing to be tested (even the father who is not even a compatibility candidate); and it is George the reptile, George the oppressive older brother, it is George who proves to be the workable match. His willingness to help is quickly given. He even deploys a private detective to locate Bill's brother in Phoenix so that Bill can also participate in the program. The connection, at last, is made; only the human hand, we recall, will do.

In the closing pages, Mark shoulders his way to confront the natural world he has so elegantly dodged. He resolves to do what we each must do within the iron grip of the immediate: accept the meaningful absurdity of suffering, the hard unscriptedness of mortality, the inevitable grief over our own temporarity, the natural anxiety over the evident simplicity with which our much vaunted presence transmutes to sheer absence. We have come a far way from our initial encounter with Mark Valerian perched, binoculars in hand, a spectator safely interred within a ghost house. By the close of the narrative, Mark understands that rejuvenation comes not from miracle clouds of radiation, not from Tarot cards, not from the enchanting spell of perfect romance, not from running away, and not from angry fantasies of resentment against those not infected, but rather from the struggle itself. Of course, the blood treatment offers no magic; indeed, AIDS demands closure. There is no survivability—a condition, by the way, that extends to anyone drawing breath and reading these words. But we close not in the cold absolute of winter; we leave Mark where, in fact, everyone at middle age is left: in a sweet problematic autumn, too far from spring and too near to winter. We watch as Mark and Bill shoulder their way to the responsibility of winter, prepare for closure: they secure the beach house for the harsher season they realize they cannot contain, cannot interrupt, cannot stop. In a moment of panic, Bill and Mark calm each other by the simplest commitment to each other, a promise that no matter what, they will stay fast by each other.

Much as the assertion of human fusion is set in *Quinn's Book* against a Civil War still raging (Lincoln has even called for a national day of fasting in an effort to bring peace), Mark and Bill, amid the carnage of a very different war, embrace (like Daniel and Maud) the slender wonder available, finally, to everyone: the (un)glittering magic of the immediate, (in)elegant and (un)scripted. Mark closes the novel planning to expand the beach house to accommodate his siblings' families for longer summer visits. Mark has come by narrative close to confront with dignity the natural world he has so long sought to reshape; it is the natural world of impermanence suggested by the Florida lake about which Matthew Black writes (with predictable disgust), one that moves, with the reassuring cycle of a "working lake," through periods of smothering algae capable of temporarily killing the lake followed by fallow periods when such growth provides oxygen and a source of food for the lake's delicate ecosystem. That balance, that (un)scripted system of coming and going that shapes the argument of the immediate (we recall the family fascination with the youngest sister's yo-yoing weight swings), is the awkward beauty Mark the decorator finally comes to accept. He turns from the implications of his own name, steps away from his valerian need to perfume, to calm, to relieve, to sedate.

We end as the autumn sun burnishes the beach, etches longer shadows, yes, but coaxes a most splendid bright yellow from the clumps of goldenrod. We close with Mark and Bill in the tower accepting what we all (save Enid Stevick, John Wheelwright, and Kate Vaiden) must: our splendid helplessness. We close not with cheesy strings of lights and miles of extension cords but rather with the cold warmth of the autumn sun and the pinpricks of starlight on autumn nights that speak a far different language of brightness. We reject the spectacle and embrace the spectacle real. Mark closes with his eyes now on the horizon, by day and by night, accepting what each of us must come to accept, a dilemma that is made frankly immediate by the AIDS virus but is nevertheless part of the inevitable growth of any human awareness: the compelling wonder over the harsh logic of animated matter in which our engendering posits termination, the stunning (dis)order of the vast system of a natural world that will not acknowledge our petty anger over our inevitable sense of a severing-too-soon, our shrill frustration over our own temporariness, our melodramatic sense of lost empowerment, but that offers as strategy only the gene-deep compulsion we intuit—whether gay or straight—to secure an open hand to enclose our own. The secret, much as with Kennedy, is fusion; we recall what dooms the Splendora project, why the rocket can never leave, is its inability to resolve the problem of fusion.

We could, then, stop here. We have departed the magic kingdom; we have engaged the difficult immediate compelled by chance and closing in the graceless cutting intrusion of mortality. We have worked from Enid's cowardly resistance to Mark's autumnal celebrations of perhaps, of possibility, of the (in)significance of our impermanence and the splendid (dis)order of the trampoline immediate. Pressured by the considerable gravity of imminent mortality, Mark Valerian forsakes the magic kingdoms he fashions by trade professionally and by choice privately. He makes the very connections Enid Stevick and John Wheelwright and Kate Vaiden refuse: to family, to mortality, to helplessness, to the risk of confluence, to the power of compassion, to the determination to continue within the struggle that is by definition beyond our control. Unlike Daniel Quinn, who embraces fusion amid such spectacle by way of inexplicable touches of the fantastic, here a character, his body shot through with an irreversible virus and preparing for a battery of debilitating tests that promises only the slenderest of perhaps, determines that the only strategy that makes sense is to forsake apartness for a partness.

It is a splendid settlement. But it leaves us, rather, in a dilemma. Must death mother such awareness? Must the affirmative dazzle of spectacle realism be reserved for those who register cell-deep the creeping invasion of death? We will move now to consider a character who must confront a similar and by now familiar sense of helplessness, a character who begins in a magic kingdom where she imagines control, a woman who must turn, finally, to face not the dramatic intervention of closure but rather the unglittering banality of the grinding routine that, at her middle age moment, has only begun the work of slowly ingesting her dreams. We turn now to track her movement toward recovering the affirmation of a dying Mark Valerian. We turn now to Anne Tyler's Maggie Moran.

6

"That Sudden Shock of Sunshine and Birdsong"

Anne Tyler, *Breathing Lessons*

I want to sit on a couch with a regular, normal husband and watch TV for a thousand years.

Serena Gill, in *Breathing Lessons*

If, as Robert Ferro shows, the affirmative impulse toward engagement, awareness, and community that defines spectacle realism faces a difficult challenge in the advent of the AIDS virus, consider such an impulse in the face of the premise of television, the fate of any challenge to affirm the immediate within a culture now conditioned for more than forty years by the virtual realities and synthetic environments of television. The more absorbed we have grown within our tube-world (and surely the explosion in cable technology during the 1980s only broadened television's tentacled reach), the more comfortable we have become within its electronic playscapes, and the more distant and inaccessible the immediate has become. The neat realities concocted within the increasingly wider frames of our television sets become our most seductive (and most accessible) magic kingdoms, the ultimate play zones, the ultimate controlled environments, open twenty-four hours a day. We have become distressingly at odds with the immediate that waits, bursting with unsuspected promise, just beyond the neat borders of the television. To borrow from Ira Moran's agoraphobic sister in Anne Tyler's *Breathing Lessons*, everything looks better on television—neater, squared, manageable. Although Tyler's 1988 novel explores the shape of a life pressured by the (ir)resistible influence of a popular culture that has gained within the last fifty years unprecedented access to our daily lives—the narrative is threaded with references to commercial films of the 1950s, to television situation comedies and daytime dramas, and to pop songs from the 1950s to the early 1970s—it is television that becomes significant subtext to the narrative of Maggie and Ira Moran and their daylong drive to Pennsylvania to help bury the husband of Serena Gill, a high school friend of Maggie's.

It is perhaps not so surprising that Tyler finds particularly attractive the "zany" world of situation comedies and the melodramatic angst of afternoon soap operas.[1] After all, sitcoms and soaps have chronicled now for nearly two generations the very terrain of Tyler's novels—the dynamics of the American home.[2] Without condescending, without handwringing, Tyler understands that to a large degree we come to measure our lives against the confections sold to us on television, that centuries hence cultural archaeologists looking into Maggie's era must look not in libraries (Maggie, who abandons plans to become an English teacher, acknowledges her library books, tomes by Dostoyevsky and Mann, have stayed "unread and seriously overdue" [218] in her car's backseat) but rather in *TV Guide*. And *Breathing Lessons* is most clearly tuned to the argument of television. Sets are on in scene after scene; they can be heard next door; they dye the scenery with their blue-staccato flicker. Even in the crossroads town of Deer Lick where Ira and Maggie drive for the funeral, television antennae are strapped to every chimney. Characters long for uneventful lives spent in the quiescence of television watching. On a Baltimore radio call-in show that asks listeners what makes an ideal marriage, one caller insists that marriage works best when "you both watch the same kind of programs on TV" (5).

So keenly is Tyler drawn to the influence of television, *Breathing Lessons* actually simulates the experience of watching television. The breezy episodic plot recalls the rhythms natural to sitcoms. Maggie's day, indeed her entire life, reads like a compilation of *TV Guide* listings: tonight, Maggie goes on and off a crazy snack-food diet; tonight, Maggie dents the car when she is sent to pick it up at the body shop; hilarity ensues tonight when Maggie recalls how she first met Ira when she mistakenly thought he had died; tonight, that zany Maggie dresses in a red wig and sunglasses to visit her own granddaughter; laughs abound tonight when a hunky store clerk mistakenly thinks Maggie is trying to pick him up; tonight, Maggie surprises her granddaughter with a kitten, only to find out she is allergic to cats; tonight's Best Bet—Maggie's plot to reunite her son and his ex-wife over a fried chicken dinner goes wildly awry; tonight, Maggie and Ira try to change a tire on a highway except that Maggie has forgotten to replace the spare; et cetera; et cetera.

In addition, Maggie and Ira both play to familiar sitcom types: Maggie, the lovable ditz, the "flibbertigibbet" (12), the "goofball" (43), the "whifflehead" (33) fighting diets and denting cars; Ira, the frazzled, long-suffering husband. Tyler's supporting cast plays on sitcom stereotypes— a cloying mother-in-law, a wacky best friend, a drifting loser of a son, a coolly distant daughter (a teenager who within the improbable logic of sitcoms wants to be a quantum physicist), an aging father-in-law convinced without medical verification of his own bad ticker, a spacey daughter-in-law who *studies* cosmetology and finds wisdom in rock and roll lyrics. Tyler's plot is sustained, as in sitcoms, by misunderstandings that only with great effort are finally ironed out; the novel offers the broad slapstick humor typical of sitcoms and frequently indulges the hyperartificial sitcom contrivance of flashbacks; and the narrative moves toward a touching moment of wisdom that freely recalls a sitcom's warm closing moments. To complete the simulacrum, Maggie and Ira encounter a registry of trademarks of commercial America that provides the narrative/sitcom with commercial breaks; it is a novel brought to you by Pepsi, Baby Ruth, Dodge, Fritos, Jell-O, Cool Whip, Kleenex, Breyer's Ice Cream, Kool-Aid, Texaco, Frisbee, Dairy Queen, Fresca, Affinity shampoo, Hershey's, Aim toothpaste, Ivory Soap, and Hallmark cards and locally by an assortment of Baltimore restaurants and businesses. And structurally, each of the novel's three sections closes in the slow fade and dissolve reminiscent of 1950s televisions; indeed, at the close of the first section, when Maggie and Ira walk in the afternoon heat to their car in the church parking lot, she imagines that because of "some trick of sunlight or heat" a stone house they pass dissolves slowly and then re-forms "solid again" (121), much like an image on an old television that is shut off and then switched back on.

But why? Why appropriate so much of television's logic? Clearly, with Maggie Moran, Tyler reveals that television has introduced into her generation a dilemma new to the arts: real influence, influence that is measured in *hours per day* we spend absorbing its narcotic calm. How have we handled this massive influence? Without voicing the elitist screeds, Tyler argues that the models for how our immediate world should work have come to emulate what we watch day and night, that we have as guide only those most accessible versions of life moments. Steeped within the casual accidents of contingency, dancing with halting step to the often brutal choreography of chance so familiar to the characters of spectacle realism, we burn for our lives to have the neatness, the unearned resolution, the sheer sanity conferred by the frame of the television. We yearn to transmute the sturdy tube of the television into a mirror; we yearn to reside in its comforting wasteland, to join in the inanity of a world where sorrow cannot touch; where wisdom is accessible; where resolution is never more than a commercial break away; where stress is merely confusion; where each resident plots the day's events with care and feels the generous benediction when such plots, in turn, generate purpose and secure dignity. As if gassed in our sleep, we have little choice but to be affected by television—after all, homes *average* three televisions. Eerily, in our most emotional moments, tonic or catastrophic, we cannot avoid sounding (as they do here in Tyler's narrative) like the innocuous palaver from an afternoon soap.

More particular to Tyler's focus, the widely embraced format of the sitcom steadily feeds us, framed as possible, families that we simply cannot mimic in our lives—cooperative homes that never splinter but rather head into syndication; families disarmingly free of the sorry trivia that routinely rends our own imperfect domestic worlds. And these families, these smiling combines of affection, humor, and understanding, these families, whom we see weekly, in some cases daily, grow more familiar to us than members of our own extended families. Without condescending, Tyler suggests that we come to measure our lives against these confections, the tyrannical assertions of now five decades of sitcoms that, in coincidental conspiracy, have manufactured such irresistible formulas without accountability, without acknowledging that our best efforts to find our way to such neatness inevitably leave us with the souring sense of accepting less. Television converts its absolute absence—after all, its physical content is a matrix of transmitted waves and light radiation—into undeniable presence, much like the dehumidifier in Maggie's basement whose hum she still imagines she hears even when it is switched off for the season. It becomes an influence impossible to resist—like the passive smoking that so alarms Maggie.

Surely, such liberal access to television sours us on what is immediate, the very geography of spectacle realism. We have become, perhaps unintentionally, agoraphobics, distanced from even the simplest encounter with the unscripted immediate. When the heavy moment comes to darken the tube, we turn uncertain how to accept the sheer banality of our lives so clearly untouched by the tube's benediction. Tyler's characters fear that their lives will drop into the vast irrelevancy of "unvaryingness" (158). Our nightly dinner talk fails to shine; our arguments with each other never approach wit; our romances will not work out; our mistakes fail to find their way to the uncomplicating sweetness of a good laugh; our most egregious "bloopers" cannot be edited and reshot; with puzzling stubbornness, our deepest emotional catastrophes will not work out in thirty minutes (twenty-two minutes with commercials); our neighbors fail to provide comic relief or unsuspected wisdom or unfailing support; our confusions stay confusing; our families rift into irresistible fissures; our love stales like bread left out; and ultimately we sag, erode, and then trundle off inelegantly to die, our significance left unsuspected by the larger world. How desperately we measure ourselves against the logic of sitcoms, fast-food entertainment that we dismiss in our saner moments as embarrassingly meager even as we covet its simplest assumptions about family, home, love, and marriage. How much we hunger for what we know is junk.

Maggie Moran, who spends most of the narrative complaining about her crash diet and craving junk food, surely demonstrates this hunger. She traffics easily in the logic of sitcom television, mushy 1950s movies, and Top 40 songs. Indeed, although she often disdains such influence, Maggie lives very much within the public space defined, illuminated, animated by such media, but most particularly by television. In Maggie Moran, Anne Tyler explores a woman who comes of age within the first generation of television; she is among that first generation of women, wives and mothers, whose immediate domestic worlds, whose emotional relationships, whose entire apprehension of the immediate would have to weigh in against the clean models fashioned within the magic kingdom of the television. But as with Daniel Quinn whose private drama inevitably revealed a cultural drama as well, Tyler's novel, so touched by the public realm of popular culture, reminds us that the massive infatuation with the logic of television extends as well to our cultural moment. Indeed, the Reagan Era to which Tyler's novel is directed, with its free abandonment of too-pressing realities, its careful manipulation of visual spectacles, its cold determination to press and mold event into uptempo plots, its easy simplification of people into manageable caricatures, plays (and replays now in a sort of perpetual political syndication) as a sort of cozy national sitcom that we sat and watched, entranced by its comforting show. *Breathing Lessons* reminds us that under the wide and generous touch of Reagan, himself a comforting talking head from the golden era of television, we reconstructed the unfolding drama of our national life into neat plot. Thus the education of Maggie Moran, indeed the entire premise of her tele-vision and her deep need for plot, speaks to its wider cultural moment.

Television has created in Maggie Moran—and within her culture—a most awkward interior tension, one familiar by now to us, between re-treat and engagement. Maggie begins her narrative just beyond midlife, unsuspecting that her life has in fact been a long strategic disengagement from the immediate; indeed, she begins the narrative with a satisfied sense of midlife security. Yet we suspect that the character's self-percep-tion is skewed; again spectacle realism deploys irony to make suspect the sympathy we generously extend to a central character. We note, for in-stance, that Maggie is always hungry: she must have a quick breakfast of "faucet coffee and cold cereal" (3) because she oversleeps, and all day she picks at junk food and never has a real meal. Maggie's hunger, which she attends to with vending machine Doritos and spoonfuls of gritty Jell-O, suggests a much greater emptiness. Indeed, at narrative opening, Maggie is heading for Deer Lick, a site that suggests providing necessary nourishment to those helpless vulnerables locked within a most unfor-giving environment.

With Maggie, we are given another character with much to learn, a character who has delayed the chore of enlightenment. Despite Maggie's age, Tyler regularly introduces education as part of the narrative. We stand on the very threshold of a massive education experience: tomor-row, Maggie's daughter, Daisy, leaves for college. Maggie herself recalls, at eighteen, despite being at the head of her high school class, deciding against her family's hopes for college to work as a lowly nursing assistant at a local retirement home; Maggie's ex-daughter-in-law, Fiona, has re-turned to cosmetology to improve her career options; in midtext, Maggie's best friend, Serena, empathetically tells Maggie that, with her nest emptying, she should resume her education; and Maggie observes that when she and Ira first stop to eat, the diner smells like a "grade-school lunchroom" (27).

Maggie begins the narrative much like the proverbial child who sat too close to the television, her vision blurred by the tube. Television, more specifically the seductive packaging of family and marriage premised by her generation's ingestion of the sitcom, has made Maggie Moran into a plotter. In her attempt to understand her life into plot, Maggie plans. But in such frenetic plotting, she is victimized by a dream that is not even hers; it comes to her secondhand, concocted by the resources of the fantasy machinery of a too-accessible popular culture. In the novel's centerpiece episode, Daniel Otis, whom the Morans meet on the road to Deer Lick, tells them that he is living out of his suitcase because he fought with his wife of fifty years over a dream she had in which he stands with both feet on a chair that she has carefully embroidered and then walks all over her other precious needlework. When she awakes, she chastises him and claims the dream showed her that he is careless man, and she wishes that fifty years earlier she had made a sounder choice. Daniel Otis becomes a victim of a dream that is not even his. His wife mistakes an illusion for the appropriate measure of real life—a dangerous confusion that here has led to a shattered home. It is our penalty, Tyler warns her character and her era, for acting as if dreams are real and then judging our lives by the criteria of such flimsy confections. Ironically, Maggie dismisses the domestic fight Otis describes: "I mean think if we all did that! Mistook our dreams for real life" (152).

Maggie conceives of her life (much as she does this Saturday) as a trip toward something, her every emotional moment part of a complex journey that, much like the simplest sitcom plot, has the grace of logic. Maggie begins the narrative resisting the ordinary, seeing in it only the assurance of quiet extinction after plodding through years of meaningless motion—the tacky stuff of the ordinary that unfolds on this side of the television tube. While talking with a waitress at the roadside diner early in the novel, Maggie recalls her daughter's accusation, asserted over Maggie's tuna casserole, that somewhere along the line Maggie must have consciously decided to "settle for being ordinary" (30). It is a notion that sends Maggie even now fumbling for her ever-present wad of Kleenex. As she quickly explains, "I mean, to *me* I'm not ordinary" (31, italics Tyler's—or, perhaps, Maggie's). When Maggie initially decides against college to work at the retirement home, her stunned mother demands to know if Maggie wants "to be just ordinary" (92). Maggie's son, Jesse, disenchanted by the first months of fatherhood and clinging to his adolescent dreams of fronting a heavy metal band, rejects outright the life of an ordinary father "with those busywork visits to the zoo and small-talk suppers at McDonald's" (203). While she is in school with Maggie, Serena flaunts most unconventional behavior, in part because as a child born out of wedlock she was naturally on the fringes of social acceptance. She comes to school in outrageous outfits, eats exotic lunches of sardines, and happily strolls about PTA meetings with a mother in leopard tights. And yet Serena dates only "plaid-shirt boys, the gym-sneaker boys," covets "everydayness," a condition she will compare when she marries a most conventional sort to "slipping off a girdle" (109). For much of the text, the ordinary represents only the ironic freedom from the demands of any emotional energy, a heavy stasis that more than justifies our deepest anxieties over its oppressive weight.

*   *   *

> *When I was just a little boy*
> *I asked my teacher, "What should I be?*
> *Should I paint pictures? Should I sing songs?"*
> *Here's what she said to me," Que sera, sera*
> *(Whatever will be, will be).*

Jay Livingston and Ray Evans, "Que Sera, Sera"

> *Same old song, just a drop of water in an endless sea.*
> *All we do crumbles to the ground, though we refuse to see.*
> *Dust in the wind—all we are is dust in the wind.*

Kerry Livgren, "Dust in the Wind"

Thus, it is plotting, not plodding, that interests Maggie. Much like Lucy Ricardo, who dominated sitcom television for Maggie's generation and who appropriately figures prominently in Maggie's characterization—her hair color (it feels coppery red in the afternoon heat), her stoic husband, her hypercontrived antics—Maggie (not Ira/Ricky) compels the action. Although Ira is behind the wheel virtually all day, Maggie directs the day's trip. She insists on attending Max Gill's funeral against the wishes of Ira, who sees the trip only as a wasted Saturday; on the way back from the funeral service, she demands that Ira turn around to help Daniel Otis; Maggie proposes the side trip to visit Fiona and their granddaughter, Leroy; Maggie maneuvers Fiona and Leroy into returning to Baltimore that afternoon to attempt what turns out to be a disastrous reunion with Jesse. Much like Daniel Quinn in his newspaper office or Mark Valerian in his gardens, Maggie finds joy in such plotting; she relishes the feeling of control, the sense of impact. For Maggie, not to plot is to accept the unacceptable: the sheer flatline of the ordinary where events stupidly knock against one another, a descendental vision of a sorry and shabby immediate that recalls traditional realistic fictions.

But in the face of the evidence of her family's collapsing construct, Maggie's rosy perceptions are disquieting; her unflagging sunniness is suspect, finally unbearable (like the blistering afternoon sun, despite its being mid-September, that so bothers both Maggie and Ira). Interestingly, Maggie's birthday is 14 February, the day when our most fervent fantasies about love and its possibilities (fueled, indeed created, by pop culture) are given their twenty-four hours, when we suspend for a moment the nagging realities of engaging emotional relationships and celebrate the true love, ideal love, many-splendored love hymned by Top 40 songs, by sitcom families, and by the Doris Day movies that are part of Maggie's development. It is the day most all of us spend in the magic kingdom, a day of illusions penned in by 364 other days when we must work on our emotional investments. Maggie recalls that when Jesse was a child he would happily plot the most imaginative tales for her while she would do her housework, fanciful tales told (much like television narratives) to beguile those otherwise gridlocked by routine. Maggie recalls Jesse's stories: a woman who feeds her children only doughnuts; a man who lives on top of a Ferris wheel; a retarded man who buys an organ with his grocery money—tales of reckless "joyousness" (230), effortless extravagance and satisfaction, magic and possibility. But they are as well tales that deny the simplest realities: the children would either die of heart-choking obesity or weary of such relentless indulgence; the man on the Ferris wheel would yearn for the reliable stability of the ground; the retarded man would starve. They are stories that—like Maggie's plottings, like those spun on television, like the edifice of Reagan's America itself—fall ironically from the weight of their own embarrassingly flimsy fantasy.

Like our other characters, then, Maggie lodges within a tensive relationship with the immediate. On the way to the memorial service, she suddenly bolts the car in a huff when Ira objects to her confiding so extensively to the waitress at the diner. Maggie walks along the hot Maryland highway and plots out a new life for herself: getting a job (waiting tables or scrubbing floors), sleeping in haystacks in open barns or in no-frills hotels, living off her two credit cards until Ira, undoubtedly, cancels them, then steadily building up her savings while living "in a perfect boarding house, dirt cheap, with kitchen privileges, full of kindhearted people" (37). For five wearying pages, Maggie happily de/reconstructs a life without her family, even sticking a blue chicory flower behind her ear in a parody of carefree counterculture freedom; the plans, with their stunning sense of areality, are more appropriate to the plot of some fluffy sitcom than the practical plans of a grown woman who has just bolted from a car in the middle of Maryland. Later, when she first meets Serena at the memorial service, she will hurriedly pull off the chicory flower, uneasy by such dopey fantasies within a pressing environment of sobering accommodation.

But Maggie does such blithe reconstructions often. To see her granddaughter when Fiona first moved away with Leroy, Maggie considered—in addition to actually dressing up in a wig and sunglasses and prowling about playgrounds—impersonating a Girl Scout leader, maybe "renting a little Girl Scout of her own" (18). At the nursing home, Maggie fell briefly under the spell of a dapper older resident named Mr. Gabriel and imagined leaving Ira, then moving into the rest home and sleeping in Mr. Gabriel's convalescence bed. The day Fiona moved out of Maggie's house when she discovered Jesse's infidelity, Maggie convinced herself that her prolonged absence most likely indicated that, while buying teething biscuits at a local convenience store, Fiona and Leroy had been taken hostage by desperate robbers. When Maggie discovered cigarette rolling papers in Daisy's room, she had all but constructed a secret life of a pothead for her brainy daughter when Daisy tells her after school that the papers helped her keep her flute keys from sticking. Maggie's is a mind fueled by the looping narrative spin of plottings; early in the day, when she hears Fiona on the Baltimore radio call-in show discussing her approaching remarriage, Maggie spins out an extraordinary plot involving Fiona's new husband, whom she of course has never met, a plot that begins with his hidden life as a child molester and ends with Maggie's fretting over who will take care of Fiona's new baby with this man, a child of course not even conceived. For most of the book, this pending remarriage ironically serves as Maggie's reality; it impels her to insist on the side trip to Cartwheel to visit Fiona and on the elaborate machinations of a reunion dinner—ironic, given that, as she later discovers, it is not even Fiona on the radio.

Maggie's tele-vision, however, marginalizes that huge discrepancy. For most of the narrative, her assumption carries the weight of (f)actuality and even Fiona's revelation of its fundamental error when they are visiting does not abate the fury of Maggie's plotting. For all but the closing pages of Tyler's narrative, illusions assume the heft of the real—like the apple pie recipe Maggie remembers that called for no apples at all, just pressed Ritz crackers soaked in cider. Maggie refuses to accommodate the immediate, much as her kitchen calendar still shows August although it is mid-September.

The novel's most extended episode—the meeting with the elderly motorist Daniel Otis—centers on just such an effortless conflation of fact and illusion. Maggie, miffed over a car's dangerously erratic swerving, eggs Ira to pass the car and then points to the car's back tire and motions to the driver that the tire is loose. Even as she is signaling, however, Maggie notes that the driver is, in fact, elderly and black, and when Ira drives off, she immediately fears the driver will think she is racist (in typical fashion, she hyperconcludes that the man will consider her a member of the Klan) and insists that Ira turn back to let the man know his tire is actually fine. They find the old man inspecting his tires on the side of the road, but when they try to reassure him, he resists. "I did see a bit of a jiggling motion to it" (142). He has Ira test-drive the car. Now Maggie acknowledges that yes, the wheel does look funny, does look "kind of squashy" (143). Effortlessly, reality and illusion slide into each other.

Maggie comfortably resides in a textwide magic kingdom where (as with television) the most outlandish assumptions are designated as real. We recall the odd circumstances under which Maggie first meets Ira. As a young woman caught between a college career and the unexpected fulfillment she finds working at the retirement home, Maggie hears at church choir practice of the accidental death in army boot camp of a young man from the church, Ira Moran. Convincing herself (and her stunned boyfriend) that she is genuinely worked up over such a loss (although she barely knows Ira), she sends off an emotional letter to the family, only to find days later, when a puzzled Ira stops in during practice, that she had been told the wrong name. That letter of condolence becomes, like all of Maggie's looping plots, (in)authentic, a most troubling sort of counterfeit; despite its appearance of engaging a difficult immediate, it is actually a wholesale retreat from it.

Maggie's determination that her family will reveal plot is not an escape (as with Enid Stevick) nor a bolting from the immediate (as with Kate Vaiden) nor even a shelter (as with John Wheelwright and Mark Valerian) but rather, like the first responsibility given to Maggie at the retirement home (washing windows), the exacting act of improvement. In the novel's opening scene, Maggie walks to a neighborhood body shop to pick up the car, "an elderly gray-blue Dodge" (4). She is pleased to find its bumpers straightened, its trunk lid replaced, its crimps ironed out, its rust dappled over with paint. It all creates a most satisfying illusion of newness that defies the sorry record of dings and scrapes that are the stuff of the car's experience so meticulously cataloged by Tyler. No need, as Ira had argued, to buy a new car; here, the illusion sustains and permits us to renege on negotiating the immediate. Tyler, of course, cannot brook such strategy—the car is bashed even as Maggie drives it out of the garage—but the logic of denial via easy restoration is evident in the narrative. On the highway, Maggie will notice a billboard advertising Bubba McDuff's School of Cosmetology, an association with cosmetic restoration linked to the miraculous by a companion billboard about Jesus' love; Fiona is improving her lot at her beauty parlor by securing a license to perform electrolysis, the painful removal of the embarrassing evidence of our too-human imperfections. Indeed, Maggie's daylong plot to reunite Fiona and Jesse is premised on simply denying the material evidence of the more than seven years of their estrangement. It is surely telling that Maggie spends so much time as they drive to Deer Lick rummaging through her purse looking for her sunglasses. With them on, "[e]verything turned muted and more elegant" (9); with them securely on, Maggie quite happily can see clearly only the "small, rounded tip" of her own nose (16).

Snugly sunglassed, Maggie will not approach the massive disappointment of her family. Like Mark Valerian, indeed like every central character within our texts, the immediate, unredeemed and woefully unscripted, cannot command her interest, much less her wonder. Maggie insists on imposing narrative line onto the sheer antidrama of her family's botched and clumsy lives. When they inevitably fail to find their way to the perfect templates proffered by pop culture, Maggie scripts her own plots. During their side trip to Cartwheel, Maggie convinces Fiona to return to Baltimore to attempt a reunion with Jesse only by telling her a much elaborated story of how Jesse, now seven years after the marriage imploded, still sleeps with Fiona's tortoiseshell plastic soapbox, a lie of such scale that Jesse himself later dismisses even the notion of such a gesture with a derisive scoff, sure that it must be a joke.

What concerns the reader, however, is that this effortlessly spun plot, so convincing and so probable, is hardly unique in Maggie's experience. Years earlier, Maggie convinces Fiona not to abort the child she conceived with Jesse because (as Maggie tells her melodramatically in front of the abortion clinic) Jesse has begun to take fatherhood so seriously that he is fashioning a homemade crib for the baby—which she later "proves" by bringing out wooden rods (which prove, ultimately, to be parts of a drying rack Ira is putting together). And later while Fiona is delivering, Maggie plays up the role of the nervous grandmother-to-be, wildly exaggerating to total strangers in the waiting room the seriousness of Fiona's early delivery. Long before, when Maggie is first dating Ira, when she barely knows him, she concocts a most dramatic series of exaggerations about Ira's irresistibility for the benefit of Ira's meddlesome father when the father suggests that Ira, so committed to his family, would never become involved with a woman. Even as part of the nursing staff at Silver Threads Retirement Village, Maggie distorts the sterner medical evidence to convince herself and her terminal patients that they are not what they are—lost causes. Importantly, Maggie refused to pursue suggestions that she become a nurse, a career that would compel her to deal honestly with the immediate.

Maggie's doomed attempt to put her family together one more time at her dining room table is yet another lost cause she refuses to abandon. Until twenty pages from the close, we feel the giddy spell of Maggie's tele-vision, the seductive pull of Maggie's magic kingdom as she entices, one by one, members of her splintered family to believe in the splendid magic of the reunion dinner, itself another spectacle, another inauthentic interlude crafted to be read as authentic, or within the logic of the Reagan Era, as authentic enough. But even as Maggie plots to bring Fiona and Leroy back to Baltimore for a fried chicken dinner with Jesse, we understand that her home has begun the tectonic shift every home must undergo, save those surreal constructions erected within the frame of television: Maggie's home has begun to revert to a house. Maggie wants only a home like those marvelous magic constructions that flicker so lifelike within the antiseptic space of television. She wants Ira to look at her the same way he did on their honeymoon; she wants her brainy teenage daughter who is so inaccessible to her (indeed, she took care of her own toilet training at thirteen months) not to leave for college (even though Daisy has already packed her teddy bears, which indicates she is not even planning regular visits); Maggie wants Fiona to return with her granddaughter (even though that marriage has stayed broken for seven years); she wants Jesse to resume his place as Leroy's father and Fiona's true love (even though he has moved far beyond that relationship). Such hopes recall an unsettling dream Maggie has late in the day even as the car bears down on Baltimore: a perfect husband and perfect wife go through the perfect movements of a perfect tender goodbye in front of a perfect house, perfect save that the man and wife are plastic, life-sized dolls.

We cannot mimic the models we absorb—day in, day out—on television or in darkened movie theaters or in the bombardment from our radios (the Muzak cascades effortlessly all about the Morans as they do their shopping at the Mighty Value Supermarket). During the reception after Max Gill's memorial service, Maggie overhears casual conversation about a man who tried to impress his wife by imitating expensive Swiss candies with liqueur centers by putting rum in a cheap chocolate Easter bunny—the results, predictably, were a disaster, "[w]orst mess you ever saw" (83). We are left again and again within the messy imperfections of our immediate as we furiously adjust to events that we cannot begin to control; it is by now the familiar sense of helplessness that so bruises characters in each of our texts and that serves ultimately as the darkly luminous backdrop for the difficult affirmation of spectacle realism.

* * *

"Well, I don't know why you're making such a fuss about it," Maggie said.
"All we've got to do is watch the road signs; anyone could manage that much."
"It's a little more complicated than that," Ira said.

Breathing Lessons

Why, then, must Maggie abandon her apparently benign determination to forge from the splinters of her family's emotional wreckage a finer, if fictive, whole? For all of Maggie's resilience, such plottings are elaborate dodges, trips to Splendora, that inevitably diminish Maggie's humanity. Under the presumption, borrowed secondhand from popular culture, that families effortlessly strike design, that love inevitably triumphs, that marriages perpetually flourish, we are like those riders in the spinning teacups at the amusement park that Maggie recalls, swirling about in apparent wild motion but actually following carefully tracked spins in predictable patterns, locked with expected turns—a virtual sort of scripted reality that (like television) leaves no room for what alone gives meaning to our lives: the crippling beauty of our necessarily reckless ad-libbing, the small but sufficient vindication of the immediate.

Consequently, when Maggie plots to rerealize the text of television within the context of her immediate life, she plays the clown. Thus Tyler makes harshly explicit what has been implicit in the cutting irony of our previous texts: that those who resist the dark wonder of the immediate are little more than fools. With the crotch of her panty hose slipping down to midthigh, forcing her to walk with "shortened, unnaturally level steps like a chunky little wind-up toy" (4), Maggie ambles into the narrative all too willing to play the clown, the earnest if bumblingly lovable ditz that from Lucy Ricardo to Tim "The Toolman" Taylor has compelled sitcom television. It is Maggie's role. But we recall that Maggie is able to convince June Moran, Ira's agoraphobic sister, to leave the refuge of her apartment only by donning an outlandish costume; to those who see her (and to the reader) June becomes, in her trampish red wig, skin-tight dress, and spiked heels, a figure without dignity, a clown painfully unaware of her own appearance. June walks about the busy streets of Baltimore much as Maggie strolls about her own narrative—confident in a strategy that all the while reveals a stunning inauthenticity, a consuming terror over the immediate, and a most disconcerting determination to withdraw from it. Indeed, the dress's design is patterned poppies, suggesting about such an outlandish charade the whiff of drugged narcotic. Maggie-as-clown, dithering about trying to bend events to her tele-vision, merely disguises the perplexing reality of our genuine helplessness amid events. Maggie recalls, in a dismal attempt to make Serena's mother feel comfortable her first day at the rest home, insisting on dressing the mother, who is newly confined to, indeed strapped into, her wheelchair, in a flamboyant clown costume for the rest home's Halloween party. Maggie discovers only as she wheels the dolled-up old woman into the home's front room, however, that the party was held the previous night. The paralytic mother is left the laughingstock—suddenly unfunny, a clown slumped, braced to a wheelchair. Maggie responds typically: she runs, simply abandons the messy predicament.

In her elaborate plottings, Maggie is akin to the very figure she so quickly abandons: a paralytic dressed absurdly as a clown. We are better, Tyler cautions, without the pretense. Once again the argument of spectacle realism is delivered by undercutting a character bent on resisting its insight. When Fiona prepares for childbirth, she rejects even the premise of breathing lessons, arguing, after all, that breathing is what comes most naturally. Such "lessons" are, of course, absurd contrivances, offering to those preparing for the (in)elegant experience of childbirth the pretense of control of a process that unfolds with its own dark, luminous logic; breathing lessons and birthing classes are exercises in the notion that "reading up on something, getting equipped for something, would put [us] in control" (254). Yet what the pregnant Fiona declaims in exasperation could serve as a premise for Tyler's take on spectacle realism: "Lay off about my breathing. I'll breathe any way I choose" (251); it is advice, of course, that signals a willingness to respond to the wild openness of the immediate, a lesson Maggie ignores—she is far too intent in her all-too-appropriate role as Fiona's breathing coach.

Maggie's reclamation of the immediate begins when she admits early in the trip to Deer Lick that the map has been left on the kitchen table. The Morans must face unassisted the unfamiliar road, a suggestive meta-phor here for the mapless world of chance and surprise. We recall that Maggie's family, in preparing for Fiona's delivery, was so in control of the birth that they selected only boys' names, only to be stunned by the ar-rival of a daughter—a potentially edifying lesson in their vulnerability that they casually negate by hanging the boy's name on the girl (Leroy). We see that, for all her plotting, Maggie's day—indeed her life—is simi-larly visited by accidents and surprise. On the first page, Maggie and Ira both accidentally oversleep. Then, in quick fashion, Maggie, sent to the garage to pick up the car for the trip, plows into a Pepsi truck as she leaves (later she will run over a mailbox in an effort to negotiate the tight line of Fiona's drive); Ira himself swerves off the road when Maggie care-lessly jabs at the car horn. Other accidents unsettle the day. When they return to Baltimore, Maggie admits to accidentally breaking Ira's an-swering machine; soda spills on Maggie's dress; Leroy's pink tank top is stained by a vivid red juice spill; and Fiona drags her suitcase along the wooden floors of Maggie's entranceway, leaving two long thin scratches.

Recollections yield other evidences of intrusive accidents. Maggie re-calls a kitten she accidentally killed in a dryer; Ira's sister's cat is killed by a car; Ira recalls his dreams of medical school are scuttled at one point when a moving van crashes into his small framing shop on Christmas Eve. Daniel Otis recalls a tumble he takes off a roof while checking for a leak in a chimney. Maggie's rest-home infatuation, the dapper Mr. Gabriel, checks himself into the retirement community because he fears the hazards of living on his own, particularly after his cook accidentally sets off a small grease fire. Fiona confides to Maggie that her most serious romantic involvement since her marriage breakup ended when she wrecked the man's car. We are given a world whose narrative line is nicked again and again by the unexpected that so compellingly terrifies characters in text after text of spectacle realism. When Maggie and Ira first hit unfamiliar country beyond the Baltimore city limits, Maggie comments (missing the wonder of it) that the open road is quite a mess, as if "[t]hings had been allowed to just happen" (14). We are ready for the education of Maggie Moran.

*   *   *

What would it be like, I wonder. . . . Just to look around you one day and have it all amaze you—where you'd arrived at, who you'd married, what kind of person you'd grown into.

Serena Gill

[The fog] had muffled every sound but [Ira's] family's close, oppressively famil-iar voices. It had wrapped them together, locked them in, while his sisters' hands dragged him down the way drowning victims drag down whoever tries to rescue them. And Ira thought, Ah, God, I have been trapped with these people all my life and I am never going to be free.

Breathing Lessons

In ways, then, that surely recall Oates's juxtapositioning of the neat zone of the boxing ring and the dangerous spontaneity of the trampoline or Kennedy's use of the hyperartificiality of Quinn's newspaper against the brutal improvisations of the Southern battlefields or the difference Ferro underscores between the neat water jets of Bill Mackey's design and the thundering wildness of the nearby waterfalls, Tyler understands that openness, of course, is what terrifies. Unlike the planned thrills of the spinning teacup ride, there are far more precarious moments once we step off the ride. It is the lesson Maggie must learn even as we watch her furiously plot, cajoling a resisting Ira, making a quick long-distance phone call under cover of a flushing toilet to ensure Jesse's cooperation, lying sweetly to a gullible Fiona. But it all cannot work. How, then, do we adjust to the immediate so stripped of our efforts to direct its unfolding momentum into convenient plot? In a strategy that recalls our other texts, Maggie will be offered two extremes—her best friend and her husband—whose responses each implicitly reject the power of the ordinary.

We begin with Serena Gill. Unlike Maggie, Serena is deeply connected to her immediate; her life has been an (in)elegant exercise in vulnerabil-ity. Her recollections of her husband's rapid decline with cancer are a sobering counterforce to Maggie's extravagant plottings. But long before that, Serena engaged a world that resisted the pleasant clichés of Maggie's tele-vision. Her father refused to leave his wife for Serena's mother and refused even to acknowledge his daughter publicly; he was a hypocrite of considerable dimensions whose comfortable middle-class life Serena observes through hedges guarded by two stone lions. She grows up with a mother who suffers the calumny of a judgmental community and who responds by flaunting herself in a flamboyant dress style that her daughter, long after, recalls uneasily. Indeed, in marrying the stolid Max Gill, Serena must live with the considerable approbation of his disapproving family, who sees in her only a career handicap. And, with the death of her husband, Serena has faced what so terrifies in our texts of spectacle realism: the graceless intervention of mortality. Her vital husband has been felled by a pernicious cancer that completes its deadly work in a few months. Her small family is now in evident collapse. Her grown daughter proves inexplicably distant in the awkward sadness of the memorial service.

Thus positioned within a difficult immediate, Serena is surely in a position to teach Maggie, a position she seems to assume naturally when she admonishes Maggie to face the immediate honestly. Maggie is distressed when Serena admits that even as her husband failed, she was angry over his illness, betrayed by his evident plan to leave her too early, an honest anger that Maggie quickly dismisses. But Serena challenges Maggie's evasion tactic: "Why do you always have to gloss things over, Maggie?" (55). And later it is Serena, reeling (like Mark Valerian) within the evidence of temporality and coming to understand the fragile grasp we have on the immediate, who first offers to Maggie the possibility of examining our life from a perspective sufficient to jar us into seeing it anew, akin, to borrow Serena's metaphor, to stripping off the curtains in a familiar room.

But in ways that recall Mark Valerian's friend Matthew Black and Daniel Quinn's tutor Will Canaday, something disturbs in Serena's argument. When she tells Maggie at the funeral reception, "What would it be like, I wonder . . . [j]ust to look around you one day and have it all amaze you" (53), she offers herself as one who exercises such acuity of vision. Yet for Serena such a remarkable rediscovery of the immediate has only deflated her enthusiasm; to her, such acuity has served only to reveal to her, in the autumnal wash of menopause (which, by her own testimony, she underwent gladly), that her husband was no Einstein, that her daughter is sadly overweight and out of reach emotionally, and that she herself is starting to slope physically in ways that resemble her own mother. To a Maggie wildly involved with the plot to reunite her son and his ex-wife, Serena offers sobering advice: let go of connections. To her, shucking children is the whole point from the moment of birthing. As her name suggests, she has found her way to a serenity of sorts, an uneasy calm that is itself a most disconcerting dodge (like Max's memorial service that she designs—one that lacks a casket and reruns her wedding), an abdication of the responsibility of engagement (she rejects Maggie's sincere offers of help during her adjustment to widowhood), a surrender of possibilities and a resolution to go-it-alone that Maggie must finally reject, much as Mark Valerian rejects the seductive cynicism of his closest friend, Matthew Black.

Ira, of course, offers a far more compelling alternative. Like Serena, Ira understands all too well the bruising nature of a life spent on the open road. For our study, Ira Moran introduces a new consideration, a character who struggles at midlife to find the reward of a long immersion in the ordinary, to touch the affirmation premised by spectacle realism amid the apparent dull stretches of time and the too-long trek toward nowhere in particular. He looks back on a life of commonplace sacrifice in which, by his own admission, he "had never accomplished one single act of consequence" (125). He was born an afterthought, long after his parents had lost interest in parenting. He recalls a distant mother who, before her death when he was fourteen, was bound up within the private world of her evangelical religion. Thereafter locked within a suffocating family that measured love only by the degree of sacrifice, Ira had to abandon plans to study medicine to run his father's small framing shop when, on the very eve of Ira's departure for the university, his father suddenly complained of a bad heart. Ira then commits his life to tending not only his father but also his sisters, one mentally handicapped, the other hopelessly agoraphobic. He meets Maggie by sheer chance. And after they marry, two unexpected pregnancies finish any hopes of his becoming a doctor. Ira has since watched his son, a high school dropout, struggle mightily against maturity and his daughter resist tendering the minimal affection any parent expects. His has been a joyless life of "plugging away day after day" in a framing business that (as it metaphorically suggests) has never expanded his narrow horizons. And now, edging past fifty, Ira has begun to confront the nearing stroke of mortality. He understands that he will die inconsequential, "unknown" (161). Unlike Maggie who so magically dispels such fears at the retirement home, Ira understands only the hard reality of it; he avoids hospitals (even when Maggie has her appendix removed and later when Fiona gives birth to Leroy), fears even a casual brush with sickness, finds uncomfortable discussions of life insurance and even the idea of being a pallbearer for Serena's husband (he begs off, complaining of a trick back).

Nevertheless, Ira has engaged the challenge of the open road, much like those heroic figures who, in the "interminable" (275) nonfiction books he reads, cross the open ocean alone. Like Serena with her apparently refreshing honesty, Ira (set against Maggie) appears resolutely bound to the immediate. Indeed, Ira's Native American ancestry separates him from Maggie's techno-media world of the mid–twentieth century and connects him to a deeper wisdom, specifically to the intuitive ability to read the unpredictable open countryside. Ira's tight gameworld of his beloved solitaire signals that, unlike Maggie, he sees a clear separation between the freewheeling experience of the immediate and the neat, cleaner borders of a game. There hangs about Maggie's schemings to reunite Jesse and Fiona the unattractive sense of a game, the manipulating of lives like gamepieces. Such games-playing is not for Ira; Maggie's plotting lasts only as long as he tolerates its clumsy execution. Unlike Maggie, Ira adapts to the immediate, suggested by his daylong adjustments to the glaring sunlight. Maggie, her sunglasses perched on her nose, inquires, "Doesn't the sunlight bother your eyes?" Ira answers simply, "No, I'm fine" (172). It is only later when Ira agrees to the visit to Fiona's, agrees to play out Maggie's scenario, that he folds down the visor, thus participating in the same protective evasion as Maggie.

Yet for Ira, clear sight has brought no joy. His gameworld of solitaire with its intricate turns fascinates him far more than the unfolding—and unscripted—dramas about him; when Maggie even attempts to play a card, he rudely commands her to "butt out" (49). His narrative chapter (which is appropriately spare, suggesting his reticence for sharing) centers on his sense of a diminished immediate and of his own enervation, a "crushing kind of tiredness" that he feels like "an actual weight on his head" (149). Tyler underscores such a perception of the immediate, the tiring going-nowhereness of it, by her use of closed tracks: Maggie recalls long afternoon waiting trackside for Jesse to complete his workout, watching the crowds of joggers moving within the tight circle of the school running track; Fiona and Jesse's marriage will implode during a family outing at Pimlico Race Track. Even Maggie's narrative day, so full of digressions and side trips, is actually a closed loop that begins and ends at home. For Ira, life on the open road has curved into the joyless round of a track where, as Maggie discovers during her afternoon at Pimlico, the experience was all expectation and letdown, the race itself a blur easily missed.

Ira attends joylessly to the demands of the immediate. All day long, he busies himself with driving, pumping gas, settling bills, working vending machines. Like those Atlantic crossers he so admires, Ira has settled into the immediate tight-lipped to navigate its perilous open ride grimly, without the bothersome need to find worth in such openness. He shares nothing, his deepest emotional responses are tendered in single words; he cannot fathom why anyone would call a radio show and air their private grievances so publicly. Confronting emotional dilemmas, he quotes the hollow clichés of his "personal heroine" Ann Landers (13). Even Maggie concedes that Ira is a "closed-in, isolated man" (13). Such stoicism has rendered Ira socially retarded—when he refuses to sing a duet with Maggie at Max's memorial service, while Maggie struggles with her part unassisted, Ira fiddles with a rubber band; during the reception after the service, Ira goes off to Serena's bedroom and plays solitaire on her bedroom bureau; later, during the awkward reunion at Fiona's, he is off in a corner inspecting a box heater—on a day of unusually high temperatures.

For Ira, veracity (so much the imperative of spectacle realism) is not an instrument of illumination. He is mercilessly bland in his inopportune introduction of the truth of things. Against a wife who compares their son's garage band to the Beatles, Ira joylessly concedes his son is a failure. During the family outing at Pimlico, Ira triggers the last great argument in Fiona and Jesse's stormy marriage by revealing long after the fact that the baby crib Fiona believed to be Jesse's had in fact been a drying rack he, Ira, had been building. The revelation years after Fiona had been so taken by Maggie's elaborate lie shatters what little faith and love Fiona had in her drifting husband. And then, with bland straightforwardness, Ira informs Fiona that Jesse is, in fact, seeing a young woman who sings in another band. And, of course, after the initial reading, we realize that Ira knows from the beginning of the trip that Jesse will not restore Maggie's hope for a functioning family, will not even be interested in the reclamation of his marriage with Fiona. Ira knows that Jesse is sleeping with another woman, a greeter at a local auto dealership.

But Ira functions as more than a bland emissary from reality amid Maggie's shadow-show. As a framer, Ira understands making do with the imperfect, taking what he is given and putting it into the best angle, much like the imperfect bits of family memories or the clumsy artifacts of amateur artisans for which he is asked to provide a neat framed and finished look. For Ira, we are simply better off accepting our lot. "Discretely sightless" (158), he fashions from such imperfections the neatest possible product. It is a lifetime of making-do. Similarly, the heart-wrenching reality of his family—a parasitic father, two dependent sisters, a wife who seldom nears reality, inaccessible children—is a ponderous weight around which Ira maneuvers with the tight-lipped control he uses as he maneuvers about the slower traffic on Route One ("the nursing home of highways" [149]). But adjustment, we are reminded by the texts of spectacle realism, is simply not sufficient. Thus, Ira does not command the narrative center.

*　　*　　*

"Music is so different now," she had said to Jesse once. "It used to be 'Love Me Forever' and now it's 'Help Me Make It through the Night.'"

"Aw, Ma," he had said, "don't you get it? In the old days they just hid it better. It was always 'Help Me Make It through the Night.'"

Breathing Lessons

The novel closes with the unraveling of Maggie's cumbersome plotting—Jesse is barely in the door when Ira lets drop the ongoing affair with the auto greeter. The novel could shudder to a bleak conclusion that would recall the descendental impulse of traditional realistic fare. Maggie could accept Serena's counsel to surrender or Ira's strategy to make do. Without the flashy optimism of plot, we suddenly front what Maggie most dreads: the threat of being ordinary. Within Maggie's logic, it is the ordinary who are left with the terrifying logic of two pop songs that become part of Maggie's day: the 1950s ballad "Que Sera, Sera (Whatever Will Be, Will Be)," which is sung at the memorial service and which offers, apart from its chirpy melody, a disturbing argument of helplessness amid raw event; and the pseudoexistentialist angst of the 1970s pop anthem "Dust in the Wind," which Maggie recalls singing to baby Leroy with an open Miller High Life balancing on her midriff and which offers a similarly disquieting vision of cosmic purposelessness. Must Maggie concede what she is: a clumsy, chubby, meddlesome, aging woman, prone to embarrassing gaffes, a woman whose emotional life has long justified a depletion of optimism?

But like other texts of spectacle realism, optimism is not the same as affirmation; clarity of vision is not simply a matter of disengaging the immediate from the possibility of affirmation, of accepting our condition as dust in the wind. It is not enough to unplug Maggie's tele-vision, not enough for her (as Ira so blandly demands) to "[w]ake up and smell the coffee" (311). In the Mighty Value Supermarket at day's close, the Morans forsake the pricey imported ice cream and buy Breyer's and decide to top it with the grocery store's brand of chocolate sauce. Similarly, Tyler asserts the mighty value of the generic, the immediate so denied significance by the machinery of pop-culture commercial America; like other writers of spectacle realism, Tyler wants us to glimpse the unsuspected radiance of the fronted fact—the fronting of the immediate so discounted by the logic of the Reagan Era. This gesture will be like the stunning moment of sudden surprise when Ira and Maggie leave church (appropriately after the funeral service) to step out into the warm September afternoon, a moment that Tyler compares to "stepping out of a daytime movie—that sudden shock of sunshine and birdsong and ordinary life that had been going on without them" (76).

At the end of her day, Maggie will come home to the very geography that television so roundly forswears—the immediate—and will find that if the immediate buries, it also lifts and sustains those who must exist, necessarily, splendidly helpless, within it. As we have seen again and again, the immediate confounds formulas, denies understanding. Maggie reflects late in the book on two accidents involving pets. A mischievous kitten is killed when Maggie accidentally traps it in the merciless tumbling of the dryer; a gerbil is eaten by a cat when Maggie "frees" it from the grinding routine of the treadmill. In one case, household routine kills; in the other, it actually protects, and when it is interrupted, disaster ensues. Maggie recalls that Max Gill's happiest memory was a night in college when fraternity brothers abandoned him, quite drunk, at Carolina Beach, far from campus. Rather than panicking when he awoke, uncertain of where he was, he was mesmerized by the layers of sky settling easily on the sea. In an impromptu moment, he shucks his clothes and flings himself into the dawn surf—his last name hinting that he can surely adapt to such a splendid new terrain. That moment of spectacle realism—embracing the stunning surprise of the ordinary, finding benediction within the most unpromising position of vulnerability—is now what awaits Maggie.

After the family reunion implodes, Maggie runs out into the night to call after Fiona and Leroy, who have bolted for Fiona's sister. Standing at the end of the sidewalk to her own house staring along the deserted street, Maggie comes to touch, like Max Gill at the oceanfront, a stirring moment of lostness and dislocation—save that, unlike Max, she is within a most familiar landscape, her own home. She glimpses a white cat that she assumes is a stray but who is suddenly claimed by a girl who flies out of an alley and then quickly disappears. From a passing car radio, she hears the play-by-play from an Orioles baseball game, "no outs and the bases loaded" (214). It is time, Tyler suggests with both images, for going home. But as Maggie—her family now shattered—starts back to her front steps, she finds she has "lost all sense of direction" (314). We have seen a tragic parody of such revelation: Max Gill, his mind battered by cancer, was found by neighbors wandering in his pajamas and lugging a huge pair of pruning shears, wholly uncertain where he was. As Serena recalls, "He said it was like he had stepped outside his own life for a minute" (52). Maggie must pursue such a revelation but without the illness that makes Max's confusion counterfeit.

Yet Maggie, like others we have seen, resists. In the cold frustration of her collapsed plotting, Maggie concedes immediately only to the simplest melodramatic despair; as she sorts through Fiona's suitcase, left behind, a despondent Maggie determines that her life was "was entirely lacking in hope" (315). Carefully washing dishes from a meal they never had, gathering her day's underclothes into the hamper, vigorously brushing her teeth and washing her face, Maggie does what Maggie has done her for most of her adult life: she discards the unpleasant and the unmentionables, spruces up the imperfect, buffs the soiled. And, much like Mark Valerian who entertains the possibility of Splendora until nearly the end of the narrative, Maggie, a spare page or two from the closing, is still plotting. As Ira busies himself with his solitaire, Maggie schemes: she wants to arrange with Fiona for Leroy to come to Baltimore for her schooling and to live with them for nine months a year, although that quickly escalates to twelve months (a scheme that in its outlandishness recalls the gay rocket to another planet).

But it is time to stop. Ira commands Maggie to look squarely at him and tells her—twice—"No." He acts like the orthopedist he always dreamed of becoming—firmly ministering to a grievous fracture, here Maggie's painful split from the immediate; it is a gesture that is therapeutic and necessary: the "bone would make a clicking sound as it returned to its rightful place, and the patient's pain would vanish utterly" (131). Show's over. Maggie, so suddenly fronting the tele-vision unplugged, considers pursuing the argument—but elects not to. She drops her hands from her hips. She is silent.

Maggie walks quietly to the window (forsaking the usual comfort-site of the television) and raises the shade—indicating a hesitant move toward the uncluttered clarity of fronting the immediate. She presses her forehead against the gritty screen. It is a summary moment of tension. Maggie is pulled between the artificial world of her plotting and the (to her) repugnant quotidian world of plodding. Appropriately, the night smells of automobile tires and lawns—a night poised, as Maggie is, between the harshly synthetic and the lushly natural. Of course, in this halting movement toward epiphany, the television lurks. Maggie hears the music from an adventure show coming from the television next door. But now, despite such promising exoticism, the television suggests entrapment—it is on in the home of the Lockes. But its influence is still large for Maggie. She sees neighbors across the street, a young couple, and imagines the romantic night they will undoubtedly enjoy; she conjures a clichéd evening of dancing, wining, splendid conversations on a "spotless white love seat" (326), all set to violin music—the tired stock images of pop-culture romance.

But, significantly, she now turns from the window—turns from the magic kingdom of such effortless tale spinning—and returns to the bed, to Ira. Her day's plottings in ruins (suggested by her bowl of ice cream that has steadily degraded into a mushy soup), she moves into her (un)glamorous immediate—and finds in a jolting moment there in bed next to Ira an unsuspected swelling in her heart, a right fronting that stirs her to acknowledge the inexplicable wonder and seductive potency of the immediate, the joyousness lodged, after all, within the ordinary. It is a gesture of a most (un)spectacular confluence that surely recalls the erotic fusion of Maud and Quinn of Kennedy's close and the commitment to endure together that confirms Mark and Bill in Ferro's close. Again and again in texts of spectacle realism, the sole consolation of our life on the open road is the vast comfort of company. As Maggie slides into the bed, Ira, diligently playing solitaire, enfolds her in the crook of his free arm. Maggie kisses Ira warmly and slides over to her side of the bed, now anticipating only the long trip tomorrow to deliver Daisy to college. Now, at narrative's close, the resilience most admirable is not Maggie's urge to plot—by narrative midpoint that had grown deliberately tiresome—but rather the difficult wisdom she asserts: to get up tomorrow and to engage the (un)limited wonder of an unscripted tomorrow, the uncertainty and maplessness of life accepted, to quote the Grateful Dead song that Ira whistles in the aftermath of Maggie's disastrous chicken dinner, as a long, strange trip.[3]

* * *

Flashing my keys out on Main Street,
Chicago, Detroit, New York, it's all the same street,
Your typical city involved in a typical daydream,
Hang it up and see what tomorrow brings.

Sometimes the lights all shining on me,
Other times I can barely see.
Lately it seems to me
What a long, strange trip it's been.

Robert Hunter, "Truckin'"

In *Breathing Lessons*, then, we come at last to the pivotal argument of spectacle realism. In a far cry from the Stevick family's sheltering strategies of evasion, which make their happy endings so darkly ironic, we come now to front an example of the narrative closure of earned affirmation that defines the very significance of spectacle realism, affirmation that comes because of, not despite, our awareness of our own vulnerabilities, our own clumsy makeshift lives spent reeling amid the blunted shocks of the immediate. In ways that Enid Stevick, John Wheelwright, and Kate Vaiden resist, we must, it turns out, forsake the luxury of maps. We are not kings of the road, the song that Ira whistles (a song that, with its parody of power, could serve as anthem for Enid Stevick, John Wheelwright, and Kate Vaiden). Rather, as Daniel Quinn perceives under the arches within Maud's embrace, and as Mark Valerian understands as he pursues the uncertain promise of a difficult blood treatment, we must lay down our roads in open country. The lush jacket illustration of the first trade hardback edition of Tyler's novel could serve as a most striking emblem of spectacle realism: double yellow lines that signal a narrow, treacherous highway painted surreally through what is obviously open countryside. We recall that Maggie is swept to tears in the hospital while waiting out Fiona's labor when she observes an old deaf man in paint-spattered overalls who responds politely to the nurses' rather loud request for a urine sample; Maggie cries, she claims, to find such "delicacy" in such a roughened character under such potentially embarrassing and deeply human circumstances, moved by the ability of the unscripted immediate to stun her and by the dignity of those who, like the old man, vulnerable and imperfect, routinely engage it.

Setting aside our "maps" and making peace with contingency, however, is only part of Tyler's parting advice. After all, how are we to take the closing scene in which two such incompatible personalities assert love, indeed even stay married? Tyler's full resolution is as traditional as the closing moments of so much sitcom television—from Ralph and Alice Kramden to Homer and Marge Simpson. In appropriating the formula of sitcom television, Tyler offers the only close she could: incompatibles inevitably balance. Maggie needs Ira; Ira needs Maggie. Honest engagement is not sufficient; finding within such engagement the stuff of wonder is not enough—confluence alone gives depth to such discovery. Maggie and Ira should surely fall apart from the weight of their differing visions. Yet Maggie cannot assert a significant solo voice (when she tries at the memorial service, she must be buttressed by an ad-libbed duet with an old friend; later she and Ira will strike up an informal duet to the Muzak in the grocery store). Maggie and Ira are never apart in the narrative present. They share every scene. They even cooperate—in alternating sections—to tell the narrative. That book jacket illustration suggests such a union: just above the jerry-built highway in open countryside is the graceful benediction of a crosspatch of birds in flight accidentally shaping the fragile image of linked wedding bands. Such imagery reminds us, finally, that the ultimate stroke of contingency is not death, which Ira (and so many others we have seen) so melodramatically fears, but rather love, the random collision of hearts that coaxes in us, nevertheless, a driving need (recall Mark Valerian and Bill Mackey) to tend another against the inevitable moment when our breathing lessens.

Consider the close of Ira's section. In the suffocating gray fog at Baltimore's Harborplace shopping complex, Ira recalls, he once took his family for a rare outing. The fog serves as suggestive metaphor for the environment of spectacle realism, the pressing contingency of a world where the familiar turns suddenly unfamiliar, where vulnerability is the very element of that engagement. In the fog, harried by a daylong struggle to keep his family in line, Ira confronts his mentally damaged sister who worshiped Elvis Presley. Feeling suddenly the burden of his family's heavy dependency, he cuts through her pleasant nullity by telling her baldly, "For God's sake, Dorrie, don't you know the guy is dead and buried?" (174). Suddenly, there in the heavy fog, Ira glimpses in his sister's shattered face her remarkable (im)perfection, her unadorned homeliness, that drives him to feel love, how much he treasures the (im)perfect world simply as it is, the very lesson of course that Maggie will find as she turns from the night world outside her gritty screen.

Ira affirms what Maggie comes to see: the awkward efforts that go into our lifelong attempts to shape experience into meaning against the narrowing options left us by forces we cannot begin to fathom much less control, how we move, all of us, through a life that seems unendurable, endless, and yet is over in a snap of the fingers. The fog does not obscure but rather sharpens Ira's perception of the immediate. But what he quickly acknowledges, there in the fog, is the persistent frustration of spectacle realism: that such a sense of benediction is a passing moment that he will not, cannot, hang on to. How tenuous is our understanding of the wonder that is so accessible, how much we struggle (like the dog Daniel Otis tells about who pokes its nose through the spindles of a chair trying to get a ball on the chair seat) to recover what is so close at hand. When Maggie decides not to pursue college, she disparages schooling as a most pointless exercise in the rote learning of useless factoids; she cites two: "Synecdoche is the use of the part to symbolize the whole" and "Ontogeny recapitulates phylogeny" (30). In rejecting such bits of information as arcane, Maggie declares she is prepared to let life teach her— and indeed her life teaches exactly these two points. In watching Maggie struggle mightily within the (extra)ordinary ad-lib dramas of love and family, we understand that Maggie repeats and summarizes the experience of the collective, of all of us caught within this "business of time's passing" (23)—and the closing affirmation is tendered as much to Maggie as it is to the reader. People have to be reminded, as Maggie intones early in the narrative as justification for her pursuit of the reunion dinner, "how they were connected. . . . The way the world was going now, it was so easy to forget" (22).

In the shattering moments immediately after Fiona and Leroy depart, Maggie considers a story told her by one of the nursing home residents that once you reach heaven, the valuables you lost on Earth would be returned. Maggie imagines St. Peter with a gunnysack waiting for her. Her catalog of items begins, predictably, with the petty and personal: misplaced earrings, discarded clothes, even a pet she misses. But in a remarkable movement toward a broader sense of valuables, Maggie moves to the (un)spectacular treasures we overlook because of their accessibility: summer evenings when noisy children play in the easy heat; chair rockers on the porch; "a bottle of wind, a box of fresh snow, and one of those looming moonlit clouds that . . . float overhead like dirigibles" (318–19). It is the very stuff of Enid Stevick's epiphanic moment on the Decker Boulevard bus, a moment she so coolly dismisses. And unlike Mark Valerian, whose similar conclusions are pressured by approaching death and for whom the promise of affirmation must be painfully brief before he must accept premature closure, Maggie—now out from her magic kingdom—fronts the terrifying exhilaration of the open road from the perspective of a midlife moment, ready to test her insights for a journey that begins, as it does for each us, at the break of tomorrow. It is not to discount the power of Mark Valerian's embrace of the immediate to point out Maggie's determination is, perhaps, that much more remarkable: to tap that same resilient determination to engage the immediate knowing that today is *not* your last, indeed that tomorrow promises yet another stretch on an open highway.

But we resist closing our study on Maggie Moran. Must spectacle realism ground its affirmation in the epiphany of a middle-aged housewife so often given to emotional excess? Indeed, how can spectacle realism justify its heady sense of engagement, its celebratory affirmation tendered in the closing decades of a bloody, absurd century that more than justifies denial and retreat? We turn now in the closing chapters to examine two massive texts in which characters will locate strikingly similar affirmations to the one Maggie intuits at the gritty screen of her bedroom window. But these texts will offer as buttressing foundation the novel arguments of two branches of late-twentieth-century science—chaos theory and genetics—arguments that have been neglected amid the noisier sciences of ballistics, thermodynamics, and atomic physics whose descendental metaphors have for so long now sanctioned only our sense of isolation and uncertainty and our grim anticipation of either graceless extinction or fiery apocalypse. We must begin, appropriately, where characters in spectacle realism always begin—amid chaos.

7

In the Jaws of the (S)napping Turtle

T. Coraghessan Boyle, *World's End*

It is a mortifying circumstance that nature often refuses to second [man's]
most profound and elaborate efforts; so that often after having invented one of
the most ingenious and natural theories imaginable, she will have the perverse-
ness to act directly in the teeth of this system, and flatly contradict his most
favorite positions.

Diedrich Knickerbocker, *History of New York*

One stifling summer afternoon in Dutch New Amsterdam, a young,
strapping Jeremias Van Brunt helps his father clear brush from a hillside
near a stagnant, dun-colored pond. His eyes stinging from sweat, he
impulsively shucks his clothes to cool off in the pond. Naked, he edges
gingerly into the muck. Suddenly, his right ankle is seized in a fierce grip.
The thick pond water quickly reddens even as Jeremias's father, who
comes running when he hears his son's cries, hacks off the horny head of
the monstrous snapping turtle whose massive jaws have clamped down
on Jeremias's leg. Even severed, the turtle's head, the size of a wagon
wheel, holds fast to the boy's ankle as the rest of it, claws still churning,
slides back into the heavy muck. Within days, Jeremias's rotting ankle,
now the sickening color of summer squash, will compel the boy's father
to amputate the infected foot with a crosscut saw and without anesthetic.

It is a uncomfortably graphic episode early in T. Coraghessan Boyle's
1987 *World's End*, a moment—a mere paragraph—that moves by amid a
sprawling narrative line where events rise and fall with manic urgency.
Indeed, when we introduce Boyle's narrative into our argument, spectacle realism finally touches the scale appropriate to its vision, specifically a narrative scope that ranges about three centuries and dozens of

characters. But this pondside episode, brief as it is, highlights a question fundamental to spectacle realism since Enid Stevick glimpsed her sweaty step-uncle at the local Armory, specifically the tension between event and plot. Is young Jeremias maimed by chance—a napping turtle blindly meandering about a still summer pond that in the silty confusion latches onto a pipestem-thin something only because of its accessibility, an event devoid of meaning or consequence? Or is this slender event part of an intriguing pattern, a plot, a conspiracy of events compelled by inexplicable forces that demand that the turtle snap and that consequently pack this unremarkable pondside incident with unsuspected import? After all, the amputation of the boy's foot will influence profoundly the unfolding drama of his family's hard struggle as tenant farmers in Dutch New Amsterdam. More to the point, Jeremias will hobble into adulthood an emotional cripple, brooding and silent. Indeed, much later, Jeremias's public humiliation, kneeling before the patroon in the public square and begging to be allowed the privilege of serving him, is foreshadowed by this amputated foot. And, more compelling, 300 years later, in a remarkable iteration in the narrative present, another young emotionally crippled Van Brunt will face a similar crippling: Walter will lose both his feet in separate motorcycle accidents. Is it, then, a napping turtle or a snapping turtle?

Do we live in the turbulent chaos of event, or do we play out something called "destiny" within the closed geometry of fate, two extremes suggested by the epigraphs that head each of the two parts of *World's End,* one taken from "Rip Van Winkle," the American primer on the disruptive intrusion of odd event; the other from Eugene O'Neill's *Desire under the Elms,* the foreboding drama of a family-qua-puppets locked within the irrevocable compulsions of their animal natures. *World's End* examines how we construct something called "plot," or, more to the point, how raw event becomes plot. More than any of our previous texts, *World's End* is supremely about event, absurd and routine, pedestrian and horrific. Chapter to chapter, even page to page, the reader shuttles back and forth among three strikingly different time periods and passes among scores of characters who with wild celerity rise and fall, love and die, prosper and crash all within the same fifteen-mile stretch of the Hudson River Valley. Thickening the trunk of the narrative line, the characters themselves are inveterate and marathon tale tellers. Amid such an assault of event, we content ourselves with the viability of a plot by noting elements of experience shared by each generation: for instance, a dramatic showdown between haves and have-nots; a fanatical loyalty to the land, "this ancestral soil business" (359); incendiary, illicit love that sparks across social taboos and then dissipates with striking suddenness; an act of emotional treason as each generation ultimately fails what it loves; horrific acts of violence, petty and great; an uneasy love between fathers and sons; the promise of a most absurd death.

As readers accustomed to traditional linear narration, as we move across centuries chapter to chapter, we grant such elements the weight of plot, giddy with the seductive arithmetic of pattern, despite the obvious—that in each generation, each historic period, these characters move about in complete free will, bounced about by contingency and accident and the inexplicable intervention of surprise, characters unbound to act in any way that will set up pattern. Plot itself becomes a sort of magic kingdom erected (with Reaganesque logic) only with the complicity of the reader. Separated by significant stretches of time—300 years in some cases—these events do not, indeed cannot, influence each other, are not dependent on each other, do not even speak to each other, directly or indirectly. Because chapters do not speak directly to what comes before or after, each chapter is its own discrete enterprise with a beginning, middle, and end. It is a most chaotic narrative, one that struggles against itself, or, more precisely, a plot that struggles for shape against the onrush of event.

To resolve this tension, Boyle works a dual narrative. Most obvious, of course, he chronicles the absorbing drama of the three representative Hudson Valley families—one, of the landed wealthy; another, of the working class; a third, of the disenfranchised Native Americans—a massive drama that shifts fugally from the seventeenth to the twentieth century with scope sufficient to frustrate any attempt to summarize its rococo story lines. Less obvious (but far more intriguing) is the subplot, relayed through the infrequent intrusions of a coy nameless narrator who explores, even marvels at, the writing of that history; his is a story not about the events themselves—although enthralling, they merely distract—but rather about how such chaotic events find their way to the architecture of plot. It is design not easily purchased. Despite the appearance and heft of a traditionally appointed realistic historic narrative, despite the opening genealogical listing that gives the narrative credible verisimilitude, despite the meticulous manipulations of the comings and goings of more than fifty characters, the narrative line deliberately subverts clean explanation. The plotline is regularly visited by intrusive ghosts from Walter's childhood and by other apparitions that are (apparently) the lingering paranormal residue of the Hudson Valley's storied Dutch settlers. At one point Walter rides his motorcycle amid an entire phalanx of these visions; at another point, as Walter contemplates the fast-approaching opportunity for a misguided act of adulterous passion with his boss's daughter, Mardi, the apparitions materialize to razz him with a choral Bronx cheer. Walter regularly "sees" his errant father, who abandoned the family some twenty years earlier, at one point even receiving from the specter a remarkably prescient warning about the approaching loss of his foot. Even Walter's dreams are more like messages that urgently speak to his unfolding present.

Far more important, the elegant neatness of any emerging plot is contested, as we have seen in other texts of spectacle realism, by the inelegant intrusion of bald chance. At a critical moment, for instance, a character suddenly slips and avoids a mortal blow of a sword—thus preserving an entire branch of the Van Brunt line. Weather abruptly turns at exactly the wrong time. Crops flourish or wither whatever attention they are paid. Freak lightning burns down a house. A thundering downpour ruins an outdoor wedding. Characters take sick with weird inexplicable maladies that defy medical treatment, or they find recovery within untraditional Native American rituals. That snapping turtle clamps down on Jeremias's ankle. Walter's motorcycle skids out of control—twice. A daydreaming Katrinchee Van Brunt accidentally drops a steaming venison dinner on her father (stunned, he bolts out of the cabin and drops—accidentally—off an all-too-nearby cliff). Walter takes the wrong turn in a hallway at work and happens to meet his boss, the very man blamed for ruining his father. Walter's wife, Jessica, surprises him one afternoon and catches him in bed with Mardi. Later, Walter shops at a massive local grocery store only to chance upon his best friend, who happens to be shopping with his new love interest, who happens to be Walter's estranged wife. At other moments, characters cross paths at moments exactly right to ignite doomed passion or to trigger nefarious political alliances; other characters turn to those they have long loved and find that sustaining emotional energy suddenly, inexplicably exhausted. The plot, even as it piles up events, mocks itself with coincidence, defies, indeed denies, accountability, causality, or explanation.

Curiously, the critical turn in the novel is never wholly explained. When Walter finds himself hospitalized for the amputation of his other foot after a second motorcycle accident, he shares a room with Piet

Aukema, the misshapen dwarf who played a large part in the political events surrounding his father's betrayal more than twenty years before. That coincidental arrangement alone sorely tests credibility, but Walter hears from Piet the critical information that his father is very much alive and living in Barrow, Alaska, and that Piet had only recently received a card from him. When Walter later meets his father, however, Truman flatly denies that Piet could possibly have known where he is living.

When the reader is denied any reliably neat plot, what emerges, of course, is Boyle's central concern: our deep *need* for plotting, for the magic kingdom of explanation, causality, against the ruthless evidence of the unfolding immediate. Plot, as Boyle uses it here, offers several levels of suggestive possibilities, each of which plays within the narrative. Most obvious, "plot" refers to the mathematical design of events within the narrative line of a text, a writerly dilemma of pushing about actions and reactions into a satisfying, probable patterning—the contract here between Boyle's nameless narrator and the reader facing a daunting tome of events that refuse to cooperate neatly into accessible linearity. Plot, however, has wider ramifications. Historians (and Boyle's concern is intimately bound with the process of shaping history—his model for this narrative was Washington Irving's *History of New York*) fashion "plot" by sequencing discrete temporal events through retrospectively applying causal linking, concocting sensible and logical arrangements known as eras or periods or ages. Rigidly empirical scientists (long an interest of Boyle's) have probed the natural world now for a millennium seeking its "plot," a reassuring sense of organization for their observed data that confers predictability onto matter, a clarifying and empowering sense of reliable laws and infallible formulas on what might be mistaken otherwise for the merciless roiling of unchartable phenomena.[1] And each of us assembles a "plot" in the exercise of our admittedly limited options in the day-to-day carnival of unfolding events, and then we impose on those choices, retrospectively, a reassuring sense of purpose or perhaps we seek such purpose within the tangled roots of our lineage or under the hard auspices of some potent deity; thus equipped, we often use such insight to indicate direction, thus conferring pattern on the hard tumble of events that make up our lives.

In each case, we earnestly, deliberately (perhaps desperately) exorcize chance to allow us the pacifying security of direction. After all, the wild play of chance frustrates historians, infuriates scientists, impoverishes novelists, and generally haunts the rest of us who must live within its alogic. It is indeed the very element of vulnerability that so vastly disturbs each central character in our texts of spectacle realism. As we have seen, we do not manage well within the loose anarchy of chance. Here, in a fit of causality, the Dutch settlers in New Amsterdam, maddened by coincidence (setbacks in the weather, to their crops, then to the general health of their village), fix blame on a recently deceased mountain man rumored to have slaughtered his family. Certain that his haunted corpse has ruined the luck of their village, they set about the grizzly job of exhuming the body, hacking it to pieces, and then consigning the pieces to a fire. So much, Boyle's narrator shudders, for the logicians of plot.

By privileging explanation and pattern, plot exhausts the wonder of event (so critical to spectacle realism) by casting about the unfolding drama of the immediate the cold rationalizing of inevitable explication. We are left again distanced from experience—victims of plot, left to carry out with unenthusiastic cooperation what genetic memory or what family legend tells us must be our fate; from a narrow handful of options we choose what we must choose and unenthusiastically hang our shingle on the family tree. Attracted by the simple neatness of plot, we demonize chance as a handmaiden of chaos. Of course, it is far easier to believe that we are fated to do what we do. The notion of private fate or destiny, whether derived from religion or economics or genetics, attracts because it simplifies life; it is like snatching the only hummable tune during an otherwise complex symphony. Like so many of our central characters, we become too easily enthralled by design. We come to accept that our actions are forecasted; we abdicate our need to navigate through experience; like John Wheelwright or Will Canaday or any of the Stevick clan or Mark Valerian or Maggie Moran, we forfeit surprise, engagement, wonder—the very elements of spectacle realism.

Boyle's narrator offers a chilling moment that suggests metaphorically this willingness to step away from experience by crying plot. In the seventeenth century, Jeremias's son, Wouter, is to be punished, along with a cousin, in the public stocks when his father refuses to help clear brush for a new road for the patroon. When his jailers are momentarily distracted to chase down the cousin who suddenly bolts, rather than make good his easy escape, the boy awkwardly sets himself down in the stocks and, fighting back his tears, eases the heavy crossbar down onto his own ankles and then onto his own hands.

We are thus torn by extremes. Event and plot—or to borrow from the crude logic of Wolf Nysen, the giant mountain man who intrudes on

Jeremias in the cornfield as he toils for the patroon, and demands with a toneless laugh, "And what are you, then—a man to forge his own destiny or somebody's nigger slave?" (150). But Boyle sees in either extreme joyless surrender. Those who struggle to meld event into plot accept the enclosing certainty of a choking determinism. Those who revel in event, rejecting the conservative geometry of plot in favor of spontaneity, inevitably surrender to joyless drift. In either extreme, Boyle cautions, we forfeit the rich reward of engagement premised by spectacle realism. Through the layering of event, through the subplot of tale telling, through the chaotic experiences of 300 years of Hudson Valley characters, Boyle's narrator tests both extremes and, finding both unworkable, urges a middle way, an alternative approach that locates (appropriately) within the hip logic of chaos theory a way for these traditional opposites to cooperate; a way, in short, for random event to find its way to plot. And along the way such narrative logic locates a most intriguing justification for the affirmation tendered by texts of spectacle realism. We begin, then, by approaching Boyle's massive chronicle as a deliberately chaotic read.[2]

* * *

He jerked open the door and the wind caught him by the throat. . . . His father stood there in the shadows of his box at the end of the world. . . . He seemed small suddenly, tiny, shrunken, wasted, no bigger than a dwarf. "No use fighting it," he said.

The wind came up, the dogs went mad.

"It's in the blood, Walter. It's in the bones."

World's End

"How does it feel?" [Mardi] asked suddenly.

"What?" he said, but he didn't have to ask.

"You know: your foot."

The rain was coming down harder now, big pregnant drops that tickled his scalp and wet his cheeks. He shrugged, "Like nothing," he said. "It feels dead."

And then, . . . she took his arm and pulled him toward her. Her voice was a whisper, a rasp. "Can I see it?"

World's End

As in our other texts, the movement here toward the affirmation of spectacle realism is achieved through testing extremes: plotters and drifters. We will begin with plotters—because here they are more numerous and more dangerous. Within the narrative, an eclectic assortment of characters divines event into pattern in strategies that surely recall plotters from John Wheelwright to Maggie Moran. Plotters here include zealous leftist intellectuals as well as university dropouts; happy flower children as well as violent rednecks; the impoverished as well as the ruthless captains of industry who dispossessed them; environmental activists as well as those who have for three centuries despoiled the Hudson River Valley. Whatever their political persuasion, cultural philosophy, education background, the plotters each survey with hyperserious earnestness the unfolding accident of event and shape plot and, most inexplicably, come to believe (with a naïveté that always verges on arrogance or ignorance) that event, thus decoded, can actually be guided into plot by their interference.

Among such a wide-ranging crew of plotters, however, Boyle's narrator fixes on Truman Van Brunt to argue the deep danger of pattern. Truman is a master plotter—a student of history and a teacher of history, a master architect of a magic kingdom. As a newlywed working forty hours a week, Truman labors through night school on a hefty thesis about an obscure colonial uprising that involved an ancestor, Wouter Van Brunt. Kicked off his land without explanation, Wouter gets caught up in the drunken vandalizing of the patroon's manor house. In a blur, Wouter finds himself pitching a crude torch onto the patroon's barn, ultimately burning it to the ground. After hiding out for six weeks in a cave and eating acorns and skinned skunks, Wouter callously turns in the others (one is his only friend and the other his half cousin); he blames the fire on his cousin, and, as reward, his life is spared while the other two are hanged. Truman's massive leather-bound thesis, which imposes clear explanation on this mess, comes to be his magic kingdom, a secure and stable zone of control.

That (re)construction of history, however, haunts Truman, narrows his perspective, and ultimately autoclaves his heart. Indeed, the more time he spends locked within his elaborate design, he becomes "increasingly withdrawn, unloving, single-minded and hostile" (219). Trapped within the iron logic of his plotting (he names Walter after this ignominious ancestor), he taps only inevitability; as he studies his ancestor's treachery he comes to accept that betrayal is in his blood, in his bones. And when Walter treks all the way to Alaska, to ask his father why he committed such a base act against his friends and his family, why he plotted with those conservative forces in Peterskill bent on destroying the socialist commune that numbered among its members Truman's own wife and most of his close friends, his father gives as answer only his worn, bound thesis that details Wouter Van Brunt's treachery against his friends 300 years earlier. This grand construction of plot has given Truman's unfolding present its shadow architecture. That history is explanation sufficient for Truman; trapped within the logic of plot's necessary assumption of accountability, Truman accepts the role he must play—betrayer. But plot has brought him no peace, no joy. He rants to his son, "Doom! History! Don't you see?" (423). Hounded by plot, he has exiled himself to the dead wastes of Alaska, has severed connections with humanity, including his family (shortly after Truman abandons his family, Walter's mother simply stops eating and quickly dies). In the northernmost spit of land available for such retreating, Truman is left alone, performing self-sustaining penance, destroyed by the elegant pseudogeometry of genealogy, destroyed by "some forgotten shit that went down hundreds of years ago" (424), destroyed, in short, by plot.

But Truman is merely the most dramatic of Boyle's plotters. We recall, from the seventeenth century, the example of Katrinchee Van Brunt. As she serves a steaming venison dinner to her family, the girl daydreams about an attractive native she eyed that day by chance; as her mind wanders, she dumps dinner in her father's lap, which sends him screaming into the night and over a cliff to his death. So certain that such an absurd unfolding of event was in fact her design, she spends what proves to be a brief, unhappy life in acts of penance, including living off by herself and cutting her beautiful hair to stubbly clumps. Ultimately, in her grief, she will wander catatonic out into a fierce winter storm and will be found, quite dead, quite blue, in early spring.

Others shape event into plot in similar exercises of simplification. The Peterskill commune of theoretical socialists, the town's Birchers and rednecks, the original settlers exploiting their way along the virginal lands of the Hudson, the Native American tribal councils who determine long before European colonization which tribes will command which tracts, the displaced Native American outlaws attempting to reclaim in the twentieth century the same precious valley land on behalf of their cheated ancestors, the earnest late-1960s environmental crusaders whose cause Walter's wife joins, wealthy Depeyster Van Wart and his ancestors who for 300 years exploit the natural resources and parcel out the wilderness—rich or poor, educated or illiterate, they all confront raw event and determine, like Truman and Katrinchee, answers to the question that Boyle's narrator raises (and indeed that all texts of spectacle realism broach) only in deepest irony: why?

The tidiness of their theories, their clean assigning of responsibility, their neat perception of good and evil, their easy ability to freeze-dry the rush of event are to the controlling narrator little more than games of defective detection that lead to what most amuses (and horrifies) Boyle's narrator: conclusions. Here, those most certain they understand history follow three alternatives that range from merely unproductive to emphatically dangerous. Some are compelled by their naïveté to pour their considerable energies into the frustrating futility of "happy horseshit" activism (399), for instance, the pleasant-valley socialists in the mid-1930s or later the happy-hippie environmentalists in the late 1960s. Others end up driven to despair over imagined responsibility for events, like Truman or Katrinchee. But by far the most dangerous are driven, like the Birchers or Depeyster Van Wart, to act on their arrogance and thus inflict the greatest evils in the narrative, including environmental holocaust, jukebox jingoism, racial and ethnic intolerance, violent mayhem, and soul-searing materialism—each, not coincidentally, a darker element of Reagan's gleaming America.

But if we cannot invoke plot without giving in to the dark clarity of paranoia and to the iron locks of determinism, we can scarcely brook the alternative—drift. The most frightening crowd in Boyle's novel is not the vicious knot of rednecks and the VFW fanatics who deliberately trigger the killing riots at Peterskill in 1949 but rather the "bead-rattling" (74) college audience that packs the gym at Vassar College for a 1968 rock concert attended by Walter's hippie friend Tom Crane. To those so embalmed by drugs, the narrator intones in an uncharacteristically lengthy intrusion, history has been emptied of significance, reduced to the disconnected bits of trivia "useful in the sixth grade for multiple-choice tests or for scoring the odd answer on a TV quiz show" (74). Stoned, cozily unaware, secure only the most basic landmarks in history (the Pilgrims, Auschwitz, and Dallas), they live without dimension, within the thin exercise of the present tense. Here, the narrator's voice is at its most intrusive, its most vitriolic, mocking the cold disregard for history, the casual arrogance of these teenage mutant existentialists who stupidly assume "that civilization began and ended with them" (74).

Much as Truman offers a pointed lesson in the dangers of plot, Mardi, the waifish daughter of the wealthy Depeyster Van Wart, best suggests the shortfall of drift. She prowls about the narrative, dispensing her sexual athleticism without thought, ingesting recreational pharmaceuticals without purpose after drifting through an expensive career at a private college financed by her distraught father. Despite her volcanic promiscuity, Mardi is frighteningly icy. Costumed in her paper microskirts, cheap fishnet stockings, and visible panties, Mardi is predatory, soulless, lost to that dimension of humanity because events have become for her merely that—events. She offers herself to a married Walter not so much out of love or even honest (if forbidden) passion but more out of a chilling curiosity to see what his amputated stump looks like. Indifferent to consequences, Mardi cannot make love—such an act, after all, requires some sense of history—rather, she can only fuck (her favorite word). With her excessive makeup and her pallid skin, her vampiric talent for a most draining sort of lust, her penchant for the night world, she is more a zombie (interestingly, Walter first fucks Mardi on a Halloween night). When Walter attempts to convert their fucking into love, to elicit from her some declaration of affection, she mocks such sentimentality and casually drifts off to other lovers. Consistently unavailable to any emotional response, she treats her father contemptibly, parading her sexual and pharmaceutical excesses in front of him without regard for his deep hurt. Before the Vassar concert begins, an announcement is made from the stage imploring the help of the stoned crowd to track down a finger that has been ripped from the hand of a gate-crasher caught gruesomely in a jutting window catch. The humane demand for the bleeding finger, however, has little effect on Mardi, who finds it actually lodged in her hair. "The expression on her face—she wasn't appalled, disgusted, panicked, didn't scream or dance on her toes—was like nothing Tom had ever seen" (77). With the merest smile, Mardi coolly tosses the severed digit away into the surging shadows of the bleachers—giving the finger, as it were, to simple decency.

Boyle's narrator, of course, cannot bear such nihilism.[3] Like plot, improvisation is finally reductive, too simplistic to serve as (re)solution. Mardi drifts through the narrative without significance, without connection, without direction. It is a posture that, ironically, suggests the ultimate condition of the plotters, who, sick with their sense of design, cannot sustain even a moment's fascination with the wild unfolding of the chaotic present. Truman Van Brunt and Mardi Van Wart, then, both immure themselves against the crippling beauty of vulnerability; both deny engagement and seek refuge within magic kingdoms, isolated, soul-dead, overwhelmed, like Kate Vaiden and Enid Stevick and John Wheel-wright, in the graceless posture of full retreat.

*   *   *

Clouds are not spheres, mountains are not cones, coastlines are not circles, and bark is not smooth, nor does lightning travel in a straight line.

Benoit Mandelbrot, chaotician, *The Fractal Geometry of Nature*

We want, then, to be more than drift—but less than plot. Reconciling just such extremes marks the intriguing achievement of Boyle's narrator and defines the text's emerging sense of spectacle realism. Through the framing narrator, who juxtaposes events from different generations chapter to chapter, the obvious tumult of unpredictability begins nevertheless to shape patterns without the bothersomely heavy linkages that provide the structural integrity of traditional realistic family histories-qua-tragedies (like O'Neill's) in which families pass behavior from generation to generation like some private virus. Here, events across generations correspond despite, not because of, each other. Audaciously, Boyle uses his assembling narrator to conflate order and disorder by tapping (in)directly the luminous logic of chaos theory, this century's last great revolution in the physical sciences, which enjoyed a wide faddish embrace by the public during the early 1980s.[4]

Chaos theory, applied to the argument of spectacle realism, has been with us all along. It governs the harsh dynamic environment of Oates's trampoline, refutes Owen Meany's elaborate webbing of explication, damns Kate's strategic bolting, justifies Kennedy's Heraclitian oxymorons, confirms what Mark glimpses at the hospital and what Maggie intuits at the screen window: that we need not fear raw chance. The argument (if not the math) of chaos theory helps define Boyle's radical ascendant sense of the immediate, a vision where randomness itself affirms reassuring pattern. Aided by the vast informational capacity of contemporary computer muscle, chaos theory has argued that those natural phenomena (for instance, weather fronts and air turbulence) long held to be unpredictable teach (in direct refutation of Newton) that such chaotic events, tracked with sufficient care, yield pattern. It is the sly arranging by Boyle's narrator that reveals that random events, here tracked for 300 years, define pattern; stunningly, contingency, confusion, chance, free will, and error recover plot—much like the grainy mineral soup that slowly settles into a fine-lined quartz crystal. Here, in more than 300 years of three families' histories, reiteration generates form; inevitability emerges amid pure possibility; pattern and turbulence cooperate dynamically.

Consider the monstrous sandwich Depeyster Van Wart artfully constructs during an oppressively hot afternoon when he returns home for lunch and a nap. By the time Depeyster has finished his lunchtime browse of the local newspaper, the carefully set layers of his sandwich—Bermuda onion, tomato, mayonnaise, Virginia ham, and pungent white cheese—have leaked one into the other. Design and chance, then, both construct the sandwich that eventually provides Depeyster a most satisfying lunch. So it is with this radical construction of this most chaotic plot. With care, the controlling narrator layers events on top of each other, moving without linkages among 300 years of experiences, and as reader-consumer we note that past and present are carefully layered and yet (un)predictably, (ir)resistibly leak one into the other—the tomato bleeds pinkish into the mayonnaise, bits of onion cling to the mayonnaise. The mayonnaise, then, maintains its integrity and yet participates in elements all about it. Not to make too much ado over a man's lunch, but such leakage creates the balanced cooperative act of chance and design—the sandwich is a perfect chaotic text.

The local newspaper that Depeyster reads as he prepares to munch his sandwich-qua-chaotic text provides an even more direct example of a chaotic narrative. Surely newspapers (recall Will Canaday's *Albany Chronicle*) domesticate contingency. They take the raw mess of daily event and shape it into neat columns, scrutinize the open vitality of event and extract plot. But when Depeyster examines his newspaper, we find a most fascinating variation on such neat plotting. He reads the account of Walter Van Brunt's motorcycle accident the night before. Boyle's narrator quotes the newspaper article in full and even sets the passage in that tiny, efficient, no-nonsense newspaper font that promises coherence and authority. But as we move through the quoted text, we find that the type has apparently been skewed somewhere in the printing process. The lines have been shuffled; typos mar the final copy; critical information about Walter's accident is missing; and in the middle appear several lines from another article, one apparently on a school board meeting over lockers for the girls' field hockey team.

Here, chance and design create a most (im)perfect record; here (appropriately in an article about an accident) accident creates design, creates the article's, albeit skewed, narrative pattern. The intermingled narratives do not cooperate; the imbedded lines stick out. We are meant to see the layers in a strategy that surely suggests the larger narrative patternings. Indeed, as Boyle's narrator moves from chapter to chapter, the characters do not, in some cases cannot, consciously parallel other historic eras, other historic characters. We must see the layers. But those layers keep leaking one into the other, cooperate despite their evident difference. The plot here is distinctly nonlinear—yet manages to strike a satisfying sense of pattern. Depeyster does not even comment on the pied type but rather accepts that jangled record as ordered, or perhaps as ordered as he can hope. Plot—whether applied as Boyle does here to an experiment in narrative or applied by scientists perusing natural phenomena or by historians puzzling over personages and events or even by individuals taking stock of their unfolding experience—our sense of "plot" is a similar amateur effort: disorder and chance create as much order as we can hope for.

Chaos theory, if introduced into our lives, reclaims a radiant pre-Enlightenment wonder over this tumultuous geography of an immediate that, despite the oppressive gravity of Newtonian laws, unfolds with stunning spontaneity and with unanticipatable turns, a geography that is the very text-site of spectacle realism. Introduced into Boyle's narrative, chaos theory reassures that its presence there does not fracture the plotline; indeed, it pulls the narrative much closer to what unfolds in our experience. Like a chaotician peering into the turbulent water hurrying around a rock in a stream or into the unruly twirlings of cream in a cup of coffee or into the apparent random moves of a weather front, Boyle's narrator peers into event and tracks its evident chaos until it yields strange attractors, fractal patterns (what we term "plot") that develop even as characters exercise free will and roil about the harsh alogic of contingency.

Like Oates's trampoline or Kennedy's Celtic disk or Ferro's thundering waterfall or Tyler's open road, the narrative proffers a handy image to suggest this balance: here, a simple onion. The onion recurs frequently amid all the eating and cooking tracked within Boyle's narrative. In addition to the layer of Depeyster's lunchtime sandwich, Walter compares his life to a peeling onion (124); Katrinchee's head, shaved out of misdirected penance for her father's death, is compared to the bulb of an onion; Walter and Jessica encounter each other in a most awkward moment at the local grocery store near an onion display and talk in front of an old man identified only as the "onion sifter"; in Alaska, Walter's father offers spam-and-onion sandwiches and holds up a huge onion; and Tom Crane includes fried onions as he cooks for Jessica in his shack. The onion argues a most stunning architecture, a clear reiterative patterning. Yet the onion—much like Boyle's chaotic sense of plot—has no clear architect, save the intrusive muscle of chance itself. Thus, chaos theory resolves rather than opposes extremes; it tells us, after all, that it is a (s)napping turtle; that it is, indeed must be, both. Despite a narrative that closes with Walter Van Brunt's horrific death by freezing, a cripple trapped in a paralyzing winter storm, Boyle celebrates not so much this sorry individual moment but rather that this shabby bit of human experience slides effortlessly into a greater pattern, a stunning achievement, really, rather like wind, whistling through bare branches, sounding an aria from Puccini. Independent, individually motivated, compelled by private choices, detoured by the absurd interventions of chance, these characters—separated by generations—achieve symmetry, rather like the sliding colored stones in a kaleidoscope tube tumbling into breathtaking design.

*   *   *

"Leave it!" Walter shouted, startled by the sound of his own voice, and he stalked up the dock. . . ."Leave it," he muttered, clomping around the piling like a puppet on a string. "This is for me to do, this is for me." He lifted his hand to his mouth, sucked at the dark blood frozen to his knuckles. And then, in a rage, he jerked the line from the piling and dropped it in the river.

World's End

To develop this chaotic narrative, we are given, in a narrative pattern familiar to texts of spectacle realism, the education of yet another poor student. Specifically, the text unfolds as a triangulation of biases among three participants: Walter Van Brunt, a most (un)heroic student of philosophy and the chief interest in the narrative present; the narrator, a practicing chaotician clearly hip to the energy tapped when chaos theory is understood sufficiently to be applied to events other than natural phenomena; and ultimately the skeptical reader, who unlike Walter (a construction of ink pressed onto paper) is lodged within the real and who must be convinced that such contentious energy is in fact capable of reassuring shape and stunning pattern. As Walter comes to understand his father, he struggles between a growing sense of his genetic doom and his understandable impulse to make his own way. In Walter's dockside act of treachery (during a blizzard, he sends off into the Hudson River a research sloop in which his wife and her lover sleep), he understands in his own way how such treachery is both inevitable and yet freely chosen. Although unavailable to the math of chaos theory, Walter surely affirms its splendid argument as he methodically fusses amid the winter storm with each of the ship's mooring lines, demanding that this act is his to do even while he performs like a "puppet on a string" (444).

It is, then, instructive to follow Walter's evolution within the narrative present. If a novel as kaleidoscopic as this one can be said to have a central narrative concern, it would be Walter—we start on his birthday; we close with his death. Yet like our other characters, for most of the narrative Walter successfully resists efforts to like him. Despite being a professional student, Walter is strikingly ignorant of history. Early on, the narrator concedes, "There was a lot of history in the area . . . George Washington and Benedict Arnold and all of that, but history really didn't do much for him" (17). Indeed, Walter has never bothered even to read the highway historic marker that he will hit with his motorcycle and that will cost him his foot. He daily passes by the closed factories along the Peterskill waterfront, indifferent to their dark historic resonance. He has never even connected the Depeyster Van Wart in whose factory he has worked for more than three months with the Depeyster Van Wart that figured in stories of his father's treachery. More to the point, Walter has little interest in his own family history. He accepts the record he has been given of his delinquent father by his adoptive parents, who deeply detest the man. Walter accepts that Truman Van Brunt is a back-stabbing traitor to his friends and to his family and to their socialist ideals, a simplification untroubled by close thought.

When we first meet Walter, he is trying hard to play modern existentialist indifferent to the bourgeois sensibility. He tries, with ironic seriousness, to live only in the moment, a most superficial sense of chic ennui he has culled from a shortlist of readings from college philosophy classes. Reading about Meursault has taught Walter only that the world is a thin geography that leaves generic extinction as sole certainty; therefore, event has no resonance—save the titillation of the appetites—and the immediate cannot touch. We are, then, bound on a tortuous road to nowhere, suggested by Walter's dead prosthetic foot flooring the accelerator of his motorcycle as it sails through the darkening night. Walter strains, then, to be pure present: he dismisses emotional debts to his adoptive family, to his fiancée, and pursues the simple thrill of experience. We meet Walter, for instance, on the evening of his birthday when, knowing a fancy family dinner awaits his return home, he dawdles at a local bar and ends up stoned, swimming naked in the Hudson River with Mardi, a young woman he barely knows; later he will commence his rather animal affair with the same woman just weeks after he is married; and when Jessica walks in on them in bed and she sends her father the next day to collect her things, Walter will blow cigarette smoke in the face of the distraught man.

Walter, to his credit, waffles uncomfortably as an existentialist. His attempts come across as strained, unconvincing performances. At a vulnerable moment after waking in the hospital and discovering his foot gone, Walter actually un-existentially swoons with the thought of Jessica and pledges love to her. And, in the hospital, he begins to work toward a constructive sense of history, giving depth to his moment. Under the considerable clout of painkillers, Walter sees the specter of his father and asks him about the 1949 riots, about the betrayal. The vision tells Walter to return to the marker he hit, tells him, in effect, to tap the power of curiosity long underdeveloped in the complacent Walter. Walter decides to explore his family's history, but he burdens this exploration with a most counterproductive bias: Walter wants plot. As he watches his doctors casually play with his new prosthetic foot, Walter demands explanation: "Why me?" (44). When he decides to track down his father, he wants to *understand* why his father cooperated with those in Peterskill opposed to the socialist commune where he and his family lived; why he then abandoned his family; why (when Walter finds midnovel that his father is still alive) he has spent forty years in self-imposed exile in the blasted reaches of Alaska. Like others in our texts back to John Wheelwright, Walter wants to flatten event into drama—as his father angrily points out, "You want black-and-white. . . . You want simple" (404)—with the obligatory heavy sense of motivation and a closing sense of rewarding good and punishing evil (we recall the Dutch settlers who viewed their lives as a tension between the benevolent Saint Nicholas and his malicious servant Knecht Ruprecht [28]).

The historic record that Walter explores as part of his father's betrayal appears to satisfy his craving for a good-guy/bad-guy plot. The 1949 Peterskill riots seem a straightforward record of the haves (the heavies) versus the have-nots (the underdogs). It is a tempting melodrama, one played out (as the narrator reveals) three centuries earlier with Wouter Van Brunt and his showdown with his oppressive patroon and again more recently in the 1929 showdown between Jeremy Mohonk, the rebellious half-breed who settles illegally on the Van Wart estate, and Rombout Van Wart, *his* "oppressor." Yet even as Walter finds such a melodrama appealing, he hears contradictory accounts: his father, it appears, is both a shit and a patriot; those innocents who organized the concert were far from naive victims but were rather savvy organizers who understood the potential value of a bloody confrontation with the local Birchers. Further, Walter finds Depeyster Van Wart, the man blamed by his foster family for corrupting Truman, the man behind the violent disruption of the 1949 free concert, accommodating and reasonable. Indeed, Walter becomes a junior executive under Depeyster's wing, defends the Vietnam War, scorns the interfering efforts of Hudson River environmentalists (among them his estranged wife), and even dons (as an exasperated Mardi observes) the "faggoty suit and fucking crew cut" of Depeyster's conservative country club set (320).

The unsettling revelations about the riots, of course, exasperate Walter. Yet these uncertainties argue persuasively to the reader that the limit of plot is its insistence that drawing up "sides" is a profitable enterprise for making sense out of event. Walter must be shown what the chaotician-narrator already understands, what spectacle realism affirms, and what—in text after text—we must learn: it is only each generation's trick of the eye, the most willful suspension of irony, that allows definitions such as "good" and "bad," "hero" and "shit" their brief tenure before they slip quickly into irony. While Walter busies himself hanging white and black hats and demanding "why, why, why in [his] heart, why" (407), what interests the narrator is not the validity but the force of such illusions, how they serve only to insulate us from what we cannot accept and what we fear: the unsettling confusion of raw event. To accept the affirmation of spectacle realism, Boyle reminds us, we must first make our peace with chance.

Not surprisingly, as Walter pieces together his father's history, he nears the inevitable conclusion: we are simply trapped by pattern. Much like our other plodding and unpromising students since Enid Stevick, Walter learns the cheapest lessons quickest: he comes to curse the world as a mean geography stricken by the logic of determinism. Early on, trying with straining effort to relish freedom, Walter acts shamelessly—hurting his loving family; cheating on a long-suffering wife for the empty excitations with the vacuous Mardi; abusing drugs and alcohol in a manic effort to embrace some sorry parody of existential freedom. The most disturbing act, however, occurs when he visits Jessica, his estranged wife, in Tom Crane's forest shack in what he hopes will be a dramatic farewell before he departs for Alaska. The farewell turns quickly grim; in some twisted effort to demonstrate that acts have no consequence, Walter attacks Jessica in what he deems Meursault-esque fashion, clumsily assaulting first her breasts and then her jeans and ultimately raping her even as she begs him to stop. He leaves her, balled up on the floor, crying, her face bruised. Problematic as drifter, Walter fares no better as plotter. When Walter finally meets his father and concludes that actions are locked within predetermined plot, he despairs melodramatically, curses his existence, and then throws up, again and again, into a bucket in a frigid closet that serves as his father's bathroom. He cannot do drift; he cannot stomach plot; he cannot play Meursault; he cannot swallow Newton. With his father, Walter pursues plot; with Mardi, he fucks around with drift. Neither satisfies.

At the novel's close, Walter will move (of course, [with]out plan) to endorse chaos as a way of ordering event; in typical chaotic fashion, he will become a student despite himself. Disaffected over his father, despondent over his wife's continuing affiliation with the jolly band of environmental crusaders (much as his father despaired over *his* wife's "happy horseshit" socialism) and more particularly over her ongoing affair with Tom Crane, Walter closes the narrative by sabotaging the new multimillion-dollar environmental research ship on which Jessica and Tom are sleeping by setting the boat adrift into the Hudson amid a blinding winter storm. He betrays his wife, his friends. But even as he apparently replays with sorry inevitability the treachery of his ancestry, even as he loosens the ship's final mooring line and sends the huge ship into its disastrous free drift into the treacherous Hudson, he expounds with certainty, "this is for me to do, this is for me" (444). Indeed, as Walter stumbles his way through the snow down to the dock, the narrator clearly indicates Walter's free will: "He could have turned right and gone home to bed. But he didn't" (440). Walter then only seems to be replaying history. When Walter sets the ship adrift, he is no actor in his father's genetics tragedy; he does so because he *wants* to and thereby does not simply fulfill a pattern but rather recovers one, salvages design amid the very confusion of unfolding events, suggested by the thickening fury of the snowstorm.

In the aftermath of the wreck of the environmental research boat, Depeyster Van Wart and his cronies, who had long opposed the efforts of the hippie-ecoraiders, content themselves assuming that Walter was a patriot. But such logic drops the crossbar across Walter's action. No more does he do what he does because of his father's treachery or because of Depeyster's influence than a colored pebble moves deliberately to strike pattern within the kaleidoscope tube. Pattern is recovered—it is not demanded, nor insisted. This final act is for Walter to do. In short, even as Walter Van Brunt betrays friends and family and repeats the treachery of his ancestors, he does so both because of history and despite history. It is the quintessential chaotic moment, the quintessential moment of spectacle realism: a fine and steady balance of symmetry and anarchy.

*   *   *

> [Depeyster] was a strong man, single-minded and tough, a man who dwelt in history and felt the pulse of generations beating in his blood. He had those thoughts, those unsettling thoughts, just once, just then, and he dismissed them, never to have them again. When at long last he turned away from the window, there was a smile on his lips. And he held that smile as he strode down the corridor, across the lobby, and through the heavy front door. He was outside, on the steps, the cool sweet air in his face and the stars spread out overhead like a benediction.

> World's End

Herein rests a dilemma. Boyle's narrator offers only the scientist's cold, satisfied aesthetic over recovered design. We must ignore the amorality of Walter's action, its dire ramifications on the lives of those on the boat, its evident cowardice, and even Walter's subsequent death in the blizzard-blown drifts, and stand enthralled by the narrator's achievement: the sustained improvisation of events has indeed recovered satisfying shape. We know that Walter will betray what he loves; yet we know that Walter will choose to do this. We relish the pattern but cannot give that recovered pattern any meaning beyond our deep fascination with its architecture. Chaos reveals that anarchy is actually structural, that our protective insistence on personal responsibility and free will is overrated as we are part of a feedback system of iterations, a dynamic, nonlinear system that bursts with improvisation. Like a weather front, like a stream of water around a rock, like curling cigarette smoke, Walter (like the rest of us) is free to shape the destiny he is destined to shape.

At initial reading, however, World's End, for all its chaotic rhythms, may seem to offer a most bleak conclusion, one reminiscent of traditional realistic narratives. Indeed, as Walter crawls about crippled in the blinding snow and begins his slow freezing death, we hear an unidentified, thin whimper that builds into a wail, "shattering and disconsolate, beyond hope or redemption" (447). We look back on nearly 500 pages of extravagant narrative and realize that Boyle's narrator-qua-chaotician has applied chaos theory to the twin experiences that most give existence "meaning"—the iterations of the tectonic experiences of love and death, the compelling energies of spectacle realism. Both are textbook nonlinear systems; despite their appearance of disorder, despite their appearance of turbulent unpredictability, charted over a vast enough area (here 300 years), they yield reliable patterns. As offered by the narrator, the experiences of love and death confound predictability, defeat probabilities, establish themselves anew within each run and yet define a most reassuring pattern to their experience—but can offer no meaning, only the pattern.

The heroic presence may seem then to be the observer-narrator, the chaotician who sets out the data, who recovers the pattern denied to the narrowed vision of each character. It is cold comfort. We are left as a species to play out over and over the same folly of greed, violence, illicit love, betrayal, and death; chaos theory, read too lightly, would seem merely to reassure us that we elect to be predictable. We are left with the cold thrill of generation itself—perpetually (re)creating event into plot, generating pattern but never touching purpose. But Boyle's narrator depends on the reader, who after all must close up the book and step back into the chaotic world, to see that such easy pessimism has no foundation in the unfolding world-in-process argued by the revolution of chaos theory. Given our participation within Boyle's text, we touch at last the affirmative impulse of spectacle realism.

In point of fact, the narrative does not end in the blizzard death of Walter Van Brunt; rather, it shuttles quickly to the maternity ward of Peterskill Community Hospital. We do not end with absurd death; rather, we close/begin with absurd birth. A baby struggles to be born (its difficult birthing will end in a cesarean). A baby intuitively fights for its place in that very same "grim" world, fighting for life against the blind intervening stroke of sour luck. It refuses to concede the obvious: surviving this dramatic test will merely launch it into a decades-long struggle against the same shattering contingencies. And not only is this baby in a difficult position physically, but the baby will face enormous emotional complications as well. This is no ordinary baby. Eight months earlier, Depeyster Van Wart, at fifty without a male child, began to make his peace with the notion that his grand ancestral line would terminate with him and that his daughter, Mardi, would offer no solace for continuity when he found his wife, Joanna, long frigid and comfortably nonengaged in the bedroom, suddenly hot for his seed. Depeyster, of course, does not know what the narrator reveals to us, that Joanna had been having a most animal affair with the half-breed Jeremy Mohonk and, when Jeremy insists on making love without protection, Joanna comes to her husband to cover the chance that she might get pregnant. Depeyster goes to the hospital in the thralls of proud papa-hood to celebrate the arrival of his heir. When he approaches the window of the maternity ward, however, he greets a son who bears the irrefutable markings of his conception: Mohonk's cat-green eyes, his shock of tar-black hair, his coppery skin. The narrative suddenly teeters near one of those family-tragedy endings typical of traditional realistic fare. Stunned by the implications of the baby's appearance, Depeyster stands in the hallway by the viewing window so long that the janitor mops around him. It is a pivotal moment akin to Maggie's lingering contemplations at the gritty screen of her Baltimore bedroom.

A chaotic universe, of course, cannot endorse melodrama nor afford despair. Chaos theory knows only relentless energy, the pulsating creative turbulence of a freewheeling universe. Every birth suggests the foundations of a chaotic universe, the very universe of spectacle realism—pure process, the stunning kinesis of creativity, the odd determination to continue, always despite, never because. Depeyster turns from the window with a wide smile that carries him out of the ward, out of the hospital, and out under a generous canopy of stars that spreads "like a benediction" (456) overhead. In that smile, he steps out from the magic kingdom, abdicates the damning need to control events (quite an achievement for one who has so singularly needed to manipulate events and people) and the equally damning temptation to bewail his "fate." The baby will be a Van Wart, yet in his blood courses the genetic signatures of the Mohonks and the Van Brunts, who share links dating back to the seventeenth-century invasion. Like the ham sandwich, like the local newspaper, like the onion, the child (a mix of Van Warts, Van Brunts, and Mohonks) is a summary chaotic text, a pied text, a layered achievement of accident and design, a confluence of event and plot, an individual act possessing its own momentum and logic and yet the cumulation of steady generations of familial production, both event and plot—every baby a part and apart. It is in that sort of generation—the complicated joy of projecting ourselves in time—that makes luminous the colder sort of generation of patterns of behavior. That (re)production, that generation, as it turns out, is this world's end, not its melodramatic closure but rather its purpose, its great-hearted mission.

Boyle's narrator closes with the birth of a marked child. Because we have followed 455 pages of iterations, we know this child's life will be no romp structured by purpose and logic. Already complicated by his crossed ancestry, he will forge his way through the same steady pull of absurdity that has compelled the 300 years recorded by this narrative— indeed by each of our texts of spectacle realism. Like characters since Enid Stevick, he will be compelled by material comforts, by disastrous love, by searing carnality; he will be terrorized by thoughts of his own mortality; and as he makes each decision freely, he will nevertheless participate in patterns as old as humanity itself and as recent as his own parents. He will be buffeted about by the unexpected, the twists and bolts of experience; he will struggle between insight and myopia, will suffer at the hands of both and will learn from neither. He will be at the very same moment passive and active. He will be compelled by a fathomless fascination with material glitter. And eventually he will stumble in some grand/petty vaudevillian fashion into death—but only after fashioning (with the [un]willing assistance of someone he is sure to let down) a descendant or two to continue the iterations. He will be exactly like his ancestry and yet strikingly unique. His unfolding life will confirm age-old patterns of human behavior and yet by virtue of his independence and self-direction will deny the determinism such inevitability suggests and grant him the terrifying reassurance of captaining his own fate. His life will be more than drift but less than plot. And the only thing that will wither such a life into stark joylessness will be if he loses the intuitive wonder over participating in its unfolding process. In short, he will live in the jaws of the (s)napping turtle, there within and amid the chaotic universe that appalls/fascinates T. C. Boyle and that figures as the very geography of spectacle realism.

*　　*　　*

"See that?" Cadwallader asked . . . indicating the frozen hindquarters of a porcupine wedged in the crotch of a tree. "When the sun warms it in spring that meat will give rise to new life." "Life?" Wouter questioned. And there, on the lesser Crane's thin lips and hairless cheeks, crouched a smile all ready to pounce. "Blowflies," he said.

World's End

It is that will to observe, that urgency to record this chaotic life that most defines the maturing Boyle. Boyle stands in the shadow of the narrator who so busily fashions the convincing evidence of chaotic (in)stability. As controlling author-ity, however, Boyle is perhaps more tuned to the vaunting ambitions of Cadwallader Crane, young Wouter's older cousin, a minor character introduced late in the narrative as part of the ill-fated revolt against the patroon's manor house in the seventeenth century. The text makes intriguing ties between this minor character and the nonintrusive author. After all, Cadwallader Crane, like Boyle, endured an uneasy relationship with organized schooling. Physically, Cadwallader recalls Boyle's scrawny frame and facial hair scheme. And Cadwallader alone of the Crane clan esteems most highly the human capacity for wonder rather than the family's more pedagogical urge for explanation. And Cadwallader will count among his descendants the 1960s hippie Tom Crane, who (coincidentally?) goes by the initials T. C.

Cadwallader Crane is our most accomplished—and most frustrating—spectacle realist. He has a restless eye; he is unschooled yet is drawn intuitively by the striking wonders of the teeming natural world; he scrutinizes patiently butterflies and moths, "worms, caterpillars, slugs and the humble nuggets of excrement" (372); he is intoxicated by the mysteries that lurk unsuspected about his every step in the (un)spoiled reaches of the Hudson Valley—a respect that he sustains even in the darkening midst of events, even as his young wife dies painfully in childbirth and the fortunes of his small farm turn disastrous. He most relishes long winter walks into a corpsed natural world, where he finds evidences of life stirring, the faintest pulse of a natural world that will not concede exhaustion or depletion. Before he backs awkwardly into his part in the "revolt," before he dies absurdly for a revolution he never conceived, much less supported, he wants only to be a naturalist, to spend his days recording the reassuring evidence of the life-and-death balance of the immediate world, its purposelessness offset grandly by its persistence. And it is this doomed naturalist, this "lover of humble worm and soaring butterfly" (384), who will offer in a passing moment within this surging narrative a most fitting summary image for Boyle's chaotic universe and by extension for the vibrant world of spectacle realism: in one winter walk, Cadwallader points to a dead frozen porcupine, nature's very refuse, bloated and wedged in the crotch of a dead tree. Confronting such stark evidence of the generic extinction that awaits all natural life,

Cadwallader understands, his face aglow, that by spring that same repulsive carcass will give rise to new life, will be alive with blowflies.

Cadwallader's "private enthusiasm for the underpinnings of nature" (371) clues us into the nature of Boyle's spectacle realist sensibilities. Refuting the Reagan Era's strategic withdrawal from the intricacies of engagement and that decade's willful participation in the grand and empty gestures of spectacles and its hunger for artifice and the serious triviality of escape, Boyle's narrative endorses engagement, fronting a spectacle immediate that spans, in this case, centuries. The steady smile of Depeyster Van Wart there under the splash of evening stars is far from the simple sunshine of Reaganesque optimism. Like Cadwallader, Boyle, in tracking the history of so much human debris and so little human heroism, finds nevertheless the splendid promise of continuity metaphorically (as Cadwallader himself does literally) in turds, bloated carcasses, worms, and slugs. But nature, freed of the onerous responsibility of meaning, finds in just such determination a way nevertheless to logic, to patterns of darks and lights that are as cripplingly beautiful as they are resilient. In the birth of the healthy bastard child, Boyle's narrative teaches the reluctant reader of nature's inclination to order, its pushing impulse to live, a system wider, fuller, more spontaneous, more directed—and more improvised—than any of us suspect. We stand at the close of Boyle's narrative under the calming wash of a star-splashed evening sky reassured that the natural world itself suggests resiliency.

And yet we resist closing our narrative on the 1980s within such a spectacle moment. Boyle has surely introduced scale into our argument; we stand at narrative close stunned by the magnificence of the sheer reach of the plot. What Maggie intuits at her bedroom screen Boyle reveals is in fact an intricate principle of architecture that can be traced through the long narrative of our species's history and affirmed by the hard data of contemporary sciences. Walter's absurd death and the equally absurd birth of the long-anticipated Van Wart heir are events that neatly balance but console only because they are played out against the backdrop of the compelling engine of a natural world that, despite our inept stewardship, ensures its own momentum. Walter and Depeyster argue that the human condition amid such noisy persistence promises little in return for our participation, save the intricate wonder of freely shaping lives we were meant to shape.

Our narrative of the 1980s is not finished—it is not the business of spectacle realism to tender such tentative affirmation. Nor can spectacle realism sustain its impact amid a narrative so determined to assert scale; the human element so critical in the argument of spectacle realism here necessarily pales beside the energy of the natural world that so enthralls young Cadwallader Crane (and so clearly powers the vision of T. C. Boyle). Intimacy, the delicate evolution of sensibility, the enduring touch of character so critical to the texts of spectacle realism is here made problematic; Boyle resists deepening characters much beyond necessary touches to sustain their form against the backdrop. Affirmation of the grander sense of operations is purchased here at the expense of accessible characters; any recognizable character here quickly flattens with too-much ease into clumsy caricature. Unlike our other characters, Walter Van Brunt and Depeyster Van Wart come to us finally like Cadwallader Crane's colorful specimens tacked on a board, "a brilliant spangle of moths and butterflies caught in hovering flight" (371). Like the polished stones of a child's kaleidoscope, Boyle's characters surely assert design and give us pause before the freewheeling architecture of chance. But their achievement cannot touch in ways that spectacle realism must. We need fully drawn human characters to understand the breadth and scope of such audacious affirmation. We lack here the deep pull of human love; for Boyle, love is vaudevillian, a careless collision that incites snickers. Thus, our work is not quite complete.

We turn, then, to Richard Powers's monumental *The Gold Bug Variations* to find a vision sufficient to tap into the energy of Cadwallader's boundless natural world but one that is counterparted by the resilient energy of the imperfect human hearts, where character—not stick figures—struggle (as we all must) to engage this staggering stochastic immediate and to participate in the splendid agony of bonding that alone confers dignity on those of us within this vast, wheeling immediate. This sense of possibility marks Powers's work as one of the highest achievements thus far of spectacle realism.

8

Humming the (In)Sufficient Heart Out

Richard Powers, *The Gold Bug Variations*

> *Over me soared the eternal sky,*
> *Full of light and of deity;*
> *Again I saw, again I heard,*
> *The rolling river, the morning bird;—*
> *Beauty through my senses stole;*
> *I yielded myself to the perfect whole.*
>
> Ralph Waldo Emerson, "Each and All"

At the close of Boyle's narrative, then, we are impressed by the furious machinery, the unsuspected author-ity, the deep plot of chance. But spectacle realism is not content to confirm an immediate that stuns by its architecture; rather, spectacle realism reclaims the right of literature to move us, to touch the common work of maneuvering about and within such splendid chaos. It is left to our closing text to bring together the scale and energy of Boyle's testimony with the need for intimacy and sheer (extra)ordinariness of Maggie Moran and the pulling recognition of the dark appropriateness of our shared finitude that shatters—and then reconfigures—Mark Valerian.

We might have selected any number of decade texts whose argument could serve to summarize this affirmation of spectacle realism: among them, Raymond Carver's *Cathedral*, Richard Ford's *The Sportswriter*, Amy Tan's *The Joy Luck Club*, Oscar Hijuelos's *The Mambo Kings Play Songs of Love*, Gloria Naylor's *The Women of Brewster Place*, Don DeLillo's *White Noise*, Norman Rush's *Mating*. But we choose Richard Powers's mammoth 1991 novel *The Gold Bug Variations* in large part because of the sheer breadth of its cultural indictment, its angry rejection of nearly all the magic kingdom premises of the Reagan Era: the era's radical turn toward simplification; its effortless conflation of fantasy and history; its fanatical gospel of self-interest; its unearned optimism; its relentless materialism; its reductive, so-seductive invocation of sham spectacle and hokey excess; its romance with surface; its cynical manipulation of the postures of childlike simplicity; its wholesale retreat from the immediate. There are other reasons. Overtired of the manipulations of irony we have watched thus far, we come to a closing text in which the struggles of the characters rest within the benevolent generosity of a writer and ultimately of the reader who in confederation recognize within the deep experience of these characters dilemmas, anxieties, passions, and profound errors that are (unlike those offered by Boyle) moving and troubling.

It is, thus, a most elegant summary text of our genre, a novel that finds vastly rewarding its confidence in the phenomenal world that reveals the possibility of wonder in the very vulnerabilities that so define our condition in the quietus of this dark century. Tapping the grand metaphor of networking suggested by computer sciences and by contemporary genetics, Powers webs a splendid and inclusive system that affirms the basic presumption of all spectacle realism: within fictions, each of us lurks. Like our other novelists, Powers seeks to revalidate wonder, to reenchant facticity for an era lulled into indifference over the intolerable weight of a stubbornly problematic immediate or willingly distracted by the sizzle of contrived spectacles. Closing the text, we are stunned—what Mark Valerian ultimately accepts, what Maggie Moran quietly intuits at the screen window, what Cadwallader Crane so nervelessly records, Powers noisily celebrates: exuberance is our right; the immediate is spectacle enough.

But, as we have seen since Walter Porter, affirmation is always despite, not because of, its context. Powers's is a world that does not easily validate wonder. For his text-sites, Powers split-focuses on the 1950s and the mid-1980s. He tracks research scientists at the University of Illinois during the High Noon paranoia of the late 1950s. With anxieties leavened with unbecoming jingoism, they react darkly to the newly launched Sputnik; they conceive quickly of a high-tech world where superpowers will collide, a world of division, paranoia, fear, a world, in short, defined by Hiroshima and sustained through the hard frost of Reagan's first term. Even as Stuart Ressler, one of the novel's central characters, dismisses Edward Teller and his ilk as mere "engineers" and disdains anything but the pure pursuit of the intricate secrets of the natural world, that immediate world—the world fashioned by this new science—is poised on self-extermination. And, twenty-five years later, Jan O'Deigh, a reference librarian in Manhattan who will come to know Ressler shortly before his death, is still living under the terrifying parabola of this closed sense of history; part of her job is to answer queries posted by patrons on cards, but when one asks why the Soviets downed the Korean civilian airliner, Jan is haunted by her inability to provide any response.

Against this paranoia so fundamental to the logic of the 1950s and to the Reagan Era, Powers taps into the ascendant metaphors suggested by the midcentury revolution in life science following the shock wave of Francis Crick and James Watson's revelation of the probable structure of DNA, a quiet revolution begun without the banner headlines that announced after Hiroshima something called the Atomic Age. The chance to understand the very mechanism of evolution and speciation enticed Ressler's generation like "the American Wilderness" (44). Stuart Ressler is himself a young promising molecular biologist hotly pursuing the genetic sequencing code that will reveal how living matter manufactures itself. By probing into the very machinery of life, we attempted to account for the ongoing reality of our own continuation, how we move from generation to generation, a movement (as Boyle argues) so relentlessly forward, so explosively resilient, that it defies the melodramatic slouching toward apocalypse implied from the theoretical work of atomic physicists. As it turns out, we have the answer to the atomic scare in our very cells. The relentless process of molecular replication, the industrial production of millions of amino acids and proteins, offers not the competing systems suggested by the midcentury world of atomic physics (and validated by the chilling rhetoric of the Reagan Era) but rather a cooperative system that argues only continuity.

Rather than cowering before contingency, life science (much like Boyle's chaos theory) marvels at the sheer prowess of chance, how it blindly erects a natural world of compelling organization, how "out of all the capricious kinds of cosmos there might have been, ours could have lucked, against all odds, into the one arrangement capable of supporting life" (336). For Ressler's generation, breaking the genetic code represented an opportunity to locate "the fundamental message unit behind the biosphere" (371). Less than a decade after the appalling lurch into the Nuclear Age with its intemperate pessimism over the imminent ravishing of the Earth, geneticists began to understand the marvelous energy of that natural world, an intricate dynamo all the more stunning because it rested on utter simplicity—a twin helixical sequencing of four bases stringing amino acids and then synthesizing proteins. As Stuart Ressler so often says, "What could be simpler?" DNA came to be understood as a twisted molecular ladder, cunningly spooled. The individuality of the organism is held in the differing rungs. That chemical makeup is spelled out at great length using a molecular alphabet of only four letters, four nucleic acids: adenine (A), thymine (T), guanine (G), and cytosine (C). One alphabet serves all animated matter, one "simple, accidental, but necessary and breathtaking generating form" (209).

Jan O'Deigh, listening to Stuart Ressler explain the world as "a single, self-buffering, interdependent organism" (324), recalls lines from Emerson's "Each and All" that she memorized in school. Indeed, Emerson's sense of the world as a single organism, thriving and cooperative, stunningly varied and yet magnificently unified by a microcosmic blueprint that creates one magnificent organic webbing was validated more than a century later by the hard data of genetics. Through Ressler, we touch a vast universe orchestrated by the inexplicable push of sheer chance and by the demand that we copy; the vast engine of the replicating gene, not the fissioning atom, becomes the most powerful force in the material universe. The meticulous record of Nobel laureates then encodes what spectacle realists argue so passionately: that continuity and cooperation fashion the simple intricacy of a natural world that, despite our best efforts to strip and plunder, maintains and thrives and should, by rights, continue to reward the eye opened wide. What Powers offers in Stuart Ressler is nothing less than the revival of the childlike passion to believe that the world can still amaze, console, teach; is, in fact, still readable, long after the rest of us have turned away, consigned it to confusion or, worse, to doom. Genetics, then, like spectacle realism, is a "voting for wonder" (412).

* * *

Es muss alles moglich zu machen seyn. (All things that are possible are real.)

Johann Sebastian Bach, quoted in *The Gold Bug Variations*

What further distinguishes Powers's narrative from our previous texts is its structural complexity. We track two central characters separated by a generation, characters who commit the same grievous error and whose educations move hesitatingly toward similar affirmations. The narrative unfolds in three narrative strands. Chronologically, the first narrative tracks Stuart Ressler, who, as part of a University of Illinois research program in 1957, conducts a brief, incendiary affair with Jeanette Koss, a married colleague who, in the course of their romance, introduces him to Bach's *Goldberg Variations* by making a gift of Glenn Gould's monumental 1955 interpretation. When she decides against pursuing the risk that Ressler represents and settles for the imperfect neutrality of her innocuous if devoted husband, Ressler dramatically abandons his career and in effect disappears in a most graceless (and by now familiar) posture of retreat.

In the second plotline, a Manhattan librarian, Jan O'Deigh, is approached at work by a stranger, a coworker, it turns out, of the same molecular biologist who now, some twenty-five years later, is comfortably sunk in the anonymity of a graveyard-shift job as a computer programmer where each night he listens to the *Variations*. The stranger, Franklin Todd, is curious about his coworker and enlists the librarian's assistance in unearthing background on the lonesome figure, certain only that at some point in his life he had attained some distinction. In the process of researching the geneticist, the librarian, drifting through a stale relationship with her own devoted if innocuous lover, falls disastrously in love with Franklin, who is himself drifting through the terminal stages of an art history dissertation on an obscure Dutch artist who he admits is available for study only because of his stunning mediocrity. In the course of her developing relationship with Franklin, however, Jan comes to be mesmerized by the deft mind of the geneticist, whom she gets to know during lengthy nighttime talk sessions at the computer center.

In the third narrative thread, nearly a year after Franklin and Jan's relationship explodes in Franklin's infidelity with a bank teller named Annie Martens, Franklin contacts Jan suddenly by postcard to tell her only that Stuart Ressler has died. Her emotions unexpectedly churned, Jan dramatically quits *her* career, resolves to live off her savings, and devotes her time to studying genetics, a subject she decides has the significance to justify such a project and that would, as well, offer a closeness to the fascinating man who is now lost to her. Indeed, the only action in the narrative present is Jan's laborious work of cerebral expansion, work that is documented for us by notebook entries that record her emerging understanding of the theories of life science that Stuart Ressler first helped define. Yet her journal entries record as well her continuing desire for Franklin Todd, and she begins to track him down using only the postmarks and other clues she finds in his few correspondences. Ultimately, as her savings dwindle and she prepares to reenter the job market, she effects a most difficult reunion with Franklin, and they prepare at the close of the novel to try their fragile relationship once more.

Powers dispatches early on any expectations of a neat linear narrative. Within each chapter, the three narrative threads are tightly intertwined, and the reader shuttles abruptly back and forth. As in Boyle's text, the narrative plots do not touch; they make no reference to each other; they do not link. Each insists on its integrity, its independence—accented by intrusive boldface headings. But unlike Boyle's narrative, Powers's has no consistent overvoice, no narrative center. Movement across the nearly twenty-five years is done within chapters; for instance, we quick-cut forward from a steamy encounter between Ressler and Jeanette in a closet of the research facility to Jan's recounting her sudden insight into DNA replication (complete with appropriate textbook-thick explanations). The novel, then, might seem a most labored experiment in violating even the simplest expectations of plot sequencing and handing the narrative over to approximate chaos.

But Powers, like Boyle, is far too much a student of contemporary sciences not to recognize that chaos is always unsuspected achitecture. The shifting between three narratives represents an ingenious approximation in the reading experience of the exacting listening experience required to hear Bach's accomplishment in the *Goldberg Variations*, the piece of music that serves as background score to each of the narrative threads. Bach's piece is no simple listen. Ears grown accustomed to the easy horizontal argument and plain drama of homophony are initially distressed by the apparent confusions of Bach's vertical polyphony. It can be like trying to keep track of three or four conversations simultaneously. And even after the demanding design of multiple-voice staggered simultaneity is explained (usually by recourse to the child's round of "Row, Row, Row Your Boat," which is to polyphony what "99 Bottles of Beer on the Wall" is to homophony), such ears frequently turn aside the music as too mathematical, architecture without passion. But Bach takes such severe mathematical formulations and devises music that has the requisite technical mastery and dense plan but possesses as well, in the working of independent voices against other independent voices, a weave that anticipates harmonic music, melodies that are expressive in ways usually not associated with polyphony. As each voice enters, each commences a separate hierarchy, a new system added like overlays in one of those anatomical maps in an encyclopedia. As each system commences, it in turn braids with the others into a most demanding vertical and horizontal cooperation.

Powers's novel, then, can only be read polyphonically. The analogy to music is central to Powers's intricate construction and to his deliberate isolation of his three controlling narrative threads. Only a careful ear can follow the intricate cooperation of Bach's multiple melodies. Like Powers's novel (and like the immense natural world that boggles Stuart Ressler), the contrapuntal exercise is oppressively vast in its apparent particulars, but once understood, it is remarkably unified and simple. To listen to Bach, the ear must move from initial indifference and/or confusion to grasping the mathematical precision of each executed variation and, then, to ultimate epiphany: the revelation of the delicate vertical beauty of contrapuntal voices that stay isolated and yet manage to tangle into a most stunning weave.

To do so, the ear must work to encode more than one melody simultaneously. In a most suggestive moment, Stuart Ressler meets a woman—the wife of a colleague—who is a whiz at processing government paperwork at work because she can take two dictation sequences simultaneously. What she mimics in her parlor trick approximates the approach Powers demands from the reader (and that Bach demands from the listener): manipulating staggered identical voices. Within the *Variations,* we recover the pattern; the variations are unified by a recurring bass line (indeed, the variations form about a traditional passacaglia), and the thirty-two variations are themselves sequenced in groups of three in which the last of each group of three is a canon at successive intervals from unison to ninth. The noncanons are themselves a rich potpourri of musical styles, but each is a careful variation on the initial passacaglia. It is, then, a most forbidding mathematics that discloses a most wonderful simplicity. Of course, those most confounded by counterpoint can simply listen, but, as with the natural world, probing only encourages awe and ignorance leads only to indifference. Reading polyphonically reveals the intricate patterns of reiteration and elaboration argued by two love affairs separated by more than a generation. Powers carefully keeps each plotline separate, much like the voices in Bach's canons. We read them much as we listen to the voices of a canon; we read them simultaneously, realizing only in their vertical juxtapositioning the impression of a fragile harmony.

This complicated structural exercise surely sets Powers's narrative apart from our other texts. Unlike those texts, which are structurally conservative, Powers's novel could be dismissed, as could Bach's *Variations*, as an arid, precious exercise in architecture, a coded puzzle that finally reveals its discussion and then exhausts itself in the explanation. Indeed, Powers has long faced the argument that he is too smart, too clever.[1] But (as when Bach's intricate architecture reveals haunting melodies) design here argues a (com)passionate theme that locates Powers's work not within the gametexts of postmodernism but rather within the strategy of spectacle realism: intricate design returns us to the immediate, reminds us that, in the contingent universe that has so distressed characters since Enid Stevick, we participate (un)knowingly in an immense round that encompasses nothing less than the species itself.

Like the other writers of spectacle realism, Powers offers as (re)solution the rich, (im)perfect experience of desire. Life is about chemistry—we are not about structure, but rather bonding. But desire is messy, akin to the inexplicable, if dramatic, pairing of the bases conducted when the DNA begins within the soup of the cell its blind, furious work of engineering living matter. And for Powers's characters, desire, despite its white-hot combustion, closes in frustration and sterility, isolation and abandonment: Jeanette leaves Ressler; a devastated Ressler abandons his career; Jan, reeling after Franklin's betrayal, retreats to her library; Franklin disappears in Europe to tend to his dissertation. Despite Powers's evident interest in polyphony and in the energy of genetic bonding, his characters seem to defy the molecular dictum to connect, the threads seem not to braid, and we are left too near the descendental vision of traditional realistic narratives where again and again the fiery need to bond incinerates those who feel it most keenly. Yet in the polyphonic rendering of their stories, Powers reminds us that such isolation is only apparent. The characters play out their individual melodies, the fundamental (and too often) disastrous movements of the craving heart, when in reality they participate in an endlessly varied yet intricately recurring design much as Bach achieved in his *Variations*. Desire is an endlessly repeated process that is, nevertheless, never the same experience. Each voice, each character's narrative, by itself unspectacular, helps create the round, and the weave would be diminished, indeed forfeited, if any one voice was removed.

This celebration of consanguinity includes, ultimately, the reader in a gesture of inclusion that marks Powers's text as critical within the argument of spectacle realism. We are all of us lodged within a vast interdependence that Powers suggests not only by the DNA signal system but also by the Manhattan On-Line computer system that employs Ressler, where the most negligible burp registers throughout the system, riffling outward in a stunning validation of interconnection. If the world is conceived as the cooperative single cell, if the voices that here grind so inevitably toward sterility and isolation all participate in a species-wide canon of desire, that single great polyphonic round must include as well the imperfect voice of the reader. We all share experience that stirs, hurts, cuts, heals, and then cuts again. Ressler comments on the audible vocalizing of Glenn Gould in his recording of the *Variations*, the fractured off-key ad-libbing accompaniment sung, hummed, and aspirated by Gould himself and caught during the recording sessions. That all-too-human, richly imperfect variation—"the pianist . . . humming his insufficient heart out" (462)—hangs above the otherwise mathematical perfection of the *Variations*. Likewise, just above the intricate construction of these characters' parallel plots, their playing out in canon splendor the argument of the bruised heart, we hang our own variation, each of us humming our own fractured variation of the heart's explosive energy. We add the crowning voice, the final variation: our own.

*   *   *

Circumstances and a certain bias of mind have led me to take interest in such riddles, and it may well be doubted whether human ingenuity can construct an enigma of the kind that human ingenuity may not, by proper application, resolve.

Edgar Allan Poe, "The Gold Bug"

The Gold Bug Variations, like our other texts of spectacle realism, is most centrally about the difficult process of learning; as with these other texts, Powers's central characters are either teachers or students. They maneuver with great agility about the most intimidating terrains of the Information Age: sprawling libraries catwalked by floors of organized facts; vast computer systems that retrieve gigabytes of information in fractions of seconds; trivial dissertations that stretch on without clear purpose; research labs crowded by those in the professional pursuit of information. Such intimidating vastness can easily trigger a most profound fear of scale. Tooney Blake, a colleague of Ressler's, spends a harrowing night locked in the university library, where he goes for shelter when a freak December tornado rakes the campus. There, he is unnerved by the sheer tonnage of information we have assembled ("words spread in all directions, an endless, continuous thread" [362]), overwhelmed by the particulars—"digging in the dirt, turning up shards, millions of shards, more than anyone expected to find" (363). Shaken, he resigns his appointment, certain that any enterprise determined to comprehend the whole—as the research team sets out to do in cracking the genetic code—is radically hopeless. "Go spend a night in the stacks. We're committed to nothing less than a point-for-point transcript of everything there is. Only one problem: the concordance is harder to use than the book" (363).

To engage the immediate tallied and cataloged by the muscle of contemporary sciences is to risk getting lost in the particulars, to lose the larger signal, a frustration that Powers compares to glimpsing into a pay-per-view telescope that "magnifies but constricts" and then abruptly "snaps shut on your quarter after a lousy two minutes" (352). During her sabbatical, Jan, a "greenhorn" to the sciences, begins to perceive exactly what the term "planet" describes. We touch the striking wonder of the immediate that spectacle realism engages. Amid pages of Whitmanesque cataloging of this "embarrassing profusion" (318), we begin to sense the sheer scale of the natural world—"the blue, species-mad world" (317) where life stirs against enormous odds and in the most inhospitable locations (deserts, ocean bottoms, arctic wastelands) to achieve an "excess of issue" (319), a catalog of species so dense that one could "memorize a hundred species a day and die not yet scratching the collection's surface" (318). But that very scale frustrates our efforts to encode it. We are stunned by the diversity of the macrolevel. Drowning in trivia, lost in the noise, we can be overwhelmed by surfaces, destroyed by factoids. Indexing the information, like Tooney Blake, we lose the magic. Stunned by the macrolevel, we ignore the microlevel, much as ears straining after melody in Bach's *Variations* miss the reassuring bass line that generates the complex exercise.

Amid such profusion, information acquisition—not celebration—is the preferred strategy for accommodation. In a strategy we have seen played out before, characters strive to understand the forbidding complexity of the surrounding immediate. Powers's two central characters—Jan O'Deigh and Stuart Ressler—pursue information obsessively. Jan, from the Reference Desk at an obscure branch library in Manhattan, guides the lost through the labyrinth of reference material. Quoting Melville (comparing an answer to "one warm spark in the Arctic crystal"), she expounds on the benediction achieved by tracking down information. Each day she receives anonymous note cards, a "community of needs" (14), each one asking perplexing questions, each one receiving her careful reply. She traffics calmly in information—the obscurest trivia on breeds of dogs, American secretaries of state, distant river systems, the weight of protein in a pound of peanuts. Jan appears to command the vastness. She is addicted to explanation; as a child she pushed her parents past patience with the cyclic interrogation of "why" (35). Indeed, burned by the disastrous affair with Franklin Todd and hurting over the stunning news of Ressler's death, Jan retreats. Her self-directed investigation into life science—"I've decided to learn something . . . exchange fact for feeling, reverse what I've done with my life to date" (86)—is a pure commitment to information without professional compensation, indeed without practical benefit—and without wonder. Jan wants only to "swim" in the "dizzy swell" of available information on genetics (89).

This odd sort of antilife, which recalls so many strategic evacuations of other characters within texts of spectacle realism, here specifically parallels behavior played out some twenty-five years earlier (and simultaneously, given the polyphonic narrative) by Stuart Ressler himself. Toting a newly minted Ph.D. in molecular biology, Ressler arrives at the research facilities in Urbana, amid rolling miles of emptiness, an outpost of information much like Jan's branch library. There Ressler proposes to lose himself, like Jan, within the study of genetics. He is uninterested in the other members of the research team. Indeed, as he listens to their chitchat he wonders how such an unpromising group could even begin the work of cracking the code. "The code must certainly be more ingenious than this crew it created. . . . Incredible comedown, awful circularity; no one to reveal us to ourselves but us" (49–50). Like Jan, Ressler, whose favorite childhood reading was a "ruinously expensive set of encyclopedias" (134), deals most confidently in information. Diligently, he plods through stacks of scientific literature garnered from the massive university library—interestingly, decorated by civil defense signs, a sort of refuge-within-a-refuge. Living on the fringes of campus, sleeping on a borrowed sofa, munching bowls of cereal and cold water, he is sustained by information. Years later, despite abandoning science, Ressler still traffics in information, save now on a stupefying level: he mans the night shift within Manhattan On-Line. There, surrounded by whirring consoles in an electronic magic kingdom plated (appropriately) by massive sheets of safety glass, Ressler monitors virtually single-handedly the flow of information feeding Manhattan's banking network.

Libraries, research facilities, computer facilities, uncompletable dissertations, notebook journals—each a magic kingdom, each a stunning play zone that thrives on the generation and compilation of information. But as we have seen again and again, from Enid Stevick to Kate Vaiden, from Daniel Quinn to Mark Valerian, spectacle realism takes issue with strategies that lead to cool disengagement. To study life here is to take a sabbatical from living. These investigators, for all their fierce cerebral locomotion, sacrifice the simplest gesture of communion that, in the formulations of the very genetics they study, is what we are about in our very cells. Despite systems that suggest intricate linkage, each information system reinforces isolation. The research team is rife with crude backstabbing; the patrons of Jan's library ("retirees and transients" [16]) huddle alone in guarded silence; the computer system merely threads a far-flung urban archipelago of financial institutions; and the dissertation is an artful isometric exercise. Jan touches her patrons only through anonymous queries on note cards; Ressler, who arrives at Urbana coldly dismissing the "plague of companionship" (43), elects, after the reckless months with Jeanette, to lead an eerily monastic life for nearly forty years. Powers finds most disturbing this easy addiction to the simple arithmetic of self-involvement, the valerian comfort of strategic retreat. Powers reminds us of the cautionary tale of Horace Wells, who "altruistically pursuing proper anesthetic dosages, discovered, instead, addiction" (117).

More important, both info-addicts move to the awareness that information, no matter how inclusive (and Ressler and Jan work to understand nothing less than the workings of all animated matter), is ultimately thin. The immediate refuses to disclose its most enticing mysteries. The day he finally resolves the knotty problem of gene sequencing, Ressler watches two university students kissing hotly in the late spring sun, indicating he is certain that they are bound for intimacies that will reveal knowledge about bonding far more significant than the information he has finally wrestled from the natural world. Indeed, the consequences of his own historic insight pale next to his desire for Jeanette Koss. Ressler wants only to talk to Jeanette, to tell her not just about his insight but that he wants her in his life whatever the complications—and they are vast as she is entangled with a conventionally doting husband. Years later, when Jan brings to Manhattan On-Line a scrap of paper on which she has copied the table describing the genetic code, the very blueprint of all living matter first defined in the early 1960s in a manner very much as Ressler argued, Ressler is "embarrassed" by the simple sheet of paper; "Doesn't look like much, does it?" (604). Ressler is not alone in discovering the limits of information. Jan, after ten months of studying genetics, understands at last bits of its argument but acknowledges the moment is imperfect; the last book she reads before she must return to the workforce informs her that the "doubling time for genetic knowledge has dropped to less than a year. Twice the field it was the day [she] started" (616). Ressler and Jan, a generation apart, resolve to study life (ironically, *Life* is the magazine sent to Urbana to profile the promising biologist) safely distanced from the larger mess of actually living, the trampoline world of spectacle realism.

Powers counterpoints this relentless quest to explain *how* bonding takes place—the pursuit of information that is exhilarating yet isolating—with the far more complicated question of *why* bonding takes place—the knowledge of desire available only in yielding to the compelling call to experience. As Jan warns, "I learn again, in my nerve endings, that information is never the same as knowledge" (15). Jeanette also concedes in her lengthy letter ending the relationship with Ressler, "I've reached a pitch of knowledge with you that I know I will never know again" (597). The bruising, exhilarating experience of bonding involves the "jump from information to knowledge" (90). Powers, himself a former computer programmer, lets loose into each character's protective system a "bug," the tectonic impulse of desire, an invasive agency that threatens the system's neat parameters and quickly crashes its sophisticated (and protective) structure.

Powers braids the metaphors of genetics, contrapuntal music, and computer networking to make vivid the very point our spectacle realists have each in turn argued: how we hunger for interdependence. Our very molecules, inert by themselves, tell us that autonomy "when pushed, probably has no meaning" (397). As we have seen since the sweaty night at the Port Oriskany Armory when Enid first glimpses her step-uncle, as particles, we want only to be part, a need that is gene deep and species wide. A colleague of Ressler's is most validated by participating in a national ratings system for television shows; he feels the remarkable security of belonging. Ressler hangs about the Illini football stadium on a fall Saturday and marvels at the 50,000 voiced collective unit. Such desire to violate our apparent isolation is mirrored by the relentless working of desire. Ressler, we are told, has "this thing about affection" (399). It is a sumptuous agony; as in our other texts, casualties of the heart litter the massive plotline. As Jan acknowledges, "Everyone I've ever loved has killed me a little" (557). When Jan and Franklin make love, it is to Mahler's sorrowful *Ruckert Leider.* Joe Lovering, a university colleague of Ressler's, is so driven by isolation that he invents an alluring mistress and enthralls colleagues with stories of his white-hot relationship. And when that tenuous fantasy no longer sustains him, he bails out of the complicated life processes by gassing himself in his garage. Dan Woytowich, another colleague, is unconditionally blown away by the marvelous reality of his infant daughter until a chance game with her alphabet blocks reveals the baby's color blindness, which he knows from his command of genetic information means the child cannot be his. The sunny openness of Annie Martens, the beautiful, pleasantly addled bank teller who regularly visits at Manhattan On-Line, suggests a conventionally happy woman. Yet despite a fling with Franklin, she reveals in an "imploring, needy, hoping" kiss that she offers to Jan, a signal that her public concession to heterosexuality belies deeper, more painful confusions.

This blind urge that drives us as to surrender our heart to another (at one point Ressler concedes that we have yet to isolate the gene that can forgive us for wanting "what we are born wanting" [350]) drives us as well to risk vulnerability, to total the heart we offer certain only that every step is a deep yet welcome mistake. That is the knowledge, rather than the information, of bonding. In experiences separated by twenty-five years, Ressler and Jan must learn that the irresistible curiosity that so drives scientists in their labs or the inquisitive urgency that compels us to burrow into libraries or the crazy locomotion that fuels the industrial replication conducted within the cell is only a thin version of the potent desire that drives the heart. It is that riddle of bonding that centers Powers's novel, how we stand confounded by the compulsive decision made virtually every moment by a heart somewhere in our species to bond against the conservative wisdom, quoted by Jan in answer to a question in the library, to "Look to your Moat" (56).

Powers finds a working metaphor for this tension between information and knowledge within the very vocabulary of life science. At a critical point when the university team is about to experiment with a genetic coding process that Ressler can see will be pointless, he alone argues in a contentious session that cracking the genetic code, that is, devising the sequencing of bases that synthesizes proteins in the cell, cannot be done by testing the process ongoing in the cell. Such in-vivo experiments, he claims, are chaotic, like reports from war correspondents under fire. Rather, he argues, the solution is a cell-free system, in-vitro experiments, that create the conditions of the cell artificially, that violate the complexity of the actual manufacturing of proteins. Such a cold reconstruction of the actual, he argues, is necessary for the retrieval of information.[2]

Information, so much the obsession of Powers's characters, comes, then, only through living in vitro, in withdrawing into the magic kingdom hermetics of libraries, laboratories, and computer terminals. We have seen such cool canopic geographies before: boxing rings, bomb shelters, music rooms, newspaper offices, empty chapels, classrooms, rambling beach houses, television soundstages, hospital rooms. Knowledge, on the other hand, comes only from in-vivo experience, in the exhilarating step away into the rough unfolding of the very process itself. Relationships here reveal what happens when science loses its calm, when life concedes to living, when in vitro becomes the terrifying vulnerability of in vivo. There is no easy attraction; it is a sort of death to offer the heart so vitally exposed (Jeanette is born on the day of the Valentine's Day Massacre, which yokes unsettling images of deep passion and sheer annihilation; Franklin's last name is a Germanic suggestion of "death"). The bonding process between hearts is capricious. But like the DNA strand, a master architect operating by sheerest chance, the fallible heart, to borrow Powers's own imagery, is a tone-deaf composer able nevertheless to execute on occasion a symphony.

*   *   *

For one human being to love another: that is perhaps the most difficult of all our tasks; the ultimate, the last test and proof, the work for which all other work is but preparation.

Rainer Maria Rilke

Like our other texts, this one is about the business of education. As with our other texts, the process of education is paralleled to resurrection, bringing back from the dead characters who curiously volunteer for figural inhumation. Powers offers a most stunning fugal-styled revival of both Stuart Ressler and Jan O'Deigh. It is the contrapuntal rejuvenation of their hearts, both long dormant, that provides our summa text of spectacle realism its most compelling affirmation. What makes Powers a most appealing summary text is that such revival is achieved against the very impulse that so terrifies in texts of spectacle realism: the human necessity to die. Stuart Ressler will come to show us what characters to this point have been unable to—how a spectacle realist is to die, how we are to distill wonder from the darkest irony of the immediate: that its massive vibrancy comes only because its every particle must die.

To understand that act of revival, we must first understand what devastates Stuart Ressler. It is familiar to us by now, it is what so often justifies retreat in spectacle realism: the detonating experience of desire. In ways that recall each of our other writers, Powers provides in this drama of bonding a most powerful anatomy of human affection, step by raw step as it is compelled from tentative attraction to fierce consummation. On the first day in Urbana, ready for the comfortable isolation of work, Ressler, in his hurry, arrives with his hair still wet from a quick morning shower. As he settles behind his desk, he receives an impromptu hair-drying massage from a coworker, Dr. Jeanette Koss, who ironically tells him such wet hair leaves him vulnerable—to infection, to a bug. After this, Ressler must contend with Jeanette's mesmerizing effect. At first, he approaches her as he would with any research problem—with information. He looks up her published work, personnel information. She becomes a most intriguing cipher to solve. He is drawn to her in the lab: "How can he remain impassive, give this woman no clue that she throws out his method, corrupts his buffer rates, soaks his equilibrium with a wash of chemical maydays?" (236). Days later, unable to shake the effects of this mysterious woman and spending yet another evening in his unkempt apartment, Ressler is again stunned by intrusion; this time Dr. Koss is at his door, bearing the gift of the Gould recording.

As spectacle realism dictates, the sheer pull of inexplicable desire drives Ressler to expose vulnerabilities protected as long as his life remained in vitro; we recall a touching scene when Ressler tries to instruct a colleague's young daughter, who is being picked on by a schoolyard bully, on the finer points of boxing. When he momentarily drops his guard, Ressler finds himself the stunned recipient of a roundhouse punch that sends him, bleeding, to the floor. Within the experience of Jeanette, he surely lowers his guard. Triggered by her notes, her unexpected phone calls late in the evening, her odd visits to his apartment, Ressler finally dares the infraction of full consummation, a hungry tearing at the flesh, a potent violation of isolation, a fiercesome rutting that explodes his simplest assumptions about something called "life" as living itself invades his protective system with irresistible absoluteness. Surely Ressler and Jeanette opt for vulnerabilities that defy the simpler lives they lead without each other; each one gets involved knowing only that such an exploration is surely a grievous error, a violation of common sense and social convention, explorations that can lead, finally, nowhere. Although Ressler finds in Jeanette a "place in cut grass, an orchard under the rushing in of dusk" (283), they both acknowledge that any revelation of their affair will surely mean they will be "dead on many levels" (345).

Importantly, the desire that compels Ressler denies the cold logic of the biological mechanisms he tracks in the laboratory. We do not replay Boyle, the benevolent naturalist. In a moment of honesty, Jeanette confesses to Ressler that she is barren. Yet at that moment Ressler most hungrily consummates his attraction for her, defying the simple laws of biological necessity: the frank and unromantic program we follow because the species will not accept its own depletion. Here, in the very savagery of their consummation, Ressler and Jeanette lift themselves—and the potent pull of the heart—away from the laboratory; living trumps the neater rules of life. Indeed, after this coupling, Ressler feels "inappropriately alive" (471). We are not, therefore, merely driven by the blind need to multiply; to argue against our eventual dispersion into death by furious procreation reduces us to breeders, where mating becomes hardly more than a suppressed scream against blankness. Powers has little regard for blind biological instinct; in a telling moment on the bus for Urbana, Ressler is appalled as he watches "the insane persistence" (44) of a line of tortoises following their mass migratory instincts across the highway and, in turn, getting squashed by passing cars.

Eventually, Ressler resolves to have Jeanette in his life, a dramatic decision that defies the logic of the tortoises, that, in fact, runs counter to the very biological dictums he is himself formulating. He decides, ironically, on the very day he finds her lengthy letter revealing her decision to stay with her husband when he departs Urbana for a new job. Within days, too impressed by the sudden weight of his particular sorrow, Ressler resigns his position at the research facility, even as he understands at last the process that would decode the genetic sequencing in which information from the DNA is translated into protein. Scalped naked by the sheer force of the knowledge he has gained into human bonding, Ressler loses not only his voracious appetite for information but his taste for the broader knowledge of desire, finds too enthralling the particulars of his own little tragedy, imagines he can withdraw from the webbing whose sheer inclusiveness he himself was just barely glimpsing, and eventually immures himself within the canopic darkness of Manhattan On-Line.

Totaled, left within the vastness of her rejection, Ressler in effect stops wrestling, retires to a long stretch of denied life, tending to his rooftop garden and writing music scores that are never played, pursuits that suggest sublimated fertility, displaced creativity, and hard isolation. It is Stuart Ressler's error that after his blowtorch experience with Jeanette he trades knowledge for information—a suicide in self-defense that recalls similar gestures by Enid Stevick, John Wheelwright, and Kate Vaiden. Manhattan On-Line is his artificial world, a magic kingdom driven by information; where when the system undergoes a cataclysmic collapse, as it does one night when Jan visits, correction is simply a programming event, convincing the computer by manipulating data that the error, whatever its size, simply never happened. The heart, of course, is no computer; Ressler's "error" cannot be so easily corrected. In the wake of Jeanette's letter, Ressler finds the immense world he tracked as a geneticist perfect now for getting lost in, to indulge the urge "to live alone in a quiet place" (383). One night, showing Jan and Franklin the computer system that employs him, Ressler demonstrates its capability for translating foreign languages by typing the spare sentence, "I am left behind" (368).

But Powers is far too much a spectacle realist to leave such bare threads—he is in the business of spinning braids. He offers a most tonic contrapuntal narrative plot in tracking the emerging relationship between Jan O'Deigh and Franklin Todd, a difficult connection that nevertheless intrigues Stuart Ressler, who, watching the deepening of the emotional tie between his two younger friends, finds the will to reengage the difficult world of the heart and to step once again away from the invulnerability of his bunker.

In polyphonic style, the revival of Stuart Ressler begins much as the experience with Jeanette did: with an unexpected touch, a violation of long-tended private space. In the library in the mid-1980s, Jan O'Deigh finds herself the recipient of an unexpected touch on the shoulder, a touch of such violence that it stuns her, testifying to the awkwardness with which Ressler attempts even the most basic connection: "the man had gone so long without touching that his muscles had simply forgotten how light a tap need be" (16). Ressler wants only to tell her that she has listed the date wrong on her Today in History Board. But this spare encounter, the benevolent intervention of a significant stranger, like the hair-drying massage, triggers a complicated sequence of events that will pull Jan's heart (and ultimately Stuart Ressler's) out of dormancy. Jan will meet Franklin Todd, who will come (by the odd machinery of chance) to the same library branch searching for information about Ressler himself. Franklin's maddeningly indirect romancing will cause Jan to forsake the entrenched lifestyle she pursues with a junior advertising executive, Keith Tuckwell (a relationship so completely devoid of magic that Powers renders the chapter devoted to its collapse in a question-and-answer format), and venture against her own common sense to commit her heart to a man whose emotional immaturity will eventually cost her so much. As Jan catalogs the advantages of her easy relationship with Tuckwell—Keith is stable, a "windbreak" (57)—she can think of only one reason to pursue Franklin: to experience "what it felt like to be alive" (315). Ressler encourages their courtship, recognizes in their hesitant steps toward each other the very (im)perfect wonder he himself engaged a generation earlier with Jeanette Koss.

And so we begin, in fugal style, the revival/education of Jan O'Deigh. During a tour Franklin conducts through the Metropolitan Museum of Art, he compares Jan to a figure in the Brueghel painting *The Harvesters*, a figure abandoned, sprawled asleep under a tree, inexplicably separated from the furious golden business of harvesting going on all about her. Like DNA bases committing themselves without clear rationale to the work of bonding, Jan and Franklin both leave the security of their current emotional states—Jan's bland cohabitation with Tuckwell (whose name suggests the unimaginative neatness of this arrangement) and Franklin's relentless moves from one beautiful woman to another. Indeed, as an artist, Franklin ("unflappable in the face of adulthood" [198]) reveals a fatal love of surfaces (he easily churns out sketches of Jan even as they talk) and an easy infatuation with sensual gratification. With her cool charm, her illuminating grace, her immense reserves of intelligence, her smoldering passion, Jan will teach him the foundation lesson of genetics: the phenotype is the distraction of the particular; the genotype is what matters.

As Jan begins to visit the night world of MOL and as Ressler watches the sure signs of her emerging interest in Franklin, Ressler acts as a facilitator, participates in the slow ignition of his friends' passion. Something in their courtship, Jan reasons, "had tricked him into thinking this time it could go right" (440). Their "happiness made *him* happy" (401, italics Powers). In such encouragement, Jan fancies Ressler a "matchmaker" (290), but in determining to assist Jan and Franklin, Ressler functions far more like the messenger RNA that he first hypothesized about during his months at Urbana. Early on, the research team wondered how the intricate blueprints necessary to replication were transferred, delivered intact from the nucleus to the larger cell. "There must be a messenger molecule, to get the message from the nucleus into the cytoplasm where translation takes place" (287). Ressler first promotes the idea of a separate messenger, an adapter RNA as he calls it, a lonely agent critical to the process, able to deliver the code but not involved in the process of replication itself, "one that can't stick around to clog the works" (425). But as he comes under the sway of Franklin and Jan's emerging desire, Ressler, in turn, begins to open up in conversation his solitary soul. He expounds patiently to Jan and Franklin on the genetic work he pioneered, on his beloved *Goldberg Variations,* on the MOL computer system and its mesmerizing complexity ("stumbling across a listener after years of having no audience but himself" [307]). But more than sharing insights into the phenomenal simplicity of nature's patterns or into the tricks of his computer network, Ressler shares with them the experience of desire. He thinks again of Jeanette, calls up her name one night during a computer search. And in one remarkable weekend when they are snowbound in New Hampshire, Ressler tells them about Jeanette in a most stunning act of self-exposure.

But Ressler must watch, as he did twenty-five years earlier, the rich possibility of desire self-destruct; he must "get ready for dissonance" (193). The disastrous resolution of Jan and Franklin's romance centers, not surprisingly in a polyphonic novel, on the same question of child-bearing that centered Ressler and Jeanette's final argument. Jan, in a frank moment that recalls Jeanette's painful confession to Ressler, tells Franklin that despite her young age (she is barely in her thirties) she has had a tubal ligation. She tells Franklin of how she helped a young mother in the library track down information on mongolism to help her shoulder the immense burden of a child who was, Jan could see, a victim of this genetic mishap. Anxious before the raw evidence she reads all around her of genetic errors, she panics—the possibilities of generation are cashiered within this enveloping fear that baby making is a sort of "Russian roulette" where she must wait for her "own blueprint to betray [her]" (385). And like the biologist Ressler, she elects withdrawal; she loses the signal. The tubal ligation disturbs Franklin and is, in part, significant rationale for his fling with Annie Martens, one of those simple beautiful forms he has such a compulsion to enjoy. After Jan happens on them in bed, Franklin explains that with Annie there is the possibility of generation, a maybe tucked away for future use. But even as Jan withdraws from the computer room where she has confronted Franklin, even as she withdraws into her library bunker, even as she surrenders before the agony of the heart, she cannot leave behind her desire. As she spends her year in closeted study in her apartment (the day Jan dedicates her immediate future to the grinding work of researching genetics, she recalls a question posed to her once by a library patron—on Hitchcock's *The Lady Vanishes*), the marathon sessions at her textbooks reveal not merely her emerging understanding of the intricate chemistry of bonding but also her lingering desire for Franklin, undiminished despite his crude betrayal. It is a maddeningly illogical pursuit that reveals how we are more than bonding agents. It is our hearts—not our cells—that fall in love.

Even as we learn of the persistence of Jan's desire, we watch the revival of Ressler's heart. Its measure is recorded in a critical set piece centering on the coworker Jimmy Steadman. When Jan, Franklin, and Ressler are marooned in the New Hampshire snowstorm, they cannot return to the city to man their shift. They leave Jimmy to process the tonnage of information at Manhattan On-Line by himself. Once again, the individual is a most vulnerable construct, and when the trio finally returns they find Jimmy frazzled. To thank him, in an impulsive gesture of kindness, Ressler and Franklin program the computer network to give Jimmy a once-only paycheck bonus. Yet, typically in a novel where gestures of the heart are never unqualified benedictions, this gesture leaves a most disastrous legacy. The paycheck benefit leaves Jimmy without insurance coverage as Ressler and Franklin fail to factor in his insurance premium. In another instance of the insufficiency of the individual, Jimmy is dropped from group insurance and finds himself now vulnerable. Suspicions over the pay benefit raised by higher-echelon watchdogs put enough stress on Jimmy to trigger a debilitating stroke at the very moment his hospitalization coverage stops.

And yet this apparent disaster triggers a powerful bonding. Together Ressler, Franklin, and Jan (despite roiling in the immediate aftermath of his infidelity) work to insert a particularly nasty bug into the computer network even as Jimmy teeters near death. The vast network of banking institutions depending on Manhattan On-Line is stunned to find in its computer readouts messages about Jimmy's insurance cancellation, warnings about shady dealings by parent banking firms, and a wealth of flip messages and trivial factoids culled from Jan's considerable library files—all harmless but unnerving—and only Ressler knows the code to stop the flow of the runaway system. When Ressler is arrested, the insurance company reinstates Jimmy, and Ressler relinquishes the code word. But that alliance shaped by the trio to help their downed colleague—each contributing to the intricate work of inserting the bug into the system— is Powers's compelling instance of a bonding that denies self-interest (Jan works side by side with Franklin; Ressler works knowing the illegality of his actions and that he is forfeiting the very benefits he is working to secure for his friend) and operates without any larger agenda than to repair a wrong and to help a friend. As genetics teaches and as spectacle realism demands, cooperation, the puzzling achievement of harmony, is the very wonder of experience.

Afterward, when the legal ramifications have been settled and each member prepares to go off, Ressler, certain now of his cancer, certain he must die, must watch his two friends separate. Before he departs for the Illinois clinic, he calls Jan late one night. Stunned by the news of his departure, Jan chokes out, "I love you." Ressler, ever the messenger, responds in a voice between "assertion and command," "You love your friend" (625). And more than a year later, long after Ressler's death, he is instrumental in reviving the love he is sure endures between the two; death, he determines, cannot be simple cold closure. Before he leaves Manhattan to go to the cancer facility, Ressler programs into the great financial network to which MOL gives him access a message keyed to Jan's bankcard. After she quits her library job, as she spends her savings with great care, she does not use her bankcard until some time after Ressler's death. To her amazement, the automatic teller machine screen goes blank and there appears a message from Ressler—who acts even from the grave like the messenger RNA—telling her, "He is a man. Take him for all in all" (631). It is further programmed to play the quodlibet from the *Goldberg*, the closing variation that capriciously twines two folk songs from Bach's childhood, two tunes unrelated yet constructed into a most delightful counterpoint. It is, of course, a most striking suggestion of the pairing of Jan and Franklin—two tunes that should not fit but nevertheless do, the hard-earned harmony of polyphonic music so familiar to texts of spectacle realism.

Powers leaves it to the ATM to articulate what is surely his great theme (and the centering premise of spectacle realism) when its screen advises Jan, "Please enter your transaction" (631). Ressler's message facilitates the reunion between Jan and Franklin that closes the book. Indeed, watching the message, Jan feels that Franklin is near. She tears off to the Metropolitan Museum of Art where they had spent so much time together. But there she is frustrated, and she decides she is not to find him here in a gallery that embalms the merely lifelike. Divested of her research, overtired of her own sabbatical, ready to reengage the raw experience of the in vivo, she is more interested now in observing the people who shuffle through the museum. Inexplicably excited, Jan heads to her apartment. But long before she arrives, she sees Franklin's familiar shadow against her drawn blinds. It is a "miracle of coincidence" (another turn of chance much like the enigmatic process of genetic replication itself)—Franklin, the only other person with a key, has returned.

Both acknowledge the long odds. "It would never last," Jan says nervously. And Franklin—feeling that splendid tremor of desire, his throat shaking, his hands gently exploring Jan's face, his eyes full "beyond measure"—reassures her that he understands the (im)perfect nature of their bonding: "Who said anything about lasting?" (638). The compelling uncertainty, the (un)easy anticipation of tomorrow that recalls Daniel Quinn and Maud Fallon under the arches, or Mark Valerian and Bill Mackey shutting up the beach house for the slow slide into winter, or Maggie and Ira Moran nestling together in their dark and emptying home—in the argument of spectacle realism, such confluence is the highest benediction of the immediate. Powers closes the novel with the last musical inscription from the *Variations*, the instructions to return to the opening aria, "Da Capo e Fine" (once more with feeling) (639). As in polyphonic music, we have come full circle and prepare to start again, the inexhaustible and bruising argument of the heart, uncertain in its eventual playing out, certain only of its resilience, the long, strange trip compelled only by its continuing engagement, the dazzling mystery of bonding, the powerful pull of desire, part error, part chance, that creates in all of us what science cannot solve, what genetics cannot reduce to a table: the twinning of hearts.

*   *   *

The poet alone knows astronomy, chemistry, vegetation, and animation, for he does not stop at these facts but employs them as signs . . . for in every word he speaks he rides on them as the horses of thought.

Ralph Waldo Emerson, "The Poet"

> *Well, I suppose a name is right if it sticks, if it becomes the name.*
>
> Jeanette Koss

But we are not quite finished. If Stuart Ressler shows us how to die and Jan O'Deigh shows us how to live, it is Powers who shows us how to communicate such news, how to touch each other with the imperfect bindings of language long held suspect in our other texts. Powers saves perhaps his most striking affirmation for the capacity of language itself to engage the freewheeling immediate. With an elegant prose line, terraced sentences that are themselves engineering marvels, Powers drives language itself to the foreground of his narrative. Indeed, unlike the other texts we have studied, whatever the subject of the narrative moment—Ressler's cereal breakfasts, DNA explication, or the characters' steamy couplings—language compels attention. And yet such foregrounding raises the dilemma first posed by Enid's diary, by Will Canaday's newspaper, by Kate's telegrams, by Splendora, by Maggie's tele-vision: surely language is a shadow of reality, a counterfeit expression, a step away, a magic kingdom shelter, a substitution for the bracing experience of the thing itself.

Early on, Ressler and Jan ponder this very dilemma. After all, Ressler, a teacher-turned-researcher-turned-computer programmer, and Jan, a librarian and later a professional student, both work pipelines of written communication. Yet they cannot make peace with the medium that so sustains them. As Jan carefully works her way through genetics textbooks, she hungers to confront the realities she studies but understands her path of information is tangled within conventional analogies—the genome is like a 5,000-volume library; the cell is like a musical score; bases are like alphabet letters; RNA is like a strip of recording tape; DNA is like a master architect—a frustrating separation from the realities of the spectacle wonders staged so casually within her very cells. Words intrude, interfere, like the tin-can telephone that muffles a message better shouted without bothering at all with the clumsy medium. And, suddenly in love, Ressler struggles to rid himself of the dependence on language. Compelled finally to tell Jeanette of his feelings, Ressler impulsively telephones her after excruciating dental surgery that leaves garbled his most earnest attempts to put his emotions into language. Jeanette, for her part, struggles against the oppressive presence of her husband in the same room. Ressler wrestles with the emerging awareness that he is "in" something that defies the neat measure of any single word. When he finally concedes to desire, the kiss he shares with Jeanette defies language. Ressler and Jeanette do not merely *kiss*—they clutch, gnaw each other, desperately savage each other in an experience for which there is no word. Skin becomes not a word but a texture, a geography, ultimately an experience. Like Jan recognizing that the most elaborate metaphors explicating the cell's processes are poor representations, Ressler, stricken by love, understands that this potent experience bankrupts words, leaves only the hunger to touch the thing itself.

Despite the struggling frustrations of Jan and Ressler, Powers will not be so easily dissuaded from the potency of language. After all, the fundamental lesson of the revolution in molecular genetics argues that the universal process of synthesizing animated matter hinges on a most effective system of delivered messages; genetic coding is an efficient, resilient exchange of stored information from genes to proteins: DNA communicates with the messenger RNA that, in turn, communicates with the ribosomes that, in turn, assemble the amino acids with loops of transfer RNA that shape, finally, chains of proteins. In our very cells, we are wondrously efficient messengers, potent communicators in a game of tin-can telephone that stretches across more than a billion years, through error and chance, and across a globeful of species. Even as the characters wrestle with language as a counterfeit reality; even as characters mouth the postmodern fretting over language's helplessly synthetic reality, how we violate the complexity of reality by affixing awkward and ill-fitting words until those words come to stand in for the experience itself; even as characters struggle with the emerging awareness that the world is only accessible through the metaphoric gamesmanship of the striking coinage of language, the reader finds a much more suasive argument for language's viability emerges in neat counterpoint, much like a second voice in a polyphonic round.

Powers takes issue with this assertion that language is an imperfect translation. Victims since Babel fractured language into competitive tongues, we have struggled to understand our emotional experiences through language. It is perhaps experience secondhand, but it is a gorgeous and splendid translation, a hand-me-down gown that still lights up a room. After all, as Stuart Ressler demands, "All things being possible, description is everything" (193). Stuart Ressler comes to see the tired observation that the world is mere translation of a reality ungraspable, beyond the power of words, as a hobgoblin of thin imaginations. Rather, he sees the natural world not as a reduction into language but rather as a challenge to measure how much a language can hold, how much it can do. It is not about "bringing Shakespeare into Bantu. It is about bringing Bantu into Shakespeare" (491). At a breaking moment of insight as he wanders about spring wildflowers with Jeanette, he perceives under the "soft, effusive enthusiasm" of her argument that flowers in fact have names, that such names, while imperfect and often amended, give human perception access, permit theorizing, promote understanding; that such verbal constructs, such apparent simulations, far from being synthetic escapes from reality, are critical ways of latching onto "it," that language itself is a fierce struggle to defy randomness, to quash ambiguity, to distinguish surfaces. Signs, then, are guideposts of reassuring familiarity that alone define the perimeters of the newer territories that, in turn, permit the first hesitant steps toward radical redefinition, the exploration, the awesome tinkering into the immediate that is pure science—and, by wondrous extension, the very premise of realistic narratology.

Language here sends messages and elicits responses. Indeed, Powers's main characters are erudite writers, proficient readers, accomplished conversationalists, letter writers; in short, people "who still love words" (59). The note cards that come to Jan's desk represent, at a basic level, messages sent, messages received, messages answered. As she becomes involved with Franklin and pays nightly visits to Manhattan On-Line, Jan becomes addicted to the marathon conversations with Ressler and Franklin conducted long into the nights, a "nervous community of words" animated by questions, philosophical and broad; by stories, intimate and historical; by readings, from *Little Women* for instance; by merciless puns, bad jokes—it is a contentment of language, an assertion of language's age-old campfire importance, an assertion of community. Even as she comes to depend on her long nights in the console room ("months of verbal drunkenness" [23]), Jan senses under the potent influence of simple conversation how someone could indeed live on words.

What good is affirmation if we distrust the only medium available for its communication? We master language, then, to touch another. Powers is fascinated by the massive suprastructure of connections determined by simple conversation; his characters are talkers, conversationalists, confiders. In brainstorming sessions, at faculty Christmas parties, in apartments, over library desks, in snowbound cabins in New Hampshire, characters open up, imperfectly, sometimes tentatively, often explosively, and discover the stunning ability of words to thread us. Words are adhesive, connective. We write to touch, to bond. Franklin, pursuing the wronged Jan in the year after their breakup, writes in a long elegant letter to Jan of his dissertation nearing completion and closes with the simplest declaration of his unflagging desire; Jan keeps a thick notebook of her attempts to master the dry theories of life science, an act of devotion that she pursues only to touch at some level the world of Stuart Ressler, and finds herself wondering more and more about Franklin; during the emotional explorations of her early months with Franklin, Jan surprises herself by turning to poetry to focus her heady emotional register; even Jeanette's farewell letter to Ressler is an imposing multipage missive, a struggle to ease the wounding, to connect even in rupture.

Powers is even more resourceful in his understanding of the power of language. It extends as well to his narrative strategies. In selecting for a third of his narrative to assume the first-person female voice of Jan, Powers leaps across the deep division of gender to explore (recall Reynolds Price) with only the vehicle of language the emotional interior of the feminine makeup. But there is more. In a novel centered on the potent force of procreation, Powers saves the most impressive creative process for the production of the novel itself. The novel we read, as it turns out, refutes its characters' apparent drag toward sterility. We find out only in the closing pages, in the reunion scene between Jan and Franklin, that the artful construction of this polyphonic novel has been, in fact, a composition for four hands (much like the *Variations* itself and, not surprisingly, most of the musical compositions Stuart Ressler has been writing in his retirement). We learn that the multiple threads of the narrative have come from the joining of two manuscripts: Jan's year-long record of her scientific pursuit spliced with the manuscript Franklin reveals to Jan the day they are reunited, a speculative biography of Stuart Ressler based on a complicated weave of his lengthy conversations with Ressler shortly before he died. Unable to bear children, Jan's tubes long ago burned shut, Franklin and Jan produce the text we have read, a creative act of mutual consent, a striking reminder of language's power to bind. In the splicing of manuscripts, twining two self-sufficient texts (the parallels to the two rails of the DNA helix are unmistakable), only in the "bioengineering" feat of splicing does language pull off the convincing experience of harmony. Language here achieves what we most fear it can only simulate: it creates confluence. Much as Powers revives the fascination with the arithmetic of polyphony, much as he revives the tonic curiosity of science, much as he revives the implosive power of desire, he restores to language its imperial right to surprise, the magician still able to stun, to pull us together like an audience of the awed.

And so we close with the achievement of Powers's magnificent work. Locked so comfortably within magic kingdoms, mesmerized by confections, entertained by the logic of illusions, in the Reagan Era we risked losing our appetite for the simply, stunningly real—the glimpsed but unsuspected. By decade's close, it was time to move out from the magic kingdom. Powers offers a stimulating testimony of possibilities, of energies unacknowledged. In a tender moment, Stuart Ressler, who will come so close to cracking the genetic code and who, in his monastic zeal for science, will set aside the more routine pleasures of love and marriage, is moved simply by watching a colleague's young daughter reciting poetry. Away from the laboratory, he is momentarily caught up by the simple miracle of this wondrous superstructure, how "a single zygote, in less time than it takes the average Civil Service gang to dig a bed for a mile of interstate, differentiates into vertebrae, liver, dimpled knees, and ears . . . splits into this terraced chemical mechanism that finds a way to say what it feels" (274). Stunned, he is moved to tears. From Ptolemy to Hawking, from Newton to Crick and Watson, science—like spectacle realism—revives the "state of wonder." To borrow from Jan's assessment of Ressler's fascination with genetics, spectacle realists continue to insist that, finally, nothing deserves wonder so much as our capacity to feel it.

Conclusion

The Gift of Spectacle(s)—(En)Closing the Reagan Era

Dr. Sayre: What's wrong?

Leonard: We've got to tell everybody. We've got to remind them how good it is.

Dr. Sayre: How good what is?

Leonard: Read the newspaper. What's it say? All bad. It's all bad. People have forgotten what life is all about. They've forgotten what it's like to be alive. They need to be reminded of what they have and what they can lose. What I feel is the joy of life, the gift of life, the freedom of life, the wonderment of life.

Awakenings

A decade, of course, never closes conveniently on its final New Year's Eve.

Indeed, a decade cannot even close dramatically. The event that comes to mark the close of any decade becomes landmark only with the passing of time sufficient to recognize the milestone quality of an event we never suspected marked the end of anything. From our position, we might ask when did the Reagan Era end? There was, after all, a most unseemly rush to pen the decade's obituary. Commentators started as early as October 1987, when the era, so fascinated by acquisition, registered a tectonic drop in stock market confidence so profound as to stir a collective recollection of a similar meltdown that signaled the close of the Jazz Era with its decadent (and illusory) sense of plenty. Or perhaps the decade ended when Reagan himself slipped offstage to slow-fade into the warm January mists of Rancho Mirage the afternoon of George Bush's inauguration or perhaps when, in the steel-cold sunshine of a Washington winter, Bill Clinton took the oath of office amid the hot buzz that the country had been once again entrusted to the newest new generation. Did the decade that began in the cold rain of the Gdansk docks and that moved to the midnight celebrations along the shattered edifice of the Berlin Wall end all too suddenly in the humid June morning of Tiananmen Square? Perhaps a decade that in many ways began when Reagan's cheerful resilience after an assassination attempt wrapped about him, despite his age, an aura of invincibility closed with the public announcement in November 1994, that Reagan was in the early stages of Alzheimer's disease with its dark suggestion of the irresistible pull of mortality and its sad movement into inevitable helplessness. Or perhaps the decade stopped dead in the night skies over Lockerbie, Scotland, at 7:17 P.M., on December 22, 1988, when TWA Flight 103 simply vanished from ground radar, an unarmed commercial jet detonated as proof that terrorism could not be dispelled by Reagan's magic. Or maybe the decade ended April 19, 1995, with a terrifying roar in the early minutes of a routine Wednesday at the Alfred P. Murrah Federal Office Complex in downtown Oklahoma City when the magnitude of the white rage first tapped by the conservative resurgence of the 1980s exploded into our awareness.

It may seem odd, however, to turn for our closing moment to the picturesque hamlet of Haymarket, Virginia, or, more exactly, to 3,000 (un)spectacular acres of unspoiled, undeveloped, undisturbed northern Virginia countryside around Haymarket, just beyond the farthest fringes of the creeping reach of Washington. But given the narrative line we have suggested for the 1980s, this narrow corridor of Virginia provided on a late September morning in 1994 a most dramatic closure for the 1980s. We have seen that, against a culture decidedly at play, a culture compelled by the premise of the magic kingdom and enthralled by the logic of unearned optimism, the decade's literary argument emerged in a resurgence of powerful realistic narratives that explored characters lured by the logic of disengagement but who affirm ultimately the need to engage despite—always despite—the complications. Given a decade that indulged the carnival excess of the contrived spectacle and that reveled amid the bombardment of the enticing play of surfaces, the 1980s ended in a gesture that signaled, much like the texts of spectacle realism, a recognition of the powerful premise of the spectacle immediate. It closed not with the political eclipse of Reagan—but rather with the hasty retreat of Disney.

The plans for the Disney America Theme Park in northern Virginia had been announced with the requisite hoopla in 1993. Disney was confident of its mission: to bring history back to an American audience poorly served by a public education system that had long ago dried up the study of history into the chalky recitation of dates and names. By bringing to bear the considerable technological muscle of its animatronics spectacles, Disney would restage critical geographies of the American historic imagination, spectacles that would bring together in a most revolutionary way the elements of a nation's historic record with the gizmos and flash of sophisticated entertainment technologies. There, on authentic historic ground, within range of the estates of an octet of presidents and a scattering of turning-point battlefields, Disney would erect another of its postmodern play zones, another giddy collage of wildly entrancing decontextualized bits; among the planned attractions, Disney would offer: a Lewis and Clark raft ride (complete with churning whitewater thrills); an "authentic" mill town featuring a high-tech roller coaster that would hurtle carfuls of screaming post-tourists through a sprawling mock steel mill, climaxing in a nauseating pitch toward a great open blast furnace; a splendid state fair mock-up complete with a towering Ferris wheel; a mock battlefield that would manipulate virtual reality technologies to give visitors the feel of participating in actual field combat. The park would include as well the obligatory Disney touches: an authentic replica (only in Disney's kingdom is such an oxymoron acceptable) of a steam train; a Hall of Presidents with a stageful of audioanimatronics chief executives declaiming bits of inaugural speeches with appropriate head rolls and meaningful arm gestures; and a Main Street of emporia complete with strolling costumed interpreters in suitable mid-Victorian getups.

And unlike nearby Williamsburg, where restored edifices stand on original foundations, this park would be uncomplicated by actual history, just bits of the American historic imagination magically reconstructed amid the Virginia countryside—historic, along Disney's logic, by association. By Disney's scale, the proposed park would be appropriately modest, a scant 100 acres, and its mission appropriately highbrow: to restore a nation's enthusiasm for its own history. To sustain such energy, of course, Disney would necessarily slight the less delightful, less entertaining aspects of our national historic record: the peculiar institution of slavery, the bloody labor upheavals compelled by the brutal rapacity of the fortunate wealthy, the horrific carnage of wars domestic and foreign, the relentless usurpation of the Native American claim to the wilderness, the methodical pillaging of a natural world that had originally so blessed the New World, the unseemly record of according partial rights of citizenship to minorities, to women, to immigrants.

Such editing notwithstanding, the point of a park visit would be to play in a managed environment of optimism and possibility so self-consciously superficial as to threaten parody—the very embodiment of the argument of the Reagan Era itself. Disney offered to what it assumed would be an appreciative culture this most elaborate environment, this confected play zone of spectacles (the noun), this marvelous triumph not of substance but of form (meticulous landscaping, careful historic costuming and detailing, innovative cutting-edge technologies, sobering platitudes about American resilience spiked by thrills and animated with the typical noise of the contemporary theme park), a collage of historic bits played off against each other, a preposterous composition offered without narrative thread and without the obligation to speculate on the implications of our often troubling historic record. It would be true-to-life and yet wholly artificial, marketing, under the aegis of history, depthless signs pulled from their historic context and fashioned into a controlled spectacle of managed thrills, scripted excitement, and packaged moments that would demand for its ultimate effect the full awareness and cooperation of its visitors. It would offer the romance of surface, the significance of the trivial—and would step wholly away from the often discomforting engagement of authentic historic investigation; it would be thus in its design and its intent the very signature of the 1980s.

And yet, on September 29, 1994, the Disney America project collapsed of its own preposterousness—defeated by a coalition of educators, historians, writers who feared Disney's inevitable distortions of history; environmentalists who foresaw only ecological disaster; and the landed aristocracy of Virginia who fretted over the inevitable invasion of hordes of the unwashed middle class. This orchestrated resistance to the suasive spell of Disney, however, offers that unsuspected significant moment that signaled the close of a decade, the moment when we finally tired of the tempting pull of play. It was not merely that Disney would distort history; historians since Herodotus have spun events into persuasive alignment. And surely even the harshest critics of Disney would concede that there would be time enough for the children drawn to a Disney park to learn about racial inequities, battlefield carnage, breadlines, government injustice; for now, let them tower above a state fair that never really existed in the basket of a Ferris wheel drawn not from history but from the way history should have been. And although Disney would inevitably vulgarize historic record—mugs and T-shirts and the goofy (pardon the pun) souvenirs that would become middle-class family heirlooms—we are surely in a time when commercialization and crassness have long since lost their ability to shock (consider the booming souvenir businesses on the steps of the courthouse wherein the O. J. Simpson double-murder trial played out or the yearlong outpouring of tasteless tribute "souvenirs" actually licensed to bear Princess Diana's countenance following her bloody death in a Paris automobile accident).

Rather, what makes the repudiation of Disney central to our reading of the 1980s was the often emotional defense, proffered by the phalanx of coalition forces, of the (un)spectacular Virginia countryside itself. That coalition accepted as sufficient the rich eloquence of the land, the unspoiled acreage of countryside simple and unretouched and surely spectacle enough. It was not so much the rejection of yet another contrived postmodern gametext as it was a bold defense of the unsuspected power of a realistic text. Disney was encroaching too boldly into a most profound geography, an immediate with depth, dazzling in the cool austerity of its plain, sweeping lines, an immediate that argued without the gaudy effects of contemporary technology the pain, heroism, frustration, joy, anguish, the compelling drama of the human experience that there stumbled its way into history. Unlike other nearby historic geographies such as the Colonial Williamsburg Restoration Park, where the historic record is so brutally obvious and so relentlessly pressing among long streets of heavily refurbished edifices and hordes of costumed interpreters, the battlefield sites that Disney pressed too near are marvelous, stunning exercises in understatement, appropriate texts of spectacle realism that tap the unacknowledged power of the unvarnished. And, as with our texts, battlefield sites demand our participation. To participate fully in the experience of the immediate at, say, Manassas is an act of willed sympathy, an intuitive sharing, an imaginative reconstruction of the terror, the glory, the (im)perfect expression of human emotions that made for the experience of battle and that link us, bond us to those who rose and fell on these (un)spectacular acres.

Let's be clear. Disney was hardly "beaten," as many commentators so quickly gloated. The repudiation of Disney America was a repudiation of this packaging, a rejection of *this* playscape. It was not a rejection of spectacle itself (we didn't run about the cultural countryside like latter-day Carry Nations, wild-eyed with axes swinging, de-constructing theme parks; indeed, the very day Disney conceded northern Virginia, long lines of restless, needful post-tourists across the country made their way into the significant retreat of magic kingdoms, Disney's and other's) but rather the embrace of a different sort of spectacle. It was not a rejection of play but rather a tonic reminder that the spectacle of play inhabits the apparently barren stretches of open fields, a defense of the careless and unscripted experience of the unadorned immediate that depends wholly on the participatory and receptive audience for its maximum effect. Like the texts of spectacle realism, this Third Battle of Manassas reminded us, quite audaciously, that the unassisted immediate merits a place amid our cultural text-sites. Endorsing the quieter ties of sympathy, respecting an immediate unassisted by the lavishing of excess and the broad diversions of artifice signals this as an appropriate closing moment for our look at the 1980s. We closed rejecting a theme/dream park and turning with new admiration to the power, the intoxicating energy of the simple immediate and to our capacity to react, to respect the enriching experience not possible within staged and antiseptic play zones. If we began the decade strolling with grateful steps along Disney's Main Street, we closed, wearied of privileging the confected, standing on the windswept Manassas battlefield, a fitting closing text of spectacle realism.

It has been the urgent responsibility of the texts of spectacle realism to remind us that as readers of the often daunting and nervy texts of massive invention and technique that have come to define the postmodern sensibility we can grow similarly weary of privileging the confected. This is not to suggest that the assertion of spectacle realism trumpets the demise of postmodern play or that we need to demonize these often marvelous texts; the edgy spirit of verbal liberation continues in the exacting works and infinite jestings of Nicholson Baker, Paul Auster, David Foster Wallace, William Vollmann, in the continuing relevancy of John Barth, and in the towering event of William Gass's 1996 *The Tunnel* or Pynchon's 1997 *Mason & Dixon*, to name only a few of the more prominent.

Nor is this to suggest that the reach of spectacle realism ended with the turn of the decade. Well into the 1990s, a most mesmerizing chorus of remarkable voices in texts of spectacle realism have continued to probe the responsibility of affirmation, the acceptance of vulnerability, the necessity of confluence and engagement, the dark beauty of the chaotic iterations of chance, and the coming to terms with the hard intervention of mortality. To mention only some of the more notable voices in the more notable texts, consider Ruby (Charles Frazier, *Cold Mountain*, 1996); Teddy Wilmot (John Updike, *In the Beauty of the Lilies*, 1996); Dolores Price (Wally Lamb, *She's Come Undone*, 1992); Swede Levov (Philip Roth, *American Pastoral*, 1997); Frank Bascombe (Richard Ford, *Independence*

Day, 1996); Daisy Stone Goodwill (Carol Shields, *The Stone Diaries*, 1994); Quoyle (E. Annie Proulx, *The Shipping News*, 1993), Stella (Terry McMillan, *How Stella Got Her Groove Back*, 1997); Margaret Bonner (Gail Godwin, *Evensong*, 1999); and the women of the Convent (Toni Morrison, *Paradise*, 1998). These are significant realistic fictions that, like our texts, audaciously transcribe an immediate that can move, engage, teach, stir, ultimately transform.

Of course, the canon of postmodern texts has offered moments, powerful and incisive, that touch the willing (if persevering) reader. Every contemporary reader has a list of such affecting moments, moments that give pause: the spare Advent service shared by Roger and Jessica amid Pynchon's war-stripped Britain; Rennie Morgan's ghastly abortion; the catastrophic evening Henry Waugh attempts to introduce Lou into the intricate system of his baseball association; the long night Billy Pilgrim hunches underground helpless while Dresden ignites. They are terroristic moments when the decay, the absurdity, the clutter, the cruelty of the twentieth-century wasteland-immediate brutally violates the otherwise spacious edifice of linguistic invulnerability, the self-contained closed structure of the postmodern spaces erected against just such pressing realities. Indeed, when, in Vonnegut or Nabokov or Pynchon or Barth, we near the reality lurking just outside and all about the privileged text-sites of their verbal exercises (funhouses, decorated showboats, tunnels, speeding cars, locked basements, jail cells, cozily claustrophobic closets, park benches, elevators), it is a reading of the world decidedly akin to the descendental texts of traditional realism. Oddly, Hamlin Garland's inarticulate dirt farmers and Nabokov's urbane professors have the same sense of the immediate: a darkling vision of a vast and emptying world of greed, aberrant sexuality, brutality, degradation, and deep boredom, a too-familiar reading of a wonderless immediate closed off to possibility and condoning, by its very entangling mess, the urge to retreat.

Life, as it turns out, is far more interesting. The moments within the postmodern canon that touch us, of course, touch on the very themes of spectacle realism we have seen: our vulnerabilities amid the stochastic turns of raw chance, our inexplicable need for the complication of another's heart, the terrifying turn toward the astounding reality of our own proximate extinction. But such moments are not, we sense, privileged within postmodern texts; they are spare and slender textual events amid the larger linguistic celebrations, moments that in their resonance are like the awkward, uneasy moment during a lavish circus when a doleful clown shuffles into the centering spotlight, thus suspending for a soulful moment the larger excess of manufactured spectacle, thus humanizing all the noise, thus introducing a deep touch of understatement that quickly fades into irony amid the ongoing rush of three-ring spectacle. Such memorable moments within the gametexts of the postmodern experience surely give pause but cannot touch, lodged as they are amid the packaged linguistic daring, the deliberate structural gamesmanship, and the sheer love of architecture that so defines these confected texts.

Like Enid Stevick suddenly wondrously short-circuited by a simple glance about her own begrimed city from a plodding city bus, we complete the texts of spectacle realism touched by the simplest confrontation; characters are brought, in some cases with significant resistance, to confront the immediate and find for their efforts the (un)easy joy of affirmation, the unexpected beauty of the unscripted mystery of the immediate. Writers castigate with satire those who reject it (Enid Stevick, John Wheelwright, Kate Vaiden) and educate with care those who resist it, those too burned by experience (Daniel Quinn, Maggie Moran, Mark Valerian, Walter Van Brunt, Depeyster Van Wart, Stuart Ressler, Jan O'Deigh). Initially, these characters seek only those elements that are crucial to the success of any theme park (and to Reagan's America)—beauty, order, control—but find the exercise of each possible only in the cool gesture of disengagement, in the rejection of the immediate that would become the signature gesture of the decade. That they need not remain in their magic kingdoms is the triumphant message of spectacle realism. The texts of spectacle realism lay claim to a most extravagant privileging of disorder; they lead us out from the magic kingdom, out into the rich reward of accepting the very helplessness and chaos that so unnerves our struggling characters. And they speak to our fin-de-siècle moment what the descendental texts of American realism and the spacious play zones of postmodern excess never bothered much to remind us: that we cannot afford to take it all for granted.

But these texts resist simple optimism—such was the counterfeit currency of the Reagan pseudoprosperity. Spectacle realism hardly reads like the insipid optimism of the enbenched Forrest Gump dumbfounded over life as a box of chocolates. Nor do these texts simply dole out chicken soup to troubled late-century souls, to borrow from a titanically popular mid-1990s series of inspirational stories and quickie parables packaged for easy consumption and geared to trigger frictionless epiphanies in crusty businessmen and harried homemakers. Readers familiar with, say, Oates or Kennedy or Powers—or any of those texts listed in the appendix for that matter—would hardly dismiss these texts as greeting cards teased out to 400-plus pages, feel-good narratives with the dopey voice-over of Rosie O'Donnell with soundtrack by Yanni. Nor are these works artificial sweeteners, part of the ruthlessly uplifting brain candy industry of our contemporary inspiration/motivation circuit riders and cable-access infomercials. As we have moved within our narrative from Enid Stevick to Jan O'Deigh, we begin to sense the work of affirmation, how different it is in feel from the spun fluff of optimism. Character to character, we have tested an assortment of strategies, responses to a trampoline-immediate, to the in-vivo life that so resists the glinting edge, that so stubbornly resists justifying even our most modest hopes.

But we have learned along with our characters—the very imperative of spectacle realism. We cannot afford retreat, we cannot be Enid Stevick; we cannot afford crabby misanthropy, to step out into a breathtaking winter morning and ponder only the dog turds, unseen, under the clean sheen of snow, we cannot be John Wheelwright; we cannot afford to shut down our heart's imperfect exercise, we cannot tolerate the shabby charade of Kate Vaiden. And so like Daniel Quinn, wounded by an immediate that seems to offer only evidence of our species's devolution into barbarism, we head to our Saratoga Spring, to be healed by the slender affirmation of touch. Like Mark Valerian, we must confront what we most fear and must resolve that struggle makes sense only when our backs are against the wall, as they are really from the moment of our engendering. Like Maggie Moran, we must all of us brace for a clean start tomorrow along an open road we cannot begin to map. Like Walter Van Brunt and Depeyster Van Wart, we must stumble about a corpsed/vital landscape in a sad/funny drama of bravery/cowardice and move with (un)erring ease between drift and plot. Like Stuart Ressler, against embracing the gesture of closure, we must opt for engagement; we must make and remake our peace with the sweet attrition of love, the bracing agony of experience—for the alternative is the sad charade of the sufficiency of the self. Like Jan O'Deigh, who completes our study's slow and sacred movement toward affirmation begun when Enid Stevick matriculates at the Westcott School of Music, we must be reminded that the immediate is a vast envelope and that participating in such a freewheeling webbing is mandated by an urge that is gene deep. This most tonic affirmation ultimately is extended to the community of contemporary readers, a dedicated band so long unstirred by best-sellers that tame the immediate into wholly manageable melodramas and by postmodern ludic texts that seduce them by their cool logic of disengagement to saunter about, overstunned, amid the spectacle of lexical funhouses. Spectacle realism, rather, suggests that the unretouched immediate—the press and feel of the turbulent ad-lib of the moment—may be brushed by wonder, that the heart finding its way to the alogic of confluence may be more than the species logic of hard survival, and, finally, that literature finds its highest validation when it reminds a doubtful and perhaps resistant audience of its right to demand nothing less than affirmation. Please, these texts argue to their characters—and to us—please, enter your transaction.

This is the gift of spectacle realism. Oddly, it is a gift that, long after the close of the Reagan Era, we struggle against, uncertain of how to handle the bald offer of affirmation without diminishing it into empty sentimentality. It is, perhaps, the critical contribution of spectacle realism to remind us that our inability to access affirmation matters. In this uncertain quietus of the twentieth century, our deep need for spectacle is too easily sustained by technology's circuited gimcracks, by the empty sideshow of big-budget films and the hokey melodramatics of athletic showdowns, and by the pornography of our virtual reality games. Inexplicably, we move into the new millennium with the stoned steps of the somnabulist, unaware of the (in)elegant immediate that would shatter our every glance.

In Penny Marshall's powerful film *Awakenings*, released in 1990 at decade's close, we meet a wardful of catatonics, locked away in the twisted wreckage of bodies ravaged years earlier by the neurologic meltdown of encephalitis. Doctor Sayre, played by Robin Williams, who has an awkward compassion for these human catastrophes, tinkers with the idea that these human shells might in fact still be quite functional inside. He investigates the possibility of bringing them around by using a risky drug treatment program. The treatments succeed, and, one by one, each patient, revived and awakened, comes to relish the simplest experiences of the immediate: a fresh breeze at an open window, loose chat with a friend, a visit from a son or daughter, a heated game of poker, a familiar bit of music, an afternoon of dancing, a simple walk in the park—pedestrian moments that had become for them over the years of their suspended animation the most unavailable luxuries. Indeed, as we watch the film, we come to understand the power of the immediate—largely because Marshall shows us the outside world of trees and sunshine and passers-by through smudged and locked windows or through window bars or in the momentary slicing light of an opened door quickly closed and then locked.

Leonard, the patient played by Robert DeNiro, who is the first to be treated, is the first who comes to understand that the drug treatments cannot work and that one by one each patient will relapse and return, helpless, to their limbo. Panicked, he rouses Dr. Sayre from sleep one night and urges the doctor to get the word out, that wonderment is our right. Later, as the drug's side effects erode Leonard's muscle control and his emotional restraint, he wrestles with Dr. Sayre and in the fracas breaks the doctor's spectacles. That night, even as he fights the hand tremors that mark his relapse, Leonard painstakingly pieces together the shattered lenses and leaves the spectacles as a gift for the doctor, who Leonard has noticed lives a most insulated sort of nonlife, a reminder from Leonard never to forget to see what is so (in)accessible and so (un)available, never to forget that it is joy sufficient to feel alive. That gift of the spectacle(s), that gift of adjusted sight, surely marks the ongoing achievement of the texts of spectacle realism. They remind us of a way to see, a reminder that emerged against a decade so enthralled by the act of turning away and against an inherited tradition of postmodern gametexts so beguiled by the possibility of private lexical wonderlands, a reminder for each of us to touch with trembling heart the terrifying wonder of the act of living.

APPENDIX

Selected Works of Spectacle Realism, 1981–1991

1981

Nobody's Angel (Thomas McGuane)
Rabbit Is Rich (John Updike)

1982

The Color Purple (Alice Walker)
Shiloh and Other Stories (Bobbie Ann Mason)
The Women of Brewster Place (Gloria Naylor)

1983

Cathedral (Raymond Carver)
During the Reign of the Queen of Persia (Joan Chase)
Ironweed (William Kennedy)

1984

Foreign Affairs (Alison Lurie)
God Knows (Joseph Heller)
Him with His Foot in His Mouth and Other Stories (Saul Bellow)
Sent for You Yesterday (John Edgar Wideman)

1985

The Accidental Tourist (Anne Tyler)
The Beans of Egypt, Maine (Carolyn Chute)
The Cider House Rules (John Irving)
Continental Drift (Russell Banks)
Lake Wobegone Days (Garrison Keillor)
Lonesome Dove (Larry McMurtry)
Love Medicine (Louise Erdrich)

Men and Angels (Mary Gordon)
White Noise (Don DeLillo)
World's Fair (E. L. Doctorow)

1986

The Beet Queen (Louise Erdrich)
Children of Light (Robert Stone)
The Lost Language of Cranes (David Leavitt)
The Sportswriter (Richard Ford)
A Summons to Memphis (Peter Taylor)

1987

All We Need of Hell (Harry Crews)
Beloved (Toni Morrison)
A Counter-Life (Philip Roth)
Crossing to Safety (Wallace Stegner)
Illumination Night (Alice Hoffman)
More Die of Heartbreak (Saul Bellow)
Temporary Shelter (Mary Gordon)

1988

At Risk (Alice Hoffman)
Good Hearts (Reynolds Price)
Mama Day (Gloria Naylor)
The Mysteries of Pittsburgh (Michael Chabon)
Prisoner's Dilemma (Richard Powers)
Roger's Version (John Updike)
Tracks (Louise Erdrich)

1989

Billy Bathgate (E. L. Doctorow)
The Joy Luck Club (Amy Tan)
The Mambo Kings Play Songs of Love (Oscar Hijuelos)
Oldest Living Confederate Widow Tells All (Allan Gurganus)
Picturing Will (Ann Beattie)
Spartina (John Casey)
The Year of the Zinc Penny (Rick DeMarinis)

1990

Afterlife (Paul Monette)

Killing Mister Watson (Peter Matthiessen)
Rabbit at Rest (John Updike)

1991

Closing Arguments (Frederick Busch)
Mating (Norman Rush)
A Thousand Acres (Jane Smiley)

NOTES

Introduction. Riding without Horses: A Reading of the 1980s

1. Ties between the 1980s and the Gilded Age and the Roaring Twenties have been made frequently—most eloquently by Haynes Johnson, Schaller, Silverman, John Taylor, and Wills. Mills, in his introduction, finds comparisons to the Gilded Age most attractive. Ginger, although making no case for the 1980s, defines several characteristics of the Gilded Age that recall Reagan's America: the acquisitive spirit; a conservative concern over slipping public morality; a revival in evangelical religion; an ugly sort of xenophobia that often sounded like thumping nationalism; the marginalization of the poor; a popular taste for escapist literature against a more serious interest among a few writers in the argument of realism; a revival of interest in self-improvement campaigns and in the entrepreneurial spirit; and political propaganda that offered a most optimistic reading of the nation's condition.

2. Blumenthal, who is seldom generous with Reagan, finds the decade restorative but quickly cites Reagan's wholesale distortions of history. Cannon speaks of Reagan "reviving national confidence" (837). Schaller points out that Reagan was elected not for his command of facts but rather because of the way he made us feel. White argues that the Reagan legacy will not be found in legislation but rather in feeling. Wills, who is perhaps the most eloquent of Reagan Era commentators, finds Reagan a "rabble-soother" (377) whose optimism was exactly what we needed to rejuvenate our emotions.

3. Blumenthal compares the decade to a daydream and calls Reagan a monarch of a "kingdom of symbolism" (299). Gelb calls the era a pleasant make-believe age of symbols where the United States lost its central place in world events to the reality of Gorbachev's courageous reform efforts. Henry finds Reagan's America little more than the imaginary America long packaged by American advertising. Haynes Johnson, who points out that studies of children of alcoholic parents (such as Reagan) indicate that they frequently grow up denying reality, argues that Reagan, a career actor, lived quite naturally in a fantasyland. Mills harshly dis-

misses the entire decade by comparing Reagan's America to a phony Hollywood facade. Rogin, who draws extensively on Reagan's Hollywood years, compares the decade to an enthralling film. Schaller compares it to a daydream and later sees Reagan as the consummate salesman. White sees the decade as a fantasy of optimism and possibility sold to us by a master pitchman. Wills assesses the Reagan appeal using "dream" and "myth" interchangeably to indicate the fantasy of Reagan's agenda. Morrow, writing in *Time* magazine at the time of the Liberty Weekend spectacle, called Reagan's America a "sleight of hand" feat and Reagan himself a "masterpiece of American magic" (12).

4. The following discussion, which uses Disney World as an example of a postmodern text, draws on the work done by Bryman, Fjellman, and Rojek, who each in turn acknowledge their debt to both Eco and Baudrillard and their notions of hyper-reality and the powerful sway of simulations that offer a "reality" more real than anything that ever existed. Schultz's useful article, while not stressing postmodernity, does work out the implications of Disney's environment of happiness that compels us to relinquish any awareness of the immediate world beyond Disney's reach. Bryman draws intriguing comparisons between Disney World and the first great age of theme parks—interestingly, for the argument here, the Gilded Age. Without using the vocabulary of postmodernism or drawing ties to the Reagan Era, Kasson, in his work on Coney Island, cites the park as America's first alternative environment of spectacle and play, a zone of excess and simulations, a playground where reality and fantasy freely elide—a most postmodern environment.

5. See Olsen, who cites the atmosphere engendered by the political clout of Reagan-Thatcher-Kohl as the impetus for the neoconservative return to realism and sees behind such a flowering a specific backlash attack on the "culture and ideals of the 1960s" (28). Kaufmann sees the return to the realism of Carver as part of Reagan's nostalgic pitch for lost values, although Kaufmann argues Carver's realism is less mimetic and more experimental à la Barthelme. Versluys, although acknowledging that realism is a most enduring tradition and really was never lost, sees in the decade the demise of postmodernism (she cites the early death of Barthelme, the disappointment of Pynchon's *Vineland,* and the general monotony of the postmodern productions that found a narrower and narrower following) and the return to realism, which she credits to the influence of television and film and the sane return to scale in an age of excess. Greiner's twin studies on gender issues and the American novel of the 1980s draw only from works squarely within the realist tradition.

6. Surely the term "a postmodern text" smacks of careless generality. Here, without steering this argument into the often treacherous waters of specification and qualification, we use a general sense of the postmodern text that is characterized (by Klinkowitz, McHale, and Varsava most helpfully) as employing a broad set of elements: a playful, restless, bold willingness to experiment with form; an ironic sense of textual self-reflexivity; the willful subversion of genre, often through parody; the opposition to narrative closure; the absence of traditional plot

and traditional nuanced characters; decontextualized bits drawn from high and low culture and fashioned into enthralling collage; self-conscious games-playing through language performance; a self-evident sense of author-ity. These novels abandon the reportorial tradition of narrative fiction, indeed forsake as unreliable the entire enterprise of recording, and indulge rather the invention of private zones, alternative worlds. These texts, lavish and self-indulgent and cerebral, abandon as unworkable traditional ethical and moral stands to explore the tonic force of language itself. As such intricate experiments, these novels place the reader in a most tensive role, aware of the act of reading and always moving about a most unreliable and deliberately tricky artificial environment.

7. Such assessments can be found in virtually any political commentator covering the 1980 election. See also Gelb, Jeffords (who finds in Hollywood's macho argument of the 1980s a rejection of Carter's apparent wimpiness), Haynes Johnson (who compares Carter's America to a bound Gulliver), Mills (who speaks dramatically of a "decade of humiliation" [12]), Orman, Schaller, and Wills. DeMause is interesting in this regard as he rehearses the same litany of anti-Carter rhetoric only to reject such apocalyptic broodings as political propaganda of the Reagan camp.

8. Although both Shi and Orvell cite the atrocities of World War II as the shattering force that closed out the era of realistic fiction, other commentators on postmodern novelistics (following both Roth's and Barth's pronouncements against realistic fiction) cite the rage for the radical that fomented during the 1960s and the acknowledgment during the Nuclear Age that rejected as unworkable the novel's attempt to record an immediate too brutal and too chaotic for ordering. See Alter, Kuehl, and particularly the passionate defense of realism as a workable convention offered by Tallis.

9. For specific approaches that find the tension between an exhausted realism and a feisty postmodern challenger, see Aldridge (who holds little hope for realistic fictions that have become to him drab and have left us all in the hands of cute fabulators); Alexander; Graff (who sees postmodernism as a revolt against realism); Kaplan (who rues the exclusion of realistic work from the national canon); Karl (who separates simple "novelists" from the "writers," those engaged in the work of self-reflexive texts); Newman (who rejects the dichotomy of technique versus vision as phony and finds a fusion in the works of Nabokov and Grass); Opdahl (who attempts to mediate the division using Updike's *Centaur* as "less literal realism"); Sauerberg (who, like Zavarzadeh, cites the rise in documentary realism as the way realism has survived); and, most eloquently, Stern, Tallis, and Wolfe. Others reject the opposition: Furst sees realism itself as a self-conscious transcription, very much like any postmodern experiment. Alter traces the division back to Cervantes but fears the most recent works of experimentation lack heart, and finds Nabokov a successful mediating figure. The work of Wilde's *Middle Ground* perhaps best anticipates the argument of spectacle realism. Wilde argues that between the extremes of the drab realism of minimalism and the cold cerebral play of reflexive texts emerged the middle fictions of Stanley Elkin and

Thomas Berger and Grace Paley (among others), who explore the ordinary and reveal its extraordinary significance and our resilient capacity to create values.

10. Reagan's "composition" has been examined by Rogin (who explores film as critical makeup of Reagan); Schaller (who cites Reagan's fondness for television and film plots); White (who cites television and film as a vast resource of Reagan's sense of Middle America); and Wills (who astutely observes Reagan's drawing from television and film offered "continuity, stability, and guideline" [375] in a contemporary world that often seems chaotic). Wills closes his study by drawing comparisons briefly between Disney and Reagan, noting that both shared an interest in edited history as a way of extending comfort. Interestingly, Blumenthal in his essay resists the notion of Reagan, for all his obvious love of kitsch, as postmodern text, arguing that Reagan lacked the irony of self-awareness necessary to such texts. Such intentionality, of course, is always subject to question—and surely irony is often the work/role of the text-consumer. The more intense the text, the deeper the irony to the critical consumer. The very lack of irony becomes itself ironic.

11. See the standard readings of realism (by Auerbach, Berthoff, Borus, Carter, Martin, Rignall), each of which indicates the compelling urgency of realistic fiction and its commitment to observational honesty—what Updike calls in his essay on Howells "the novel as a means of grasping reality" (80). Such readings indicate how realistic writers brought immediacy to fiction by the commitment to record and observe with candor against the gentility of much of the sentimental (and popular) fiction of the Gilded Age. Such efforts, however, offer a literature that is often somber, bitter, inelegant, anxious, bleak; see Kaplan's argument that realism asserted control and order in a world that so obviously resisted such shaping. Levin and Levine, although interested in European realism, suggest the realistic eye is often pessimistic as it records the brutality and materialism and dullness of the ordinary. The American movement in realistic literature, headed by Howells, is often cited for its lame sense of sunny optimism, although in its time it treated head-on the more damning evidences of the tawdry in human behavior. Sundquist offers that the difficulty in recording objectively the immediate compelled writers in the next generation to take the imperative of candor and bring it to bear on the interior self.

12. This standard list of elements of realistic literature drawn from the first great flowering in American literature comes from the overviews provided by Becker (in his introduction), Bell, Berthoff, Kolb, Martin, Pizer, and more recently by Shi.

13. Although beyond the scope of this book, this fugal counterforce of work and play can also be traced in the decade's music, film, and television. In music, we counterpoised the obvious postmodern texts of deliberate spectacle and pastiche and playful self-projection (Michael Jackson, Madonna, David Byrne, Prince) with the hard-eyed blue-collar gospels of Bruce Springsteen, the political activism of nuclear resistance and AIDS awareness, the street poetry of rap, and the industry-wide interest in hunger relief. The decade's signature moments in big-budget films—whirling special effects, dizzyingly simple plotlines, winsome manageable

worlds of elegant villains and campy heroes—found counterforce in the small-budget works of Barry Levinson and John Sayles, the string of big-budget historic epics and biopics that dominated the Oscars, and the occasional gestures of realistic filmmaking—*Terms of Endearment, Rain Man, Driving Miss Daisy, The Color Purple*—that managed to hold their own even at the box office. On television, the seductive fantasies of *Cosby, Dallas, Dynasty,* and *Miami Vice* were balanced by the decidedly quotidian sets of *Roseanne* and *Married . . . with Children* and by the operating rooms of *St. Elsewhere* and the gritty precincts of Hill Street and *Cagney and Lacey.*

Chapter 1. Reading Ringside: Joyce Carol Oates's
You Must Remember This

1. See, for instance, Strandberg, who sees the novel as a contest between Spinoza and Schopenhauer or more specifically between control and will; or Wesley, who sees it as a contest between power and impotence; or Redmon, who draws on the contest between body and spirit; or Greg Johnson, who tracks the contest between appetite and civilization; and Creighton, who sees passion and control as the central matchup with unholy love and holy love on the undercard; Daly pairs off innocence and self-knowledge.

2. Readings of the novel's close trace particularly the lovemaking between Hannah and Lyle as a gloss to Joyce's closing pages of *Ulysses,* another sort of autumnal defrosting within a troubled marriage—although the present reading would suggest that any gloss to *Ulysses* is clearly parody. Indeed, given the nature of Lyle's fantasizing (which Strandberg oddly terms memory), there are few more chilling words that the closing "Thank you" and the "I love you" exchanged by the Stevicks. Daly and Redmon suggest that Enid emerges into womanhood. Indeed, Daly accepts Felix's dramatic turn to marriage as authentic and Lyle's bomb shelter as honest confrontation with imminent apocalypse. Redmon sees Enid going off to music school as a sort of Ishmael-survivor who will come to be the "soul" of the world. Strandberg celebrates the resurgence of Eros but cannot account for its sudden implosion—he even accepts Felix's turn toward monogamy without irony. Creighton celebrates Oates's "mellow" spirit (76) but again offers little in the way of explaining this anomaly in Oates's fiction.

3. See particularly Updike's review and Wesley, who both draw extensively on the boxing ring as suggestive symbol of the tumultuous real world.

Chapter 2. Strange Gods before Us: John Irving's
A Prayer for Owen Meany

1. For a complete discussion of Irving's fascination with this predominantly violent vision of contemporary life, see Lounsberry and Miller. That we struggle amid such chaotic violence to impose order in some measure (usually through the sheer muscle of artistic endeavor) is the argument of Priestley's essay and one made by Irving himself in his piece on Piggy Sneed.

2. For all this documented scorn for the elitism of much postmodern experimenting (see particularly his comments in the McCaffery interview), Irving has often worked out intricate experiments in the relationship between narrator and author, especially in his earlier, pre-*Garp* works; see Harter and Thompson, and Miller.

3. See Sheppard, Pritchard (who dismisses Wheelwright as a character of "little interest"). Page, in a more illuminating study, suggests that the text deliberately denies Owen any status, any definition—that Owen is pure sign. Unlike other analyses, Page cites Wheelwright's surly unreliability. Page decides that Irving parodies both the need to know and the open universe that denies satisfying conclusion. We are then left with nothing to affirm, a reading that pitches the narrative into a far darker reading than that offered here. Greiner finds fascinating Owen Meany and Hester as part of Irving's replay of Hawthorne's *The Scarlet Letter*, but finds Wheelwright merely a retreating male who bonds by virtue of the baseball accident with Owen. Although Towers confesses the narrator does little to inspire "confidence," his uneasiness over Wheelwright never explores the broad satirizing argued here.

4. The definition of a contemporary Christian here comes largely from the luminous theological writings of novelist Frederick Buechner, Irving's prep school teacher to whom he dedicates the novel.

5. That Irving has used broad satire through his narrators has been noted by Gabriel Miller, Harter and Thompson, and Page and discussed more completely by Cosgrove, who, using largely the example of *Garp*, finds in Irving a heavy use of irony and satire in which Garp is the narrative voice of sanity—a formula that *Owen Meany* reverses.

6. The promise of family, the rewards of parenting, the bond of family as part of Irving's offering against the confusions and chaos of contemporary life are detailed by Epstein, Gabriel Miller, and Harter and Thompson's introductory chapter.

Chapter 3. A Necessary Time to Bolt: Reynolds Price's *Kate Vaiden*

1. Price himself develops the multiple meanings of the word "bolt": he uses it to mean both the active (to run suddenly without explanation) and the passive (to be firmly attached to another).

2. The argument here is based on Gilligan, who has defined the problem of autonomy and compassion as central to the female sensibility; Rich, who has examined the struggle to define the self against the imperative of reproduction; and MacKethan, who traces the female struggle for voice within southern literature, where the urge toward individuality is complicated by a persistent agrarian culture that idealizes women.

3. Critical response found such a deliberate speaking device "highly distinctive" (Towers); "homely" if a bit unbelievable for its cleverness (Clemons); "exhaustingly rich" (Wilson).

4. This central dilemma in Price's work has been pointed out by Shepherd, Eichelberger, and to a much greater extent in the introduction to Rooke's study.

5. The following discussion on androgyny draws on the work of Heilbrun, Singer, and Kimbrough. Price's remarks are taken from his essay "Men Creating Women," which appeared shortly before the publication of *Kate Vaiden*. It might be interesting to compare Price's fusion of a male author with a female narrator to Alan Gurganus's *Oldest Living Confederate Widow Tells All* (1984), a stunning example of spectacle realism.

6. Walter was largely ignored by critical responses. Brown alone mentions him, only to dismiss him with the withering epithet "saintly," her admiration leavened with skepticism.

Chapter 4. "The Twin-Peaked Glory of Bothness": William Kennedy's *Quinn's Book*

1. Kennedy as realistic writer, of course, is something of a knotty problem. Standard readings of Kennedy have tended to stress his place either within the gritty urban realist school of Dreiser, Crane, Bellow, Algren or within the magic realist school of Marquez and Kafka. Van Dover speaks of the use of magic realism; Reilly places Kennedy within the urban realist tradition. Reilly also argues that Kennedy finds realism a dead end and thus introduces elements of the surreal, the inexplicable. In a limited study, Black introduces both elements as part of a reading of *Ironweed*. Boyle finds elements of both traditions in *Quinn's Book* but stays largely within the first twenty or so pages.

2. The critical exegesis on the works of Heraclitus is, of course, quite extensive. The present discussion draws on the standard commentaries of Hussey, Manley-Robinson, and Wheelwright.

3. The novel's interest in language has only been briefly noted, usually with dismay. Prescott and Birkerts, for instance, find the work simply overwritten, that Kennedy is perhaps too impressed by the vehicle to worry much about where it might be going.

4. Oddly enough, this speech has been hailed as riveting and important in understanding Kennedy's antiwar interest as part of Quinn's education. Even Boyle, in an otherwise perceptive piece, finds the speech quite harrowing. That Quinn might be engaged in rhetorical simplification is suggested, of course, by the fact that this speech does not close the novel but comes at a point where Quinn clearly has much left to learn.

5. Van Dover weakly argues that Quinn is of value as he confronts his time, although that confrontation apparently bears little on Quinn's private life. Indeed, Van Dover finds no ties to the United States of the 1980s and suggests the novel teaches lessons about the "American world of the 1850s and 1860s" (108). Reilly dismisses the use of public events as simply too much for the plot to handle. Birkerts finds the novel straining for the cinematic. Boyle cites the harrowing prose that re-creates the draft riots, the immigrant scenes, and the war stories—but does not relate such events either to Quinn's development or to the contemporary cul-

ture. Gray finds the plot is picaresque and allows only that the public and private are "counterbalanced."

6. For background to this use of melodrama and its rise in American culture of the mid–nineteenth century, see Grimsted and Toll.

Chapter 5. Speaking the Language of Brightness: Robert Ferro's *Second Son*

1. The canon of AIDS narratives is quite massive and suggesting anything such as a single theme is, of course, helpful only as a generality. But the preponderance of narratives of handling the disease, the sheer volume of elegies and diaries and reportorial accounts, has been often cited. See, for instance, Kruger, who divides AIDS narratives into narratives of growth (more historic and social examinations of the disease itself) and narratives of decay (personal and private records of infected individuals). See Pastore's essay for a masterful brief overview of the direction of AIDS literature and see also Poirier's lucid introduction.

2. Although listing such intriguing treatments is not within the scope of this book, Kruger works out a most illuminating summary of these positions, including his own fascinating reading of the virus as information system. In addition, Kruger's bibliography indicates the reach of such postmodern readings.

3. See my essay on Ferro's work for a fuller treatment of this fascination.

4. Indeed, *Second Son*, as one of the earliest and more critically acclaimed treatments of the AIDS virus, has received scholarly attention, but each time within a context of other AIDS narratives or other gay fiction: see my essay in Nelson; see James W. Jones, James Miller, and brief mentions by Kruger.

5. Along with Ferro's decision to include a subplot involving interplanetary space travel, the decision not to name the virus directly within the narrative has sparked the most heated critical response, although Ferro himself indicated he did not want the novel bound to its time. James W. Jones argues such a strategy moves the disease from the narrative center and puts in its place rather the nature of relationships, but Jones goes on to say that by refusing to name AIDS directly Ferro allows the fantasy element of Splendora to dominate the narrative and to permit the possibility of magic and fantasy. Kruger, in a brief and puzzling argument, suggests that the refusal to name the virus directly is somehow a strategy of avoiding reality; but he does not bother to indicate how Ferro so carefully maneuvers around such simplistic escapism and comes by narrative end to a character who demands confrontation and accepts the immediate. For Ferro's interest in avoiding making his narrative a period piece, see my biographical essay on Ferro's novels.

6. In addition to the aesthetic inclinations of the second son, his travels overseas, and the nature of his infection, Ferro draws much of the narrative line from autobiography. These similarities include the structure of the East Coast urban Catholic, upper-class family and the personalities of each family member and the makeup of their individual families, as well as his father's business life and his difficult adjustments to his son's homosexuality. Interestingly, one indication of Ferro's distancing from his own character is that Mark Valerian has had little inter-

est in the commitment and responsibilities of monogamous relationships—Ferro committed himself to a nearly twenty-year relationship with artist Michael Grumley, who died some months before Ferro did.

7. James Miller provides the most involved treatment of the Splendora fantasy, but he offers only that Ferro gently satirizes the notion of such escape although Miller is apparently unimpressed by the obvious darker element of Matthew Black's letters. Jones does offer that Ferro resists the invitation to indulge Splendora but does leave the idea that Ferro condones escapism generally by suggesting, indirectly, that the Berkshire retreat is somehow a closing narrative position rather than what it actually is: a most problematic midtext posture. James W. Jones closes by arguing that the narrative has indeed transformed Mark Valerian; but Jones argues that Mark emerges from the narrative a "triumphant lover" (241), thus highlighting the very urge that Ferro minimizes by narrative end. It is not the work of passion (genital connection is at best an opening move for Mark) but rather the inclusive work of compassion, the turn toward family and the support structure that does not involve sexual identity, that permits Mark his closing status as narrative hero.

Chapter 6. "That Sudden Shock of Sunshine and Birdsong": Anne Tyler's *Breathing Lessons*

1. The connection between *Breathing Lessons* and such popular television formats has been examined (see particularly Betts, Gilbert, and Voelker). Other critical responses (Powers, McPhillips, Hoagland) argue that Maggie plots but do not trace to television the origins of such tale spinning.

2. The interest in the family is central in Tyler criticism; see Voelker, Carroll, Petry, and Anne G. Jones. The sitcom interest in the family is well defined by Frances Gray and Taylor.

3. Critical response is divided on the closing. Betts, for instance, finds Maggie's conversion unconvincing and at best "semi-final" (14). Voelker finds the closing nearly despairing in Maggie's concession to the ordinary. Koppel, oddly, asserts that Maggie has "touched on the futility" of her life (285) but insists, nevertheless, that this is somehow a positive ending. Kissel finds the close affirming the traditional feminine values of relatedness, Maggie making her peace with her domestic role against her text-long pull toward separating the self, an odd reading given Maggie's daylong plotting to reassemble her nest. Carroll, in her *Frontiers* essay examining Maggie as a model for postmenopausal women, sees the close as an unsatisfying, sentimental gesture akin to the close of *Gone with the Wind* when assertions about the promise of tomorrow are made against panic and anxieties.

Chapter 7. In the Jaws of the (S)napping Turtle: T. Coraghessan Boyle's *World's End*

1. Boyle has long used science, particularly evolution and astronomy, as a way to approach his "studies" of humanity, a scientific posture that he has used to describe his role as a writer in both Friend's article and in the Adams interview.

2. It is, of course, conjecture to approach the novel through chaos theory because Boyle has never directly indicated that influence. And yet it is a workable rubric to approach Boyle's black comic world, his bleak sense of hopelessness always coupled with a cheery disposition to continue. And it gives a new dimension to his long fascination with accidents and how the smallest trivial event can have enormous consequences—all within the logic of chaos. Indeed, it would be far more within the freewheeling logic of chaos theory to deny such influence while demonstrating its pervasiveness within the narrative. Boyle has long been struck by the workings of determinism, and this text has been particularly cited in initial reviews for its oppressive sense of foredoomed action. Clearly, the events here repeat, shape patterns, but each character acts freely—a clear application of the logic (if not the math) of chaos theory, a way for Boyle to preserve both his iron sense of predetermination and his insistence that the novel is nevertheless "comic" (Adams 54).

3. Boyle has long been seen as a rather grim pessimist; even by his own admission in interviews he admits, "I wish I had better news" (Adams 53). Clute finds Boyle's characters here destroyed by a "crushing machine." And Walker, in a devastating piece on Boyle's short fiction, cites Boyle's inclinations to bleak fictions devoid of any redeeming ethical dimension. DeMott senses this novel possesses "a belief in human range," although he can offer no logic for such affirmation (53).

4. The mass of standard literature produced in the late 1980s that explicates chaos theory for a lay audience is so great, only a few critical titles need to be cited here as sources for the understanding of the theory that informs this reading Boyle's narrative: Hayles, Stewart, Briggs and Peat, Lorenz, Gleick, Kellert, and Lampton, and the collection edited by Hall.

Chapter 8. Humming the (In)sufficient Heart Out: Richard Powers's *The Gold Bug Variations*

1. Critical response to Powers has frequently cited the young novelist, certified in his early thirties as a "genius" by the MacArthur Foundation, of showing off. In his review of *Gold Bug*, Porter testily accused Powers of a "zany obsession with data" that ultimately threatens to destroy the narrative love stories. *Time's* Paul Gray praised the book (indeed, the magazine would name the novel its book of the year) but felt compelled to warn readers about the book's "constant hum" of intellectual activity. For a fuller examination of the critical struggle in Powers's work between the head and the heart, see my essay on his first five novels.

2. It is possible that Powers modeled Stuart Ressler on Marshall Nirenberg, a promising molecular biologist who (like Ressler) took his doctorate in 1957 and who (like Ressler) worked at a government-funded research outpost. Nirenberg, like Ressler, posited the existence of a messenger RNA and suggested evidence was available through the use of a cell-free system to build amino acids into proteins.

BIBLIOGRAPHY

Primary and Secondary Works Cited or Consulted

Adams, Elizabeth. "An Interview with T. Coraghessan Boyle." *Chicago Review* 37, 2–3 (1991): 51–63.

Aldridge, John W. *The American Novel and the Way We Live Now.* New York: Oxford University Press, 1983.

Alexander, Marguerite. *Flights from Realism: Themes and Strategies in Postmodernist British and American Fiction.* London: Arnold, 1990.

Alter, Robert. *Partial Magic: The Novel as a Self-Conscious Genre.* Berkeley: University of California Press, 1975.

Auerbach, Erich. *Mimesis: The Representation of Reality in Western Literature.* Trans. Willard R. Trask. Princeton: Princeton University Press, 1953.

Baker, John F. "Richard Powers: Interview." *Publishers Weekly,* 16 August 1991, 37–38.

Baudrillard, Jean. *Simulacra and Simulation.* Trans. Sheila Glaser. Ann Arbor: University of Michigan Press, 1994. (Originally published in 1981.)

Becker, George J. *Realism in Modern Literature.* New York: Ungar, 1980.

———, ed. Introduction. *Documents of Modern Literary Realism.* Princeton: Princeton University Press, 1963.

Bell, David F. *Circumstances: Chance in the Literary Text.* Lincoln: University of Nebraska Press, 1993.

Berthoff, Warner. *The Ferment of Realism: American Literature, 1884–1919.* New York: Free Press, 1965.

Betts, Doris. "The Fiction of Anne Tyler." *Southern Quarterly* 21, no. 4 (1983): 23–37.

———. "Tyler's Marriage of Opposites." In *The Fiction of Anne Tyler,* ed. C. Ralph Stephens, 1–15. Jackson: University Press of Mississippi, 1990.

Birkerts, Sven. "O Albany." Review of *Quinn's Book. New Republic,* 27 June 1988, 41–42.

Black, David. "The Fusion of Past and Present in William Kennedy's *Ironweed.*" *Critique* 27, no. 1 (1986): 177–84.

Blumenthal, Sidney. *Our Long National Daydream: A Political Pageant of the Reagan Era.* New York: Harper, 1988.

———. "Reaganism and the Neokitsch Aesthetic." In *The Reagan Legacy*, ed. Sidney Blumenthal and Thomas Byrne Edsall, 251–94. New York: Pantheon, 1988.

Borus, Daniel H. *Writing Realism: Howells, James, and Norris in the Mass Market.* Chapel Hill: University of North Carolina Press, 1989.

Boyle, T. Coraghessan. "Into the Heart of Old Albany." Review of *Quinn's Book. New York Times Book Review*, 22 May 1988, 1, 32–33.

———. *World's End.* New York: Viking, 1989. (Originally published in 1988.)

———. *World's End: A Videorecording.* New York: In Our Times Arts Media, 1991.

Briggs, John, and F. David Peat. *Turbulent Mirror: An Illustrated Guide to Chaos Theory and the Science of Wholeness.* New York: Harper, 1989.

Brown, Rosellen. "Travels with a Dangerous Woman." Review of *Kate Vaiden. New York Times Book Review*, 29 June 1986, 1, 40–41.

Bryman, Alan. *Disney and His Worlds.* London: Routledge, 1995.

Buechner, Frederick. *The Alphabet of Grace.* New York: Seabury, 1969.

———. *The Hungering Dark.* San Francisco: Harper, 1969.

———. *The Magnificent Defeat.* New York: Seabury, 1966.

———. *The Sacred Journey.* San Francisco: Harper, 1982.

Cannon, Lou. *President Reagan: The Role of a Lifetime.* New York: Simon and Schuster, 1991.

Caramello, Charles. *Silverless Mirrors: Book, Self, and Postmodern American Fiction.* Tallahassee: University Presses of Florida, 1983.

Carroll, Virginia Schaeffer. "The Nature of Kinship in the Novels of Anne Tyler." In *The Fiction of Anne Tyler*, ed. C. Ralph Stephens, 16–27. Jackson: University Press of Mississippi, 1990.

———. "Wrestling with Change: Discourse Strategies in Anne Tyler." *Frontiers* 19 (1998): 86–109.

Carter, Everett. *Howells and the Age of Realism.* Philadelphia: Lippincott, 1954.

Clemons, Walter. "The Ballad of a Country Girl on the Run." Review of *Kate Vaiden. Newsweek*, 23 June 1986, 78.

Clute, John. "Van Warts and All." Review of *World's End. Times Literary Supplement*, 26 August–1 September 1988, 927.

Combs, James. *The Reagan Range: The Nostalgic Myth in American Politics.* Bowling Green, Ohio: Bowling Green State University Press, 1993.

Cosgrove, William. *"The World According to Garp* as Fabulation." *South Carolina Review* 19. no. 2 (1987): 52–58.

Creighton, Joanne V. *Joyce Carol Oates: Novels of the Middle Years.* New York: Twayne, 1992.

Daly, Brenda. "Porous Boundaries: Daughters, Families, and the Body Politic in Recent Novels of the 1980s." In *Lavish Self-Divisions: The Novels of Joyce Carol Oates*, 179–204. Jackson: University Press of Mississippi, 1996.

DeMause, Lloyd. *Reagan's America.* New York: Creative Roots, 1984.

DeMott, Benjamin. "Ghost Ships on the Hudson." Review of *World's End. New York Times Book Review*, 27 September 1987, 1, 52–53.

Dewey, Joseph. "Dwelling in Possibility: The Fiction of Richard Powers." *Hollins Critic* 33, no. 2 (1996): 1–16.

———. "Hooking the Nose of the Leviathan: Knowledge, Information, and the Mysteries of Bonding in *The Gold Bug Variations*." *Review of Contemporary Literature* 18, no. 3 (Fall 1998): 51–66.

———. "Music for a Closing: Responses to AIDS in Three American Novels." In *AIDS: The Literary Response*. ed. Emmanuel S. Nelson, 23–38. New York: Twayne, 1992.

———. "Robert Ferro: 1941–88." In *Contemporary Gay American Novelists*, ed. Emmanuel S. Nelson, 128–39. Westport: Greenwood Press, 1993.

———. "A Time to Bolt: Suicide, Androgyny, and the Dislocation of the Self in Reynolds Price's *Kate Vaiden*." *Mississippi Quarterly* 45, no.1 (1991–92): 9–28.

Doty, Alexander. "The Cabinet of Lucy Ricardo: Lucille Ball's Star Image." *Cinema Journal* 29, no. 4 (1990): 3–22.

Eco, Umberto. *Travels in Hyper Reality*, 3–58. Trans. William Weaver. San Diego: Harcourt, 1986. (Originally published in 1975.)

Eichelberger, Clayton L. "Reynolds Price: 'A Banner in Defeat.'" *Journal of Popular Culture* 1 (1972): 410–17.

Epstein, Joseph. "Why John Irving Is So Popular." *Commentary*, June 1982, 59–63.

Feifer, Maxine. *Tourism in History: From Imperial Rome to the Present*. New York: Stein and Day, 1985.

Ferro, Robert. *Second Son*. New York: Crown, 1988.

Fjellman, Stephen M. *Vinyl Leaves: Walt Disney World and America*. Boulder, Colo.: Westview, 1992.

Friedman, Ellen G. *Joyce Carol Oates*. New York: Ungar, 1980.

Friend, Tad. Interview with T. C. Boyle. *New York Times Magazine*, 9 December 1990, 50, 66, 67, 68.

Furst, Lilian. *All Is True: The Claims and Strategies of Realist Fiction*. Durham: Duke University Press, 1995.

Gardner, John. *On Moral Fiction*. New York: Basic, 1978.

Gelb, Leslie H. "The Mind of the President." *New York Times Magazine*, 6 October 1985, 20–24, 28, 30, 32, 103, 112.

Gilbert, Susan. "Private Lives and Public Issues: Anne Tyler's Prize-winning Novels." In *The Fiction of Anne Tyler*, ed. C. Ralph Stephens, 136–44. Jackson: University Press of Mississippi, 1990.

Gilligan, Carol. *In a Different Voice: Psychological Theory and Women's Development*. Cambridge, Mass.: Harvard University Press, 1982.

Ginger, Ray. *Age of Excess: The United States from 1877 to 1914*. New York: Macmillan, 1965.

Gleick, James. *Chaos: Making a New Science*. New York: Viking, 1987.

Graff, Gerald. *Literature against Itself: Literary Ideas in Modern Society*. Chicago: University of Chicago Press, 1979.

Grant, Mary Kathryn. *The Tragic Vision of Joyce Carol Oates*. Durham: Duke University Press, 1978.

Gray, Frances. *Women and Laughter.* Charlottesville: University Press of Virginia, 1994.

Gray, Paul. "An Eyewitness to Paradox." Review of *Quinn's Book. Time,* 16 May 1988, 92–93.

———. "What Is the Meaning of Life?" Review of *The Gold Bug Variations. Time,* 2 September 1991, 68.

Greiner, Donald J. *Women Enter the Wilderness: Male Bonding and the American Novel of the 1980s.* Columbia: University of South Carolina Press, 1991.

———. *Women without Men: Female Bonding and the American Novel of the 1980s.* Columbia: University of South Carolina Press, 1993.

Grimsted, David. *Melodrama Unveiled: American Theater and Culture, 1800–1850.* Chicago: University of Chicago Press, 1968.

Hall, Nina, ed. *Exploring Chaos: A Guide to the New Science of Disorder.* New York: Norton, 1993.

Harter, Carol C., and James R. Thompson. *John Irving.* Twayne's United States Authors Series (TUSAS) 502. Boston: Twayne, 1986.

Hayles, N. Katherine. *Chaos Bound: Orderly Disorder in Contemporary Literature and Science.* Ithaca: Cornell University Press, 1990.

Heilbrun, Carolyn G. *Toward a Recognition of Androgyny.* New York: Knopf, 1973.

Henry, William A. *Visions of America: How We Saw the 1984 Election.* Boston: Atlantic Monthly Press, 1985.

Hill, Jane Bowers. "John Irving's Aesthetics of Accessibility: Setting Free the Novel." *South Carolina Review* 16, no. 1 (1983): 38–44.

Hoagland, Edward. "About Maggie, Who Tried Too Hard." Review of *Breathing Lessons. New York Times Book Review,* 11 September 1988, 1, 43–44.

Humphries, Jefferson, ed. *Conversations with Reynolds Price.* Jackson: University Press of Mississippi, 1990.

Hussey, Edward. "Heraclitus." In *The Presocratics,* 32–59. New York: Scribner's, 1972.

Irving, John. "The Aesthetics of Accessibility: Kurt Vonnegut and His Critics." *New Republic,* 22 September 1979, 41–49.

———. *A Prayer for Owen Meany.* New York: Morrow, 1989.

———. "Trying to Save Piggy Sneed." *New York Times Book Review,* 22 August 1982, 3, 20–22.

Jeffords, Susan. *Hard Bodies: Hollywood Masculinity in the Reagan Era.* New Brunswick, N.J.: Rutgers University Press, 1994.

Johnson, Greg. *Understanding Joyce Carol Oates.* Columbia: University of South Carolina Press, 1987.

Johnson, Haynes. *Sleepwalking through History: America in the Reagan Years.* New York: Norton, 1991.

Jones, Anne G. "Home At Last, and Homesick Again: The Ten Novels of Anne Tyler." *Hollins Critic* 23, no. 2 (1986): 1–14.

Jones, James W. "Refusing the Name: The Absence of AIDS in Recent American Gay Fiction." In *Writing AIDS: Gay Literature, Language, and Analysis,* ed. Timothy F. Murphy and Suzanne Poirier, 225–43. New York: Columbia University Press, 1993.

Kaminsky, Alice. "On Literary Realism." In *The Theory of the Novel: New Essays,* ed. John Halperin, 213–43. New York: Oxford University Press, 1974.

Kaplan, Amy. *The Social Construction of American Realism.* Chicago: University of Chicago Press, 1988.

Karl, Frederick R. *American Fictions, 1940–1980.* New York: Harper, 1983.

Kasson, John F. *Amusing the Million: Coney Island at the Turn of the Century.* New York: Hill and Wang, 1978.

Kaufmann, David. "Yuppie Postmodernism." *Arizona Quarterly* 47, no. 2 (1991): 93–116.

Kazin, Alfred. "God's Own Little Squirt." Review of *A Prayer for Owen Meany. New York Times Book Review,* 12 March 1989, 1, 30–31.

Kellert, Stephen H. *In the Wake of Chaos: Unpredictable Order in Dynamical Systems.* Chicago: University of Chicago Press, 1993.

Kennedy, William. *Quinn's Book.* New York: Viking, 1988.

Kimbrough, Robert. *Shakespeare and the Art of Humankindness: An Essay toward Androgyny.* Atlantic Highlands, N.J.: Humanities Press, 1990.

Kissel, Susan S. *Moving On: The Heroines of Shirley Ann Grau, Anne Tyler, and Gail Godwin,* 69–98. Bowling Green, Ohio: Bowling Green State University Press, 1996.

Klinkowitz, Jerome. *Literary Disruptions: The Making of a Post-Contemporary American Fiction.* Urbana: University of Illinois Press, 1975.

Kolb, Harold, Jr. *The Illusion of Life: American Realism as a Literary Form.* Charlottesville: University Press of Virginia, 1969.

Koppel, Gene. "Maggie Moran, Anne Tyler's Madcap Heroine: A Game-Approach to *Breathing Lessons.*" *Essays in Literature* 18, no. 2 (1991): 276–87.

Kruger, Steven F. *AIDS Narratives: Gender and Sexuality, Fiction and Science.* New York: Garland, 1996.

Kuehl, John. *Alternate Worlds: A Study of Postmodern Antirealistic American Fiction.* New York: New York University Press, 1989.

Lampton, Christopher. *Science of Chaos.* New York: Venture, 1992.

Levin, Harry. *The Gates of Horn: A Study of Five French Realists.* New York: Oxford University Press, 1963.

Levine, George. "Realism Reconsidered." In *The Theory of the Novel: New Essays,* ed. John Halperin, 233–56. New York: Oxford University Press, 1974.

———. *The Realistic Imagination: English Fiction from Frankenstein to Lady Chatterley.* Chicago: University of Chicago Press, 1981.

Lorenz, Edward N. *The Essence of Chaos.* Seattle: University of Washington Press, 1993.

Lounsberry, Barbara. "The Terrible Under Toad: Violence as Excessive Imagination in *The World According to Garp.*" *Thalia* 5, no. 2 (1983): 30–35.

MacKethan, Lucinda. *Daughters of Time: Creating Woman's Voice in Southern Story.* Athens: University of Georgia Press, 1990.

Mansley-Robinson, John. "Heraclitus." In *An Introduction to Early Greek Philosophy,* 87–105. Boston: Houghton, 1968.

Martin, Jay. *Harvests of Change: American Literature, 1865–1914.* Englewood Cliffs, N.J.: Prentice-Hall, 1967.

McCaffery, Larry. "An Interview with John Irving." *Contemporary Literature* 23 (1982): 1–18.

McHale, Brian. *Postmodernist Fiction.* New York: Methuen, 1987.

McKay, Janet Holmgren. *Narration and Discourse in American Realistic Fiction.* Philadelphia: University of Pennsylvania Press, 1982.

McPhillips, Robert. "The Baltimore Chop." Review of *Breathing Lessons. The Nation,* 7 November 1988, 464–66.

Miller, Gabriel. *John Irving.* New York: Ungar, 1982.

Miller, James. "Dante on Fire Island: Reinventing Heaven in the AIDS Elegy." In *Writing AIDS: Gay Literature, Language, and Analysis,* ed. Timothy F. Murphy and Suzanne Poirier, 55–72. New York: Columbia University Press, 1993.

Mills, Nicolaus. "The Culture of Triumph and the Spirit of the Times." In *Culture in an Age of Money: The Legacy of the 1980s in America,* ed. Nicolaus Mills, 1–29. Chicago: Dee, 1990.

Morrow, Lance. "Yankee Doodle Magic." *Time,* 7 July 1986, 12–16.

Newman, Charles. *The Post-Modern Aura: The Act of Fiction in an Age of Inflation.* Evanston, Ill.: Northwestern University Press, 1985.

Oates, Joyce Carol. *You Must Remember This.* New York: Harper, 1988. (Originally published in 1987.)

Olsen, Lance. *Circus of the Mind in Motion: Postmodernism and the Comic Vision.* Detroit: Wayne State University Press, 1990.

Olster, Stacey. *Reminiscence and Re-Creation in Contemporary American Fiction.* Cambridge: Cambridge University Press, 1989.

Opdahl, Keith. "The Nine Lives of Literary Realism." In *Contemporary American Fiction,* ed. Malcolm Bradbury and Sigmund Ro, 1–15. London: Arnold, 1987.

Orman, John M. *Comparing Presidential Behavior: Carter, Reagan, and the Macho Presidential Style.* New York: Greenwood Press, 1987.

Orvell, Miles. *The Real Thing: Imitation and Authenticity in American Culture, 1880–1940.* Chapel Hill: University of North Carolina Press, 1989.

Page, Philip. "Hero Worship and Hermeneutic Dialectics: John Irving's *A Prayer for Owen Meany.*" *Mosaic* 28, no. 3 (1995): 137–56.

Pastore, Judith Laurence. "What Are the Responsibilities of Representing AIDS?" In *Confronting AIDS through Literature: The Responsibilities of Representation,* ed. Judith Laurence Pastore, 15–35. Urbana: University of Illinois Press, 1993.

Petry, Alice Hall. "*Breathing Lessons.*" In *Understanding Anne Tyler,* 233–53. Columbia: University of South Carolina Press, 1990.

Pizer, Donald. *Twentieth-Century American Literary Naturalism: An Interpretation.* Carbondale: Southern Illinois University Press, 1982.

Poirier, Suzanne. "On Writing AIDS: An Introduction." In *Writing AIDS: Gay Literature, Language, and Analysis*, ed. Timothy F. Murphy and Suzanne Poirier, 1–8. New York: Columbia University Press, 1993.

Porter, Roy. "Data for Data's Sake." Review of *The Gold Bug Variations*. *Times Literary Supplement*, 8 May 1992, 20.

Powers, Richard. *The Gold Bug Variations*. New York: Morrow, 1991.

Prescott, Peter S. "The Romance of Olde Albany." Review of *Quinn's Book*. *Newsweek*, 9 May 1988, 76.

Price, Reynolds. *Kate Vaiden*. New York: Atheneum, 1986.

———. "Men Creating Women." *New York Times Book Review*, 9 November 1986, 1, 16, 18, 20.

Priestley, Michael. "Structure in the Worlds of John Irving." *Critique* 23, no. 1 (1981): 82–96.

Pritchard, William. "Small-Town Saint." Review of *A Prayer for Owen Meany*. *New Republic*, 22 May 1989, 36–38.

Quinn, Peter A. "Incandescent Albany." Review of *Quinn's Book*. *Commonweal*, 20 May 1988, 308–9.

Redmon, Anne. "Vision and Risk." Review of *You Must Remember This*. *Michigan Quarterly Review* 2, no. 1 (1988): 203–13.

Reilly, Edward C. *William Kennedy*. TUSAS 570. Boston: Twayne, 1991.

Rich, Adrienne. *Of Woman Born: Motherhood as Experience and Institution*. New York: Norton, 1976.

Rignall, John. *Realist Fiction and the Strolling Player*. London: Routledge, 1992.

Rogin, Michael. *Ronald Reagan, the Movie and Other Episodes in Political Demonology*. Berkeley: University of California Press, 1987. 1–43.

Rojek, Chris. *Ways of Escape: Modern Transformation in Leisure and Travel*. Lanham: Rowman, 1993.

Rooke, Constance. *Reynolds Price*. TUSAS 450. Boston: Twayne, 1983.

Rugoff, Milton. *America's Gilded Age: Personalities in an Era of Extravagance and Change: 1850–1890*. New York: Holt, 1989.

Sauerberg, Lars. *Fact into Fiction: Documentary Realism in the Contemporary Novel*. New York: St. Martin's, 1991.

Schaller, Michael. *Reckoning with Reagan: America and Its President in the 1980s*. New York: Oxford University Press, 1992.

Schultz, John. "The Fabulous Presumption of Disney World: Magic Kingdom in the Wilderness." *Georgia Review* 42 (1988): 275–312.

Shepherd, Allen. "Love (and Marriage) in *A Long, Happy Life*." *Twentieth-Century Literature* 17 (1971): 29–35.

Sheppard, R. Z. "The Message Is the Message." Review of *A Prayer for Owen Meany*. *Time*, 3 April 1989, 80.

Shi, David E. *Facing Facts: Realism in American Thought and Culture, 1850–1920*. New York: Oxford University Press, 1995.

Silverman, Debora. *Selling Culture: Bloomingdale's, Diana Vreeland, and the New Aristocracy of Taste in Reagan's America*. New York: Pantheon, 1986.

Singer, June. *Androgyny: Toward a New Theory of Sexuality.* Garden City, N.Y.: Anchor, 1976.

Spigel, Lynn. *Make Room for TV: Television and the Family Ideal in Postwar America.* Chicago: University of Chicago Press, 1992.

Steele, H. Meili. *Realism and the Drama of Reference: Strategies of Representation in Balzac, Flaubert, and James.* University Park: Pennsylvania State University Press, 1988.

Stephens, C. Ralph, ed. *The Fiction of Anne Tyler.* Jackson: University Press of Mississippi, 1990.

Stern, J. P. *On Realism.* London: Routledge, 1973.

Stewart, Ian. *Does God Play Dice?: The Mathematics of Chaos.* New York: Oxford University Press, 1989.

Strandberg, Victor. "Sex, Violence, and Philosophy in *You Must Remember This.*" *Studies in American Fiction* 17, no. 1 (1989): 3–17.

Sundquist, Eric J., ed. Introduction. *American Realism: New Essays.* Baltimore: Johns Hopkins University Press, 1982.

Tallis, Raymond. *In Defence of Realism.* London: Arnold, 1988.

Tanner Tony. *City of Words: American Fiction, 1950–1970.* New York: Harper, 1971.

Taylor, Ella. *Prime-Time Families: Television Culture in Postwar America.* Berkeley: University of California Press, 1989.

Taylor, John. *Circus of Ambition: The Culture of Wealth and Power in the Eighties.* 1989. New York: Warner Trade, 1990.

Toll, Robert C. *On with the Show! The First Century of Show Business in America.* New York: Oxford University Press, 1976.

Towers, Robert. "Roughing It." Review of *Breathing Lessons. New York Review of Books,* 10 November 1988, 40–41.

———. "Ways down South." Review of *Kate Vaiden. New York Review of Books,* 25 September 1986, 55–56.

Towers, Tom. Review of *A Prayer for Owen Meany. New York Review of Books,* 20 July 1989, 10.

Trachtenberg, Stanley, ed. Introduction. *Critical Essays on American Postmodernism.* New York: Hall, 1995.

Tyler, Anne. *Breathing Lessons.* New York: Knopf, 1988.

Updike, John. "Howells as Anti-Novelist." *New Yorker,* 13 July 1987, 78–88.

———. "What You Deserve Is What You Get." Review of *You Must Remember This. New Yorker,* 28 December 1987, 119–23.

Van Dover, J. K. *Understanding William Kennedy.* Columbia: University of South Carolina Press, 1991.

Varsava, Jerry A. *Contingent Meanings: Postmodern Fiction, Mimesis, and the Reader.* Gainesville: University Presses of Florida, 1990.

Versluys, Kristiaan, ed. Introduction. *Neo-Realism in Contemporary American Fiction.* Amsterdam: Rodopi, 1992.

Voelker, Joseph C. *Art and the Accidental in Anne Tyler.* Columbia: University of Missouri Press, 1989.

Wagner-Martin, Linda. "Panoramic, Unpredictable, and Human: Joyce Carol Oates's Recent Novels." In *Traditions, Voices, and Dreams: The American Novel since the 1960s,* ed. Melvin J. Friedman and Ben Siegel, 196–209. Newark: University of Delaware Press, 1995.

Walker, Michael. "Boyle's 'Greasy Lake' and the Moral Failure of Postmodernism." *Studies in Short Fiction* 31, no. 2 (1994): 247–55.

Wall, James M. "Owen Meany and the Presence of God." *Christian Century,* 22–29 March 1989, 299–300.

Watt, Ian. *The Rise of the Novel: Studies in Defoe, Richardson, and Fielding.* Berkeley: University of California Press, 1967.

Weinraub, Bernard. "The Reagan Legacy." *New York Times Magazine,* 22 June 1986, 12–21.

Wesley, Marilyn. "On Sport: Magic and Masculinity in Joyce Carol Oates' Fiction." *LIT* 3, no. 1 (1991): 65–75.

Wheelwright, Philip. *Heraclitus.* New York: Atheneum, 1959.

White, John Kenneth. *The New Politics of Old Values.* Hanover, N.H.: University Press of New England, 1990.

Wilde, Alan. *Middle Grounds: Studies in Contemporary American Fiction.* Philadelphia: University of Pennsylvania Press, 1987.

Williams, D. A., ed. Introduction. *The Monster in the Mirror: Studies in Nineteenth-Century Realism.* Oxford: Oxford University Press, 1978.

Williams, Raymond. "Realism and the Contemporary Novel." *Partisan Review* 26 (1959): 200–217.

Wills, Garry. *Reagan's America: Innocents at Home.* Garden City, N.Y.: Doubleday, 1987.

Wilson, Robert. "Confessions of a Country Girl." Review of *Kate Vaiden. New Republic,* 29 September 1986, 40–41.

Wolfe, Tom. "Stalking the Billion-Footed Beast." *Harper's,* November 1989, 45–56.

Zavarzadeh, Mas'ud. *The Mythopoeic Reality: The Postwar American Nonfiction Novel.* Urbana: University of Illinois Press, 1976.

INDEX

Price, Reynolds, 24, 249. *See also Kate Vaiden*
Pynchon, Thomas, 32, 256, 257

Quinn's Book (William Kennedy), 31, 115, **116–42**, 144, 145, 149, 151, 166, 167, 175, 185, 192, 193, 202, 208, 209, 210, 234, 245, 246, 258, 259; as example of spectacle realism, 116–17, 122–24, 128–32, 141–42; and Heraclitus, 116, 123–25, 126, 127, 129, 130, 131, 134, 135, 140, 141; and the impossibility of certainty, 118–22, 130–35; and the logic of melodrama, 136–38; and the oxymoron, 122–25, 130–31, 134–35; and the Reagan Era, 135–41; and the theater as metaphor, 117–118; and the use of language, 125–29, 134. *See also* Kennedy, William

Reagan Era (the 1980s): definition of, 1–5, 6–7, 28, 40, 254, 255, 258; end to, 13, 251–55, 260; and the Gilded Age, 5, 6, 26, 27, 266–67n; and the new realism, 24–26; and the 1920s, 5, 6; popular literature of, 25, 32; as rejection of the Carter years, 11–12, 13; reactions to, 6–7; resistance to, 19; as theme park, 8–9, 13–15, 18–19, 32–33; *See also* individual chapter novels
Reagan, Ronald, 9, 266n; popularity of, 7, 13–14, 18, 252; as postmodern phenomenon, 17–19, 269n; shooting of, 16
realism before the Reagan Era: conventions of, 11, 20, 21, 26–27, 268n, 269n; dark vision of, 21–23; and postmodern literature, 11–12
realism during the Reagan Era: critical reactions to, 25–26; compared to realism of the Gilded Age, 26–27; as different from traditional realism, 21, 23, 25, 27; as reaction to Reagan Era, 20–23, 33–34, 267n; varieties of, 28–30. *See also* spectacle realism; individual chapter novels
Roth, Philip, 11, 39, 256, 268n

Second Son (Robert Ferro), 31, **143–67**, 168, 175, 178, 179, 185, 190, 192, 193, 194, 196, 202, 208, 210, 223, 224, 234, 245, 246, 258, 259; and death, 148–149, 159–62, 164–67; as example of AIDS narrative, 146–48; as example of spectacle realism, 143–44, 145–49, 158, 160, 163–67; and the Reagan Era, 143, 147, 156, 163; and the solution of love, 155–57; and speculative fiction subplot, 162–64; and the theme of disconnection, 144–45, 149, 151–55, 157–59. *See also* Ferro, Robert
Shaw, Irwin, 11
She's Come Undone (Wally Lamb), 256
Shipping News, The (E. Annie Proulx), 257
Smiley, Jane, 30
spectacle realism: definition of 27–33, 256–61; as different from postmodern literature, 30–33; pre-1980s examples, 23–24; as Reagan Era phenomenon, 24–28, 30, 32. *See also* realism during the Reagan Era; individual chapter novels
Sportswriter, The (Richard Ford), 223
Springsteen, Bruce, 18, 24, 140, 269n
Stone Diaries, The (Carol Shields), 257
Styron, William, 11, 12, 15

Tanner, Tony, 11
Taylor, Peter, 23
theme park, 8, 14–15, 252–54, 258. *See also* Disney America Theme Park; Disney World
Tyler, Anne, 24, 32. *See also Breathing Lessons*

Updike, John, 12, 23, 30, 256, 268n, 269n, 270n

Varsava, Jerry A., 267–68n
Vollmann, William, 256
Vonnegut, Kurt, 257

Wagner-Martin, Linda, 36
Wallace, David Foster, 256